Nineteenth-Century Major Lives and Letters

Series Editor: Marilyn Gaull

This series presents original biographical, critical, and scholarly studies of literary works and public figures in Great Britain, North America, and continental Europe during the nineteenth century. The volumes in *Nineteenth-Century Major Lives and Letters* evoke the energies, achievements, contributions, cultural traditions, and individuals who reflected and generated them during the Romantic and Victorian period. The topics: critical, textual, and historical scholarship, literary and book history, biography, cultural and comparative studies, critical theory, art, architecture, science, politics, religion, music, language, philosophy, aesthetics, law, publication, translation, domestic and public life, popular culture, and anything that influenced, impinges upon, expresses or contributes to an understanding of the authors, works, and events of the nineteenth century. The authors consist of political figures, artists, scientists, and cultural icons including William Blake, Thomas Hardy, Charles Darwin, William Wordsworth, William Butler Yeats, Samuel Taylor, and their contemporaries.

The series editor is Marilyn Gaull, PhD (Indiana University), FEA. She has taught at William and Mary, Temple University, New York University, and is Research Professor at the Editorial Institute at Boston University. She is the founder and editor of *The Wordsworth Circle* and the author of *English Romanticism: The Human Context*, and editions, essays, and reviews in journals. She lectures internationally on British Romanticism, folklore, and narrative theory, intellectual history, publishing procedures, and history of science.

PUBLISHED BY PALGRAVE:

Shelley's German Afterlives, by Susanne Schmid
Coleridge, the Bible, and Religion, by Jeffrey W. Barbeau
Romantic Literature, Race, and Colonial Encounter, by Peter J. Kitson
Byron, edited by Cheryl A. Wilson
Romantic Migrations, by Michael Wiley
The Long and Winding Road from Blake to the Beatles, by Matthew Schneider
British Periodicals and Romantic Identity, by Mark Schoenfield
Women Writers and Nineteenth-Century Medievalism, by Clare Broome Saunders
British Victorian Women's Periodicals, by Kathryn Ledbetter
Romantic Diasporas, by Toby R. Benis
Romantic Literary Families, by Scott Krawczyk
Victorian Christmas in Print, by Tara Moore
Culinary Aesthetics and Practices in Nineteenth-Century American Literature, edited by Monika Elbert and Marie Drews
Reading Popular Culture in Victorian Print, by Alberto Gabriele
Romanticism and the Object, edited by Larry H. Peer
Poetics en passant, by Anne Jamison
From Song to Print, by Terence Hoagwood
Gothic Romanticism, by Tom Duggett
Victorian Medicine and Social Reform, by Louise Penner
Populism, Gender, and Sympathy in the Romantic Novel, by James P. Carson
Byron and the Rhetoric of Italian Nationalism, by Arnold A. Schmidt
Poetry and Public Discourse in Nineteenth-Century America, by Shira Wolosky
The Discourses of Food in Nineteenth-Century British Fiction, by Annette Cozzi
Romanticism and Pleasure, edited by Thomas H. Schmid and Michelle Faubert
Royal Romances, by Kristin Flieger Samuelian

Trauma, Transcendence, and Trust, by Thomas J. Brennan, S.J.
The Business of Literary Circles in Nineteenth-Century America, by David Dowling
Popular Medievalism in Romantic-Era Britain, by Clare A. Simmons
Beyond Romantic Ecocriticism, by Ashton Nichols
The Poetry of Mary Robinson, by Daniel Robinson
Romanticism and the City, edited by Larry H. Peer

FORTHCOMING TITLES:

Coleridge and the Daemonic Imagination, by Gregory Leadbetter
Romantic Dharma, by Mark Lussier
Regions of Sara Coleridge's Thought, by Peter Swaab

ROMANTICISM AND THE CITY

Edited by

Larry H. Peer

ROMANTICISM AND THE CITY
Copyright © Larry H. Peer, 2011.

All rights reserved.

First published in 2011 by
PALGRAVE MACMILLAN®
in the United States—a division of St. Martin's Press LLC,
175 Fifth Avenue, New York, NY 10010.

Where this book is distributed in the UK, Europe and the rest of the world, this is by Palgrave Macmillan, a division of Macmillan Publishers Limited, registered in England, company number 785998, of Houndmills, Basingstoke, Hampshire RG21 6XS.

Palgrave Macmillan is the global academic imprint of the above companies and has companies and representatives throughout the world.

Palgrave® and Macmillan® are registered trademarks in the United States, the United Kingdom, Europe and other countries.

ISBN: 978–0–230–10883–7

Library of Congress Cataloging-in-Publication Data

    Romanticism and the city / edited by Larry H. Peer.
      p. cm.—(Nineteenth-century major lives and letters)
    Includes bibliographical references.
    ISBN 978–0–230–10883–7
     1. Romanticism. 2. Cities and towns in literature. 3. Public spaces in literature 4. Literature, Modern—19th century—History and criticism. 5. Literature, Modern—18th century—History and criticism.
    I. Peer, Larry H.

PN56.R7R655 2011
809'.93358209732—dc22   2010038977

A catalogue record of the book is available from the British Library.

Design by Newgen Imaging Systems (P) Ltd., Chennai, India.

First edition: March 2011

10 9 8 7 6 5 4 3 2 1

Printed in the United States of America.

In memory of Jean-Pierre Barricelli and Henry H. H. Remak

For dedicated members of the International Conference on Romanticism and its annual meeting coordinators, particularly Joshua Wilner, and for Janet Priday Peer, at one in the quest.

Contents

Acknowledgments   ix

Notes on the Contributors   xi

Introduction   The Infernal and Celestial City of Romanticism   1
Larry H. Peer

Part I   Theories of the City

1. Nerve Theory, Sensibility, and Romantic Metrosexuals   9
   Michelle Faubert
2. Wordsworth's Double-Take   25
   William Galperin
3. John Galt, Happy Colonialist: The Case of "The Apostate; Or, Atlantis Destroyed"   43
   Jeffrey Cass
4. The Gothic Chapbook and the Urban Reader   55
   Diane Long Hoeveler
5. Romantic Science and the City   73
   Marilyn Gaull

Part II   Continental Cities

6. Phenomenal Beauty: Rousseau in Venice   87
   Nancy Yousef
7. E. T. A. Hoffmann's Marketplace Vision of Berlin   105
   Alexander Schlutz
8. Renzo in Milan   135
   Ernesto Livorni
9. Rome Above Rome: Nikolai Gogol's Romantic Vision of the Eternal City   157
   Tatiana V. Barnett

Part III London

10 Wordsworth's Invigorating Hell: London in
    Book 7 of *The Prelude* (1805) 181
    Eugene Stelzig

11 Blake's Golgonoosa: London and/as the Eternal City of Art 197
    Mark Lussier

12 London's Immortal Druggists: Pharmaceutical Science
    and Business in Romanticism 209
    Thomas H. Schmid

13 Wordsworth's "Illustrated Books and Newspapers"
    and Media of the City 223
    Peter J. Manning

14 Babylon and Jerusalem on the Old Kent Road 241
    Tim Fulford

Works Cited 261

Index 279

Acknowledgments

This book, although about an important topic in Romanticism studies, is also about the finer aspects of scholarly support, respect, and cooperation. Colleagues from around the world, with remarkable insight, have participated in seen and unseen ways in bringing this work to light. I am grateful for the sustaining power of their goodwill.

Without the expertise of Brooke Downs, Jana Porter, and the editorial staff at Palgrave Macmillan, with each person crucial at various stages of this project's development and completion, this book would not have come to print.

I offer particular thanks to The Wordsworth Circle for permission to use earlier versions of the essays by Jeffrey Cass, William Galperin, Diane Long Hoeveler, and Thomas H. Schmid, all appearing in volume XLI, number 3 (2010).

Contributors

TATIANA V. BARNETT is currently an independent scholar in America, and formerly associate professor of Comparative Literature and chair of the Department of World Cultures at the State University in Bishkek, Kyrgyzstan. She has held a Fulbright Fellowship.

JEFFREY CASS is professor of English and dean of the College of Arts and Sciences at the University of Louisiana, Monroe. He is the coeditor of *Romantic Border Crossings* and *Interrogating Orientalism* as well as author of a number of essays on the British Romantics.

MICHELLE FAUBERT is assistant professor of English at the University of Manitoba. Her book *Rhyming Reason: The Poetry of Romantic Era Psychologists* connects many insights already proffered in the coedited *Romanticism and Pleasure* and *Cultural Constructions of Madness in the Eighteenth Century*.

TIM FULFORD is professor of English at Nottingham Trent University and author of numerous books and essays on British Romanticism and eighteenth-century culture. His most recent book, *Romantic Indians*, will be joined by his forthcoming *The Late Poetry of the Early Romantics*.

WILLIAM GALPERIN is professor of English at Rutgers University. Among his many publications are the books *Revision and Authority in Wordsworth*, *The Return of the Visible in British Romanticism*, and *The Historical Austen*.

MARILYN GAULL is research professor in the Editorial Institute at Boston University. Her publications include the book *English Romanticism: The Human Context*. She is the founder of the Wordsworth Circle and editor of its comprehensive journal and is a frequent lecturer in international academic venues.

DIANE LONG HOEVELER is professor of English at Marquette University. She is the author of *Romantic Androgyny*, *Gothic Feminism*, and *Gothic Riffs*, editor or coeditor of fifteen books and has published more than five dozen essays on a variety of literary topics.

ERNESTO LIVORNI is professor of Italian Language and Literature and affiliate of the Comparative Literature Program at the University of Wisconsin. His thirty published essays and three books include studies of Montale, T. S. Eliot, Ted Hughes, Papini, D'Annunzio, Marinette, Ungaretti, Quasimodo, Joyce, and Pound.

MARK LUSSIER is professor of English at Arizona State University. He is the author of *Romantic Dynamics* and *Engaged Romanticism*. Joining his published essays in *Arts Quarterly*, *New Orleans Review*, *Nineteenth-Century Contexts*, and *Studies in Romanticism* are forthcoming books on Romantic Dharma and on reading Blake through the lens of Lacan.

PETER J. MANNING is professor of English at the State University of New York, Stony Brook. He is the author of *Byron and His Fictions* and *Reading Romantics* as well as numerous essays on the British Romantic poets and prose writers. He has received fellowships from the National Endowment for the Humanities and the Guggenheim Memorial Foundation.

LARRY H. PEER is professor of Comparative Literature at Brigham Young University, editor of the journal *Prism(s): Essays in Romanticism*, and Executive Director of the International Conference on Romanticism. His books and essays on Manzoni, Goethe, Stendhal, Pushkin, Friedrich Schlegel, Byron, the Brontes, the Romantic Manifesto, and Romantic literary theory are joined by two books of his poetry.

ALEXANDER SCHLUTZ is associate professor of English at John Jay College, City University of New York. Published essays on Coleridge, Poe, Beckett, and Salman Rushdie are joined by his book *Mind's World: Imagination and Subjectivity From Descartes to Romanticism*, winner of the 2009 Barricelli Book Prize of the International Conference on Romanticism.

THOMAS H. SCHMID is associate professor of English at the University of Texas, El Paso and winner of the Rocky Mountain Modern Language Association Book Award for *Humor and Transgression in Peacock, Shelley, and Byron*. He has been awarded fellowships from the National Endowment for the Humanities and the Huntington Library.

EUGENE STELZIG is distinguished teaching professor of English at the State University of New York, Geneseo. In addition to many articles on Romantic literature, his groundbreaking book *Romantic Autobiography in England* puts him at the forefront of scholarship on the relationship between Romanticism and autobiography as a genre.

Contributors

NANCY YOUSEF is associate professor of English at The Graduate Center and Baruch College, City University of New York. A specialist in the ethics and narratology of Enlightenment and Romantic literature, she is the author of *Isolated Cases: The Anxieties of Autonomy*.

Introduction

The Infernal and Celestial City of Romanticism

Larry H. Peer

Western world literature "is and has always been at war with given reality. The world, as given, is disliked: it is disliked in large part just because it is given."[1] What is "given" today is a suburbanized culture based on the dominance of industrialization and the advance of technology, a situation decried in post-Romantic decades as a process that obliterates the natural environment by a valorization of the urban.[2] The role of late eighteenth- and early nineteenth-century Romanticism in this contemporary "given" is important for the understanding of modernism and postmodernism and crucial to an understanding of Romanticism per se.

Romanticism is a complex and reticulated system of norms undergirding a panoptic vision of both physical and metaphysical reality. It has been clearly and often demonstrated that one of the chief, if not *the* chief characteristic of this system is its almost obsessive engagement with the natural world.[3] Conceptual structures, images, and settings taken from the natural landscape and its weather are present everywhere in European Romantic art. The poems of Hölderlin, Petöfi, Leopardi, and Goethe, for example, reflect this characteristic, as do the novels of the Brontes, of Manzoni and Chateaubriand, and of *Sturm und Drang* drama. The philosophical systems of Fichte and Schelling stem from it. The paintings of Turner, Constable, and Friedrich would be blank without it.

Romanticism clearly represents a desire for identification with the elemental natural world. Nature is alive and, for the artist to be intensely alive, he or she must fuse with that world and attain a highly individualized mystical experience that digs down into the core of reality. Wordsworth's excursion takes him there, as does Beethoven's pastoral symphony, Turner's steamship in a snowstorm, and Emily Bronte's wild and wind swept heights. The discourse of Romantic identification with and merging into dynamic, dangerous, and mysterious nature contrasts with that of pre-Romantic Western culture and constitutes a shift of profound proportions in philosophical attitude.[4] At the beginning of this shift lie Vico's *La scienza nuova prima* (1725) and Rousseau's *L'origine et les fondements de l'inégalité parmi les hommes* (1754), in which is found the beginning of Romantic preoccupation with the interaction of the poet with nature, and on the reverie in nature so crucial to the act of contemplation, both of which lead to a mature critique of civilized society in the 1820s and beyond.

It is, however, easy to see this preoccupation of Romantic poets simple mindedly. Another concern of Romantic thinking is the mutual interdependence of the individual with society, a relationship not always at its most profound in raw nature. For example, Schiller, in his powerfully influential essay *Über naive und sentimentalische Dichtung* (1795–96), argues that the realization of the deepest individual development requires the emergence of a moral society, a kind of ethically mature "city." Fundamental questions of social power and social order are at stake and, ultimately, human beings need to live together in such a way that self-interest and public interest mesh. Although there inevitably is tension between these interests, they are always brought into harmony by "aesthetic education," a kind of cultivation, possible in urban spaces as well as in nature, that brings about a free, although ideal and not yet achieved, society. In other words, art is the solution to the problem of the individual's alienation from and in urban space. The power of aesthetic artifacts to bring people together in creative and harmonious ways is a subtle valorization of the city as Romantic space.

Thus, it is the *tension* between city and country, and the possibility of an *ideal* urban space that powers much of the metaphorical positioning of Romantic art. Vico would say that in Schiller's ideal city the people are speaking with *sapienza poetica*, the robust and "true" language at an individual's core, lost not only by separation from nature, but also by a tendency of human beings to separate the art they produce from the society that makes such production possible. That is, a return to nature without a parallel return to relevant urban space produces mere sentimentality, not the Romanticism toward which Vico moves and in which Schiller thinks. It is necessary to remember that Romantic art always seeks the *transcendental*, looks for that which is beyond the world of appearances, revealing the infinite and unfathomable, or

Geist, in Hegel's terms. The radically individualized and transcendental orientation of Romantic art actualizes the tension between and possible harmony of city and country.

In this book Romantic views and metaphorical uses of urban space are explored. The first part of the book opens a series of chapters on the theory of the city, Michelle Faubert's "Nerve Theory, Sensibility, and Romantic Metrosexuals" offers a view of the relationship between Romanticism and the psychology of urban sensibility. Her groundbreaking argument about the emotion engendered by urban space leads to a consideration of how such feeling is used as a trope and setting in the works of the movement. William Galperin ("Wordsworth's Double-Take") explores Wordsworth's poetry as a Romantic example of moving back and forth between conceptions of art as imagination on the one hand and, on the other, of the creative process as stemming from simple ordinary experience. A poet teetering on the edge of the ordinary before he becomes a visionary is central to the creative process of Romanticism and finds a trenchant example in the encounter with the blind beggar in Book 7 of *The Prelude*, which recounts Wordsworth's residence in London with its urban ordinary extraordinariness. Jeffrey Cass ("John Galt, Happy Colonialist: The Case of 'The Apostate; Or, Atlantis Destroyed'") studies the complex use of the mythical city of Galt's work, making a case for *The Apostate* as iconic example of how Romanticism mythologizes the city in ways new to Western culture. Diane Long Hoeveler's "The Gothic Chapbook and the Urban Reader" points out that in 1800 a three-volume gothic novel could cost as much as two weeks' wages for a laborer, so the cheaper chapbooks, as redactions of longer Gothic novels and dramas, were affordable and became the chief reading material of the vast population longing to be "in fashion." And it is precisely in the city that readers lived at the boundary between the more sophisticated reading and the essentially illiterate nonreading publics, making the city the site of "pop Romanticism." Finally, Marilyn Gaull ("Romantic Science and the City") concisely summarizes the chief issues in the development of the hard sciences in Romanticism, seeing in that development the rise of urban life as key to an understanding of the history of science.

The second part of the book deals with Romanticism and Continental cities. Nancy Yousef ("Phenomenal Beauty: Rousseau in Venice") explores the problem of Rousseau's recollection of his sojourn in Venice, in *Les Confessions,* where, as an urban space, Venice itself is virtually invisible. Arguing that in Romanticism beauty insinuates itself as an unstable mediator between sensually determined perception of the other and an ethically determined appreciation and respect for the other, Yousef shows that, for Rousseau, Venice represents the philosophical problem of the city as possible site for transcendental beauty. Another ambiguous use of the city is studied by Alexander Schlutz in "E. T. A. Hoffmann's Marketplace Vision of Berlin." In addition to the fact that Hoffmann provides the first sustained description of Berlin as a cityscape, he demonstrates an acute awareness of the narrative quality of acts of perception through which we construct reality: Schlutz sees Hoffmann's description of the city as a kind of "test case" for Romantic narratology. Ernesto Livorni ("Renzo in Milan") analyzes the view of the city in Manzoni's *I promessi sposi,* an ambivalent look at urbanity as intellectual, social, and artistic labyrinth in which one inevitably will lose oneself but only sometimes will find oneself again. The city as a hellish place, contrasted with the idyllic countryside, is in Manzoni's novel raised to a new metaphorical level, a level at which individual freedom and its relationship to providence and history is explored. Tatiana V. Barnett, in "Rome Above Rome: Nikolai Gogol's Romantic Vision of the Eternal City," shows how Rome was a place of cultural refuge for Gogol in contrast to Paris, a place of emotional emptiness. This contrast figures forth Romantic interpretations of urban space, of ancient versus contemporary, of North versus South, and of Romanticism as the dislocation of the antique world.

The third group of chapters focuses on Romanticism and London. We are accustomed to thinking of Wordsworth as the poet of nature, but he is also the poet of the city, as Eugene Stelzig argues in "Wordsworth's Invigorating Hell: London in Book 7 of *The Prelude* (1805)." The poet's extended presentation of London in Book 7 of "The Prelude" not only shares in a negative perception of the urban as a kind of necropolis, but also sees its role as highly stimulating to the imagination. This ultimately ambivalent view of the city is more common in Romanticism than has heretofore been recognized. Mark Lussier ("Blake's Golgonooza: London and/as the Eternal City of Art") examines Blake's appropriation of discrete sections of London as the foundation for his imaginary city of art, pointing out that through Blake we have a visionary cartography of how the gates of this city open onto the work of other authors and other post-Romantic historical moments. In "London's Immortal Druggists: Pharmaceutical Science and Business in Romanticism," Thomas H. Schmid points out that the early nineteenth century marked the beginning of London's, and Great Britain's, modern drug industry, with its complex interplay of research, manufacturing, and marketing, the more negative implications of which led to greater legislative regulation and oversight later in the century. The drug business was a permanent feature of London's cityscape in Romanticism and, properly understood, cast new light on works such as De Quincey's *Confessions of an English Opium Eater.*

Peter J. Manning ("Wordsworth's 'Illustrated Books and Newspapers' and Media of the City") explores the dual engagement with the quality of urban life and the media it fosters, as exemplified by Wordsworth's experience with the complicated contexts of London, and Tim Fulford ("Babylon and Jerusalem on the Old Kent Road") shows how London was seen by many Romantic artists as the modern Babylon on the verge of being turned into the New Jerusalem. Arguing that in Romanticism a permanent split between the rural and the urban occurred, he suggests that Romanticism either necessitates a concentrated poetic synthesis of the two or else requires an acknowledgment of a deep night of bifurcated human experience.

This book is a further articulation of complexities coterminous with the rise of Romanticism in the arts. It is instructive to think back to 1752, when Bambini and his musicians first brought the music of Scarlatti and Pergolesi to Paris, engendering a battle over this new kind of music reflected in the writings of Rousseau, D'Alembert, and Grimm: or, to remember Thomas Girtin's search for "structured luminosity" (a catchword for Romantic visual representation) that led him in 1800 to an ambitious scheme to paint a panorama of London. In both cases, the city functions as both the site and symbol of an inclusionary power fostered by Romantic art, of the insistence that to be Romantic meant not just to be a dreamer, but to be one who faces the developing and powerful realities of the time, especially the reality of an increasingly urban landscape in Western culture.

Notes

1. George Kateb, "Technology and Philosophy," *Social Research* 64:3 (1997): 1241.
2. See, for example, F. R. Leavis and Denys Thompson, *Culture and Environment: The Training of Critical Awareness*, London: Chatto, 1933; Jonathan Bate, *The Song of the Earth*, Cambridge, MA: Harvard UP, 2000; Michel Serres, *Le contrat naturel*, Paris: Bourin, 1990; and Michael E. Ziimmerman, *Contesting Earth's Future: Radical Ecology and Postmodernity*, Berkeley: U of California P, 1994.
3. Numerous scholarly studies of this point have been made during the last five decades, including these exceptional examples: James C. McKusick, *Green Writing: Romanticism and Ecology*, New York: St. Martin's, 2000; Irving Babbitt, *Rousseau and Romanticism*, New York: Houghton, 1919; and Simon Schama, *Landscape and Memory*, New York: Knopf, 1995.
4. See Chapter 17 of H. G. Schenk's *The Mind of the European Romantics*, New York: Doubleday, 1969, for a succinct explanation of this difference.

Part I

Theories of the City

1

Nerve Theory, Sensibility, and Romantic Metrosexuals

Michelle Faubert

Since G. S. Rousseau proposed the link between nerve theory and the literature of sentiment in his groundbreaking article from 1976, "Nerves, Spirits, and Fibres: Towards Defining the Origins of Sensibility," a few commonly accepted notions appear in criticism about Romantic-era literature and nerve theory, for example, that the nervous illness of hysteria and hypochondria afflicts city dwellers most violently, as both George Grinnell and Martin Wallen have shown with reference to Thomas Beddoes's text on nerves, *Hygëia: or, Essays Moral and Medical on the Causes Affecting the Personal State of our Middling and Affluent Classes*, and that this metropolitan nervous body is plagued by weak borders, a contention that derives from Michel Foucault's focus on the nervous diseases of hysteria as a disease of the permeable spaces of the female body and its "brother" disease, hypochondria, as one that affects the more solid mass of the male body. In this chapter, I will begin by showing that this neat paradigm is not, in fact, borne out by some of the most influential texts of nerve theory in the early Romantic period. Indeed, Beddoes's famous text, as well as the influential text of nerve theory by Thomas Trotter called *A View of the Nervous Temperament*, trouble Foucault's distinction between the male and female body as one that is "firm and resistant,...[and in which the] internal space is dense, organized, and solidly heterogenous in its different regions" in the former case and one that is plagued by weak borders in the latter (149). These Romantic-era nerve theorists show that, in opposition to hale and hearty rural men, metropolitan males can become feminized, the victims of weakened boundaries and their bodies as prone to collapse as those of women from a Foucauldian perspective. In short, that most bracing of divisions—what separates the male from the female—dissolves when people transgress another important border, the one between the city and the country. Moreover, I will show that two novels of sentiment, Frances Burney's *Evelina* and Elizabeth Inchbald's *A Simple Story*, complicate the tidy formula that Foucault presents, as well as Beddoes's and Trotter's ideas about the effects of the city on the nervous female body. These female novelists thereby offer a subtle feminist challenge to the distinctly male medical establishment of the Romantic period through a literary type that has been lambasted as misogynistic by many, including Mary Wollstonecraft herself.[1]

In *Evelina* and *A Simple Story*, male representatives of the metropolis are feminized, a reflection not only of their weakened nerves, as Beddoes and Trotter conceived the matter, but also of the authors' understanding of a basic principle from nerve theory regarding the debilitating effect of the city upon the body. Notably, though, the fictional heroines' gender identities also change in London, and they begin to show more masculine traits, a response to the stimulation of the city that does not appear in Beddoes's and Trotter's texts of nerve theory. To summarize, Beddoes and Trotter warn that the cramped spaces and desk jobs of the city are associated with feminized men; unlike in rural life, they explain, the lack of fresh air and exercise shattered metropolitan men's nerves, and the resulting condition expressed itself as effeminate fragility—and the nerve theorists extend this paradigm to encompass women, arguing that the city further debilitated their already-fragile bodies. Burney and Inchbald evoke this paradigm in their treatment of citified male characters to establish their novels as recognizable contributions to the cultural conversation about sensibility, but, in their treatment of their female protagonists, they reform the paradigm and challenge traditional, male-authored notions about women's gender identity in nerve theory and the broader culture of sensibility by presenting masculinized metrosexual heroines. By giving fictional life to an alternate view of the effects of the city upon women's bodies in their novels of sensibility, Burney and Inchbald problematize popular ideas about gender, nervousness, and the city as conceived by male nerve theorists and thereby suggest that there existed "many cults of sensibility," as G. S. Rousseau notes (153), or, indeed, various "culture[s] of sensibility," to modify G. J. Barker-Benfield's well-known phrase. Viewed thus, Burney's and Inchbald's novels of sensibility acquire a feminist *frisson* that is not often recognized in a literary type more notable for its celebration of weak and submissive women as a feminine ideal. Using the bodies and characters of their female protagonists as staging-grounds for ideological rebellion, these authors present the reader with surprisingly powerful women of sensibility and modify notions from the markedly male realm of medicine regarding the effects of environment on the female body.[2]

All contemporary historians of medicine and literary critics who study the intersection of nerve theory and the literature of sensibility owe a debt to Foucault, who suggests in *Madness and Civilization* that the realms of medicine and literature shared the same social space, the culture of sensibility, in a "classical era" exchange of ideas that can be traced through a number of texts, imaginative and otherwise. Foucault identifies the very notion of nervous illness as guided by "the theme of a dynamic upheaval of corporeal space," a theme that was modified in the eighteenth century, when "a morality of sensibility" was added to this conceptualization (146). He notes that "if corporeal space is perceived as a solid and continuous whole, the disordered movement of hysteria and of hypochondria could result only from an element whose extreme tenuousness and incessant mobility permitted it to penetrate into the place occupied by the solids themselves" (146–47). Through his description of hysteria as the breakdown of bodily borders and subsequent delineation of sensibility as a culture-wide phenomenon that dissolves ideological divisions between medicine and literature, Foucault encourages a reassessment of concepts about nervous illness in early Romanticism. That is, he suggests that the key characteristic of ideas about nervousness was not in the aetiology or symptoms of the illness itself, nor even in the relationship between the nervous patient and doctor alone, but, rather, in the outlines that circumscribed these conceptualizations, or, as related to these ideas, the spaces, borders, and transgression thereof.

Viewed thus, English ideas about nervous illness in the Romantic period seem to express social anxiety about changing and weakened spatial boundaries in the early days of the Industrial Revolution, when people were flocking to the city to acquire work and London was beginning to take shape as an overwhelmingly bustling metropolis. Foucault claims that, at the end of what he calls the classical period, "All life was finally judged by...[a] degree of irritation: abuse of things that were not natural, the sedentary life of cities, novel reading, theatergoing, immoderate thirst for knowledge" (157). In this potent statement, Foucault adumbrates the links between medical texts, literature, and the role played by the city in ideas about nervous illness, called either "a hypochondriacal disease when it attacks men...[or] a hysterical affection when it attacks women" (145). He also links this sentiment to notions about gender: "So few women are hysterical when they are accustomed to a hard and laborious life, yet strongly incline to become so when they lead a soft, idle, luxurious, and lax existence" (149). In a few key pages of *Madness and Civilization*, Foucault provides all the elements on which my argument is based, especially since he also gestures to the issue of labor and bodily exercise as the root of why nervous illness was thought to have afflicted some people and not others, an idea that is central to my discussion. However, unlike in my approach, Foucault does not examine this issue of exercise and laxity closely and, without the complicating influence of this concept, he outlines an overly simplistic gendered paradigm of nervous illness I contend. As I will show, two of the most influential nerve theorists of the late classical period, Trotter and Beddoes, present this issue of bodily exercise and physical freedom as so essential to the expression of nervous illness that it has the power to destroy what is, to many, an undisputed border: the division between male and female.

Although Foucault presents eighteenth-century nerve theory as establishing a definitive difference between the male and female body—such that the bodies of female "hysterical sufferers" express a breakdown of internal borders that "hypochondriacs possess[…], on the contrary, in a relatively blunted form" (153)—Trotter maintains that men's bodies can become as fluid and soft as those of women. In short, he differentiates between female and male characteristics in a way consistent with Foucault's reportage of classical-era nerve theory by attributing weak bodily borders to women and more solid physical boundaries to men, but Trotter complicates this paradigm by suggesting that certain lifestyles and environments, specifically the constricted life of the city, can turn men into what we would call "metrosexuals" today.

Trotter is extraordinarily concerned about the feminizing effects, via the nerves, of city life on men. He posits a mythical English past, in which "real men" abounded, a vigorous, Germanic race of rural hunters, log-breakers, and stone-smashers with ropey nerves, who were, alas, replaced in the Romantic era by a citified lot of sissies. In *A View of the Nervous Temperament*, the first chapter of which is entitled "The Health of the Savage State Compared with Modern Times," Trotter describes this golden age: "Our rude ancestors, born and brought up in a hut or a hovel, almost naked from infancy to manhood, and constantly exposed to the weather, whether employed in agriculture, tending herds and flocks, or the more laborious pursuits of hunting and fishing, had few bodily disorders" (16). Framing the matter in a modern context, he later opposes "the slim soft-fibred man-milliner" with "the firm and brawny ploughman," as well as "the nervous cramp of the delicate lady" with a rustic woman, adding that, as a man moves from a job in the countryside to a career in town, "he forsakes a mode of life that had been presented to him by nature; and in adopting a new situation he becomes the creature of art" (22–23). He becomes, in short, affected, which is part of Trotter's definition of nervous illness in *A View of the Nervous Temperament*:

> An inaptitude to muscular action, or some pain in exerting it; an irksomeness, or dislike to attend to business and the common affairs of life; a selfish desire of engrossing the sympathy and attention of others to the narration of their own sufferings; with fickleness and unsteadiness of temper, even to irascibility; and accompanied more of less with dyspeptic symptoms are the leading characteristicks of *nervous disorders*. (xii)

This nervous patient is a "creature of art" in another way, too, for Trotter's definition is also an apt description of many characters in novels of sensibility. "Sympathy," the "narration of…sufferings," and "unsteadiness of temper"—or what we might call "histrionics"—are all common features of novels of sensibility.

The link between cities, bad nerves, and the realm of literature Trotter would not question; indeed, he notes the "numerous instances of dyspepsia, hypochondriasis, and melancholia, in the literary character" (36) in his chapter on the dangers of cities. However, he would question the gender of what he denotes a whole "class" of metropolitan men. About clerks in dress shops, he opines,

> Not a few of them behind the counter, approach in external form towards the female constitution; and they seem to borrow from their fair customers an effeminacy of manners, and a smallness of voice, that sometimes makes their sex doubtful. Such degeneracies in corporeal structure, cannot fail of engendering a predisposition to diseases of the nervous kind. (38)

In this description of the Romantic-era metrosexual's effeminate body, Trotter uses words that recall Foucault's description of nervous illness as a breakdown of borders, a fluidity between the body's spaces that should remain independent of each other: these fashionable sissies "borrow" physical characteristics from their female customers, and the "degeneracies in [their] corporeal structure" mirror the permeable and disintegrating borders of the feminine form. In the city, Trotter contends, men are almost indistinguishable from women. As I will show, Dr. Beddoes, agrees.

Essential to an understanding of Beddoes's role as a "doctor of society," as Roy Porter has so aptly dubbed him, is the significance of nerve theory in his medical writings. In "Coleridge, Thomas Beddoes and

Brunonian Medicine," Neil Vickers shows convincingly that Beddoes was an associationist of such dedication and originality that he replaced David Hartley's associationist theory with one that accounted for the important links between emotions and ideas, instead of only how ideas lead to inevitably successive ideas. However, some critics, such as Wallen, Grinnell, and Paul Youngquist, have treated Beddoes, by and large, as a nerve theorist in focusing almost solely on *Hygëia*, which treats of hypochondria and hysteria. Moreover, Beddoes's approach to nerve theory is closely aligned with that of Trotter: both doctors identify nervous illness as linked to a metropolitan environment and list effeminacy as a major symptom for nervous men. In a commentary on what he calls the "forms of misery" that are nervous illnesses or states of excessive sensibility, Beddoes mentions that Jean-Jacques Rousseau recommends the rejection of "social refinement" and retreat "from the institutions of polished society" into isolation to counteract the source of such disease, like the luxuries found in the city (1: 87). He adds, with reference to what he terms "town-effeminacy," "Every circumstance of modern life conspires to soothe a man into the excess of effeminacy" and "unmanly delicacy" (1: 2), and, just like Trotter, he prescribes shunning the metropolis and celebrates the rural lifestyle of precivilized Germanic peoples as the model for maintaining nervous fortitude. Beddoes's remedy is "active occupation"; he states, "No species of nervous disorder easily fastens upon persons who devote a part of their time to moderate labour" (3: 91). Exercise, it appears, is key to the maintenance of healthy nerves—and a stable gender identity for men. Labor in the city is too soft and produces "girlie men," as Arnold Schwarzenegger would say. But what about women? Like Trotter, Beddoes warns against excessive sensibility in women, for it creates "drooping, blighted creatures, frequently half-insane," who "abuse [...] their animal powers till their sensibility acquire[s] the unnatural property of deriving pain from the slightest impression" (87). Reading this statement, the post-Foucauldian critic studying the links between nerve theory and the literature of sentiment is on familiar territory among swooning heroines dying for love and the female readers who aspire to such lovely illness. Notably, though, two of the most popular novels of sentiment written by women, Burney's *Evelina* and Inchbald's *A Simple Story*, trouble this widely accepted image of the woman of sensibility, even as the narratives reinforce with remarkable specificity the figure of the effeminate metropolitan male as depicted by Trotter and Beddoes. Indeed, Burney and Inchbald suggest that the gender-bending effects of the metropolis are more total than hitherto imagined—to the extent that the city masculinizes women.

Burney and Inchbald are two of the best-known writers of literary sentiment, the eighteenth-century literary fashion that "encouraged a sensitivity to—and spontaneous display of—virtuous feelings, especially those of pity, sympathy, benevolence, of the open heart as opposed to the prudent mind" (Vickers, *Doctors* ix).[3] Certainly, there are many classic markers of sensibility in the heroines of our novels. In *Evelina*, the eponymous hero reports in a letter to Miss Mirvan on the scene when she is once again reunited with Mr. Villars, her protector and "the most venerable of men":

> How did my heart throb with joy!...I thought it would have burst my bosom!—I opened the chaise-door myself, I flew,—for my feet did not seem to touch the ground,—I sprung forward with a pleasure that bordered upon agony, I embraced his knees, I kissed his hands, I wept over them, but could not speak. (254)

Similarly, in *A Simple Story*, Miss Milner falls to pieces while composing a response to a letter from her beloved, Dorriforth: "Her hand trembled, and her heart beat with rapture while she wrote" (136). Such descriptions firmly establish these novels as literary representatives of the culture of sensibility, but they do not simply confirm a static set of markers of sensibility. Rather, like all novels of sensibility, I maintain, these novels engage actively in redefining the very concept of sensibility and endeavor—in ways too numerous to mention here—to distinguish true sensibility from false sensibility. Dispersed among announcements of their membership in the cult of sensibility through standard descriptions like the above quotations, these novels devote themselves, however subtly, to the important business of expanding their audiences' perception of both sensibility and—because the form is so closely connected with conceptualizations of femininity and attracted mostly female readers—what it means to be female.[4]

The suggestion that novels of sensibility can be covertly feminist documents will strike many as ludicrous. After all, Mary Wollstonecraft, the Romantic-era mother of feminism, singled out such novelists for special castigation in *A Vindication of the Rights of Woman*, where she rails,

> Another instance of that feminine weakness of character, often produced by a confined education, is a romantic twist of the mind, which has been very properly termed sentimental....[W]omen...are amused by the reveries of stupid novelists, who, knowing little of human nature, work up stale tales, and describe meretricious scenes, all retailed in a sentimental jargon, which equally tend to corrupt the taste, and draw the heart aside from its daily duties. (330)

Although Inchbald and Burney trace the usual love-plot in their novels of sensibility, I argue that they also present an image of the sentimental woman that, in some ways, reforms the typical sickly heroine, whose "senses," Wollstonecraft complains, "are inflamed, and their understanding neglected, [and who] consequently...become the prey of their senses, delicately termed sensibility, and are blown about by every momentary gust of feeling" (177). However, Wollstonecraft could not deny the attraction of the culture of sensibility, for she penned *Mary, A Fiction,* which may well be identified as a novel of sentiment.[5] In keeping with other novels of sentiment, Inchbald and Burney offer recognizably sentimental heroines in these novels. However, in opposition to male nerve theorists' definitions of nervous women of sensibility, these protagonists show masculine characteristics in the city, even as the authors echo Beddoes's and Trotter's descriptions of the metropolitan sissy through their male characters. The potential consequences of the novelists' challenge to contemporary ideas about gender are great: through these means, Inchbald and Burney attempt to redefine Romantic-era femininity, which, as Wollstonecraft points out, was heavily influenced by novels of sensibility.

The representation of the metrosexual male in *A Simple Story* and *Evelina* is remarkably similar to that of the same figure in Trotter's and Beddoes's texts of nerve theory. Especially in Burney's novel, effeminate city-males are associated with clothes, like Trotter's "man-milliners" and Beddoes's dress-shop clerks, while, as I will show, Inchbald takes up the subject of clothes to show the gender-bending qualities of her female protagonist. Significantly, the first man that our rural heroine, Evelina, meets at her inaugural ball in the "great city" of London is a simpering, sissified fool named Lovel, who advances to meet her "on tiptoe" in "foppish," or overly elaborate, dress (30). Although Evelina soon thereafter meets Lord Orville, whose manliness the narrator confirms, significantly, through reference to his clothes—he is "gayly, but not foppishly dressed" (31)—Burney evokes popular Romantic-era ideas about the feminizing effects of the city by presenting Lovel as the first male representative of London that Evelina meets. No less notable is Evelina's laughter at the effeminate male clerks at the shops of "milliners" and "mantua-makers": she reflects, "Such men! so finical, so affected! they seemed to understand every part of a woman's dress better than we do ourselves; and they recommended caps and ribbands with an air of so much importance, that I wished to ask them how long they had left off wearing them!" (29). Lovel, too, confirms his status as a fashionista by claiming to have invented three styles of dress, whereupon Lady Louisa confirms that he "lead[s] the *ton* in the *beau monde*" (393). Just as Beddoes and Trotter present effeminate male shopkeepers as evidence of their theories about the deleterious effects of the city upon a man's nerves and very masculinity, Burney, too, focuses on feminine male fashion-mongers.

Clothes as a marker of metrosexuality may be associated with the cultural belief that a taste for fine clothes and adorning the body is a feminine trait, or that clothes—being covers for the natural body, as William Blake would remind us—are artificial and unnatural, which these feminine men are in other ways. Certainly, Beddoes and Trotter seem to focus on "man-milliners" and other men in the business of retailing women's clothes for these reasons. Notably, though, in the hands of a female novelist like Burney, this association between women's clothes and effeminate men acquires another layer of meaning that is distinctly feminist. At the end of the eighteenth century, numerous radical tracts lambasted men for stealing jobs that, their authors claimed, should be filled by women, such as careers in the field of women's dress. Some twenty years after Burney's novel appeared, Priscilla Bell Wakefield wrote of the differences between the availability of honorable, well-paying jobs for men and women in *Reflections on the Present Condition of the Female Sex; with Suggestions for its Improvement*:

> It is a subject of great regret, that this inequality should prevail, even where an equal share of skill and application are exerted. Male stay-makers, mantua-makers, and hair-dressers are better paid than female artists of the same professions; but surely it will never be urged as an apology for this disproportion, that women are not as capable of making stays, gowns, dressing hair, and similar arts, as men. (330)

Moreover, Bell Wakefield, perhaps like Burney, attempts to shame men out of such positions by mocking those who occupy them for being feminine:

> The occasion for this remark is a disgrace upon those who patronize such a brood of effeminate beings in the garb of men.... [W]ere the multitudes of men, who are constantly employed in measuring linen, gauze, ribbons, and lace; selling perfumes and cosmetics; setting a value on feathers and trinkets; and displaying their talents in praising the elegance of bonnets and caps, to withdraw, they might benefit the community, by exchanging such frivolous avocations for something more worthy of the masculine character. (330)

A year later, Mary Anne Radcliffe's *The Female Advocate; or An Attempt to Recover the Rights of Women from Male Usurpation* established the same point and, again, by accusing men in jobs associated with women's clothing of being effeminate: "What can be said in favour of men-milliners, professions, such as hair-dressers, &c. &c.; all of which occupations are much more calculated for women than men.... Men may be much better employed than in filling women's occupations" (333). As such, the link between women's clothes and effeminate metropolitan men in novels of sensibility may function to confirm a familiar late-eighteenth-century feminist message, as well as to develop a trope from the annals of nerve theory (in which, however, the medical authors do not argue for women's rights to these jobs, according to my research). In this light, Burney's depiction of gender appears to be more provocative than readers have usually understood it to be.

Inchbald, for her part, traces the metropolitan threat to masculinity in much broader narrative terms: her hero, Lord Elmwood (formerly Dorriforth when he was a priest),[6] submits to the more powerful and sexually aggressive Miss Milner while they are in the city, but he asserts his macho and controlling side when the narrative moves to the countryside. In London, Miss Milner is the sexual aggressor in her relationship with Elmwood; formerly, as a good (or, at least, celibate) Catholic priest, Dorriforth does not even consider her in a romantic light until Miss Woodley confesses Miss Milner's affection for him upon his exit from the priesthood and transformation from Dorriforth into Lord Elmwood (165). When Elmwood responds to these overtures positively, Miss Milner shows her masculine aggression by trying to assert her control over him, which, she notes, makes Elmwood behave like a sentimental belle swooning with love: "He trembled...and that manly, firm voice faltered, as mine does some times" (202). Inchbald thus gestures to Elmwood's effeminacy not directly, such as through his clothes, but indirectly: through his relationship with the increasingly masculine traits of Miss Milner. She defies Dorriforth's male authority even before they are lovers—indeed, the Jesuit Sandford finds "his friend Dorriforth frequently perplexed in the management of his ward" (92)—and thereby establishes her own authority, a part of Miss Milner's increasingly masculine character in the city. In other words, while the culture of sensibility as it is expressed in the city is linked to male metrosexuals—men who appear and act like women—this combination also seems to create female metrosexuals who are more masculine than other ladies. Far from being the ever-passive victims of their environments, as male nerve theorists and commentators describe them, these female sentimental heroines appear to be fortified by their metropolitan surroundings.

Typical of novels of sensibility, both fictions trace "a young lady's entrance into the world," to echo the subtitle of Burney's novel, and both detail their lovely protagonists' introductions to and early trials in the great metropolis of London. Evelina is introduced to us as a shy and naïve (and therefore appropriately feminine) country bumpkin, fresh from Villars's country estate, while Miss Milner has arrived at Dorriforth's London doorstep from a Protestant boarding school. Before long in London, both young ladies show a new side. Our sentimental heroines do not follow the trajectory of increasing nervous debility in the city, as Beddoes's and Trotter's works suggest they should. Burney and Inchbald seem to assert that the city makes women more assertive, courageous, and even aggressive—in a word, more masculine.

To varying degrees, both novelists indicate that their sentimental heroines develop a masculine edge during their time in London. This pattern is most evident in *A Simple Story*. Miss Milner's masculinity is most obviously on display when she indulges in the temptations of the great city, such as partying. Inchbald associates partygoing with city living early in the novel when she writes of Miss Milner's first morning in London: "After a night's rest,... her thoughts [were] pleasingly occupied with the reflection [that] she was in that gay metropolis—a wild rapturous picture of which her active fancy had often formed" (68). Later in the novel, Miss Milner illustrates her autonomy in the face of male control by going to a masquerade party against Elmwood's wishes—and she does so dressed as a man, according to her footman. In response to the footman's assertion to Elmwood and Sandford that Miss Milner wore boots to the party—apparel that belonged only in a masculine wardrobe in the period, and usually as a part of military gear—Miss Milner's loyal maid retorts, "They were not boots.... [I]ndeed,... they were only half boots," to which the Jesuit Sandford replies, "What has a woman to do with *any* boots?" (191–92; emphasis in original).[7] Precisely because they were associated with the military, boots are an apt expression of Miss Milner's increasing masculine power—and Inchbald's opposition to popular ideas in nerve theory about the effects of the city upon women. While Beddoes and Trotter claim that the nervous woman of sensibility, a proto-Patmorian "Angel in the House," is weak, almost bodiless, so fragile are her fleshly borders, and that the city only intensifies her debility, Inchbald implies that London cures, at least partially, these troubling symptoms of Romantic-era femininity.

As for Burney's Evelina, subtle signs of her increasingly powerful character appear throughout the novel. This protagonist can hardly be called "masculine," but she does move from being what Villars dubs a "little angel" (21) of the country estate to a woman who is less naïve, much more independent, and even courageous in the city. One of the major markers of her increasing strength is her ability to speak in the presence of men, which she could not do early in the novel, so timid was she (e.g., 32, 43). By the middle of the tale, Evelina's courage and strength are undeniable, for she *wrestles loaded pistols away from a suicidal* man, Mr. Macartney (183–85)! If Miss Milner appears militaristic for wearing boots, then Evelina is a regular Rambo in this episode. True, she "trembles," is called an "angel" by Macartney and is constantly on the verge of fainting during this scene—all signs that she retains her place as an ideal woman of sensibility—but she nevertheless succeeds in wresting loaded guns away from the suicidal Macartney and, when he attempts to reclaim them, to maintain her control over the weapons (184). This scene illustrates powerfully how the city has changed the character of our "little rustic." If Evelina is, nevertheless, not quite manly, she is a good deal more macho than her shy, retiring, rural self—or, for that matter, Lovel.

Unexpected as these masculinized metropolitan females in novels of sensibility may be—given that the female protagonists of such fictions are traditionally portrayed as weak and always fainting, in keeping with nerve theorists' descriptions of nervous illness in women—perhaps more surprising is the fact that these same texts of nerve theory inadvertently provide an aetiology for the manly health and robustness of Miss Milner and Evelina. Trotter and Beddoes suggest that a lack of exercise and confinement to cramped quarters, like shop-fronts, are to blame for the effeminacy of the male metrosexual. By the same token, I suggest, these female heroines of sensibility appear to have gained fortitude through the freedom and activity that the city offers to them. Perhaps Burney and Inchbald imply that the new activities associated with the city, such as going to balls, shopping and walking in pleasure gardens, strengthen the woman of sensibility. Burney emphasizes that her protagonist is swept up in a whirlwind of activity on reaching the capital. Evelina moves from "humble retirement" with Villars, in a "retired place, to which Dorchester, the nearest town, is seven miles distant" (21), to London "in full splendour," as Evelina describes it, in anticipation of its "Two Playhouses...—the Opera-House,—Renelagh,—the Pantheon" (25), each of which she visits—and as soon as possible. She writes in her first letter to Villars from London, "This moment arrived. Just going to Drury-Lane theatre" (27). In another early letter to Villars, she notes, "We came home from the ridotto so late, or rather, so early, that it was not possible for me to write" (41). Evelina goes out so much in London that she begins to tire of it: "I would not live here for the world. I don't care how soon we leave town. London soon grows so tiresome," she complains on Tuesday (38). Yet, when she turns down the opportunity for more activity on Thursday, she feels trapped and bored:

> This morning was destined for seeing sights, auctions, curious shops, and so forth; but my head ached, and I was not in a humour to be

amused, and so I made them go without me, though very unwillingly.... And now I am sorry I did not accompany them, for I know not what to do with myself. (39)

That these activities involve some degree of exercise is confirmed in Evelina's description of the "cascade" at Vauxhall: she writes that her walking companion, Mr. Smith, "hurried me away, mixing with a crowd of people, all running with so much velocity, that I could not imagine what had raised such an alarm" (195). For Evelina, London is a place of constant activity and exercise.

Similarly, in *A Simple Story*, Miss Milner's days revolve around parties, shopping, and visits. The narrator muses, "Six weeks have now elapsed since Miss Milner has been in London, partaking with delight in all its pleasures," so much so that Dorriforth can scarcely snatch a moment to speak to her between her "visits and visitors," but, when he does, he "pressed the necessity of 'time not always passed in society; of reflection; of reading; of thought for a future state'" (72). Evidently, Miss Milner does not partake in these restful activities, or he would not recommend them to her. Also tellingly, Miss Milner informs Miss Woodley, "if he [Elmwood] will not submit to be my lover, I will not submit to be his wife" (187); since the masquerade ball is the occasion of the final battle of wills between the lovers before they marry, the subject of Miss Milner's party going becomes linked to her masculine boldness, which threatens to destroy her relationship with her fiancé. Thus, both novels of sentiment present the city as a place of increased activity and masculinity for their female protagonists and suggest, however subtly, that male-authored representations of the nervous woman of sensibility in the city are inaccurate. Just as Evelina defies male physical power in the gun-snatching scene and Miss Milner challenges male authority by repeatedly flouting Elmwood/Dorriforth's commands, Burney and Inchbald undermine male medical authority by presenting metropolitan women of sensibility who are, to varying degrees, masculine.

My theory about the gender-bending properties of the city in texts that contribute to the Romantic-era culture of sensibility—whether they be novels of sensibility or treatises on nerve theory—is not borne out by all works of either kind, or even with perfect consistency within these novels.[8] Significantly, though, the female protagonists and several of the male characters of these highly representative novels of sensibility illuminate claims made by influential nerve theorists regarding the effect of the city on the expression of one's gender. In their treatment of male characters, Inchbald and Burney seem to illustrate very accurately Beddoes's and Trotter's theories; Inchbald even mocks the feminine manners of male clerks in women's clothes-stores exactly as Beddoes and Trotter do. However, both female novelists suggest that the city has a rousing and masculinizing effect on women. The city, they seem to assert, offers women room to stretch their limbs and fortify their nervous constitutions. The same locale of cramped desk-jobs and milliners' shops that debilitate their male counterparts is, for women, the scene of increased freedom and physical activity. In relation to an ideal of male activity, city life is positively stultifying, weakening, but, in relation to the lifestyle of the upper-class rural woman, the city offers a range of new activities. Beddoes and Trotter link the negative effects of the city upon the nerves of men and women with the lack of exercise available to city-dwellers, but Inchbald's and Burney's famous novels suggest that Romantic-era nerve theory did not assess the lived experience of women accurately. These female authors appear to use the literary realm to challenge influential medical and distinctly masculine notions of the effects of the city upon women's bodies, and especially their nervous constitutions. By offering their fictional narratives as correctives to male medical authority, Inchbald and Burney achieve a kind of feminist *coup*—and by couching their challenge in a literary form widely thought to celebrate and preserve female passivity, these authors accomplish their ideological rebellion from within the ranks of the opposition.

Notes

I would like to thank the Faculty of Arts Dean's Office at the University of Manitoba and SSHRC for providing me with funding to attend the ICR 2009 conference in New York City, where I presented the conference paper from which this chapter is derived. I would also like to thank Larry H. Peer for inviting me to submit this essay, the organizers of ICR 2009, especially Josh Wilner, and, for their invaluable feedback, those who presented at and attended the panel on which I presented the conference paper.

1. I do not suggest that Inchbald and Burney were influenced by or challenged directly Beddoes's and Trotter's texts specifically, but that these novelists contributed to the culture of sensibility to which male nerve theorists also contributed, and that Beddoes's and Trotter's well-known texts are representative of the (entirely male) medical establishment's view of nervous illness in the early Romantic era. Also, although I use general terms such as "men" and "women" in this chapter, the specific subject of these texts of nerve theory, the literature of sentiment, and, thus, my chapter is the middle- to upper-class English person.

2. In the Romantic period, the medical profession as a whole was becoming increasingly specialized, and doctors seeking to protect their chosen fields from apothecaries and midwives with no formal education,

as well as from "gossips" (local women who dispensed medical advice and prescriptions for traditional cures), began lobbying for stricter rules regarding the qualifications necessary to practice medicine. Physicians asserted that their specialized, university-level education, from which women were barred, warranted them alone to practice medicine. Except for the apothecaries, most of the traditional, nonacademic health-care workers were women, either "gossips" or midwives. As such, the division that physicians were attempting to establish was, simultaneously, the initiation of a masculinist medical authority over a feminine and domestic medical authority.
3. I do not distinguish between "sensibility" and "sentimentalism" (or, here, "sentiment"), as G. S. Rousseau does (141).
4. That Miss Milner "falls" through adultery in the third volume of *A Simple Story* may be offered as a rebuttal to the suggestion that Inchbald presents her protagonist as a woman of sensibility. However, since Inchbald's is, undeniably, a novel of sensibility and Miss Milner is its heroine, we must consider that the author uses the character to comment on the form and its ideals in some way.
5. In Wollstonecraft's novella, the protagonist, Mary, writes a "rhapsody on sensibility," in which she hails it as "the foundation of all our happiness" (50), and describes sensibility as

   this quickness, this delicacy of feeling... which expands the soul, gives an enthusiastic greatness, mixed with tenderness, when we view the magnificent objects of nature; or hear of a good action.... Softened by tenderness; the soul is disposed to be virtuous. Is any sensual gratification to be compared to that of feeling the eyes moistened after having comforted the unfortunate? (49–50)
6. I refer to Dorriforth/Elmwood by using the name with which he is identified at the point in the novel that I describe.
7. Inchbald also describes Miss Milner's costume as distinctly feminine in other ways, writing, "although it was the representative of the goddess of Chastity,... it had, on the first glance, the appearance of a female much less virtuous" (187). This description furnishes further material for a consideration of Inchbald's challenge to traditional ideas about feminine identity. Indeed, through these clothes, Miss Milner represents both aspects of the angel/whore dichotomy at once, a seemingly impossible situation that undercuts the viability of these limiting roles. Inchbald also seems to encourage her readers to consider the significance of this scene by giving her protagonist a name that suggests the importance of clothes for her: "Milner" (like "milliner").
8. For example, the weak and weepy Mr. Villars dwells in the countryside and is therefore no hale and hearty rustic.

2

Wordsworth's Double-Take

William Galperin

> *At issue…is history as our own unassimilable alterity, our difference from the directions in which "history" is pushing us…a different conception of history—one where historical thinking is the dimension in which thought becomes responsible to what is other, lost, unconscious, or potential, yet to be.*
>
> Raja Tilottama, "Imagining History" *(428, 433)*
>
> [T]he world is Eden enough, all the Eden there can be, and what is more, all the world there is.… Romanticism's work… [is] the task of bringing the world back, as to life.
>
> Stanley Cavell, In Quest of the Ordinary *(52–53)*

"It was, in truth, / An ordinary sight, but…" So writes Wordsworth in one of *The Prelude*'s more memorable segues that I have deliberately truncated. I have done so because my interest, following the poet's own intuition, is with the "ordinary…but"—with the ordinary as something more or extra—rather than with the sublime interiority or "visionary dreariness" to which Wordsworth immediately assigns the sight in a characteristic, if possibly erroneous, move. My truncation might well be viewed as a truncation of romanticism itself, which commentators from Coleridge to Paul de Man have variously identified as incorporating a movement of mind from the particular to the universal or, in de Man's lexicon, from the "earthly and material" to the "mental and celestial" (13). And indeed an otherwise "ordinary sight"—"A Girl who bore a pitcher on her head / And seemed with difficult steps to force her way / Against the blowing wind" (306–8)—ultimately rises in Wordsworth's description to the level of vision. But equally important is the way the ordinary irrupts here only to evanesce. For the ordinary's evanescence—in this case, into something personal and aesthetic—is not simply a foregone conclusion that the transitional conjunction ("but") anticipates and abets; it is an introjection as well in which something at once ordinary and not (again, the "ordinary...but") is palpably reconfigured, even counterfeited, as a romantic and mnemonic surplus. Although decades-old and necessarily a feature of memory, the passage of the ordinary into vision is as much an anterior negotiation as an abiding and still-pressing obligation: "It was, in truth, / An ordinary sight; but I should need / Colours and words that are unknown to man / To paint the visionary dreariness / Which, while I looked round for my lost guide, / Did at that time invest the naked Pool, / The Beacon on the lonely Eminence, / The Woman, and her garments vexed and tossed / By the strong wind" (308–16).

Wordsworth, by his own admission, is no painter. And were he a painter, he would have encountered considerable difficulty here, since the scene before him is really a condensation of three discrete events that took place ostensibly in sequence when Wordsworth was about five years old: his separation from his riding companion and guide; his coming upon a place where "in former times / A Murderer had been hung" (288–89) and where someone had then "carved the murderer's name" on the "turf" (294, 292); and lastly, his sighting of the woman with the pitcher upon "reascending the bare Common" (303). The traumatic conjunction of these events, involving an encounter with memorials of violence in the wake of what seemed like abandonment to a young boy, amply accounts for the additional freight that the "ordinary sight" is summoned to bear. But there is a sense, too, both in the image of the woman, and in the poet's backhanded and retrospective wish for painterly skills, that the peculiar excess of the only "ordinary" event of the three owes at least as much to a lived and residual actuality, to something palpable and material, that a painter might better capture. Wordsworth is no painter. Still, neither his inadequacy as a visual artist, nor his implicit critique of painting as inadequate to the scene as he recalls it, work entirely to the benefit of his present business: namely poetry. If painting does not exactly serve the interests of interiority and memory, it is the case too that "words"—Wordsworth's words—are far from the vehicle par excellence for representing the ordinary or, again, the "ordinary...but." By writing *his* story rather than painting it, Wordsworth allows the "real"—the historical and material real—to "perish into art" (in Walter Benjamin's strikingly apt description [47]) in the same way that the poet's *inability* to render the "ordinary sight" by visual means, or even by a combination of words and colors, provides a momentary reprieve from death by representation. By no means am I arguing that painting rather than poetry is the answerable medium for representing the ordinary, however charged. My point is that the force of the ordinary is such, even decades later, that its internalization is chalked up to a *failure* of representation even as it remains, as both the poet warrants and as numerous commentators have shown, a triumph of mind. Thus while painting per se is deemed inadequate to the event, something akin to an impossible or "unknown" version of painting is simultaneously projected as the only way to do justice to a sight whose transformation into vision is also something of a missed opportunity, at least in representational terms. Although the problem confronting Wordsworth appears to be art's failure in this instance to capture a particularly charged moment, the real failure here lies in the misrecognition—administered by "but" 's passage from qualifier to conjunction—by which an otherwise "ordinary sight" is written out of history into Wordsworth's story.

If this contortion with Wordsworth reveals anything—beyond the now-obligatory practice of contorting Wordsworth's poetry to one exegetical purpose or other—it is the necessary connection between the misrecognition that defines and characterizes poetical representation in these lines and "what" is otherwise missed or transfigured in what Michel de Certeau has termed "the writing of history." For in verging on a history of what was before it somehow wasn't, or in encountering the "ordinary" in a guise so arresting that it is immediately refigured as the work of imagination and interiority, Wordsworth makes art's failure to grasp what is close by, pitching its tents before him as he moves, a confirmation of something lived and something real. In other words, far from a problematic tic, or even a vitiation, of the "romantic ideology," it is a characteristic, and I would argue representative, feature of Wordsworth's writing here that the material opportunities it variously misses—or that variously evanesce—are both recoverable and acutely palpable in consequence of being missed (or misrepresented) in what amounts to a "history of missed opportunities." In such a history, the claim to historicity is advanced in a manner that the characteristic—indeed temporalized—movement of something earthly into something imagined is very much a "history...of departed things" (to borrow a phrase from the Prospectus to *The Recluse* [50]) in which things appear to evanesce (or appear *only* to evanesce) in a characteristically romantic process that is intermittently readable as an illusion.

In making such "a history," which necessarily honors what it rules out of bounds, a matter of literary and cultural history, I am motivated by the same empirical legacy that drove Romantics such as Coleridge to different, more idealistic, paradigms and to more definitive versions of romanticism, where subjectivity and imagination are the hallmarks of individuality and genius.[1] The principal goad to romanticism in this humanistic formation remains a largely contrary, uniformitarian, view of human nature and interiority by which people are undifferentiated through various mental processes and by the hardwiring to which these mental activities point. At the same time, the bearing of empirical thinking on a real so recessive now that it amounts to a "history only of departed things"—beyond the fact that that real is no longer in doubt or a matter of skepticism—is more immediately lodged in the Prospectus's counterproposal of a "fiction of what...was" (51). Such a notion not only describes the probabilistic writing with which the rise of the novel, particularly as a realistic instrument, was largely coextensive at this time; but it also describes the "fiction" that informs (or, as de Certeau argues, "haunts") the writing of history at this same moment (*Heterologies* 219). The very protocols in fact to which history writing was being urged to conform by Hume and others in the eighteenth century were virtually identical to those that Frances Burney articulated in urging her sister novelists to take "aid from Sober Probability" (8). To Hume, anterior "objects of which we have no experience" must be made to resemble "those of which we have [experience]" in history writing because "what we have found to be most usual is always most probable" and likely to have been that way (124). Whether this customary view of things, in which the usual is extended diachronically as well as synchronically, was responsible in the end for a more social or general conception of history against the more traditional form, which had focused on exemplary, individual agents and the extraordinary events they had either shaped or encountered, is still a matter of speculation.[2] But what seems especially pertinent to many literary texts of this period, romantic and otherwise, has surprisingly little to do with the antihumanistic bent of empirically based understanding to which romantic voluntarism and individualism were obvious reactions. Central to these texts is the romantic, or again period-bound, reaction to a more subtle development that Wordsworth actually flags in both *The Prelude* and elsewhere: namely, the separation or growing nonequivalence of the probable, on the one hand, and the ordinary or the everyday, on the other, whose implicit opposition to both probabilizing and *idealizing* initiatives marks it not just for evanescence (as we have seen) but, paradoxically or so it seems, for return—in this case as an emergent category for which history, specifically a history of something missed and overlooked, is primarily a placeholder.

Based therefore on a seemingly contingent relationship of means and ends, or between certain retrospective procedures and their emergent or conceptual yield, the various mechanisms by which the ordinary or the everyday comes initially into view in romantic-period writing require a much tighter focus than the current tendency to think in longer intervals, and with longer historical narratives at issue, typically warrants. For what the mechanisms associated with the everyday's emergence urge, beginning indeed with the antiempirical hypothesis, is a particular kind of attention, or slowing down, by which literature, in this case, is sufficiently estranged from its own procedures to be text and context at once. Far from duplicating certain generic norms, literature of the romantic period, be it Wordsworth's poetry or Austen's fiction, frequently counterposes what are effectively two modes of history: one that uses the past, and in the case of empiricism an aggregated past, as a template for generalizing about human life and human nature, and another mode—a "retrospect of what might have been" (to borrow a phrase from *Mansfield Park* [415]—in which something prior is sufficiently unprecedented to undermine its reproducibility in any form apart from something that *may* have happened. Literature of the period, in other words, harbors possibilities not simply in the way certain events, certain ordinary events, are able to emerge from the amnesia of generic interdiction and but also in the way certain assumptions about the period, notably the anti-empirical hypothesis, are sharply qualified by that emergence. It is not of course that the anti-empirical hypothesis lacks proof, whether practically or theoretically; it is rather that in positing a rather tendentious distinction between the "English idealism" of Hume or Berkeley (as Henri Bergson termed it [239]) and that of Coleridge, the hypothesis loses traction in disregarding a new category of experience that, while seemingly cognate, is distinct, again, from what empiricists call the probable. A brief look at the OED would appear to confirm this. The everyday (as opposed to the ordinary which had primarily been a class designation) clearly developed into a concept in need of a term sometime in the mid-eighteenth century, eventually achieving an apotheosis in the notion of "everydayness" in the 1840s. But what this also means is that the particulars of this development, which appears to have crystallized in the new century, are all that we have to go on. As a category *in process*, the everyday registers a series of distinctions now, or better still separations, that are quite minimal, whether in Austen's narratives, where circumstantial detail complicates the probabilism of plot and setting,[3] or in Wordsworth's poetry, which verges on a world that regardless of its historicity is strangely emergent.

II

We can take as an illustration of this emergence a poem by Wordsworth that is not just synonymous with British romanticism in its conventional or received formation but a work as well whose principal task is to separate what the mind or the imagination apparently offers the subject in contrast to the material and temporal vicissitudes of ordinary life. The poem is the well-known "Ode" (later subtitled "Intimations of Immortality from Recollections of Early Childhood"), which seeks to guarantee the persistence of a "visionary gleam" or sense of "glory" that has fled the world with the passage of time. Readers will remember very clearly the probabilistic course of human existence that the poem outlines in place of what in either *The Prelude* or in "Tintern Abbey" is a more clearly defined developmental trajectory involving a "paradise regained" through the interaction of mind and nature. The "Ode" is more qualified. After a four-stanza beginning in which the barely remembered plenitude of childhood is juxtaposed to a present marked by disenchantment, the poem proceeds haphazardly to answer the question on which its inaugural stanzas and, not coincidentally, its initial phase of composition came to an abrupt halt: "Whither is fled the visionary gleam? / Where is it now the glory and the dream?" (56–57).

We might consider the two years during which Wordsworth fashioned an answer to these questions as an interval in which something like historical distance was either achieved or interposed by way of validating what is already implied in the form of the initial questions: namely, that the glory and the dream—if they are anywhere—are proximate and close at hand ("Where is it now...?"). For what stands as history in the poem thus far is sharply dissociated not only from the present, where the glories of the past are pretty much nonexistent, but also from anything that might have been a present at some point. If the two years that Wordsworth took to complete the "Ode" involved anything like retrospection on his part, therefore, it was less "a retrospect of what might have been—but what never can be now" (to quote Austen's statement in full), than a retrospection of what might have been because it "is" and presumably *was*.

But how exactly does one fashion such a history? The answer is "very quickly" or as rapidly as it takes for there to be an interval to create historical distance. We can take as an example of such fashioning the ordinary or "meanest flower" in "Ode"'s final lines, the one that famously gives "thoughts that do often lie too deep for tears" (206–7). This is the same flower, presumably, glimpsed earlier in the poem: first, as a personification and, in virtually that same instant, as something less mystified and more natural:

> —But there's a Tree, of many, one,
> A single Field which I have looked upon,
> Both of them speak of something that is gone:

>   The Pansy at my feet
>   Doth the same tale repeat:
>   Whither is fled the visionary gleam?
>   Where is it now, the glory and the dream? (51–57)

Without belaboring the difference between a declarative statement of loss and a question that bears the promise, at least rhetorically, of some recovery in the present, it is clear that the pansy does not just repeat the tale inferred from either the tree or the field. It alters the tale in quickly segueing from a debased or fallen present to something equally present if indeterminate. Out of nowhere, or so it seems, the prosopopoeia is inverted in deference to the flower, whose speech is more properly ventriloquized and whose pressure as a thing rather than a figure—and eventually a meanest or ordinary thing—is additionally registered in an interrogative that turns on "it." This double-take is fundamentally a retroactive procedure in which something prior or "before" the subject is restored to an original and ordinary state. And it happens—at least for Wordsworth—with a suddenness best encapsulated by a phrase from Austen's *Emma* (and from the memorable character of Miss Bates) who in a rare moment of economy states flatly, "What is before me, I see" (157). "Before" is more than just a spatial designation, indicating something that, as Miss Bates routinely reminds us, is independent of the self and demands deference; it points, in Wordsworth and in Austen (whose discovery of the everyday is largely apotheosized in Miss Bates), to something alternately prior and present.[4]

On the face of it, this seems counterintuitive, especially for Wordsworth, whose characteristic move is often from the material and debased present to a privileged and internalized past. But the double-take actually reverses that process in removing the initial perception from internalization and from the pathetic fallacies deployed to register interiority. The double-take, accordingly, not only identifies the initial take as a mis-take; it identifies it as a supervention upon something anterior if still fathomable, so that a retrojection of "what" *is* becomes, in a single stroke, a projection simultaneously of "what" really was.

Such a maneuver is far from self-evident, especially in a poem where memory, particularly of childhood, is enlarged and privileged as a form of vision. And so for the duration of the "Ode" the history of missed opportunities is a counterpart, and a mostly silent one, to a probabilistic account of things, chiefly the progress of life from the "heaven-born freedom" of childhood to the "earthly freight" of "custom" or experience (129–30). Unlike Austen, however, for whom probability is part of a dialectic and linked to truths that, as Miss Bates reminds us, are alternately irrevocable and a foreclosure on what is "before" us, probability is for the most part a register of despair in the "Ode" rather than an acknowledgment, however qualified, of an empirical worldview. This distinction becomes especially obvious in the poem's final stanzas when the speaker departs from the probabilistic collective of humans he had been speaking of (and on whose behalf) in the first-person plural to talk specifically about himself and about the separate peace or compensation he has managed to secure. Most readings of the poem follow the poet's own mythologizing here, chalking this compensation up to a heroic, highly individualized, act of recovery through imagination and memory. However the concluding turn is perhaps better explained by recognizing that the speaker's sudden valuation of things registered by sensory means actually represents a step back from a strictly phenomenological or idealistic stance to the world.

In the context of the poem's argument, such stepping backward would appear to mark a return, administered by memory, imagination or both, to an earlier, proto-phenomenological state, which the speaker nevertheless distinguishes from the "simple creed / Of Childhood" (139–40):

> Not for these I raise
> The song of thanks and praise;
> But for those obstinate questionings
> Of sense and outward things,
> Fallings from us, vanishings;
> Blank misgivings of a Creature
> Moving about in worlds not realized,
> High instincts, before which our mortal Nature
> Did tremble like a guilty Thing surprized. (142–50)

To be sure, things get a little murky here, especially in the way imagination or high instinct is oddly dissociated from its source in the mind. That is because what the poem and the poet are verging toward, and what has been shadowing the probabilistic argument from the beginning, is not so much the condition described in the earlier or primal scene earlier but something at once prior *and* more present—what Harry Harootunian has, in a different context, called a "noncontemporaneous contemporary" (477). This "noncontemporaneous contemporary" is the "everyday." And its status as an experience distinct from either an empirical or an idealistic one is demarcated in a clinching observation after which the pansy reemerges as something other than an armature of expression. The "thoughts that do often lie too deep for tears" that the "meanest flower" provokes at the poem's end certainly presuppose a deep interiority consistent with our received sense of British romanticism. But this concluding move to depth and singularity—which is intermittent and disarticulated in any case from the expressive functions typically associated with romanticism—is preceded as well by a sudden and clinching turn to a condition and to a mode of sustenance that is distinctly nonindividuated and presented as a human dispensation in general:

> Though nothing can bring back the hour
> Of splendour in the grass, of glory in the flower
> We will grieve not, rather find
> Strength in what remains behind. (180–83)

"Behind," like Miss Bates's "before," refers not only to the residue of the present. It refers simultaneously to something before or prior that alternately precedes and supersedes the "romantic" response to empiricism, which the subsequent description of "what remains" as being here and there, as subjective and objective—as something at once "primal," "philosophic," and counterintuitive ("the soothing thoughts that spring / Out of human suffering"... "the faith that looks through death")—nicely approximates (184–89). For in this way, the final turn, some might argue return, to the individuated speaker ("To me the meanest flower that blows....") is also a turning away. In gaining access finally to something previously overlooked, and in making that access the signature of a subjectivity that is representative but not necessarily uniform or probabilistic (a "heart of hearts" [193]), the single self that emerges in the poem's last lines is a decidedly different or rediscovered self: one sufficiently immured in the everyday now that "alone" (22) is no longer or perforce the qualifier of "me."

Coleridge of course saw things quite differently. It was Wordsworth's achievement, he recalled, "to give the charm of novelty to things of every day... by awakening the mind's attention from the lethargy of custom, and directing it to the loveliness and the wonders of the world before us; an inexhaustible treasure, but for which in consequence of the film of familiarity and selfish solicitude we have eyes, yet see not, ears that hear not, and hearts that neither feel nor understand" (2: 7). This may well have been the aim when Wordsworth and Coleridge were collaborating on *Lyrical Ballads* but it was not long before everything that Coleridge is describing here was exposed to a second look. While Coleridge is clearly tarrying with a missed opportunity that Wordsworth's poetry restores in some fashion, the particular recovery that the double take performs in Wordsworth is very much at cross-purposes with what he outlines. What the double take facilitates is not just a disarticulation of the "every day" from "the charm of novelty," and from the particular, indeed "selfish," endowment that was and remains Wordsworthian "custom," but a disarticulation, however temporary, of history and memory by which the Wordsworthian subject temporarily joins those unexpressive but also unimposing "hearts" from whom he was previously isolated. This last may appear to be nothing more than a simple retrenchment to a more nebulous "preromantic" condition of sociability and uniformity. But it is also—and by the "new historicism" that provokes it—a development *upon* "English idealism" and a "third way" back to the future. Or, borrowing from the "Ode" itself, the "one delight" that the speaker claims to have "relinquished" finally—namely "to live beneath [the] habitual sway" (193–94) of the "Fountains, Meadows, Hills and Groves" (190)—moves processually, in effect, from an idealized, barely memorable, immersion in a world that is irretrievable and, for all practical purposes, prehistoric, to other opportunities *in time* that have been missed or discounted. For in a restaging of the doubletake, this time at the level of argument, "to live beneath" or within the habitual sway of nature and the world is no sooner a "delight" that has been "relinquished" than a condition, or better still a precondition, for the recompense such relinquishment affords: in the "Brooks" (195), in the "new-born Day" (197), in the "Clouds that gather round the setting sun" (199) and, last but hardly least, in the "meanest flower that blows," all of which are viewed again and for the first time.

III

For all its success in establishing an alternative to the probable, the "Intimations Ode" is somewhat less clear in demarcating an alternative to the marvelous and to the conventionally romantic. That's because the ordinary here, unlike the ordinary sight with which we began, is located entirely in nature, which remains a mystified category despite its overdetermination. A more indicative poem, then—one in which the double-take opens onto something palpably distinct from both the customary *and* the ideal—is the brief sketch from *Lyrical Ballads* (1798), "Old Man Travelling" subtitled "Animal Tranquillity and Decay." As in *Prelude* 11, the ordinary is defined by a person in this instance, whose ordinariness (as opposed to objecthood) is linked not only to the method of its disclosure (in this case the double-take) but to a disclosure where the perceiving or poetical subject is once again estranged from himself and his procedures.

> The little hedge-row birds,
> That peck along the road, regard him not.
> He travels on, and in his face, his step,

> His gait, is one expression; every limb,
> His look and bending figure, all bespeak
> A man who does not move with pain, but moves
> With thought—He is insensibly subdued
> To settled quiet: he is one by whom
> All effort seems forgotten, one to whom
> Long patience has such mild composure given,
> That patience now doth seem a thing, of which
> He hath no need. He is by nature led
> To peace so perfect, that the young behold
> With envy, what the old man hardly feels.
> —I asked him whither he was bound, and what
> The object of his journey; he replied
> "Sir! I am going many miles to take
> A last leave of my son, a mariner,
> Who from a sea-fight has been brought to Falmouth,
> And there is dying in an hospital."

The corrective that the "old man" administers to the speaker's eloquent, if extravagant, surmise would appear on the surface to represent a return to the ordinary, especially as a subset of what Wordsworth, in the Preface to *Lyrical Ballads*, terms the "more than common" (595).

But if the ordinary is ultimately *anywhere* in the poem, it is located and characteristically *missing* in the space between the two linguistic moments. The initial description, which constitutes most of the poem, is nothing less than poetry itself or a particular version of representation aligned with interior or imaginative projection. And the poem more or less concedes this, attesting not only to the old man's subjugation, but also to the way he moves and is thus animated "with thought." Correspondingly, the man's reply, which necessarily jolts the poem out of poetry into social and geopolitical reality, seems equally stagy and generic. Less an instance of what Wordsworth, in the Preface to *Lyrical Ballads*, terms "the very language of men" (600), particularly those whom he would have encountered in either the Lake District or the West Country, the reply bears a normative elegance of a kind that we associate with Dr. Johnson, especially reported by Boswell. This normativizing drive, which critics from Coleridge to John Barrell have picked up on by way of disputing Wordsworth's democratizing initiative, at least in matters of diction, is probably less sinister than either Coleridge's praise or Barrell's blame might suggest. Rather, the continuity of the man's diction with poetic diction projects a sociability or uniformity reflective of the peculiar leveling that empiricism performs in its generalizing view of human nature. And leveling, to be sure, is what "Animal Tranquillity and Decay" accomplishes in radically separating poetic utterance from its subtitular trajectory.

But there is one more thing that happens or that the poem can be said to project. And it takes place at the moment that the speaker shifts from projective contemplation to social interaction. That moment is marked only by a space between the lines or more immediately by the dash preceding "I asked." But the question that ensues, which is the supplement or manifestation of a curiosity *over something*, tells us a great deal. What it tells—or permits us to fathom in the pause prior to the man's reply—is the force of something more than common, something ordinary again, that neither imaginative projection nor recuperated speech, nor even the man's disclosure about his son can justify, much less figure. It is not that the man's reply lacks force or even a kind of sublimity. It is simply that the force of his reply is different again from whatever roused the speaker to question him in the first place, interrupting the *work* of poetry in two senses.

A related, possibly better, example of this interruption in Wordsworth, and of the history and the ordinariness it inscribes in something analogous to invisible ink, may be found in "The Two April Mornings," which appeared in the 1800 edition of *Lyrical Ballads*. Like the majority of the Matthew poems in both editions of *Lyrical Ballads*, the poem records a conversation between Matthew and his Wordsworthian interlocutor, which is quickly displaced by Matthew's recollection of "a day like this...Full thirty years behind" (23–24). On that day, Matthew recalls, as "The self-same crimson hew / Fell from the sky...The same which I now view" (26–28), he came upon the grave of his daughter, Emma, who had died at the age of nine and whom he remembers loving "more" at that moment "than...[he] e'er had loved before" (39–40):

> And, turning from her grave, I met
> Beside the church-yard Yew
> A blooming Girl, whose hair was wet
> With points of morning dew.
> A basket on her head she bare,
> Her brow was smooth and white,
> To see a Child so very fair,
> It was a pure delight! (41–48)

It may be fortuitous that it is a female carrying something on her head who is the placeholder again for what is both contingent and more than common. But the transfiguration that follows, where the "girl" is immediately likened to a "happy...wave...danc[ing] on the sea" (51–52), is hardly accidental and typical rather of the "intentional structures" to which the object world invariably conforms in Wordsworth. Where in *Prelude* 11 this symbolic movement to "vision" is largely unidirectional, it is limited and perpetually reversible in "The Two April Mornings." This is so thanks to a now-stubborn materiality that, to borrow from the inaugural Matthew poem, "Expostulation and Reply," operates not just "with" but ultimately "against" the subject's "will" (20):

> There came from me a sigh of pain
> Which I could ill confine;
> I looked at her and looked again
> —And did not wish her mine. (53–56)

Although the pain that Matthew experienced owes presumably to the recognition that the blooming girl before him is *not* his daughter, it issues, at least by recollection, from a subject not exactly or continuously self-identical with the grieving father. This is even truer of the double-take that follows, where Matthew is also divided: first, between looking and looking, and then, between wishing and not wishing. It would appear that it is the second look, rather than the first, that creates division leading to divestiture, where the prerogative of ownership is relinquished along with the subject's self-possession, making any reassertion of the will a largely negative way ("I did not wish"), where desire and lack are (quoting the Matthew poem that precedes this one in the 1800 edition) "are all that must remain of [Matthew]" (33).

But the real point of the anecdote, along with the doubling of the two mornings—specifically those of the poem's past and of Matthew's past—devolves upon the double-take again, the look and the look. Like the pain within that comes seemingly from elsewhere, the looking and looking is not just an endless loop or circuit. It represents a new or different mode of seeing—a distension or splitting of the "look" over time (marked here, as in "Old Man Travelling," by a dash)—in which something lost or missed, specifically the blooming girl, is recovered despite the equally palpable and wrenching loss that had threatened to subsume her. This recovery is also painful since it involves (as the Matthew's sigh alerts us) a letting go of the pain and love that are properly constitutive of the subject in mourning. But what emerges at the end "The Two April Mornings," especially in the final stanza, is a dynamic if still evanescent sense of the ordinary, where the movement or oscillation between one look and another leads nowhere but to the blooming girl or, in the speaker's version of this same experience, to Matthew in a "now" different and defamiliarized formation:

> Matthew is in his grave, yet now
> Methinks I see him stand,
> As at that moment, with his bough
> Of wilding in his hand. (57–60)

The act of seeing Matthew so long after the fact is no doubt an act of imagination. Still, it is typical of the trajectory of this poem that, far from disappearing in a moment of vision, the ordinary emerges from the welter of both memory and thought in the recollection of Matthew attached to a very particular *thing*. There may be some ambiguity as to which moment is actually "that moment," and it is arguably the case that, like Matthew's double-take, the moment of Matthew standing condenses the speaker's recollection of him at the "moment" of interlocution and the reported moment of encounter and letting go.

Nevertheless, it is the effect of the poem overall, along with the history it inscribes (however fleeting), that it ironizes and subverts the titular pun by introducing a mode of remembrance—a temporalization of perception itself where exterior or real time supersedes interior time—in opposition to the work of mourning or grieving. This is not to suggest that the concluding image of Matthew standing is not still an imaginative representation or recovery. Rather it is that the illusion at the poem's close ("Methinks I see him stand") is less a bravura or sublime dilation on the order, say, of the first part of "Old Man Travelling," or the visionary dreariness of *Prelude* 11, than an image whose force remains tied to the way the speaker's remembrance actually narrows to a very particular materiality shorn of virtually all affect and meaning. Like the letting-go, then, administered by Matthew's double take, the emergence of the ordinary at the poem's close, where something demonstrably overlooked or missed irrupts to bear the freight of closure, is a telling divestiture: a submission to the world where, in a reversal of Benjamin's axiom (quoted earlier), art and subjectivity disappear into the real.

IV

I turn finally to the most overdetermined such encounter in the Wordsworthian oeuvre: the Blind Beggar in Book 7 of *The Prelude*. I do so because in the same way that the everyday has no meaning other than its emergence at this juncture, or apart from the toll that that emergence exacts on the subject/object dyad, the encounter with the beggar, for all its demonstrable yield critically and theoretically, is also an exegetical dead end. As I have written elsewhere, this episode in the section recounting Wordsworth's residence in London and the spectacle to which London is generally tantamount in the poet's view, follows upon Wordsworth's experience there in struggling, with very little success, to enlarge a mostly sensory experience into a moment of vision akin to the poem's other "spots of time" (Galperin, *The Return of the Visible* 99–128). But now I want to change direction somewhat and focus on the way the encounter with the beggar opens, like the "spot of time" with which I began, onto an emergent category of experience defined primarily by subtraction or by what is *not*: namely something neither probable nor marvelous. In Book 11, this definition comes in the stutter or hesitation marked by "but," where the traumatic memory on which the visionary is based, gives way, just briefly, to something equally anterior and distinct from the dreary condensation that words alone can barely describe. In Book 7, that process is reversed and distended as the people of London and, by turns, the beggar effectively wrest themselves—this time with the poet's cooperation—not only from the visionary formations to which *The Prelude* generally inclines but from the uniformity as well into which the city simultaneously dissolves.

Any reader of *The Prelude* remembers very well how the experience of London or of the mathematical sublime that *is* London thwarts all aspirations to a "romantic sublime"[5] in which the imagination might hold sway: a blockage that comes to both crisis and exegesis in the moment preceding the encounter with the beggar where Wordsworth describes a recurrent experience in the city:

> How often in the overflowing Streets,
> Have I gone forwards with the Crowd, and said
> Unto myself, the face of every one
> That passes by me is a mystery.
> Thus have I looked, nor ceased to look, oppressed
> By thoughts of what, and whither, when and how,
> Until the shapes before my eyes became
> A second-sight procession, such as glides
> Over still mountains, or appears in dreams;
> And all the ballast of familiar life—
> The present, and the past, hope, fear, all stays,
> All laws of acting, thinking, speaking man
> Went from me, neither knowing me, nor known. (595–607)

The mystery that the faces of London variously evoke resembles the mystery onto which the speaker of "Old Man Travelling" earlier stumbles and that his eventual question to the old man is intended to clarify and to illuminate. Here, however, the mystery is protracted by a mode of perception that, in the description at least, resembles a double-take ("Thus have I looked, nor ceased to look"), which ultimately involves a splitting of the subject into two: one who looks and looks again, submitting in effect to what he cannot comprehend, and another whose double-take eventually dissolves into its near-cousin, second sight, the effects of which, no matter how phantasmal, manage to bracket "familiar" or phenomenological "life" from everyday urban life.

It is at this point, then—with this distinction of the "familiar" and the "everyday" at the fore—that the speaker segues to the blind beggar:

> Amid the moving pageant, 'twas my chance
> Abruptly to be smitten with the view
> Of a blind Beggar, who, with upright face,
> Stood propped against a Wall, upon his Chest
> Wearing a written paper, to explain
> The story of the Man, and who he was.
> My mind did at this spectacle turn round
> As with the might of waters, and it seemed
> To me that in this Label was a type
> Or emblem of the utmost that we know
> Both of ourselves and of the universe;
> And, on the shape of this unmoving man,
> His fixed face and sightless eyes, I looked,
> As if admonished from another world. (610–23)

The final line in this passage makes more sense if we regard the analogy as bearing not just on the speaker's sense of being warned or cautioned or, even better, "put in mind of a thing forgotten, overlooked or unknown" (OED definition 5), but on the "world" as well from which the reminder emanates. This latter sense—admonished "as if...from another world"—captures perfectly a sense of something close at hand and of *this world* whose seeming remoteness or mystery, driving its emergence now as an admonishment, turns out to be a matter of perspective more than one of either fact or imagination.

It is particularly fitting that this culminating apercu is immediately preceded by "I looked," which in the context of the description overall references a second look in contrast to a "view" of the beggar that is alternately spectacular and rife with meaning. For this second look or double-take, which runs arguably through the entire description, beginning with the contingent sighting, juxtaposes materiality and deductive dilation in such a way that any synthesis that the "mind" might be inclined perform is forestalled. We see this in the speaker's struggle to move figuratively, in effect, from the figure propped before him, where the effort to find the *mot* or *figure juste,* beginning with the highly metaphorical description of the mind's movement, is impeded by something not unlike the "second-sight procession" described in the passage preceding this one. The difference is that where such a procession is truly phantasmagoric on the order, say, of Poor Susan's pastoralization of London in the poem named for her, where "bright volumes of vapour through Lothbury glide, / And a river flows on through the vale of Cheapside" (7–8), it is an after-image now of something stationary, abiding and "unmoving." More akin, in other words, to what Henri Lefebvre, in later describing everydayness, has called a "residual deposit" (2: 64), the beggar introduces something both here and there, both beyond and close at hand, both past and present, that, Wordsworth, in anticipation of that other apostle of everydayness—Martin Heidegger—calls the "world" (91–148): not "another world" or the one to which Wordsworth frequently recurs both in this poem and elsewhere, but "as if...another world."

Notes

1. This is the central theme of Coleridge's *Biographia Literaria.* The modern analog of this account is of course Abrams's *The Mirror and the Lamp.*
2. See especially Phillips.
3. I treat this aspect of Austen, first noted by her earliest readers, in *The Historical Austen.*
4. This becomes especially apparent when, in Miss Bates's company, both the protagonist and the narrative pegged to her viewpoint must acknowledge an always-present but otherwise unnoticed world of other people and other things of which Miss Bates is always mindful.
5. For discussion the Romantic sublime, see Weiskel, Ferguson, and with particular relevance to this passage in Book 7, Hertz.

3

John Galt, Happy Colonialist: The Case of "The Apostate; or, Atlantis Destroyed"

Jeffrey Cass

> At the same time, and an age later, or more, the inhabitants of the great Atlantis did flourish. For though the narration and description, which is made by a great man with you; that the descendants of Neptune planted there; and of the magnificent temple, palace, city and hill; and the manifold streams of goodly navigable rivers...yet so much is true, that the said country of Atlantis, as well as that of Peru, then called Coya, as that of Mexico, then named Tyrambel, were mighty and proud kingdoms in arms, shipping and riches. (12)
>
> —Francis Bacon, The New Atlantis

Bacon's *New Atlantis* has recently sparked interest in his relationship to the problem of colonialism, and whether or not the work, as is often believed, validates British expansion into the New World. Sarah Irving argues that Bacon's utopian fantasy actually reveals colonial anxieties about the dispossession of indigenous peoples, the moral dimensions of colonial occupation, and the legitimacy and reliability of the scientific knowledge produced in colonial outposts.[1] Suzanne Smith deconstructs the work over and against those who would make the *New Atlantis* an apologia for Christian thought, as well as those who believe that Bacon uses Christian tropes to promote a scientific rationalism that would advance social and culture welfare of the nation's citizens and ultimately diminish the role of religion within the State. She writes, "The

New Atlantis does not offer a consistent portrait of an ideally organized state that may be viewed in opposition to its degraded European counterpart, but rather an image of a state that is torn between the rival claims of science and religion concerning the order of nature, instead of the rival claims of different forms of Christianity" (99). Regardless of whether his work embodies Christian apologetics, scientific smugness, or colonial anxiety, however, Bacon's Atlantis becomes a master trope, an island and city-state linked to utopian progress and imperialist designs; in fact, the State's ability to colonize is a leading indicator of its success at establishing and translating its cultural capital and bureaucratic machinery into global prestige and authority. The "Great" Atlantis, which is depicted in the earlier epigraph, is the first city of Atlantis before a flood destroys it. Although Bacon's "New" Atlantis seemingly represents the attempt to recapture the grandeur of the original city, and is in that sense nostalgic, the narrative is scarcely an early modern narrative of liberal acceptance of or longing for the New World Other since science ultimately becomes the means of cultural subjugation, not the basis for intercultural exchange. As Claire Jowitt has indicated, "The New Atlantan policy insists that contact with other cultures be a one-way process" (136). In effect, through the utopian ideals envisioned by its scientocracy, Bacon's *New Atlantis* ideologically embraces the colonizer's dreams of commercial avarice and natural bounty that the original city of Atlantis naturally contained. True, Atlantis simultaneously looks back to a lost Edenic paradise, but it also looks forward to a profitable utopia for those intrepid enough to find it.

The isolation and singularity of Atlantis play, therefore, an important role in the colonialist paradigm that underwrites Bacon's vision. With its advocacy of scientific progress as the basis for social improvement, Bacon's *New Atlantis* remains an important foundational text well into the eighteenth century. As Roy Porter formulates Bacon's influence on eighteenth-century philosophical thought: "Drawing on [his] championing of science as the key to human progress, enlightened *philosophes* modeled man as *faber suae fortunae*, the author if his own destiny" (8). Baconian science buttresses what Stephanides and Bassnett refer to as "the positivist scientific and rationalist discourse of the Enlightenment" (9), which "survive[s] into the nineteenth and twentieth centuries especially in the discourses of anthropology, geology, botany, and zoology where islands are perceived as the sites of isolated life forms" (9). But science can be as profitable as it is useful, and as recent work on Romanticism and science has shown, global commercial networks forged close linkages between science and imperialism. Insidiously, scientific endeavor appears to have spurred both the production of knowledge and its commercial exploitation. As Fulford,

Kitson, and Lee suggest, "When science codified explorers' journeys, it acquired authority...Science and literature thus increased their social status as they processed information that was acquired as apart of an effort to exploit foreign peoples. As bodies of knowledge, they grew strong by acquiring knowledge of new bodies" (6). As island, as nation, as lost transatlantic city, Atlantis is certainly, at one level, an important image for an unrecoverable past and a bracing, visionary future. In short, Atlantis points to the spread of a colonialist *ethos*. As transatlantic city, Atlantis is not merely the avatar for social and cultural attainment; it reifies as well British imperialist logics by drawing explorers, wanderers, and conquerors into the mythological confines of its power, riches, and fame.

Not surprisingly, then, Bacon's *New Atlantis* is the most important intertext for one of the great defenders of colonialism in the Romantic period, John Galt, who ultimately emigrates to Canada, not entirely successfully, to solve some of his more intractable financial problems.[2] Many Romantic writers who were disappointed and mortified by the developments of post-revolutionary France viewed the New World with great optimism and hope for social and cultural change. "In other words," as Michael Wiley asserts, "North America became for many British radical writers a space to refocus their displaced political, social, and religious energy after France failed to fulfill its early revolutionary promise: A space in which to establish new selves" (57). By contrast, Galt primarily sees profit and loss, getting and spending, a far less spiritual and far greater material opportunity for success than he had had in Scotland. Atlantis, that fabled space between the New and the Old Worlds, becomes an appropriate starting point for evaluating Galt's exploration of a new space in which "to establish a new self." In effect, Galt stages the colonization of Atlantis in anticipation of his own personal foray into the imperial fray of North American commerce and exploration.

The Apostate; *Or*, *Atlantis Destroyed* (1815), one of John Galt's plays from his four-volume collection *The New British Theatre*, enacts many of the social, political, and cultural anxieties of empire that attend the public's attitudes and views of an evolving British *imperium*, an argument that Daniel O'Quinn has captured in his recent book *Staging Governance*. As O'Quinn suggests, "Because of the temporality of the performance, the mélange of stock plays and new productions that made up a typical season not only reactivated past representations but also put forth new representational paradigms to explore present social problematics" (6). "On any given night," O'Quinn continues, "Events in the transformation of British imperial society were brought to the stage, often mediated by the sexual and commercial relations that accompanied all class interactions in the metropole at this time" (6). While O'Quinn's arguments cover a period of British drama slightly before the publication of Galt's *The Apostate*, the principal difference between Galt's play and those encompassed by O'Quinn is that Galt's "new" plays are intended for a nuanced *reader*ship, rather than for a "nightly" theatrical performance, indeed for staging at all. This reading public is for Galt an audience that remains uneasy about Britain's national and international interests, uncertain about their connection to untrammeled colonial expansion throughout the globe, and dubious about the commodification of British exploration. Moreover, Galt's Scottish allegiances complicate an interpretation of the new "British" theater since Scotland's overtly nationalist claims of its own identity make it a "critical site for the invention or production of 'Romanticism'" (10), to use Ian Duncan's phrase, "but always as a part of a larger political, economic, and cultural geography, encompassing not only 'Britain'—London, Northern England, Ireland—but Europe, North America, and an expanding world-horizon of colonized and dominated territories" (10). Galt's play *The Apostate; Or, Atlantis Destroyed* reifies a "world-horizon" that finally appears hopelessly fractured and unstoppably violent. But it would be a mistake to assume that Galt himself is an uneasy colonialist within this "world horizon" or that he has doubts about the long-term power and prestige of (or need for) the British Empire.

The subtitle of Galt's *The New British Theatre*, "A Selection of Original Dramas, not yet acted; some of which have been offered for Representation but not accepted with critical remarks from the Editor," confirms the suspicion that Galt uses these plays "not yet acted" as a broadside against the establishment that controls theatrical productions in London and that he does so for ideological reasons. As Philip Cox reminds us, "The stated intention of [Galt's] anthology is to challenge the contemporary restrictive management practices of the London theaters: "Galt claims that his hope is that a collection of 'rejected pieces' would enable the lovers of the drama to appreciate the taste and the judgement with which the management of the theaters is conducted" (13). Thoughtful, highly dramatized plays such as Galt's are too esoteric for the debased taste of contemporary audiences who prefer pantomimic plays with magician's tricks, such as Farley's *Harlequin and Asmodeus; Or, Cupid on Crutches* (1810), Dibdin's *Harlequin and Humpo: Or, Columbine by Candlelight* (1812), and William Corri's *Harlequin and Sinbad the Sailor; Or, The Genii of the Diamond Valley* (1814). For Galt, theatrical reliance on machinery or trickery to induce audience approval, whether clever or delightful, is an affront to the true nature of drama. In his remarks on *Love, Honor and Interest*, also included in *The New British Theatre*, Galt writes, "There is such an austere simplicity in Nature that her physical operations cannot be changed but by the interference of a moral cause, nor the necessary course of her moral proceedings altered without employing physical force" (287). Furthermore, he writes,

> The transformations of the pantomime...both interest and delight in despite of the understanding, but the delight and the interest is very different from those enjoyments which we expect from the drama. Mechanical effects are not legitimate dramatic incidents. They are contrary to the first principles of the drama, which is an imitation of those actions of men which originate in moral considerations. (287)

Galt's philosophy finds artificial theatricality unnatural or, as Jane Moody might have it, illegitimate.[3] Jeffrey N. Cox and Michael Gamer write, "Romantic theater not only offered a reimagined and revitalized tragedy; it was also an exciting dramatic laboratory in which playwrights experimented with a wealth of new forms and technologies" (xviii). As a kind of conservative about theatrical production, Galt frowned upon the ways in which Romantic drama diverged from standard practices. That pantomime was commercially popular only further eroded Galt's confidence in the theater establishment's ability to look beyond profits and produce moral, introspective, and "natural" drama. Galt's attitude appears to contradict his later feelings about colonization and profit in the New World, but his ideological stance about drama's moral dimensions is of a piece with his belief that our "understanding" be put in the service of imperial expansion and national character. The audience should not merely remain entrenched at the level of "interest and delight," but should be engaged, as he indicates earlier, with "legitimate dramatic incidents" that promote thoughtful insight about the nature of the world and not merely indulge in contrivance for its own sake. As Porter argues, "Theatrical make-believe revealed how temptingly easy it was to slip out of one part and into another" (272). Galt understands the power of illusion to lead the audience away from truth, which is why he disapproves of the theater establishment's exploitation of that power.

Moreover, for Galt, drama should produce better British citizens, more productive subjects. When drama is reduced to entertainment, it is detrimental to the national character. As Galt suggests in his remarks to the ironically titled, *A Search After Perfection*, whose setting is fashionable London, "But what is more to our present purpose is, the historical fact, that since the court has neglected to exercise any influence over the stage, the dramatic genius of the country has appeared to decline.... The cause may, perhaps, not be owing so much to any alteration of disposition in the court, as to a change in the general economy of the country, with respect to amusements" (92). Consistent with other remarks about the nature of drama, Galt explicitly ties his theories of drama and theater management to the politics of the nation:

> It is, in our opinion, an essential part of the duty of the crown, if not to regulate, at least, to influence the public amusements.... This is now perhaps the more necessary, as the public play-houses have been so long left to the management of the patentees, that nay attempt of the Lord Chamberlain to re-assume his ancient authority over them, would be felt as ungracious.... [However] without some interference on the part of the court, to encourage the regular drama, we have no hope of effectually redeeming the British stage from the contempt in which it is held by all foreigners of taste. (92–93)

Still, in this passage, Galt is not entirely making an aesthetic judgment about play production, as much as he is leveraging the theater for social and political ends, which as we shall see in *The Apostate* lie in the realm of colonialist expansion.

Galt's pointed remarks about the current condition of the British theater eventually point to a manipulation of geography in the service of British imperial interests. Not surprisingly, many of the plays Galt collects in *The New British Theatre* make use of foreign settings and historical periods to launch his ideas about the nature of drama and its ideological effects on the reading public. Again, Galt does not attempt this for good, liberal reasons, such as making the other more familiar and thereby less strange to the British reader. Instead, he defamiliarizes the foreign, so the thought of widespread colonization is more palatable to the reader, its breathtaking scope easier to swallow. The setting for *Love, Honor and Interest* is Rotterdam, while *Sixteen and Sixty* opens with troops returning from the battlefields of Spain and Portugal. *Selim and Zuleika* opens in Anatolia near Abydos. *Hector* and *The Prophetess* explore ancient Greece; *Gozzanga* takes place in an Italian castle somewhere on the Adriatic. *The Fair Crusader* has no named location, but its Orientalized geography, a grotto between two rocks, lies somewhere in the East. And perhaps the most mysterious of Galt's foreign settings is the lost continent of Atlantis in *The Apostate*. Mythical and real, European and Oriental, Atlantis is the lost land bridge between the New World and the Old World, between homeland and colony, between metropole and periphery. It is the connection among foreign and exotic geographies, where issues of race, religion, social class, and cultural norms are interrogated. It is the place where territoriality and colonization emerge as the principal markers for Galt's ideological spin on the anxieties surrounding the British Empire, but they are anxieties, which for him, can be surmounted. Galt's tragedy plays out these anxieties, culminating in the destruction of the city of Atlantis. Yet Galt does not intend that destruction as a cautionary tale about the problematic nature of colonialist intervention; to the contrary, the tragedy for Galt lies in Antonio's deviation from the colonialist *ethos*. Antonio does not properly complete his mission, which is to expand European interests and to develop new markets.

It is true that Galt's drama hinges on decentering the national European subject. The ambiguously named Antonio (Spanish? Italian? Austrian?) has imported Enlightenment principles and Christian doctrine to Atlantis, and its king, Yamos, enthusiastically embraces Antonio's philosophical arguments, which themselves feed into a colonialist paradigm that allows European expansion into Atlantis. Yamos effuses,

> How rich in knowledge has thou made us all!
> Teaching our docile youth the arts of peace;
> The all-cementing harmony of law,
> And like the new moon, out of darkness born,
> Still more and more, to the full round of light,
> Brightening our souls, thou with the dim reflex
> Of eternal truth, which in thy land
> Sheds the warm mid-day beam.... (4)

But Antonio's ideological imports have transformed Atlantis's culture into a colonial outpost for European hegemony. Cloaked under "the arts of peace" and the "all-cementing harmony of law," phrases that would not look out of place in Blackstone's *Commentaries*, Atlantis becomes a legal outpost of Europe. In addition, Yamos's contextualization of Atlantis's law within the "eternal truth" of Christianity provides another transformation within his culture that supports European entry into the New World. In short, Antonio has made Yamos a believer in the virtues and benefits of imperialism. For his part, Antonio praises Yamos for his graciousness but reminds him that Atlantis's tilt toward the European side is not merely an embracement of belief systems. It is prophylaxis against Oriental invasion:

> The time will come, when from the Eastern world,
> With spreading sail, some daring mariner
> Will this way steer. Then all these unknown scenes
> Of inland seas and forests infinite
> Shall be reveal'd. Oft, sir, as I have told,
> Their winged vessels would the way explore,

> And that in which I 'scaped the waves to you,
> Was sent in quest of this great continent,
> On which some dark report had long prevail'd:—
> And when they come and find the arts of Europe
> In sweet communion with the Christian faith,
> My name shall rise to an equality
> With that of Cadmus, of Bacchus, those
> Who in the elder time brought westward truth. (4–5)

In this passage, the explorers "from the Eastern world" will plainly see Atlantis's allegiances and the manner in which the "sweet communion with Christian faith" reveals them to be allies of Europe and skilled in its "arts." Moreover, and rather curiously, Antonio compares himself to Cadmus, the founder of Thebes and brother of the abducted Europa. He is thus mythologically linked to a founder of a great city (like Atlantis) and to a city and a continent that requires the protection of an older brother, lest the Eastern enemies of Europe "rape" Atlantis (as was the case in the myth of Europa) and deprive it of its natural resources, which appear to be pristine and ample ("inland seas" and "forests infinite"). Unfortunately, Antonio betrays Yamos by having an affair with Idda, his wife, who is ultimately condemned to die in exile on a rock. Her willing seduction is Galt's parable about colonial mismanagement. For Galt, the colonized should see the colonizer's offer of aid as magnanimous, a gesture of civilized and enlightened sympathy. Consumption of natural resources and profit taking are merely understandable parts of the imperial process. Antonio ruins the opportunity by not remaining vigilant about the goals of the colonialist enterprise; he is drawn into the familial and cultural politics of Atlantis when he should be looking out for the interests of Europe.

That Antonio's magnanimity is tainted by his love for a woman from Atlantis is not revealed until after the damage to the indigenous inhabitants is irreparable. Regardless of the indigenous response, a return to precontact innocence is impossible. Antonio tragically transforms Atlantis into an apostate culture that abandons its traditions and cannot recover them, not only because the contact with European ideas cannot be erased, but because they have as well shown the inhabitants of Atlantis the ideological and practical emptiness of their nativism and old beliefs. When the high priest Orooko retreats into the forest, presiding over "vast mountains and cataracts," he bemoans the loss of the "country's gods"—their "sacred rites and old simplicity"—but European ideas, rightly or wrongly, have effectively replaced native superstition and unscientific thinking. The loss of the old order is determined. Furthermore, Orooko's vision of Atlantine Nature is hardly pacific. Yamos's attempt to construct a modern European city adumbrates a violent apocalypse, for the "dread gods, whose secret throne of fires, / Deep in the hollow of the mountain glows, / Will burst the earth, and sweep in floods of flame / Th'apostates and their perishable homes" (3). At the end of the play, the inhabitants of Atlantis, in fear of their sins, set fire to the new Atlantis, but the final conflagration, which destroys the entire continent, is not divine retribution. Yamos attempts to turn the burning of the new city into anti-urban lesson: "Come now, Atlantines, hurl your brands around, / Till but the ashes of the sacrifice / Be all the trace of our apostacy.—/ Hosts of our sires, pause in your airy chase, / And, as the flames of these proud towers ascend; / Around in hov'ring circles, view them burn" (37–38). Galt frames this incineration as the result of "penal fire," the unstoppable punishment for civilization's "two great crimes"—adultery and suicide. If anything, Atlantis's reversion to the purity of their beliefs through fire is itself a sign of their utter conversion to European ideology since their punishment has been converted from simple disobedience against their gods to a breach of Christian ethics and morality.

When Antonio hears that Idda has perished, he commits suicide by stabbing himself. At this point, even Orooko refers to Antonio's "truth and science" (37), and he no longer conceives divinity as embedded in Nature. Rather, he exclaims to Yamos with language reflective of the new religion:

> Heavenly truth,
> Like the bright sun's unquenchable effulgence,
> Which, from the foul and aguey fen, exhales
> The foggy pestilence and dries its poison;
> Receives no blemish from terrestrial vapor;
> Serene, sublime, it holds its destin'd course
> Above the momentary clouds that shadow
> The human Chrysalis, whose mortal term,
> By the slight tissue, spun from its own breast
> Is pass'd in darkness and captivity. (37)

Orooko's oration about "heavenly truth" and the "human chrysalis" reflects Atlantis's acceptance of Christianity's "tale of fancy" (31), which Orooko had earlier decried.

But the speech also indicates that Atlantis is no longer an independent nation/state, distinct from the colonialist paradigm that has thoroughly infected it. Instead, it is now an assimilated colony that has lost its sovereignty, both from the perspective of Orooko's ancient traditions that govern the behavior of Atlantis's subjects and from Yamos's figurehead edicts, which only give him the appearance of sovereign authority over his subjects. As Daniel O'Quinn observes, "The state's juridical control of its subjects is integrated with the institutional management of bodies and populations" (9). Orooko and Yamos no longer truly have regulatory power because they have unknowingly submitted to a colonial *ethos* that shapes their public actions and decisions; hence, neither has any ability to manage the citizens of Atlantis. The burning of Atlantis the city is the rehearsal for the destruction of the entire continent, and its destruction, in turn, signifies the impossibility of truly managing "bodies and populations" through imperial networks.

Despite the continent's horrifying destruction, however, which is directly linked to colonial intervention, Galt never condemns Antonio for his colonialist designs, only his mismanaged affairs. Indeed, far from actually feeling angst about his imperial ambitions, Galt is actually a happy colonialist, content to offer advice about taking over land and dealing with indigenous inhabitants. In *The Canadas: As They At Present Commend Themselves to The Enterprise Of Emigrants, Colonists, And Capitalists* (1832), Galt unironically characterizes the "subject" of Canadian emigration and colonization as one connected to "the employment of capital, not less than the employment of labour; the relief of distressed trades, of overpeopled districts, of individuals and their families struggling vainly without hope, and of overflowing manufactures seeking a market and a beneficial return" (1). For Galt, the benefits of emigration and colonization are self-evident: "But the comparative nearness of the Canadas to the mother-country; the known salubrity of the climate, and their being peopled in general by persons of European habits, who differ but little from those of the emigrant; must ever make this the first country looked to for the choice of British subjects" (23). Like Atlantis, the Canadas have rich resources, a "salubrious" climate, apparently docile indigenes, and new markets. His own family, Galt writes, "is supported with respectability and comfort, having abundance in all the necessaries of life within [his] farm, and [his] pay enabling [him] to supply all other requisites" (17). In short, Galt is an idealized Antonio, the colonialist who gets it right.

Galt tells the story, in his travel narrative, *Letters from the Levant*, about German ropedancers who provide entertainment to a general audience. The Janissaries, guarding the entrance to the event, attempt to keep some sailors from entering, and in a scuffle one of the Janissaries is killed. The killer escapes to the Russian Consul, who does not immediately turn him into the Turkish authorities. "The Turks, no longer able to endure the evident trick that was playing against justice, set fire to the street where the Franks resided, and almost every house and store, along with a vast quantity of property, was consumed" (270). Galt continues, "A massacre of Greeks followed, and it was some time before the fire could be got under, or the rioters reduced to order" (270). Galt makes no comment about the disproportionate Turkish response, other than to say that the Turks had "just cause for their indignation," a rather casual conclusion to a fiery conflagration that destroyed businesses and families. Galt's indifference to the fate of the Greeks accords with his capitalist and colonialist ethic since the government has to manage its populations in ways that are efficient and beneficial to it. Without such management, colonialism would not be profitable, would not provide the living to emigrants that it can provide. Galt's anecdote reveals that European involvement in the cultures of others may result in unthinking destruction, where even innocent contact can pose immense danger to all; nonetheless, he anticipates benefits for all the Atlantises who await engagement with the British Empire, even if, sadly, some of them are destroyed. Galt is cognizant of the moral ambiguities attending colonialism; they just do not bother him.

Notes

1. Many new readings of Francis Bacon have contributed to a reexamination of the *New Atlantis*, including those cited earlier. Others include the following: Travis DeCook, "The Ark and Immediate Revelation in Francis Bacon's *New Atlantis*"; Stephanie Shirilan, "Francis Bacon, Robert Burton, and the Thick Skin of the World"; Dana Jalobeanu, "Bacon's Brotherhood and Its Classical Sources: Producing and Communicating Knowledge in the Project of the Great Instauration"; José Maria Rodriguez García, "Patterns of Conversion in Francis Bacon's *New Atlantis*"; and Chloë Houston, "'An Idea for a Principality'? Encountering the East in Bacon's *New Atlantis*."
2. For additional information about John Galt and his family in Canada, see Ian A. Gordon's book, *John Galt: The Life of a Writer*; H. B. Timothy, *The Galts: A Canadian Odyssey, John Galt, 1779–1839*; and Elizabeth Waterston (ed.), *John Galt: Reappraisals*.
3. Jane Moody's description of "illegitimate" theater represents a violation of genre, a dramatic hybridity that disturbed Galt's notion of pure dramatic form and appropriate theatrical conventions. "In particular," Moody writes, "critics mocked the miscellaneous interweaving of music and visual spectacle with elaborate stage machinery, virtuosic dance and, in the case of pantomime, the silent, gestural language of mime" (12).

4

THE GOTHIC CHAPBOOK AND THE URBAN READER

Diane Long Hoeveler

Gothic bluebooks and chapbooks have been something of the step-child of gothic scholarship, most frequently ignored because of their derivative nature, as well as their lack of artistic sophistication, depth, or significance.[1] Montague Summers claims that they were the reading material of "schoolboys, prentices, servant-girls, by the whole of that vast population which longed to be in the fashion, to steep themselves in the Gothic Romance." They are, in fact, commonly referred to as "the remainder trade" or "the trade Gothic" (84–85). More recently, William St Clair has claimed that, in fact, the chapbooks were read by

> adults in the country areas, and young people in both the town and the country. It would be a mistake, therefore, to regard the ancient popular print as confined to those whose education fitted them for nothing longer or textually more difficult. Many readers, whether adults or children, lived at the boundary between the reading and the non-reading nations. They were the marginal reading constituency whose numbers fell when prices rose and rose when prices fell. (343–44)

Whatever the exact class of their readership, I would claim that gothic bluebooks and eventually the gothic short tale's importance can be appreciated only by understanding that they carried the ambivalent agenda of secularization within their slim and flimsy covers. It is not for nothing that Percy and Mary Shelley, along with Byron, Claire Clairmont, and John Polidori, were reading aloud from a collection of German tales of terror the night before Mary Shelley began writing *Frankenstein* (1818) and Polidori penned *The Vampyre* (1819). These German short stories began their literary life as *Das Gespensterbuch* (*The Ghost Book*), a five-volume collection of tales by Johann August Apel and Friedrich Laun that were first translated into French by J. B. B. Eyriès as *Fantasmagoriana; ou Recueil d'Histoires d'Apparitions, de Spectres* (1812), and then as *Tales of the Dead* (1813), when they were translated into English by Sarah Utterson. During the summer of 1816, the Diodati circle were very fashionably reading from the French collection.

Most interesting to me as a scholar of the gothic is the sheer number of chapbooks that no one has studied or copied and which are in my opinion interesting as mediations on the ideology of secularization. The gothic chapbook: what is one to make of this strange cast-off genre? Frederick Frank certainly had no time for it:

> Low quality Gothic fiction [was] denoted by its garish blue coverings or wrappers. The Gothic bluebook is a primitive paperback or ur-pulp publication, cheaply manufactured, sometimes garishly illustrated, and meant to be thrown away after being "read to piece."... The reader of the bluebook received a single dose of Gothicism between the blue covers. Almost all of the hundreds of bluebooks published during the period are pirated abridgments of full-length Gothic novels. (433)

But Angela Koch claims that, of the 220 chapbooks that she has examined, only 63 were adaptations of the longer, full-length gothic novels, while the others were works that used "the same Gothic paraphernalia, such as family feud, illicit love, and the intervention of supernatural powers" ("Gothic Bluebooks" 3), but were original so far as any "formula" fiction can be. Clearly delimited as a genre that flourished between 1770 and 1820, the gothic chapbook has been discussed in largely accusatory tones by earlier critics who blame it for the eventual decline of the canonical gothic novel's status and popularity. David Punter, for instance, observes that

> popular writers in the genre appear to have become increasingly able to turn out a formulaic product in a matter of weeks, and the eventual decline in Gothic's popularity was clearly at least partially to do with a flooding of the market, and also with the way in which the hold of the early Gothic masters tended to stultify originality. (114)

As there are at least one thousand gothic chapbooks currently extant in Britain alone,[2] it is virtually impossible to provide anything other than a snapshot or freeze-frame portrait of the genre. I have chosen to look at a handful of representative types to suggest the tremendous range to be found in this mode of writing. Certainly by the time Edgar Allan Poe was writing his short tales of terror (e.g., "The Tell-Tale Heart" in 1843), he had mastered the formulae necessary to produce a taut and macabre study in gothic psychology and action. Any claim that the gothic tale was moribund by this date is patently false given the artistry that Poe brought to the genre, not to mention that developed by Maupassant in France or Hoffman in Germany.[3] Between William Mudford's "The Iron Shroud, or Italian Revenge" (1839), a tale in which a man is crushed to death in a room that collapses on him, and Poe's "The Pit and the Pendulum" (1842), however, there is a considerable artistic gulf, and it is my intention to try to explain how that gap was bridged through an examination of the evolution and eventual refinement of the subjectivities presented in the gothic tale.[4]

In many ways, the short gothic tales found in the chapbooks represent examples of what Charles Taylor has called cultural technologies or textual practices that serve to instantiate the ambivalent moral agenda of what he calls "secularization 3."[5] The usual interpretation of the secularizing process—dubbed "subtraction stories" by Taylor (22)—is that either religion in "public spaces" diminished during the origins of modernity (called "secularization 1" by Taylor), or that "religious beliefs and practices" declined (called "secularization 2"). Taylor argues that both of these approaches are inadequate because, while there is certainly less religion in modern Europe, this is not a universal feature of the Western experience (the United States being the prime counterexample). Nor is it true to say that the separation of the public and religious spheres is rigorously observed. Taylor argues instead that while the creation of a Western "secular age" is indeed historically unique, its defining feature is not a diminution in religion, but a change in the "background" of the public "imaginary" (13). Using Heidegger and Wittgenstein, Taylor defines "background" as the prephilosophical understanding that conditions thought by being universal, within culture, and invisible to its citizens (13). During the Enlightenment, there was a unique change in this "background," one that asserted for the first time that human beings have the choice as to whether they locate the experience of "fullness" in the quotidian realm of everyday life or in the transcendent and spiritual, or in some other construction that allowed them to simultaneously embrace both worldviews. For Taylor, the final stage of secularization can be understood as a matter of personal choice as to whether one locates supreme value in the supernatural and transcendent, in mundane "human flourishing," or in a "cosmology" that combines the two (a locus that he calls "secularization 3," [2–4]). As Taylor observes, "There has been a titanic change in our western civilization. We have changed not just from a condition where most people lived 'naïvely' in a construal (part Christian, part related to 'spirits' of pagan origin) as simple reality, to one in which almost no one is capable of this, but all see their option as one among many" (12).

For Taylor, this transition in subjectivity occurred when the concern for and emphasis on earthly "human flourishing" replaced the high value that had been placed on accumulating "merit" in an afterlife:

> I would like to claim that the coming of modern secularity in my sense has been coterminous with the rise of a society in which for the first time in history a purely self-sufficient humanism came to be a widely available option. I mean by this a humanism accepting no final goals beyond human flourishing, nor any allegiance to anything else beyond this flourishing. Of no previous society was this true. (18)

Taylor also argues that, paradoxically, this modern secular mindset was largely fostered in the eighteenth century by religious reforms and enthusiasms—what he calls "Providential Deism"—an argument supported by modern historical opinion, which tends to see schools of French rationalism, for instance, as the exception during an eighteenth century that was otherwise marked by a revival of religious feelings and beliefs (19). According to Taylor, this change of mindset—this fundamental alteration in the Western "background" (13)—did not happen by accident. On the contrary, it was the product of several newly invented cultural practices and technologies, and I would claim that some of those technologies can be seen in the development of the highly gothicized phantasmagoria, the melodrama, the chapbook, and the opera, all of which performed their cultural work by transforming that "background" through iteration and repetition.

But for Taylor, the work of the social imaginary is not a simple matter of "re-enchantment" as Max Weber has employed the concept. Instead, he argues that the development of "secularity 3" was based on "images, stories, legends" developed initially by an elite and then spread through the wider culture (172) through "new inventions, newly constructed self-understandings and related practices" (22). These cultural practices paradoxically revealed the uncanny doubleness at the heart of secularization 3, that is, that it was possible to continue to believe simultaneously in both the realms of the supernatural and the natural, the enchanted and the disenchanted, at the same (uneasy) time. For Taylor, this "repertory of collective actions at the disposal of a given group of society" (173) actually encouraged the development of what he calls a "social imaginary" that advocated a sort of imaginative pluralism that in turn fostered the coexistence of the transcendent and the immanent realms:

> The great invention of the West was that of an immanent order in Nature, whose working could be systematically understood and explained in its own terms, leaving open the question whether this whole order had a deeper significance, and whether, if it did, we should infer a transcendent Creator beyond it. This notion of the "immanent" involved denying—or at least isolating and problematizing—any form of interpenetration between the things of Nature, on one hand, and "the supernatural" on the other, be this understood in terms of the one transcendent God, or of Gods or spirits, or magic forces, or whatever. (15–16)

Within the "background" of the popular cultural imagination, a variety of attempts were made to resolve the metaphysical split between the material and transcendent realms that had occurred during the Enlightenment period. For instance, it is significant that the Minerva Press, the most successful purveyor of gothic chapbooks in Britain and with their fingers firmly pressed to the pulse of their lower and middle-class reading public, also promoted a variety of socially and politically conservative values in its publications. On one hand, the chapbooks were invested in an imminent Protestant, rationalistic, and Enlightenment agenda, while on the other hand, they were riddled with ghosts, superstitions, and reanimations of the world of anima. This bifurcated subjectivity is at the heart of ambivalent secularization, and in the chapbooks we can also examine how class came to play a crucial role in defining the transformations of the gothic uncanny.

Scholars most frequently claim that the short gothic tale or chapbook grew out of the earlier tradition of cheap broadside (because printed on one side of the paper) ballads or street literature, and certainly one can see in the shorter eight-page chapbooks the residue of this direct oral to written tradition. Gary Kelly has recently observed that this early street literature is characterized by its "emphasis on destiny, chance, fortune and leveling forces such as death, express[ing] the centuries-old experience of common people...with little or no control over the conditions of their lives....For these people, life was a lottery" (Introduction x). According to Kelly, the fact that the lower classes were the target audience of these early productions is also obvious from their very heavy use of narrative repetition, their emphasis on incident and adventure, and their episodic and anecdotal structures. The other major difference between lower and middle-class reading materials is the absence in the lower-class works of any extended depictions of subjectivity or emotions in the protagonists (x; xv). One example of this lower-class ideology at work can be found in *Tales of Superstition: or Relations of Apparitions* (see figures 4.1 and 4.2), a work that is extremely similar to Isabella Lewis's *Terrific Tales* (1804), a series of short vignettes that purport to be true, although the contents are fantastical and reveal an interesting mix of residual supernaturalism combined with rationalizing Christian moral exempla. For instance, one tale concerns an aristocrat, "of very inordinate passions," who is kidnapped by a spirit who arrived on horseback. Obviously a prose revision and redaction of the Germanic ballad "Lenore," the homily at the conclusion remarks on his abduction as "a punishment for his excessive passions" (7). What is most interesting about all of these collections of tales, besides their repetitive use of specters, devils, ghosts in chains, warnings from Purgatory, and clouds of sulphur, is their persistent assurance that the afterworld and the realm of the transcendent do indeed exist. In one tale, a dead man appears to his friend to exclaim, "Michael, Michael! Nothing is more true than what has been said of the other world" (61), and such a message is the major reason for the popularity of these works. The supernatural was not supposed to be explained away, but instead confirmed as real. Although the elite and the intelligentsia might have been willing to accept the stark lessons of materialism and the finality of death, the lower class was not able to do so, and the gothic chapbook reveals in all its convolutions the persistence and continuing power of the supernatural in the social imaginary.

In 1800 a three-volume gothic novel could cost as much as two weeks' wages for a laborer, and we know that, for the most part, the library fees at a circulating library also would have been out of their reach. The longer (thirty-six and seventy-two-page) prose chapbooks cost from sixpence to a shilling, or the price of a meal or a cheap theater seat (Kelly, "Fiction and the Working Classes" 218), and they seem to have had a written rather than a purely oral origin. The gothic chapbooks can best be understood in two ways: first, as adaptations of the extremely popular European fairy tale, and second, as redactions of the longer gothic novels and dramas. Circulating widely between 1750 and 1820, these tales are European culture's first "bestsellers." In fact, G. Ross Roy claims that a conservative estimate of the sale of Scottish chapbooks during this period runs to more than two hundred thousand a year, a huge number given the fact that they were purchased largely by members of the working class. Originally running as twenty-four pages of single sheet, duodecimo, these truncated tales were frequently bound in course blue paper and sometimes illustrated with rough woodcuts and printed in a rude and unfinished style of typography.

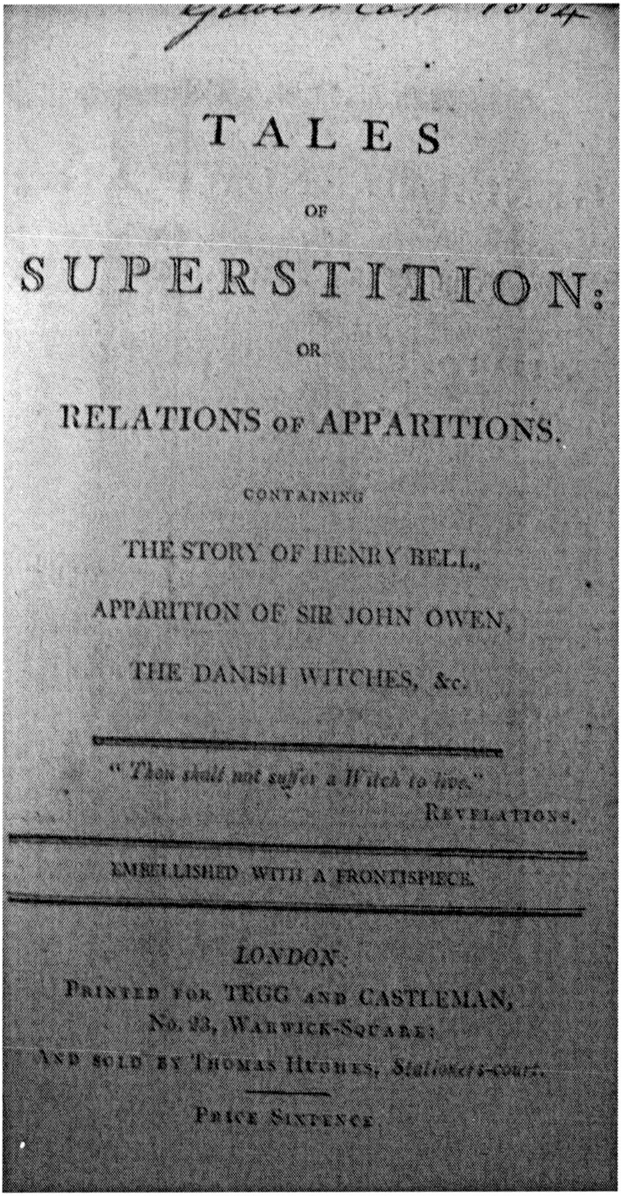

TALES

OF

SUPERSTITION:

OR

RELATIONS OF APPARITIONS.

CONTAINING

THE STORY OF HENRY BELL,

APPARITION OF SIR JOHN OWEN,

THE DANISH WITCHES, &c.

" *Thou shalt not suffer a Witch to live.*"

REVELATIONS.

EMBELLISHED WITH A FRONTISPIECE.

LONDON:

PRINTED FOR TEGG AND CASTLEMAN,

No. 23, WARWICK-SQUARE;

AND SOLD BY THOMAS HUGHES, *Stationers-court.*

PRICE SIXPENCE.

Figure 4.1 *Tales of Superstition* (London: Tegg, 1803).

Source: All figures used with permission from the Sadleir-Black collection, University of Virginia Library.

Figure 4.2 *Tales of Superstition* frontispiece (London: Tegg, 1803).

The earlier "lottery mentality" that was operative in the lower-class chapbooks was eventually replaced during the late eighteenth century by what Kelly calls a dominant "investment mentality" that we can see evidenced in the emerging middle-class chapbooks. This "investment mentality" was characterized by the Protestant ideologies of self-improvement, self-advancement, modernization, and self-discipline, or "the middle-class discourse of merit" (Introduction x; xxiii). Increasingly hostile to lower-class street literature, which it saw as politically subversive and at the same time spiritually reactionary, the middle class effectively displaced street literature by co-opting it. Hence Hannah More published her *Cheap Repository Tracts* (1795–98) for the lower classes, actually imitating cheap broadside and ballad chapbooks and suffusing them not with the "lottery" but with the "investment" mentality that she and her cohorts were attempting to promulgate: a disdain for immediate gratification, a focus on the disastrous consequences of moral relativism, and a stress on the accumulation of "solid and useful" knowledge for middle-class life.[6] This strategy is identical to the one that John Guillory has identified as "covert pastoralism" (124) and claimed as operating in Wordsworth's *Preface* to the *Lyrical Ballads*. Sensing that they are being marginalized by a bourgeois reading public that has begun to exert power in the literary marketplace, Wordsworth and More create a binary of lower class and aristocrat and actually begin to present themselves as aristocrats in peasant dress.

But if there was a middle-class attempt to co-opt the chapbooks, there was also a concerted effort to condemn their popularity altogether. For instance, Coleridge, in his *Biographia Literaria* (1817) specifically condemned the "devotees of the circulating library" for indulging in

> a sort of beggarly day-dreaming during which the mind of the dreamer furnishes for itself nothing but laziness and a little mawkish sensibility; while the whole *material* and imagery of the doze is supplied *ab extra* by a sort of mental *camera obscura* manufactured at the printing office, which *pro tempore* fixes, reflects and transmits the moving phantasms of one man's delirium, so as to people the barrenness of an hundred other brains afflicted with the same trance or suspension of all common sense and all definite purpose. (3: 36; his italics)

There is a certain amount of fear as well as class resentment expressed here about an unregulated (non-elitist) press pandering to what Wordsworth had called the "fickle tastes, and fickle appetites" of the lower-class reading public (*Preface* to the *Lyrical Ballads*, 1800).

The gothic chapbook tradition is split between lower- and middle-class agendas, both of which were presenting alternative versions of the secularized uncanny to their readers. One group of tales—the middle-class variety—made claims for the powers of reason, rationality, and secularized education, while, ambivalently, it kept alive the vestiges of a belief in a mythic and sacred past of divine beings. As Kelly notes, the representation of subjectivity is much more developed in these works, but in a writer like John Aikin, a Protestant dissenter and author of "Sir Bertrand: A Fragment" (1773), a short gothic tale that was written to demonstrate the aesthetic principles put forward in his sister Anna Barbauld's essay "On the Pleasure Derived from Objects of Terror" (1773), this subjectivity is severely "disciplined" so that the new bourgeois citizens are those who control their emotions in even the most perilous of situations (Introduction xix). The other group of tales—the lower-class variety—persisted in promulgating a "lottery" view of life, with fate, magic, or luck as the ultimate and inscrutable arbiters in all matters and with human beings still presented as what Taylor calls "porous selves" or pawns in the hands of tyrannical forces they could not fully understand.

For Kelly, the subjectivity that occasionally appears in lower-class chapbooks is

> like the simulation of richer fabrics on cheap printed cottons of the period, [it] is a form of symbolic consumption rather than ideological and cultural instruction for the text's readers. It is as if the readers of the street Gothics were aware that there was a certain model of subjectivity prized in middle-class and upper middle-class culture, but that subjectivity in itself was of little interest, or perhaps supposed to be of little use or value, for these readers. (Introduction xxiii)

One cannot discuss the gothic chapbook phenomenon without also briefly addressing the development of the circulating library as a "front" so to speak for its own publishing house, William Lane's Minerva Press being the most famous example. Lane's Circulating Library opened in 1770 in London and had ten thousand items in circulation by 1794. We know that circulating libraries were widespread and viewed with some class suspicion by 1775, as evidenced by Richard Sheridan's comedy *The Rivals,* with its famous metaphor of circulating libraries as trees. I suggest that the metaphor indicates that although chapbooks may be useless trees, the fruit of the trees is the possession of culture, class, and civilization that easy access to libraries provide for the working class. But just as circulating libraries were viewed with suspicion by the upper classes for the easy access they provided to gaining a modicum of culture, so were they seen as important for the role they played as moral guardians to the working class. In the how-to pamphlet *The Use of Circulating Libraries Considered* (1797), circulating libraries were specifically encouraged to avoid stocking too many chapbooks and pamphlets, but to have 79 percent of their stock in fiction. However, library proprietors were also urged to consider the following advice: "Reading and instruction should be universal—the humbler walks of life require much culture; for this purpose I would recommend to their perusal, books of authenticity, in preference to those of entertainment only." From this advice we can infer that the preferable form of fiction was of the morally didactic variety ("the novel") rather than of the "romance" (or gothic) type. The very existence of these libraries, though, was seen as playing a disruptive role in the distribution of cultural materials that were viewed by the upper classes as encouraging the working classes in their misguided and even dangerous social aspirations.[7]

As literacy rates increased among the lower classes (Stone), the demand for reading materials for them proportionally increased as well. It is difficult to know exactly what proportion of the working class purchased their own chapbooks or opted instead to obtain them through a circulating library as either a subscriber or a day-borrower (the latter option would have been the much more economical route to borrowing). Either way, through the act of reading the chapbooks, the lower classes were participating in the ideological and intellectual struggles of their culture. If they could not afford to attend the opera or theater productions in even the "illegitimate" theaters of London, then they could read highly condensed redactions and much simplified abridged versions of Walpole, Reeve, Radcliffe, or Lewis's long novels. Doing so allowed the working classes, they thought, to have the same reading experience that the elite experienced and therefore the same access to and ownership of their culture's luxury items. By the early nineteenth century, however, the tales were being collected into longer anthologies that frequently contained up to five previously published stories, while the popular *Tell-Tale, or Universal Museum* (1805) began reprinting popular stories by authors like Sarah Wilkinson in its six volumes.

As I have noted earlier, literary critics have been slighting if not downright hostile to the popularity and prevalence of the gothic chapbooks during the early nineteenth century in Britain, France, and Germany. We know, for instance, that Percy Shelley, Robert Southey, and Walter Scott read them as children (Potter 37), and there is a certain appeal in their childlike simplicity, their distillation of plot, and their flattening of character. More interesting, however, is the confused spiritual ideology they promulgated for their reading audience: alternately advocating either a bourgeois, moralistic, and "investment" mentality (what Taylor calls the "buffered self") or a "lottery," lower-class, and fatalistic attitude toward life (the "porous self"). By examining one work of one particular gothic chapbook author, we can see the sometimes confused struggle between these two attitudes. Along with Isaac Crookenden (1777–1820), Sarah Scudgell Wilkinson (1779–1831) was one of the most prolific writers of gothic chapbooks, the author of some twenty-nine volumes of fiction and more than one hundred short works, at least half of which are gothic. Working at times as a writer (and perhaps editor) for Ann Lemoine's *Tell-Tale Magazine*, or independently trying to support her mother and (possibly illegitimate) daughter Amelia, Wilkinson scratched along as a "scribbler" and owner of a circulating library until she was forced on more than one occasion to apply for financial assistance to the Royal Literary Fund, a form of welfare for indigent and worthy authors. I will examine one of her best-known works, "The White Pilgrim" (based on Pixérécourt's drama *Le Pèlerin Blanc* [1802]), as representative of the genre. What is most interesting in this work is its confused and at times frantic heteroglossia, its parasitic grasping after every known gothic mode in the attempt to produce yet another new and marketable genre, the gothic tale of terror.[8]

Wilkinson has received a certain amount of critical attention recently, largely because of attempts to recover "lost" female writers and to place the chapbook tradition itself into its larger cultural and literary context. As one of the only female "hack" writers that we know by name, Wilkinson's works and career can be fruitfully examined as a case study of middling to lower-class female authorship during the early nineteenth century. In fact, her very prolific publishing profile recalls Bradford Mudge's observation that the development of mass culture during this period was linked to the dominance of women as the authors as well as readers of circulating library materials. But this female-inflected mass culture was increasingly figured at least by the Regency and the early-Victorian periods as a diseased, metastatic type of female reproduction because it challenged the hegemonic model of the realistic novel (92).

Wilkinson's biography is bleak reading indeed (Potter 109–15), and it illustrates that the high point of the gothic trade occurred roughly between 1800 and 1815, its decline causing Wilkinson to turn to writing children's books by 1820 in order to survive. Within five years, however, that market had also shrunk to such an extent that she was again appealing to the Royal Literary Fund: "I need not point out to you that the depression in the Book trade and consequently scantiness of employ in Juvenile works has been great.... *Forsake me and I perish*" (RLF, December 12, 1825). Casting herself as the gothic heroine of her own life story, Wilkinson was, unfortunately, prescient. But before the very bleak death she suffered in 1831 at St. Margaret's Workhouse, Westminster, she was determined to produce gothic chapbooks that would appeal to a growing reading audience of literate lower-class females.[9] As she herself observed in the Preface to her last gothic novel, *The Spectre of Lanmere Abbey; or, The Mystery of the Blue and Silver Bag: A Romance* (1820):

> Authors are, *proverbially*, poor; and therefore under the necessity of racking their wits for a bare subsistence. Perhaps, this is my case, and knowing how eager the fair sex are for something *new* and *romantic*, I determined on an attempt to *please* my fair sisterhood, hoping to profit myself thereby. If the following volumes tend to that effect, I shall be gratified; but if they meet with a rapid sale, and fill my pockets, I shall be elated.

It would seem that whatever "elation" Wilkinson had as an author of gothic chapbooks was short-lived, while her claim to be producing "new" works is a bit disingenuous. Before her sad end, however, she did write a number of works that disseminated the major gothic tropes to a very wide, lower-class reading public and helped codify the lower classes' understanding of "romantic" as "gothic."

A good deal of ideological ambivalence can be seen in Wilkinson's "The White Pilgrim; or, Castle of Olival" (see figure 4.3). Based on the earlier Pixérécourt drama as translated into English in 1817 by Henry R. Bishop as "The Wandering Boys; or The Castle of Olival," Wilkinson's version suggests that she was adapting and publishing gothic chapbooks at least as late as 1818. As the story begins we are introduced to the Count of Castelli, "the truly amiable and liberal" Horatio, living with his beautiful wife Amabel and their two sons in a castle in Berne, Switzerland. Devoted to their sons and the welfare of their tenants and dependents, the young couple has made their domain "a second Eden," unaware that there are serpents lurking in the guise of attendants, namely the Chevalier Roland, Seneschal of the castle, and his assistant Otho, Captain of the Guard. Pregnant again, Amabel has a "fearful dream" the night before her husband is to make a short trip to settle some legal affairs with his friend Count Vassali. When she informs her husband of her forebodings, he responds, "What Amabel superstitious? This is indeed a novelty, for which I was unprepared."

Figure 4.3 Sarah Wilkinson, *The White Pilgrim* frontispiece (London: Dean, 1820).

Mocking his wife's primitive "superstitions," Horatio next ignores the warning cries of "screech-owls and crows" as he begins his journey with his servant Claude, who warns him that the cries of the birds are "ill-omens." The consummately rational man, Horatio ignores all of these warnings only to leave his family defenseless to the schemes of Roland.

Upon his return, Horatio is informed that his wife has fled the castle, her maid Theresa asserting that she has absconded with a paramour ("a near relation of her own, whom you had forbid the castle") seen lurking around the grounds. When all the evidence points to the truth of this story, Horatio resigns himself to caring for his sons until he grows restless for travel and a change of scene. Leaving his sons with a tutor, Horatio sets out for England, where he coincidentally discovers the missing maid Theresa, who tells him that she and her father had been bribed by Roland to stage the disappearance of Amabel during Horatio's absence. Horatio further learns that Amabel has in fact been held captive these past three years in a "subterranean cavity" on the castle grounds, and so he begins to plot his revenge by letting it be known that he has perished in a shipwreck during the channel crossing. The resolution of the story occurs when the reader is informed that Roland is the illegitimate brother of Horatio, the son of the former Count and a woman who was "of obscure birth and illiterate manners." When he learns that Horatio has died at sea, Roland now produces a will that allows him to claim all of Horatio's estates. At this very moment, the reading of the suspicious will, a pilgrim, "clad in white, his robes, his hat, and staff were all of that virgin hue," appears asking for refuge "after performing his vow of pilgrimage to the shrine of our Lady of Loretto." The appearance of this man is almost atavistic, antediluvian, suggesting the uncanniness of the Catholic past, its ability to erupt as the not-quite repressed that still figures on the edges of this culture. But the white pilgrim is also a melodramatic figure because he is introduced by Roland as "deaf," reminiscent of the "deaf and dumb" characters that form the melodramatic core of Thomas Holcroft's gothicized dramatic adaptations.[10]

Thinking that he can safely discuss his plans in the presence of the white pilgrim, Roland reveals to Otho that he intends to poison the orphan boys and kill their mother: "She had long since become an object of disgust and hatred to her betrayer, for she had nobly resisted every attempt to despoil her of her honor and fidelity." The servant Ruffo enables Amabel to escape her dungeon, and she tells an abbreviated tale of abuse and misery that recalls the fate of Agnes, the pregnant and imprisoned nun in Lewis's *The Monk*: "She was delivered prematurely of a child, who died the same night; she was allowed no assistance, and having wept many days over her dear blossom, she buried it with her own hands in one corner of the damp dungeon." Whereas her story recalls a literary source, the intended fates of her sons recall a particularly gothic moment in British history, the murder of the two princes in the Tower of London by Richard III in 1483. In an almost-repetition of that crime, this text instead allows the white pilgrim to save the children in the nick of time by substituting a safe potion for the intended poison. We learn later that all of these actions have been orchestrated by the white pilgrim, the avenging husband and father Horatio in disguise. Vassali brings the king's troops to storm the castle, and at the decisive moment, the white pilgrim strips himself of his robes and appears as "the real Count Olival" to denounce the evil machinations of his illegitimate half-brother.

"The White Pilgrim" positions religious as well as class ideologies front and center. The lower class is pandered to in the privileging of premonitions and ill-omened birds, while bourgeois attitudes can be detected in the descent of Roland from an "illiterate" mother. There are clearly "lottery" elements in this work, as Horatio, an aristocrat, is frequently saved by the most chance-like occurrences (literally running into Theresa on a street in London). There are also bourgeois attitudes present, as Horatio rescues his family through cunning, skill, and what we would almost call omniscience. Originally written as a melodrama in France in 1801 and then recast as a British chapbook by Wilkinson around 1818, the text suggests the revenant power of Catholicism and the persistence of superstitions among lower-class readers. In fact, John Kerr's 1820 dramatic version of the work, titled "The Wandering Boys," continued to be so popular that it was performed in the British repertory and published as late as 1894.

The question that is most frequently begged in so many discussions of the gothic chapbooks is the reason for their popularity. Frederick Frank claimed that they appealed to "the type of reader who had neither the time nor the taste for a leisurely Gothic experience. That there were many such readers during the Gothic craze is a well-documented fact" (420). But this is just another way of saying that you will always have the poor with you. A more important question might be to ask, why were the gothic chapbooks so fractured by both class and religious issues? One possible explanation is offered by Ann McWhir, who notes that

> in the very process of rejecting superstition, one suspects that these authors take pleasure in it, though their genre prevents them from completing the transition from shocked incredulity to imaginative suspension of disbelief. The completion of the movement towards suspension of a disbelief that can be assumed and therefore deliberately

transgressed moves us from superstitious anecdote or supernatural tale to Gothic fiction. (36)

As part of its secularizing and modernizing agenda, this culture saw a dramatic rise of literacy among the lower class, and the circulating library emerged as an important component of the public sphere in which commercial interests would ideally be complemented by secularizing and moralizing trends. In a culture in which literacy was seen as advancing the bourgeois cause of promulgating moral and civic responsibilities and inculcating "investment" values, the library and its publication arm, even one as lowly as the Minerva Press, produced works that would attempt to accomplish important civilizing work at the same time they made a profit. But finally, the gothic chapbook presented its lower-class readers with yet another instance of ambivalent secularization, a literary technology that was predicated on the notion that many different belief systems could coexist, and that the mixing of traditional spirituality with newer rationalistic approaches to life would allow them to remake themselves as effective citizens of the new nation-state.

Notes

I would like to thank the librarians at the Sadleir-Black Collection at the University of Virginia Library—in particular Gayle Cooper, Sharon Defibaugh, Margaret Hrabe, and Regina Rush—for their assistance and patience during my month of research there. The Sadleir-Black catalogue of gothic chapbooks can be accessed at http://www2.lib.virginia.edu/small/collections/sadleir-black/

1. Varma deplored the development of the genre, seeing it "as an index of the sensation-craze into which the Gothic vogue degenerated in its declining years," also observing that the gothic bluebook "catered to the perverted taste for excitement among degenerate readers" (189). Frank writes,

    Why were the Gothic writers so often drawn to the use of fairytale and folklore motifs of the kinds found throughout the chapbooks? The answer may be that the grotesque motifs and violent patterns of action of these primitive stories provided the distortions of reality and amoral disorientation that the Gothic writers depended upon for rendering their powerful effects. The motifs themselves are variations of the malignant sublime. (415)

2. Potter provides two appendices that list some 650 titles for gothic chapbooks and tales published between 1799 and 1835. It seems safe to say that at least another three to four hundred were published during the earlier phase of the genre (1764–99). St. Clair claims that the height of the "chapbook gothic" craze occurred around 1810 (349). Scholarly

sources on the earlier phase include Birkhead, who argues that "in these brief, blood-curdling romances we may find the origin of the short tale of terror" (186).
3. Richter has claimed the "Gothic is to all intents and purposes dead by 1822" (125), while Mayo asserts that "from 1796 to 1806 at least one-third of all novels published in Great Britain were Gothic in character" (766); earlier he had observed that "the popular vogue for romances of terror was over in 1814, but their appeal was still fresh in the minds of readers" (64).
4. Baldick claims that Poe's tales are distinctly different from the earlier gothic tales, which he sees as inferior and merely redactions of the longer gothic novels (xvi). One of the earliest scholarly attempts to discuss the genre can be found in W. Watt, who argues that "shilling shockers" are the transitional link between the late eighteenth-century gothic novels and the short tales of terror as developed by Poe, Maupassant, and LeFanu.
5. My book, *Gothic Riffs: Secularizing the Uncanny in the European Imaginary, 1780–1820*, uses Charles Taylor's *A Secular Age* to examine a variety of gothic genres as one of those newly invented cultural practices that advocate for what he calls "secularization 3," or the ability to hold several competing and contradictory beliefs at the same time.
6. Mayo was the first critic to recognize the essentially bourgeois moralizing tone of the gothic tale as published in the periodicals, while he asserted that the gothic bluebook was too crude to appeal to the rising middle-class reader (448). In a later article (1950), he focused on the chilly reception given to the bluebooks by "many critics, editors, and members of the general reading audience in whose eyes *romance* was the hallmark for barbarous superstition, unreason, moral depravity, and bad taste" (787; his emphasis).
7. *The Use of Circulating Libraries Considered*, an anonymous how-to manual for proprietors of circulating libraries, 195–203. The Edmonton Circulating Library (England) stated its terms for subscription as five shilling a quarter, nine shillings for six months, and sixteen shillings a year. Extremely detailed discussions of the evolution, economics, and patronage of circulating libraries in Britain can be found in a number of sources: Blakey 111–24; Jacobs 157–235; Potter 114–36; and R. Hume. Richter connects the rise of circulating libraries with the increase in more naïve readers (126), while Punter argues the opposite, claiming that the "confidence trick" that gothic authors play on their readers (making them believe in phantoms only to sneer at the belief) actually "demands a type of discrimination largely unnecessary in the reading of earlier realist fiction" (96).
8. Frank characterizes Wilkinson's writings as "plundering" (412) and "automatic Gothicism produced and marketed for the reader's fee of six pence" (413). James discusses the authors of gothic chapbooks as "hack writers" and "lower-class writers... [who] had not enough skill to create

through atmosphere a suspension of disbelief" (80–81). More recently, Kelly has stated bluntly, "Wilkinson was a hack" (Introduction xxi).

9. A bibliography and analysis of the critical reaction to gothic romances can be found in Gallaway and Haworth.

10. Another one of the many examples of French melodramas making their way to the British shore as first dramas and then chapbooks can be seen in Thomas Holcroft's drama, *Deaf and Dumb*, translated by him from the French drama by J. N. Bouilly, *L'Abbé de l'Epée* (1800). Initially the drama became Holcroft's *Deaf and Dumb, or the Orphan Protected* (Drury Lane, 1801), and then the chapbook for children, *Julius, or the Deaf and Dumb Orphan; A Tale for Youth of Both Sexes: Founded on the The Popular Play of Deaf and Dumb* (third edition. London: Harris, 1806). See Holcroft.

5

Romantic Science and the City

Marilyn Gaull

In New York City, the American Academy of Science sponsors a website with weekly updates listing more than three hundred science-related activities open to the public, some educational, social, and even some performance art. There are no distinctions among the sciences, the real and pseudo, the life and earth sciences, the observational, theoretical, experimental, recreational, narrative, visual, field or laboratory, or even between science and technology. The disciplines include astronomy, oceanography, mathematics, anatomy, computers, anthropology, political science, psychiatry, sociology, medicine, botany, biology, chemistry, physics, geology, the history of, the sociology of, and the philosophy of any of them and hybrids as well—sociobiology or the history of smell. Name it and someone in New York City, probably in London, Rome, Tokyo, Berlin, and Paris, or any large urban center will demonstrate, lecture, publish, perform, illustrate, promote, evaluate, record, finance, and talk about it. Here is urban science, the variety, ingenuity, and popularity. In form and practice such public science began in the Romantic period in London mostly, but also Glasgow, Edinburgh, Manchester, Bristol, Bath, Newcastle, Birmingham, where the Lunar Society reputedly began the Industrial Revolution, and in Philadelphia in America. In European cities, public energies were focused on war, survival, religion, politics, and defining a national identity.

Except for medicine, very little science actually takes place in any city, then and now. I wondered why—and that question led me into intellectual conflicts comparable to the humanities culture wars of the 90s with similarly conflicting ideologies, styles, and implacable opponents. Scientists (a word coined by William Whewell in 1833, at Coleridge's request, as an analogue to artist), both applied and theoretical, and historians of science, the formalists, theorists, and culturalists, all divided into smaller and oppositional sects. For the sciences as for the humanities, the conflicts are equally divisive and, in the same way, rewarding.

In the neo-Romantic period of the 1960s, before Thomas Kuhn's sociological analysis of the history of science, *The Structure of Scientific Revolutions* (1962), a topic such as science and anything would have been marginal, even rare. Most scientists believed that science offers an explanation of the real world: use the right language, manipulate the right materials, ask the right questions, look far enough, and be rewarded with something true—something that can be verified, replicated, communicated, and validated; they are the universalists, purists, Platonists, if you like. In popular culture, they are often Faustian, secretive, elitist, demonic, and possibly deranged. Their primary interest is the secret of life, from alchemy to string theory, all the obscure, impractical, and even dangerous concepts behind the laws of nature and of human behavior. To them, the culture of science, the life and times, the form and substance, the literature and experience, and where it takes place are not relevant, are not science.

Before Kuhn, historians were not particularly interested in science. Priestley's discovery of oxygen, how people require air to live, was not so important as his radical politics. Napoleon's conquering Europe was more interesting than Mary Anning's fossils and their evidence of "deep time" or William Herschel's revelation of an infinite and evolving universe. In *The Structure of Scientific Revolutions,* Kuhn initiated the very paradigm shift in science studies that he had identified in the sciences. After Kuhn, a new breed of historians of science called constructivists reclaimed the human place of science, the culture of science.

Scientific constructivists believe that contextual variables such as politics, economics, race, class, gender, nationality, and even opportunity condition the selection of scientific problems, what is studied, by whom, how and where, how the dissemination of scientific knowledge shapes the problem and the solution, how "the medium shapes the message," as Marshal McLuhan, Kuhn's contemporary said, often. Philosophically, constructivists do not discover anything in nature or even reveal it. Their narratives and theories reflect them, their world, their historical context, and deal with nature only obliquely. They consider the scientist as much as the science, the gender, class, race, ethnicity, location—when and where the science was practiced, in an industrial, academic, pastoral, or urban setting, the motive and reception of the science (Golinski, 1998).

Historians of science like biography. To them, as Blake said, the perception is shaped by the perceiver, "As a man is, so he sees," even women, even in science. Objectivity is an illusion. Blake's contemporary, James Hutton, the greatest geologist in this Golden Age of Geology, saw the danger: "Man is made for science; he reasons from effects to causes, and from causes to effects; but he does not always reason without error.... care must be taken how we generalize; we should be cautious not to attribute to nature, laws which may perhaps be only of our own invention" (*Transactions of the Royal Society of Edinburgh* [1788], 1, 273.) Marx in a classic constructivist reading observed that Darwin's theory of struggle for survival reflected the paradigm of his own competitive and greedy society, which he projected on the history of nature—and Marx may have been right. There have always been constructivists: they just did not have a name.

Constructivists are more concerned with the philosophies, sociologies, even geographies of science than with science itself. For constructivists, following Kuhn, the pivotal moment in the history and institutionalization of science was the Romantic period in England when all the disciplines, learned societies, and publications appeared, when, science, just as nature and art, was urbanized. They know, these constructivists, as many literary people overlook, that the modern city and everything in it is an expression of Romanticism, that the literature could not have been published or the art displayed, and that creative people, however secluded, depended on and participated in the new urban culture.

What about nature, the subject of both science and Romanticism? "Man, Nature, and Human Life," as Wordsworth identifies the subject of *The Excursion,* were always the subjects and themes of all literature, painting, theology, and science. Culture itself includes the study and representation of nature long before the Romantic period, before *Tintern Abbey* and *Frost at Midnight*. But, this cultural knowledge of nature began in texts, illustrations, letters, paintings, stories, poems, and conventions; nature was analyzed, interpreted, painted in studios, represented in galleries, examined in laboratories, collected in libraries, domesticated, removed from experience, a second-hand knowledge. For example, the longest loco-descriptive poem in English, William Cowper's *The Task* (1785) was composed from his sofa in a parlor. The country poor, vagrants, farmers, shepherds, vagabonds, traders, knew nature, its lore and signals, lived "in the eye of nature," as Wordsworth describes the Old Cumberland Beggar in *Lyrical Ballads*. As a primary source, the lore and signs of nature had traditionally belonged to them: science discovered it as it were a new country, a new plant, and Romantic poets and painters learned to see and to depict it, its form and meaning.

By 1770, in Great Britain mostly, artists, poets, philosophers, and a new category called tourists were leaving their sheltered spaces, took to the roads and countryside, on foot as well as in carriages, while farmers, shepherds, vagabonds, and criminals, for various reasons, some legal and some economic, became urbanized, found places in factories, domestic service, trade, poor houses, or migrated to distant lands and took their natural knowledge, their nature lore, with them. A new excursive generation of writers, philosophers, and artists, supplemented, challenged, or replaced the textual knowledge of nature—the conventions that shaped their lives, the images of clouds and oceans, mountains and cities, depicted in European art, Mediterranean-style pastoral painting, Eastern philosophies and theologies—with experience, with knowledges of encounter. The scientists produced what Richard Holmes has aptly called in the title of his book, *The Age of Wonder: How the Romantic Generation Discovered the Wonder and Terror of Science* (2009). The Romantic writers and painters have been held responsible for a *return* to or the *discovery* of nature, as if it were ever hidden, lost, or forgotten.

To literary scholars, this exchange of place sounds too familiar to mention; there are whole books on walking, the picturesque, colonization, and natural theology. These books and essays explain the results, the artistic effects, but not the causes: why did individuals, working in science, art, and literature, choose independently, to leave the laboratories, libraries, studios, and parlors, to become an excursive generation, why did they depart from the domestic settings where they were expected to write, paint, or discover the laws of nature and go out of doors? From Rousseau's *La Rêveries du promeneur Solitaire* (1770), a source for the poet in *Alastor,* to Wordsworth's exhortation, "Come forth into the light of things / Let Nature be your teacher" ("The Tables Turned," *Last Poems,* 15–16), writers celebrated not the textual tradition from which they acquired their craft and to which they were contributing, but observational knowledge and with it the oral tradition, the one that had always flourished outdoors, the popular narratives and nature-lore.

I find no explanation for what drew the scientists, the natural philosophers as they were still called into the 1840s, into the open air, but the most characteristic and significant discoveries from 1770 to 1830 were out of doors: Joseph Priestley, like Ben Franklin, gathered electricity standing out in a thunder storm; James Hutton overturned the biblical narrative of creation while sitting on a hillside watching the wind and water shape the landscape. And William Herschel, a German musician living in Bath, one of the windiest, rainiest, muddiest cities imaginable, the least likely place for an astronomer, went out of doors and unsheltered, on rare, cold and clear nights, discovered an infinite universe through telescopes he invented and shared with anyone passing by.

These natural, life, or earth sciences were all narrative, easily illustrated, nontechnical, and relevant. They suited the new popular culture, the theater, newspapers, magazines, lecture halls, and the new collective life that was growing up in urban centers. Although astronomy was practiced at night, it was public and inherently social (Olson and Pasachoff). Comets were occasions for parties, and telescopes were common parlor decorations, or set up in public places such as Leicester Square, a scene Wordsworth described so well in "The Stargazers":

> What crowd is this? what have we here! we must not pass it by;
> A Telescope upon its frame, and pointed at the sky;
> Long is it as a barber's pole, or mast of little boat,
> Some little pleasure-skiff, that doth on Thames waters float.
> The showman chooses well his place, 'tis Leicester's busy Square;
> And is as happy in his night, for the heavens are blue and fair;
> Calm though impatient, is the crowd; each stands ready with the fee,
> And envies him that's looking—what an insight must it be (1–8)

Similar to other natural sciences, however, in urban settings, astronomy was known obliquely, through technologies that compressed and familiarized it, or through representation, models, simulations, diorama, panorama, cosmorama, all ramas, as a spectacle in lectures, an exotic setting such as *The Man in the Moon* performed at Sadler's Wells, or the giant orrery that Adam Walker displayed by candle light in the Haymarket Theater (Inkster, Altick). In such sheltered spaces and visual representations, astronomers and those who promoted astronomy as a popular entertainment even in 1800 created a virtual reality while the real universe was up there, outside. Contemporary museums, such as the monumental Rose Science Center in New York City at the Museum of Natural History, aspire to be not just a model but a substitute for the entire universe.

In 1793, the year historians remember for the Reign of Terror, seventeen years after the Declaration of Independence, human beings finally discovered the mechanism by which they live, that they require oxygen, which had been unknown before, and that it is produced by photosynthesis, the interaction of green and growing things with sun and rain. Ironically, photosynthesis, to me the most important discovery of the period, the very basis of modern green culture, acquired no urban audience during the Romantic period. While the understanding of the gases, the interactions, the mechanism originated in laboratories and refined by Priestley, illustrated by Joseph Wright of Derby as demonstrable in a parlor, photosynthesis too subtle, invisible, and common for the theater or lecture hall. Consequently, although quintessentially Romantic, photosynthesis is often overlooked in discussions of science during the period. It is nature, and simply through breathing, human beings become an extension of nature, an instrument in the cycle, binding the human need for air and carbohydrates to plants and converting the toxic gases humans exhale or create into the a necessity for plant life. However belatedly it was discovered, this knowledge was surely the most crucial knowledge of all, challenging the very hierarchy of life from its divine source to a natural sustenance. But photosynthesis lacks the drama of electricity, the visual appeal of comets, and risk of balloon flights.

Balloon flight and other aeronautical experiments were urban based and fashionable, so popular that from about 1783, when the first balloon was launched over Paris, the British and French populace was taken up with "balloonacy," each ascent accompanied by such crazed public gatherings that soldiers were called in to keep order. Fancifully decorated with astrological signs, Greek gods and goddesses, often in erotic poses, fringes, sparkles, and brilliant colors, balloons, like electricity and nitrous oxide, were too frivolous and popular to have any scientific use. At best, some thought they could be used for tourism, communication, stratospheric research in weather, or, as Ben Franklin feared, the means by which the French could invade England. At best, balloon flight introduced the aerial perspective reproduced mechanically in panoramic views of London, Paris, Rome (Tucker).

Similarly, electricity was discovered out of doors both by Joseph Priestley and Benjamin Franklin using kites to attract lightening. But what was it and what use would it serve? It took at least another century before all its applications became evident in machine power, communication, transportation, and illumination, dispelling the urban darkness. Before it became a topic for philosophic debate as a source of life, or perhaps life itself, electricity was an entertainment brought into the urban environment and popularized by the magicians and sorcerers familiar in British culture from Merlin, Prospero, Faustus, in nursery tales, folklore, and even the poetry of the period, especially and Keats (Taylor). Challenged by the church and local civil authorities, magicians traditionally lived as vagrants, hermits, wizards, sorcerers, conjurers, tricksters, even healers, surviving for centuries in the country fairs and among the rural populations where they told tales, performed tricks, invoked ghosts, and even predicted the weather. Displaced along with country people into urban settings, they found new audiences, in urban street culture, the theaters and lecture halls. For credibility, they affiliated with the new sciences, donned formal costumes, took titles such as "Professor of Scientific Experiment" and offered what they called "philosophical entertainments." They introduced the working-class urban population to magnetism and electricity, and, for a time, perhaps still, magic and science shared the same space and audience—both required the "willing suspension of disbelief" that Coleridge considered essential to poetic faith.

As entertainment electricity could make dead frogs or dead criminals twitch, or, if one had a few shillings, attend Dr. James Graham's Temple of Health where he used electrical currents and magnetic beds to "invigorate the whole body," he said in his advertisement, remedy "all physical defects," cure infertility and sexual dysfunctions (Altick, 65, 519, 551). At the same time, serious scientists, such as Humphry Davy lectured on electricity in legitimate venues such as the Royal Society and, at the Royal Institution, founded in 1799, performed legitimate electrical experiments for the working-class audience and instituted Christmas lectures for these same adults and children, which are, like the pantomime, still part of the holiday season.

As these urban institutes became technical, selective, and expensive, they attracted the fashionable middle class who were interested in or wanted to appear at such philosophical exchanges such as Dr. John Abernethy and Dr. William Lawrence at the Royal College of Surgeons debating vitalism, whether electricity was life itself and dependent on form or was added to form. Thus, Mary Shelley's own invention, Dr. Frankenstein, either the novel or on stage had a ready London audience (Holmes, chapter VII). For the working class, Jacob Perkins and William Sturgeon, a legitimate but self-taught physicist, founded the National Gallery of Practical Science, later known as the Adlaide Gallery, where for free, or for pennies, the public could view a living electric eel, a hydromicroscope trained on the otherwise invisible creatures in the Thames, a steam cannon that shot one thousand bullets a minute, and working models of steam engines and electrical machines. Open daily, from 10 a.m. to 5 p.m. and from 7 p.m. to 10 p.m., free to the public, it was successful for about a decade of lectures and showmanship before it was replaced by a marionette theater (Morus, 80).

Electricity, known simply, then and now, as power was popular, and life changing, attracting the widest urban audiences, challenging religion as nothing else before Darwin's *Origin of Species*, even before it was understood and applied to medicine, communication, transportation, and industry. Electricity still defines the urban environment—as an urban power-outage demonstrates. Unfortunately, by the end of the twentieth century, the production and urbanization of electricity had produced 40 percent of the gases and pollution that obscure the very skies from which Priestley and Franklin originally collected it, and light itself, even while it made urban life possible, became a pollutant and ended urban-based astronomy (Fleming).

Chemistry, electricity, and astronomy were urbanized because, among other things, they could be demonstrated, performed, and appealed to paying audiences. Other sciences such as geology, paleontology, zoology, and botany originate in the countryside and took on an urban identity as specimens, fragmented, displaced like the rural population, and appealing to the national mania for collecting (Pascoe, 6). They collected, brought to the city, and exhibited, exchanged, or sold shells, bones, feathers, stones, butterflies, locks of hair, the Elgin Marbles, fossils, living plants and animals, anything unusual, unfamiliar, portable, and deviating from expectation. As science, however, such collections were unrepresentative, the settings inappropriate, the information unreliable and misleading.

Consider, for example, the zoo: Zoological Society of London, founded in 1826, sponsored the Zoological Gardens, the first public collection of living and exotic animals in London. In 1829, a record of two hundred thousand visitors came to see the elephants, giraffes, peacocks, ostriches, moneys, and lions, the great symbol of monarchy. The whole collection was an expression of British colonial power housed in Regency Park, the anomalously elegant neoclassical setting designed by John Nashe. The zoo, which is still a major attraction, was enriched by the donation of the Royal Menagerie, a collection of exotic animals, mostly gifts to the crown, kept for over six centuries at the Tower of London (Hahn, 227–230). Founded as the first scientific zoo, for teaching and research, the science consisted mostly of anatomy, dissecting animal corpses, an extension of the successful Hunterian Museum, which displayed a continuum of analogous body parts of animals and humans. In effect, the Zoological Gardens were less a laboratory than an extension of the animal shows, the curiosities that had been displayed to the believing public at country fairs, the "horse of knowledge," "the learned pigs," the cats that could make coffee, the shaved monkey passed off as an angel. Among the human curiosities, the Hottentot Venus, a living native African native, was brought to London and displayed, as science, naked in a cage for a paying public (Altick, 318, 270–272; Fulford, Lee, and Kitson).

In this urban environment, dead bodies, anatomical museums, stuffed animals, and human "curiosities," once they were labeled, explained, historicized, and organized, became science, an extension of the street culture. Wordsworth described in *The Prelude*, recounting St. Bartholomew's fair:

> All moveables of wonder, from all parts,
>   Are here—Albinos, painted Indians, Dwarfs,
>   The Horse of knowledge, and the learned Pig,
>   The Stone-eater, the man that swallows fire,
>   Giants, Ventriloquists, the Invisible Girl,   710
>   The Bust that speaks and moves its goggling eyes,
>   The Wax-work, Clock-work, all the marvellous craft
>   Of modern Merlins, Wild Beasts, Puppet-shows,
>   All out-o'-the-way, far-fetched, perverted things,
>   All freaks of nature, all Promethean thoughts
>   Of man, his dullness, madness, and their feats
>   All jumbled up together, to compose
>   A Parliament of Monsters. (VII, 706–708)

Geology was also essentially excursive, studied out of doors, in the field, a knowledge of encounter. James Hutton, an urban gentleman himself, sitting on a hillside pondering the mysteries of arable land realized that the forces around him, the wind, rain, sun, tides were responsible for shaping and even creating the landscape, that creation itself was beyond human knowledge. His discoveries were confirmed by observation in Edinburgh where the outcroppings at Arthur's Seat and Holyrood Park revealed strata comparable to those William Smith was uncovering digging canals near Bristol. The theories all made sense at the Edinburgh Royal Society, where the evidence could be confirmed outside the door, but in London at the London Royal Society, the theory was contested by a countergeology, a textual, and a theoretical one. George Cuvier's Catastrophism was based on the Old Testament, appealing to the aesthetic taste for the sublime, a revolutionary political climate, the mania for collection, and the urban inclination to see oneself reflected in what passes for science. As Shelley dramatized in *Prometheus Unbound*: "The wrecks beside of many a city vast, … see, they lie, / their monstrous works and uncouth skeletons, / Their statues, homes, and fanes, prodigious shapes/Huddled in gray annihilation" (IV, 296–301). Urban apocalypse with contemporary implications, a recurrent theme in catastrophic geology, accounted for the effect of Catastrophism on the culture though not the science. Inherently visual and unaccountably social, it lingered into the 1830s when John Martin painted "The Flood."

Catastrophism stimulated another science that also migrated from the countryside to urban life, paleontology, the recovery of ancient animal bones. In 1802, the first complete mammoth skeleton in Europe was displayed in London, brought over from New York (an interesting reversal) and shown for two shillings. Working from apocryphal biblical sources such as the Book of Enoch, to Byron and other Romantic writers, dinosaurs and all their relatives among prehistoric beasts were the deformed offspring of angels, God's sons, and human women. Whatever their origins, they were and remain the stars of natural history museums, celebrities among fossils, as genuine specimens or reconstructions, exhibited like so many other natural anomalies in panorama, diorama, and monsterrama.

Hutton, William Smith, all the field geologists and fossil hunters evolved a unified theory of origins and development that acquired an even more inclusive and wonderful narrative in Darwin's *Origin of Species*. But, in the artificial context of urban life, geology, paleontology, earth history are represented in fragments, as dislocated as the Elgin Marbles in the British Museum. No matter how authentic or accurate, these urban simulations were neither science nor art, at best, as domestications of nature and its potentially deadly forces, even in fragments, the fossils were great comfort in the postcatastrophic period. Geologists, however, from the field and the forces they studied, recognized that nature is unpredictable, mysterious, perilous— the earthquakes, tornadoes, floods, volcanic eruptions, extreme and unpredictable weather events, the very forces that shape the landscape (Gaull, VII, "Natural History and its Illusions" 208–226).

As a science, meteorology is a Romantic invention. It developed only because a generation of human beings took Wordsworth's advice, went out into "light of things" and, like other excursive sciences, achieved an organization, developed a collective body of knowledge, standards, and professional status in an urban setting. The textual knowledge of weather had been based on Mediterranean and European paintings, poetry, drama, and it had always been inappropriate in a British setting. Indeed, much British writing and painting had had no weather at all. Yet weather, rather than nature, is decisive in Romantic writing, art, and the sciences, especially geology, photosynthesis, astronomy, and electricity.

To become a science, weather required instruments to measure and record temperature, air pressure, wind, rainfall, even time on international gauges, thermometers and barometers that registered the same in Russia as in France and Canada, on land or sea. Understanding weather required patient and accurate records and communication from one place to another, in time the telegraph and balloons, and eventually, the capacity to interpret data for prediction—which is still a work in progress. So however preoccupied people were with weather, and even more with climate, understanding it was as belated as understanding breathing.

In an *Essay on the Modification of Clouds*, first published in1803, Luke Howard, a Quaker chemist living in London, classified, named, and described the shape and behavior of clouds, British clouds. His drawings and publications influenced Constable, Shelley, and even Goethe who wrote a poem about him (Wood). As an urban scientist, in *The Climate of London* (1833), he described for the first time the concept of the urban heat island. Although he had no understanding of convection, weather systems, and, without the essential means of communication to test his theories in other places, he recognized that London and therefore similar urban places are warmer than the country side during the day because of human heat and because the sides of buildings absorb radiation. At night, these same buildings give off heat and, along with the fires and the smoke people generate, maintain a warmer temperature than the countryside.

Between 1783 and 1816, several generations had endured traumatic weather events: four earthquakes, five volcanic eruptions, including Mount Tambora, the effects of which are familiar to readers of Byron's *Darkness*, the last throes of the little ice age (though they did not know it was ending), polluted the atmosphere, produced noxious fogs, brutally cold winters, years without summer, famine, plague, riots, and migrations to urban centers. Howard's heat island offered an urban refuge, an explanation, a sense that human beings might participate in the climate and not just become weather-victims. For Luke Howard, London was a laboratory, an urban ecology, where human beings and buildings influenced the environment and possibly reclaimed a humanly habitable space in a natural world that appeared to be winding down. Luke Howard's meteorology would become the only authentic urban science practiced in the period.

Conclusion

Although the Romantic sciences are characterized by genuine, fresh, and imaginative encounters with the natural world, excursions, as Wordsworth so rightly called his epic, they were dependant on urban culture to survive. But these sciences, just as Luke Howard's climate, were also altered by urban life. In this urban context, science had to be visual, performable, verbal, nontechnical, emotionally appealing, and, if possible, profitable, competitive with other entertainments. In adapting to the urban environment, these sciences were fragmented, displaced, even fictionalized. The most appealing, influential, and successful were curiosities, eccentricities (a word from astronomy adapted to human deviation), the monstrous, rare, and heroic. They generated the heroic science narratives that remain so engaging: the martyrs, eureka moments, misunderstood genius, political and religious rebels: Galileo and the Inquisition, Darwin on the Beagle, Einstein's eureka moment, the first this, the biggest that, the only something else. They appealed to the same depraved appetites for sensation, horror, and "outrageous stimulation" that Wordsworth complained about in the Preface to *Lyrical Ballads*, that "blunt" the discriminating powers of the mind and the "great and permanent powers that act upon it." In Humphry Davy, who edited the text before it went to press, Wordsworth had a scientific ally.

Part II

Continental Cities

6

PHENOMENAL BEAUTY: ROUSSEAU IN VENICE

Nancy Yousef

This chapter is about the unlikely intersection of Rousseau and Kant in Venice. The two philosophers meet there over the coincidence of aesthetics and ethics. Of course, I do not refer to an actual encounter (the two thinkers did not, in fact, ever meet), nor even to contrasting views of the same place (Kant, notoriously, did not travel), but rather to a conceptual space, which brings typically Rousseauvian anxieties about the transparency of others into close proximity with typically Kantian determinations about the recognition due to others. This wholly theoretical encounter unfolds within Rousseau's recollections of the famously beautiful city that he rather perversely does not seem to have seen at all. Although the urban space is virtually invisible in the memories Rousseau sets down in *The Confessions*, Venice does appear as the site of frustrated efforts to perceive a correspondence between physical and moral beauty, and I will be proposing that this underlying theme amounts to a kind of conceptual portrait of the cultural aura of that city in its eighteenth-century decadence. My conjecture is that the city is represented as a philosophical problem and that the Venetian scene is a uniquely appropriate setting for the collision of Rousseauvian and Kantian attempts to conceive of beauty as an irresistible impression of human value.

LOCATING ROUSSEAU IN VENICE

Rousseau's sojourn in Venice as secretary (to then French ambassador Pierre François de Montaigu) hardly counts among the more memorable episodes in *The Confessions*. Nevertheless its place in the narrative presents intriguing interpretive possibilities alongside its difficulties. On the one hand, it seems to prolong the tale of wayward, unsettled youth beyond its appropriate, formal culmination in the ending of the affair with "Maman" (Louise de Warens) that closes Part One of the autobiography. The secretarial post Rousseau assumed in 1743 is the culmination of several unsuccessful efforts to secure some livelihood in the service of well-connected families. The pattern of shameful resentment at his position of dependence, frustrated pride at his failure to be recognized for his merit, and suspicion of malicious intrigue against him comes to a climax with the violations of dignity Rousseau endures in Venice, leading him to the resolution "never again to attach myself to anyone, but to maintain my independence by making use of my talents."[1] On the other hand, the Venetian recollections preface the abrupt intellectual debut that sets the trajectory of Part Two of *The Confessions,* occurring just before Rousseau's account of the inspired composition of the prize-winning *Discourse on the Arts and Sciences*—that "moment's madness" from which "all the rest of my life and of my misfortunes followed inevitably" (328/351). Thus the Venetian interlude constitutes a kind of narrative interregnum, or detour, between the recollections of unsettled and romantically disappointed early years and the frequently rueful, defensive account of a life determined by a career in letters. Venice is a transitional space in *The Confessions,* one at which Rousseau arrives after the constitutive affective patterns of youth have been established, but before those patterns have been transformed into and by philosophical work.

Within the chronology of the autobiography, Rousseau's recollections of Venice belong to the period just before the composition of his earliest social critique. But, as part of *The Confessions* as a whole, the episode belongs to the final phase of his career—one distinctively marked by an unremitting intersubjective despair, a paranoid sensibility, a hardened disillusionment with the possibility of knowing other minds.[2] Venice is merely another place in *The Confessions* where Rousseau's preoccupation with the cleft between being and appearance leaves a memorable impression—consistent with the early traumatic discovery that other persons are not "Gods who read our hearts" (30/21), the recurring lament that "beneath a mask of feeling it is always self-interest or vanity that speaks" (144/147), as well as the cumulative misunderstandings, suspected betrayals, explosive ruptures, and estrangements that dominate the second part of the autobiography. Both a prelude to the scathing cultural critique of the early Discourses, and symptomatic of the anxieties, at once personalized and existential, that are endemic to the late autobiographical writings, the Venetian episode allows consideration of both the earliest Rousseauvian diagnosis of intersubjective impenetrability and its final articulation, after the apparent exhaustion of his efforts, in mid-career works such as *The Social Contract* and *Julie,* to imagine a system, a community, a political order in which individuals would be transparent to one another.

Bearing this in mind, let us recollect the famous distinction between "being" and "appearance" that Rousseau laments in both the first and second Discourses: to attract the "regard" of others, he writes, "one had to seem other than one in fact was. To be and to appear became two entirely different things, and from this distinction arose ostentatious display, deceitful cunning, and all the vices that follow in their wake."[3] Rousseau's formulation of intersubjective inscrutability—the fact, as he puts it in the first Discourse, that "one will never really know with whom one is dealing"—conflates epistemological ambition—to know with certainty who the other is—and ethical aspiration—to trust in the humanity of the other. "Vices must attend upon such uncertainty," Rousseau explains, as "suspicion, offenses, fears, coolness, reserve, hatred, betrayal" are safely hidden behind the "deceitful veil" of impenetrable faces.[4] Appearance masks above all the drive to exploit or make use of the other—the "hidden desire to profit at another's expense"—and in that sense what Rousseau calls appearance masks the corruption or deformation of what Kant later identifies as the essence of our humanity as moral agents—that recognition of the dignity of the other as an end-in-herself.[5] In the first Discourse, Rousseau imagines this corruption as symptomatic of cultural decadence, invoking a mythic prehistory "before Art fashioned our manners," when "men found their security in how easily they saw through one another" and "outer appearances were always the likeness of the heart's dispositions."[6] No longer able to see through one another, dwelling in what Rousseau calls "uncertainty," the ethical possibilities of relationship he specifies as "sincere friendship," "real esteem," and "well-founded trust" are foreclosed.[7] Whether it is the object of nostalgic yearning (as in the first Discourse) or of utopian longing (as in the *Social Contract* and *Julie*), intersubjective certainty is always, in Rousseau, an epistemic ideal beyond the bounds of perceptual limitations. Appearances are all we have of one another.

In the terms of contemporary philosopher Stanley Cavell, Rousseau's anxious preoccupation with how "the body of the other seals me out, and the other in" is symptomatic of "living skepticism" with regard to other minds, of a chronic "disappointment" with our knowledge of others "as though we have, or have lost, some picture of what knowing another would really come to—a harmony, a concord, a union, a transparence." For Cavell, acknowledgment "that I cannot close my eyes to my doubts of others...that my relations with others are restricted, that I cannot trust them blindly" is precisely the point at which epistemic ambition is forsaken and the ethical challenges of life among others discerned, if not necessarily met.[8] I want to suggest that such an insight is implicitly embedded in Kant's austere imagination of ethical regard for others as wholly, necessarily free of empirical determination.[9] In Rousseau's work, however, what Cavell calls our "disappointment" in the possibilities of knowledge is recurrently, compulsively aggravated by a stubborn confounding of epistemic security and ethical imperative, an insuperable sense that loving, trusting, befriending, and respecting depend on knowing.

I offer this brief review of the ethical and epistemological implications of the divide between "being" and "appearance" as an initial approach to the flagrant eruption of this problem in Venice when, in a remarkably abrupt phenomenological shift, the irresistible impression of a woman's beauty suddenly gives way to an equally irresistible perception of her monstrosity. In a famously portentous introduction of his awkward, unconsummated encounter with the Venetian prostitute named Zulietta, Rousseau distinguishes it as "the one incident in my life which plainly reveals my character" (*300/320*).[10] It is tempting to take Rousseau's extravagant claim as a light irony, deflecting embarrassment at his own awkwardness by an exaggerated self-deprecation at once disproportionate to the incident and cleverly designed to titillate and deflate his readers' aroused interest. "Forcibly reminding myself of the purpose of my book, I shall have strength to despise the false modesty which might prevent my fulfilling it": thus Rousseau challenges the reader to meet his strength with the "courage to read the next two or three pages," and so to attain "complete knowledge of Jean-Jacques Rousseau" (*300/320*). The promise certainly heightens the voyeuristic interest with which the reader follows Rousseau into the courtesan's room, only to be quickly disappointed by the sudden dissolution of sexual anticipation and drive into trembling, weeping impotence. But this erotic misadventure cannot so easily be assimilated with other flirtations and amorous exploits lightheartedly recounted in the narrative, and so the challenge Rousseau issues ahead of this particular confession ought not be wholly disregarded.[11] To credit the importance Rousseau grants this strangely failed encounter is to ask how it "plainly reveals" an autobiographer who has consistently presented himself as acutely anxious about the possibility of knowing and being known by others, and how it is particularly telling of an autobiographical subject who is soon to transpose that anxiety into a damning cultural diagnosis of the existential rift between being and appearing. Insofar as it typifies the problem of intersubjective opacity in *The Confessions*, the episode is certainly significant, but what makes it distinctive is how the category of beauty enters into and complicates Rousseau's typical conflation of epistemic and ethical judgment. This experience in—and of—Venice is singular precisely because beauty insinuates itself as an unstable mediator between physical appearance and moral being, between sensually determined perception of the other and ethically determined appreciation or respect for the other.

THE INVISIBLE BEAUTY OF VENICE

As I mentioned at the outset, the Venetian interlude in *The Confessions* is remarkable for the absolute poverty of Rousseau's account of the city. No single art work, or building, or public space finds its way into Rousseau's memories of a period that he seems to have spent, or wasted, immersed in quarrels with his employer and petty maneuverings for distinction among his fellow employees at the French embassy during his eleven-month sojourn there from September 1743 to August 1744. The material beauty of the urban space—its water-filled streets and floating palaces—goes completely unremarked. Of course Venice was not—in the mid-eighteenth century—what it would become in the European cultural imagination during the nineteenth century. It was not yet the scene of an elegiac Romanticism, not yet the most exquisite corpse of cities.[12] But Venice has never been unremarkable and so Rousseau's silence, or blindness, merits attention. The veritable inundation of foreign visitors during the eighteenth century is evinced by a large and lively body of travel memoirs almost all of which attest to the impossibility of saying anything new about a city already so well known.[13] Rousseau does not even offer the kind of demurral Goethe feels compelled to make as he approaches Venice (in 1786) with the wary sense that too much had already been said and written about a place that "can only be compared to itself"—an impression, at least, both of the singularity of the city and of the unique provocation it has always posed to travelers to record their impressions of it.[14]

The invisibility of Venice in Rousseau's recollections begins to make philosophical sense as an absence Rousseau fills in with an immaterial form of beauty that is associated with appreciation of what Kant terms the "humanity in a person," and what Rousseau identifies as the "soul." Venetian beauty makes its first impression on Rousseau when he finds himself exquisitely moved by a concert at the Church of the Mendicanti—associated with one of the four charitable *scuole* devoted to the musical instruction of orphaned girls and renowned, in the period, for their choral performances.[15] Rousseau is convinced that the irresistible "beauty of the voices" issues from equally beautiful faces, and so he is "distressed" by the "accursed grilles" screening the singers from the audience. "Angels of beauty" stand behind the screen, he complains, "concealed...from my sight" (295/315). But when finally granted an opportunity to come face to face with them, Rousseau meets with the disappointing fact of their ugliness. One of the girls was "hideous" he recalls, another had "only one eye," a third had been "disfigured by smallpox," and "scarcely one of them was without some notable defect" (296/315). This unpleasant surprise consists not only of the ironic deflation of aroused erotic interest. Rousseau's reaction also exposes a more profound conviction inspired by the "beauty of the voices"—a kind of philosophical presupposition about what the beauty of the voices necessarily signifies. "'No one can sing like that without a soul,' I said to myself. 'They have souls,'" Rousseau assures himself (296/315). It is important to be precise here: Rousseau does not assume a correspondence between beautiful voices and beautiful souls; rather, the beauty of the voices is the certain sign of no more and no less than the bare presence of "soul." The girls must be beautiful not because they have beautiful voices, but because of the "soul" evinced by their beautiful singing. Aesthetic impression—beauty—underwrites a judgment that is ethical in substance—the other bears a soul—and this correspondence is affirmed rather than shaken by the girls' physical unsightliness. Beauty, in this case, is preserved by a willful denial of what is plain to see. "In the end, my way of looking at them was so changed," Rousseau recalls, "I continued to find their singing delightful, and their voices lent such imaginary charm to their faces that so long as they were singing I persisted in finding them beautiful, notwithstanding the evidence of my eyes" (296/315). (The French "*leurs voix fardoient si bien leurs visages*" more suggestively proposes that the beautiful voices cosmetically alter or make over the faces.)

Several interpretive possibilities might account for this insistent impression of beauty despite the irresistible, contradictory "evidence" of the eyes. "My way of looking at them was so changed": We might say that, no longer distorted by prurient desire, Rousseau's gaze now falls on objects of aesthetic rather than erotic interest. We might say that superficial judgment yields to penetrating observation, so that Rousseau ultimately sees through the girls' appearance to their being (although the impression of both beauty and soul here involves the overlaid "*fard*" of the voice rather than infiltration of a surface). Or we might say that in this scene Rousseau's "way of looking" is stubbornly determined by an underlying expectation of correspondence between body and soul ("*je m'obstinois en dépit de mes yeux à les trouver belles*") that is almost formal or categorical in nature. It is not, after all, any particular feature of the girls' characters or virtues that impresses

Rousseau more powerfully than the evidence of his eyes, but rather the generic presence of their souls. The disconcerting disjunction between being and appearance arises from the obstinately held conviction that beauty evinces soul—where soul suggests mere humanity with the body as its habitation, and where beauty names no more and no less than the perception of this embodiment. In Kantian terms, Rousseau's taste for this beauty is neither free nor disinterested but guided and constrained by a "concept of what the object ought to be."[16]

The human form, in the *Critique of Judgment*, belongs to the category of things that cannot be judged apart from an idea of their end, and appreciation of human beauty inextricably bound to the idea of the human as that which "has the end of its existence in itself" (17).[17] Kant's remarks on human beauty are rarely discussed because they are both marginal to and at odds with his central arguments about the structure of aesthetic experience as a harmonious free play between intellect and imagination, the universal validity of aesthetic judgments, and the necessarily disinterested form of aesthetic appreciation. However anomalous in the *Critique,* the claims about the human form in 17, "On the Ideal of Beauty," are consistent with related observations on the judgment of character in the *Anthropology* and on the origins of love and the taste for human beauty in the "Conjectural Beginning of Human History."[18] Unlike the "purposive purposelessness" of the pure object of aesthetic judgment in the third *Critique,* the beauty of the human form "adheres" or "depends" on an idea of the "ends of humanity." Thus the human figure in Kant strikes us as beautiful because of its "visible expression of moral ideas," of "everything that our understanding connects with the morally good" (17). Something like this correlation inspires the imaginative idealism involved in Rousseau's "persistent finding" of beauty in the girls at the Mendicanti, physical appearance aside. The "soul," authentically bodied forth in voice, literally "makes up" beauty.

Venetian Scenes

Rousseau's silence about the impressive art, architecture, and setting of Venice might be understood to foreground an interest in beauty as a mode of appreciating or valuing the intrinsic humanity, or soul, of the other. But such a conjecture cannot fully account for his reticence about the city. Lovers of Venice might wonder about Rousseau's blindness to its visual allure, but readers of Rousseau will be more inclined to wonder at the absence of his contempt. After all eighteenth-century Venetian society—in fact and in reputation—rather perfectly exemplifies the corruption and decadence Rousseau would launch his career denouncing.[19] What Rousseau did not care to admire—the beauty of palaces, churches, squares—he might at least have been roused to condemn—as, for example, Montesquieu did in his travels of the 1720s: "My eyes are very pleased by Venice," he conceded, "my heart and mind are not."[20] What Montesquieu and others were responding to was not just the apparent dissipation of a civic life given over to pleasurable amusements, festivals, theater, and gambling, but also the astonishing, frankly tolerated sexual license of a city in which married women freely consorted with companions (*cicisbeii*) and in which prostitution was widespread and openly practiced.[21]

In the remainder of this chapter I want to propose how we might read Rousseau's most memorable experience *in* Venice as an indirect but incisive impression *of* Venice during this period of unprecedented and disturbingly compounded license and liberty. His troubling encounter with the beautiful prostitute allegorizes a certain aspect of eighteenth-century Venice, the philosophical implications of which involve the association and disassociation of aesthetic impression and ethical judgment that I have been sketching out. Let me begin by giving this claim visual form by touching on the work of a Venetian painter, exactly Rousseau's contemporary, whose images materialize impressions the philosopher condenses into narrative.

As is well known, the development of tourism in eighteenth-century Venice helped foster a genre of view paintings and cityscapes by artists such as Luca Carelevaris, Michiel Marieschi, and Giovanni Antonio Canal ("Canaletto"). The work of Francesco Guardi (born, like Rousseau, in 1712) is both representative of the genre and distinctively unsettling (figure 6.1).

What is characteristic about Guardi's work, especially in comparison to his more prolific Venetian contemporary Canaletto, is the delicate, expressive brushwork he uses both to capture detail and to convey the impression of a vulnerable ethereality. Wisps of paint conjure human activity in a fragile, liquefying space, contributing to what art historians consider the elegiac quality of his work in the waning decades of the Republic.[22] While not broken or ruined, Guardi's Venice seems in the process of dissolution.

Although he is best known for his cityscapes, Guardi's interior scenes of the *ridotto* at Palazzo San Dandolo transpose his sensibility onto a typical—and particularly Venetian—social setting (figure 6.2).[23]

The *ridotto* was a licensed public gaming house which, along with more than a hundred smaller casinos lodged in informal apartments or rooms in private palaces, operated as nightclubs where the upper and middle classes mingled freely, immersing themselves in gambling, drinking, and dancing. These were also ideal and notorious sites for

Figure 6.1 Francesco Guardi. *Venice from the Bacino di San Marco.* c. 1780. Oil on canvas (61.9 x 95.3 cm). Kimbell Art Foundation.

Figure 6.2 Francesco Guardi. *Il Ridotto.* c. 1745–58. Oil on canvas (108 x 208 cm). Ca'Rezzonico.

seduction, illicit assignations, and the engagement of prostitutes. Admission to the *ridotto* was officially restricted to patricians and to anyone else wearing a mask, so the rooms were crowded with masked guests, creating a "theater of vice" (in one contemporary account), "a detestable intermingling of gentlemen and foreigners, officers and plebeians, honest women and public prostitutes."[24] The mask, which was worn six months of the year during this period (Rousseau himself donned one while he was there), was certainly a condition for the possibility of the liberties enjoyed at the *ridotto* and similar venues. More than a costume for special occasions, the mask had become a defining feature of Venetian social experience in the last decades of the Republic. In Montesquieu's estimation, the mask permitted a kind of "freedom that the majority of decent people would not care to have."[25] "It was secrecy, anonymity," comments the historian Henri Zerner, allowing "secure impunity" and "licensed folly."[26]

Unlike paintings of the same setting by his contemporary Pietro Longhi, Guardi's paintings offer no evident, visual, or narrative focal point (figure 6.3).[27]

Arrayed on the canvas as on a stage, seen from a distance, and masked, his figures are individuated only by posture and gesture. The chromatic scheme manages to mingle sumptuousness and sordidness—rendered in a kind of bronze brown, the gilt splendor of the rooms appears dingy and muddied. Guardi's images of the *ridotto* evoke the uneasy coexistence of civility and dissipation in Venice, of something vaguely sinister and corrupt attending elegance and refinement—the very social ills Rousseau would excoriate in the two discourses that initiated his career—but that is not all. This particular painting has also

Figure 6.3 Pietro Longhi. *Il Ridotto*. Oil on canvas (84 x 115 cm). c. 1740s. Private collection.

frequently provoked interpretive disputes generally centered around the masked lady on the left: is she a prostitute about to be engaged or an innocent young lady dangerously vulnerable to seduction? Is the gentleman's bow predatory or solicitous? Do the masks conceal virtue or vice? As the historical record does not decide the matter, the painting is free to convey precisely this undecidability.[28] The Venetian mask, obscuring the expressions and identities of the two figures, functions as a kind of synecdoche—or material figuration—of intersubjective inscrutability. In Guardi's style, critics read a "perceptual nervousness" that conveys "awareness of the complexity and fragility" of the act of seeing itself.[29] The ambiguity of *Il Ridotto* compounds self-consciousness about the act of perception with moral indiscernibility—and this is precisely what we might choose to see as the pictorial form of the anxieties about appearance Rousseau begins to articulate in the first Discourse and dramatizes in his unconsummated encounter with the prostitute named Zulietta.

Rousseau and the Beautiful Body of Venice

Clichéd praise of Zulietta's attractions ("great men and princes should be her slaves"; "the houris of Paradise are less enticing") distracts from, but does not obscure Rousseau's enunciation of the same standard of judgment he applied to the girls at the Mendicanti. "She is not only charming and beautiful," he observes, "but good also and generous"; "I could never have believed it possible to feel anything like the emotion she inspired in me, without my also feeling a respect and esteem for her" (300–1/*320–21*). "Respect and esteem" are terms, that here in Rousseau as later in Kant, name that fundamental recognition of the inherent value of the other. Rousseau's hyperbolic appreciation of Zulietta as a worthy object of worship (he calls her "Nature's masterpiece," "a divinity") is in fact an iteration rather than an inflation of the more basic perception of her as worthy of "respect." The agitated confusion that afflicts Rousseau arises from his effort to reconcile this ethical recognition of the other's humanity, inspired and affirmed by the evidence of his senses (her "charm and beauty"), with the unconcealed fact that Zulietta is also "a wretched street-walker, on sale to the world," a "thing" at the disposal of others (300–1/*320–21*). "There is something incomprehensible about this," Rousseau observes, and I would suggest that what exceeds the understanding in this scene is not the discordance between a trivial fantasy about Zulietta's worth ("Sceptres should lie at her feet") and her real condition ("a worthless slut") but the discordance between her absolute human value—evinced by her beauty—and her equally evident availability as "a thing at my disposal." Her being belies her appearance, not because she pretends to be something other than she is, but because she has turned herself into an object.

Deciding "either my heart deceives me, deludes my senses and makes me the dupe of a worthless slut, or some secret flaw that I do not see destroys the value of her charms," Rousseau looks ever more carefully at Zulietta's body for the visible sign of the human value degraded or deformed into a thing with a price. "I began to seek for that flaw with a singular persistence," he recalls, finally finding, at the very the instant when scrutiny would yield to intimate contact, the apparent mark that destroys her beauty and betrays her as some thing other than human.

> Just as I was about to sink upon a breast which seemed about to suffer a man's lips and hand for the first time, I perceived that she had a malformed nipple. I beat my brow, looked harder, and made certain... I was struck by the thought that it resulted from some remarkable imperfection of Nature and, after turning this idea over in my head, I saw as clear as daylight that instead of the most charming creature I could possibly imagine I held in my arms some kind of monster, rejected by Nature, men, and love. (301/321–22)[30]

Important here is not the arbitrariness of the physical imperfection, but the willful activity of thought and imagination through which it comes to count as a revelatory sign of inner deformity. Empirical certainties ("I perceived," "I looked harder," "made certain," "saw as clear as daylight") lead to the fantastic conclusion that Zulietta's body belongs to a "monster." The discovery of this physical defect restores a correspondence between apparent and real being, a correspondence that can only be established and affirmed in aesthetic terms. The monstrosity of a soul that has made itself a thing for sale—ideally and evidently cannot reside in a beautiful body.

Thus far I have followed Rousseau's account, linking his sudden revulsion and disgust with Zulietta to a scrupulous sense that beauty is incompatible with her being a "mere thing," that she is beautiful only insofar as she is "worthy of respect and esteem." But there is another side to the story, even as Rousseau tells it. His uneasiness and barely concealed disgust elicit a response; Zulietta blushes, adjusts her clothes, and retreats from Rousseau's scrutiny. What Rousseau has seen in Zulietta is displaced by a glimpse of Zulietta's apprehension of Rousseau's appraisal. And this is where Kant enters the scene, standing somewhere over Zulietta's shoulder, affirming Rousseau's surmise that "human beings... have no right to hand themselves over for profit, as things for another's use," but also insisting that the intrinsic value of the other, that which makes the other worthy of respect, can never be a matter of empirical certainty.[31] In Kant's terms, Rousseau does the right thing for the wrong reasons, or rather for no *reason* at all. Reflected by Zulietta's uncomfortable withdrawal from Rousseau's eyes, his revulsion redounds back upon him as the legible symptom of conceptual confusion between perception of the other and ethical regard for the other.

Beauty is phenomenal, but in Venice appearances do not mask being in the way that Rousseau typically fears. Zulietta is indeed both a "thing on sale to the world" and a "being worthy of respect." Her beautiful body is disturbing not because it is a deceptive appearance but because it is the site of diverse, conflicting impressions of value that cannot be resolved by merely looking more closely. Ultimately, the hermeneutic challenge of Zulietta's attractions defies not only Rousseau's effort to find beauty "good" and "worthy of respect," but also Kant's austere insistence on the irreconcilability of erotic interest in the other, ethical regard for the other, and appreciation of human beauty.

Notes

1. *The Confessions.* Trans. J. M. Cohen. New York: Penguin, 1953. 308. *Oeuvres complètes.* Ed. Bernard Gagnebin and Marcel Raymond. Paris: Gallimard, 1959. 1: 329. Subsequent page references to the translation and French language text (in italics) will appear parenthetically in the text.
2. Rousseau's French biographer remarks that his subject's "genuine discovery" was that "no one ever understands anyone else," and his most comprehensive interpreter understands *The Confessions* to evolve from the child's early discovery "that minds are separate from one another." Jean Guéhenno, *Jean-Jacques Rousseau.* Trans. John Weightman and Doreen Weightman. New York: Columbia UP, 1962. 2:187. Jean Starobinski, *Transparency and Obstruction.* Trans. Arthur Goldhammer. Chicago: Chicago UP, 1971. 8.
3. *Discourse on the Origins of Inequality among Men. The Discourses and Other Early Political Writings.* Trans.Victor Gourevitch. Cambridge: Cambridge UP, 1997. 170. *Oeuvres complètes* 3: 174.
4. *Discourse on the Arts and Sciences. The Discourses and Other Early Political Writings*, 8. *Oeuvres complètes*, 8.
5. *Discourse on Inequality, 171/175.* The conception of the human being as an "end in himself" ("something that may not be used merely as a means") grounds what Kant calls "dignity" and "respect" in the *Groundwork of the Metaphysics of Morals.* This recognition of the other's absolute worth enjoins all "to use humanity whether in your own person or in the person of any other, always as an end, never merely as a means." *Groundwork of the Metaphysics of Morals.* Trans. Mary Gregor. Cambridge: Cambridge UP, 1998. 37–38.

6. *Discourse on the Arts and Sciences,* 7–8/7–8.
7. *Discourse on the Arts and Sciences,* 8/8.
8. *The Claim of Reason.* Oxford: Oxford UP, 1979. 427; 440; 432. On the intersection between epistemological disappointment and moral aspiration with respect to the knowledge of other minds, see especially, 420–63.
9. On Kant's complex debt to Rousseau see Ernst Cassirer, *Rousseau, Kant, Goethe,* Princeton: Princeton UP, 1945, and, more recently, Richard Velkley, *Freedom and the End of Reason,* Chicago: Chicago UP, 1989.
10. Cohen's translation does not capture the provocative paradox of the original: "*une circonstance de ma vie qui peigne bien mon naturel.*" While the figurative sense of "*peindre*" (to depict, to represent, to show) is consistent with the promise of revelation, the implications of its literal meanings (to cover with paint, to color over) should be borne in mind.

    Recent thoughtful interpretations of this episode include Sarah Herbold, "Well-placed Reflections: (Post) Modern Woman as Symptom of (Post) Modern Man," *Signs* 21.1 (1995): 94–106; Michael Sheringham, *French Autobiography: Devices and Desires,* Oxford: Oxford UP, 1993, 60–66.
11. Compare, for example, the excursion to Tourne with Mlle. Galley and Mlle. Gaddenfriend (133–36/*135–39*) and the diverting "traveller's love affair" with Mme. de Larnage (237–41/ *248–52*).
12. On the compounding of death and desire in the nineteenth-century cultural imagination of Venice, see John Pemble, *Venice Rediscovered,* Oxford: Clarendon, 1995, and Tony Tanner, *Venice Desired,* Cambridge: Harvard UP, 1992.
13. "The description of the situation of Venice every one knows," wrote William Freeman in 1729, "but still it surprises" (Black 39). On eighteenth-century travel to the city see Bruce Redford, *Venice and the Grand Tour,* New Haven: Yale UP, 1996; Christopher Hibbert, *Venice: The Biography of a City,* New York: Norton, 1989, 152–96; Jeremy Black, *Italy and the Grand Tour,* New Haven: Yale UP, 2003, 33–45.
14. *Italian Journey.* Trans. W. H. Auden and Elizabeth Mayer. New York: Penguin, 1970. 77.
15. Antonio Vivaldi was maestro of the *scuola* at the Church of the Pietà; Baldassare Galuppi (subject of Robert Browning's "A Toccata of Galuppi's") presided at the Mendicanti when Rousseau attended. Goethe also praises the "music...of infinite beauty" he enjoyed at the Mendicanti during his visit in 1786 (*Italian Journey* 83). On the music of the *scuole,* see Hibbert, 169–170; M. V. Constable, "The Venetian '*Figlie del coro*': Their Environment and Achievement," *Music and Letters* 63 (1982): 181–212; Dennis Arnold, "Music at the Mendicanti in the Eighteenth Century," *Music and Letters* 65 (1984): 345–56.

16. *Critique of the Power of Judgment.* Trans. Paul Guyer and Eric Matthews. Cambridge: Cambridge UP, 2000. 16. Subsequent references to this edition will be identified by section number parenthetically in the text.
17. Useful recent discussions of this troublesome section in the *Critique of Judgment* include Angelica Nuzzo, *Ideal Embodiment: Kant's Theory of Sensibility,* Bloomington: Indiana UP, 2008, 298–302; Robert Wicks, "Kant on Beautifying the Human Body," *British Journal of Aesthetics* 39.2 (1999): 163–78; Rachel Zuckert, "Boring Beauty and Universal Morality: Kant on the Ideal of Beauty," *Inquiry* 48.2 (2005): 107–30.
18. On "cognizing the interior of the human being from the exterior," see Immanuel Kant, *Anthropology from a Pragmatic Point of View.* Trans. Robert Louden, Cambridge: Cambridge UP, 2006, 185–203. On the movement from "sensual to idealistic attractions," the origins of appreciation for human beauty, and the "first hint of man's formation into a moral creature," see the "Conjectural Beginning of Human History" in *Perpetual Peace and Other Essays,* trans. Ted Humphrey, Indianapolis: Hackett, 1983, 51–52.
19. The "decadence" of Venetian culture and society during the century before the fall of the Republic in 1797 has been a constant, virtually undisputed theme in both popular and scholarly histories of the city from the nineteenth century to the present day. See, for example, Hibbert, 153–184; Philippe Monnier, *Venice in the Eighteenth Century.* Trans. Monnier, London: Chatto, 1907; Maurice Rowden, *The Silver Age of Venice,* New York: Praeger, 1970; Maurice Andrieux, *Daily Life in Venice in the Time of Casanova.* Trans. Mary Fitton, New York: Praeger, 1969, and most recently, Margaret Plant's meticulously researched *Venice: Fragile City,* New Haven: Yale UP, 2002, 7–39; 461–69. Pompeo Molmenti's compendious nineteenth-century history of the city draws on a range of public archives, private letters, and memoirs, and remains a useful resource. For the eighteenth century, see Horatio Brown's translation of Pompeo Molmenti, Part III: "The Decadence." *Venice: Its Individual Growth from the Earliest Beginnings to the Fall of the Republic.* Trans. Horatio Brown, London: Murray, 1880.
20. *Voyages de Montesquieu.* Ed. Albert de Montesquieu. Bordeaux: Gounouilhou, 1894. 1: 41 (my translation).
21. Montesquieu's travel notes frequently return to the theme of sexual turpitude. He is astonished to find young gentlemen supporting and even marrying courtesans, to witness prostitutes making engagements in the churches (23, 25), and he disapproves the liberties enjoyed by Venetian gentlewomen who "go wherever they want and with whomever they want" in their gondolas (33). Historians confirm these observations. The "government itself, though it carefully regulated prostitution, did not attempt to suppress it," according to Molmenti. During the eighteenth century, Venetian women

enjoyed greater liberties and "vied with the courtesans in all the arts of seduction and in the shamelessness of their indulgence" (III: 2: 93, 96). Similarly, Rowden remarks that "nowhere in Europe was a wife externally more independent of her husband," linking the "freedom of women" to an "open sexual market" in which both courtesans and "respectable women" circulated (105, 114). See also Andrieux 154–57 and Hibbert 177–81. On eighteenth-century prostitution in Venice, see Giovanni Scarabello, "Le 'Signore' della Repubblica," *Il Gioco dell'Amore: Le Cortigiane di Venezia dal Trecento al Settecento*, Milan: Berenice, 1990, 28–30.

22. On Guardi see, Michael Levey, *Painting in Eighteenth Century Venice*, London: Phaidon, 1959, 42–46; 96–105; Michael Merling, "The Brothers Guardi" *The Glory of Venice: Art in the Eighteenth Century*, New Haven: Yale UP, 1994, 293–328; Antonio Morassi, *Antonio e Francesco Guardi*, 2 vols., Venice: Alfieri, 1973; George Simonson, *Francesco Guardi*, London: Metheun, 1904; Dario Succi, *Francesco Guardi: itenarario dell'avventura artistica*, Milan: Silvana, 1993.

Michael Levey characterizes Guardi as "a rebel against the Canalettesque set-piece of hard light and shade" (96) describing his style as "fluid, wavering and capricious" (43), his brushstrokes "erratic and flickering" (97). In his paintings "Venice raises its facades and towers almost tentatively into the stormy atmospheric world where the elements buffet what man has built" (98) and human figures become "mere specks of color, a running squiggle of white paint, a black dot, shorthand to express the population of the most moribund of European states" (102). Michael Merling also notes Guardi's "conscious rejection of Canaletto's example" in the "nervous and irregular movement of his brush" (317). On the elegiac tone of Guardi's cityscapes, see also Plant, 14–15, and Succi, 118.

23. The Ca'Rezzonico canvas is the most famous of several related paintings of the *ridotto* by Guardi. One of the paintings hangs at the Metropolitan Museum of Art in New York, another at the Fitzwilliam Museum in Cambridge, and three others are in private collections.

24. *Giocchi e ridotti proibiti* (1703), quoted in Alberto Fiorin, "Azzardo e Piacere: Relazioni Pericolose," in Bruno, *Il Gioco dell'Amore*, 45 (my translation). Descriptions of the *ridotto* at Palazzo San Dandolo emphasize both the ruinous intensity of the gambling there and its notoriety as a site for romantic assignations and solicitation of prostitutes. The Italian historian Pietro Giannone complained, or marveled, that "women of every condition, married, maid or widow, mingle freely with professional prostitutes, for the mask levels all distinctions": in his *Grand Tour* (1749), Thomas Nugent recalls that "here you meet ladies of pleasure, and married women who under the protection of the mask, enjoy all the diversions of the carnival...Here the gentlemen are at liberty to rally and address the ladies" (quoted in Hibbert 162 and 171–72). Many of the private casinos, as well, were "lairs where a squalid rabble of rogues and harlots mingled with the best blood of

Venice; places that admitted anyone in a mask" (Andrieux 132). See also Rowden 44–47 and Molmenti III: 1: 170–75.
25. *Voyages* 1: 24 (my translation). The specific liberties "honest men" would not want include "going out in broad daylight with ladies of pleasure" and "being entirely unknown and independent."
26. Material fact and evocative symbol at once, the semiotics of the mask proves irresistible to historians of Venice. "The mask habit swamped Venetian life. It took away every barrier there had been. Working girls could sit next to patrician women at the gambling tables…under it every woman was a *zentildonna*, class and even sex were cancelled out, and everyone became a secret spectator" (Rowden 84). "Watertight anonymity was in fact the great lure of the Carnival…All the barriers were down…Dissembling was suddenly good behavior and deviousness a merit, as the elite of the underworld rubbed shoulders with the worthier multitude" (Andrieux 121). "Young and old, noble and plebeian, rich and poor, all indiscriminately donned the mask, under cover of which they carried out their intrigues, and which was, so to speak, a symbol of the lost equality of all Venetian citizens, every rank of life fraternizing behind the quaint and bizarre disguises" (Molmenti, 3: 1: 143). For Zerner, see unpaginated preface to Monnier.
27. Longhi's and Guardi's paintings are strikingly similar, and it is frequently suggested that Guardi based his composition on that of Longhi. In both images, the gambling house is represented as a scene of amorous intrigue and assignation, though Longhi's painting makes explicit much that Guardi chooses to obscure in his ensemble of sweeping gowns and veiled figures. Particularly notable is the handing over of keys to the couple in the right foreground of Longhi's canvas, presumably to a back room given over to private transactions. See Filippo Pedrocco, "Iconografia delle Cortigiane di Venezia," *Il Gioco dell'Amore*, 90. On the relationship between the two paintings see Michael Merling's catalog entry on Guardi in *The Glory of Venice*, 455–56.
28. Fiorin speculates that Guardi exploits the relatively ambiguous lines between professional prostitutes and "women of the world" in the period (45). See also Merling, 455.
29. Merling, 317. Guardi's expressive style and emphasis on dissolution, transience, and "lyrical gift for transposing reality in his own highly personal terms" (Levey 105) have been seen as anticipating nineteenth-century innovations (Impressionism for Morassi, I: 270; J. M. W. Turner for Simonson, 70).
30. Lost in Cohen's translation is Rousseau's evocative designation "*téton borgne*" (literally a nipple blind in one eye). Sarah Herbold suggests that insofar as "*borgne*" also signifies "low in a moral and social sense," the deformed breast "securely identifies Zulietta as a low-class reprehensible slut," thereby allowing Rousseau to sustain his "cherished—but already crumbling—illusion that physical and moral beauty…perfectly correspond." Herbold reads this episode in Zizekian terms, as

a retreat to "patriarchal fictions regarding the inseparability of material and metaphysical meaning and value," but like me she identifies the crisis of the moment with the "loss of epistemological certainty" (94–106). See also James O'Rourke's discussion of the incommensurability between the "rhetoric of interiority, which produces the domain of love, shame, intentions, remorse" in *The Confessions* and the "rhetoric of ethics," which exposes the "intimate exchanges of power" in sexual transactions. *Sex, Lies and Autobiography.* Charlottesville: U of Virginia P, 2006. 62.

31. *Lectures on Ethics.* Trans. Peter Heath. Cambridge: Cambridge UP, 1997. 157. Insofar as Kant regards the object of sexual desire as the body of the other, sexual relations necessarily entail a "debasement of humanity." Only in marriage, understood as a mutual dedication of the "whole person" to another, is sexual intercourse "possible without debasement of humanity or violation of morality" (158). Christine Korsgaard links the reciprocal "self-surrender" of marriage in Kant to Rousseau's account of the social contract. *Creating the Kingdom of Ends.* Cambridge: Harvard UP, 1996. 194–96; 215.

7

E. T. A. Hoffmann's Marketplace Vision of Berlin

Alexander Schlutz

A fantastical Berlin features prominently in many of E. T. A. Hoffmann's stories and novellas: secret trysts and occult rituals take place in the *Tiergarten,* an incongruous abandoned house on the luxurious avenue *Unter den Linden* becomes an object of dangerous obsession, brides show their faces from the tower of the old town hall at midnight on summer solstice, revenants and sorcerers mingle with petty Prussian bureaucrats, frequent local wine cellars and cake shops, and enigmatic women turn the heads of well-established noblemen, causing them to disastrously breach protocol at the fashionable tea parties of Berlin high society. In Hoffmann's 1821 story "The Errancies" Berlin even becomes an object of reverse ethnology in the fragmentary notes of a quite possibly imaginary Greek princess—notes that reveal her bewilderment about the city's exotic building materials and the strange dress of its inhabitants, in particular the men's tall, black and cylindrical headgear, and ultimately leave little to recommend for the would-be visitor but the *quadriga* on the *Brandenburg Gate.*

With his keen sense for the fantastic, the uncanny, the grotesque, and the absurd, in story after story, Hoffmann creates his very own indelible literary version of Berlin, the capital of the German Enlightenment and one of the centers of German Romanticism, and in so doing, he was one of the first, as Walter Benjamin remarks in a 1930 Berlin radio broadcast for children, "The Demonic Berlin," to put Berlin on the European literary map. Hoffmann, Benjamin suggests, could well be called "the father of the Berlin novel," and Benjamin draws a direct line from Hoffmann's stories to Alfred Döblin's *Berlin Alexanderplatz* (90, 92). Hoffmann's purpose in his writing, Benjamin contends, is *physiognomic* and stems from his ability to see the extraordinary in the concrete and the everyday; it is "to show, that this dull, sober, enlightened, sensible Berlin is, not only in its medieval corners, out-of-the-way streets, deserted houses, but also in its working population of all classes and neighborhoods, full of things that excite the story-teller, and which one only has to trace, which one has to see in them." It hence seems like a parting lesson to Benjamin that one of Hoffmann's last stories, dictated on his deathbed, is "actually nothing other but such a course in physiognomical seeing" (91).[1] The text in question is *My Cousin's Corner Window*, published a few months before Hoffmann's death in 1822, a novella that indeed puts both the art of seeing and the people of Berlin at the center of the reader's attention.

Benjamin is by no means the only one to look at Hoffmann's text as a parting lesson, and assessments of *My Cousin's Corner Window* as a literary testament are quite common in Hoffmann scholarship. Yet, as David Darby points out in a recent essay, while there is general consensus about the importance of the novella, critical interpretations of the art of seeing the text imparts and of the actual content of the testament Hoffmann may have wished to leave behind differ widely. Such discrepant readings can be traced back to the structural complexities of the text itself, for its aesthetic and stylistic rhetorical strategies are threefold: it not only offers a course in eighteenth-century modes of physiognomical seeing, but it also presents an elaboration of Hoffmann's own "Serapiontic" poetic principles, while its specific observations of socioeconomic realities in post-Napoleonic Berlin, rather unusual in their realism for Hoffmann's work, equally allow the novella to be read as performing a shift in Hoffmann's aesthetic priorities and as an anticipation of the "poetic realism" German writers would develop by the mid-nineteenth century. The novella can thus be seen to simultaneously champion three seemingly contradictory aesthetic credos: an Enlightenment aesthetics based on assumptions about the world's readability; Hoffmann's own late-Romantic poetics of creative narrative vision; and a nascent aesthetics of nineteenth-century realism. Undoubtedly, Hoffmann's narrative achievement lies in holding all three of these stylistic directions together in one relatively short text, and any balanced interpretation of *My Cousin's Corner Window*, as Darby rightfully suggests, will need to consider their "complex interweaving" in Hoffmann's novella (283).

Beyond these narrative and stylistic complexities, Walter Benjamin's comments on *My Cousin's Corner Window* in his unfinished book on Charles Baudelaire, *Charles Baudelaire: A Lyric Poet in the Era of High Capitalism* (rather than those in the little-known "The Demonic Berlin") have had a considerable effect on the critical discussion of the novella, which has consequently also been drawn into the orbit of the critical debate about the nineteenth-century modern urban aesthetics of the flaneur. For that reason, this chapter, as it attempts to unravel the intricacies of the "art of seeing" developed in *My Cousin's Corner Window*, also engages the question whether the novella could be understood as a flaneur's testament, a claim Benjamin makes in one of the notes for his *Arcades Project*. In fact, Benjamin's own—quite contradictory—assessments of Hoffmann's text on different occasions faithfully mirror the novella's narrative complexities, and they can usefully serve as a guiding thread connecting the discussion of its aesthetic strategies. An untangling of the text's aesthetic play with stylistic modes and narrative perspective will then not only reveal how physiognomical practices continue to inform the flaneur's urban vision, but it will also demonstrate that the text's ultimate narrative positioning, its true art of seeing as well as its modernity, lie in a metanarrative perspective that remains unconfined by the respective visions of the text's two protagonists. Only from this self-reflexive position of narrative distance can we possibly hope to attain a glimpse of the vision Hoffmann's "literary testament" may provide, both in terms of aesthetics and with respect to the socioeconomic realities of post-Napoleonic Berlin.

A Flaneur at the Window?

Both in "The Paris of the Second Empire in Baudelaire" and in its partial revision, "On Several Motives in Baudelaire," Benjamin briefly discusses Hoffmann's novella in a few short paragraphs, and his judgment about Hoffmann's text here is much less flattering than the one he had pronounced a few years earlier in his radio broadcast (551–52, 628–29). While Benjamin still calls the novella "probably one of the earliest attempts to grasp and conceive the street scape of a bigger city," he does not look at Hoffmann's text as a point of origin for a modern urban genre, but rather uses it as a foil that serves to highlight the modernity of Poe's short story "The Man of the Crowd," which interests him in his discussion of the modern flaneur (628). Benjamin, in fact, now pays little mind to Hoffmann's art of seeing or the structural complexities of his novella, which seems almost like a straw man in the discussion of Poe and Baudelaire, and the "course in physiognomical seeing" now turns into a presentation of "all sorts of little genre pictures," interpreted by "edifying comments" for a bourgeois audience (551; 629). Hoffmann, the keen observer and master of the fantastic, whom Benjamin knew so well, has disappeared, and *My Cousin's Corner Window* turns into an example of Berlin *Biedermeier* that does not hold up to scrutiny in comparison to Poe's London and Baudelaire's Paris of the 1840s. Berlin in 1822, its rapid rise to a fully industrialized metropolis still ahead, is not yet a true capital of the nineteenth century, and Hoffmann's vision not yet quite modern. Had he ever visited London or Paris, Benjamin now speculates, Hoffmann might have written differently.[2]

Benjamin, however, is only too aware that the last thing that could fittingly describe the writings of E. T. A. Hoffmann is a *Biedermeier* sensibility. In another radio broadcast of 1930 devoted to E. T. A. Hoffmann and Oskar Panizza, Benjamin strongly emphasizes Hoffmann's pronounced hatred of the everyday and his conviction that the virtues of the "good citizen" are the product of an artificial, mechanical, and ultimately satanic sensibility: "The ordinary person [Alltagsmensch], at whom his whole hatred had always been aimed, seemed to him more and more, in his virtues as well as his beauties, the product of a despicable artificial mechanism, the innermost core of which is governed by satan" (643–44). In this broadcast, even more so than in "The Demonic Berlin," Benjamin captures in a few short paragraphs the essence of Hoffmann's artistic convictions, and it is unlikely that Benjamin was fully convinced that *My Cousin's Corner Window* could have been written for the edification of a bourgeois audience. Indeed, Benjamin seems to have had some misgivings about his drastic juxtaposition of Hoffmann and Poe in "The Paris of the Second Empire in Baudelaire," for he adds, almost as a note of caution, "And yet Hoffmann was in his disposition part of the family of the Poe and Baudelaire" (551). Benjamin quotes Hoffmann's friend and biographer Julius Eduard Hitzig, who notes Hoffmann's enjoyment of observing and interacting with people and highlights his need and desire to be in human company whenever possible. Hoffmann, too, Benjamin implies, was by his nature an urbanite and a flaneur like Poe and Baudelaire, an assessment that he makes much more explicitly in one of the unused entries in the *Arcades Project,* which describes "E. T. A. Hoffmann as the type of the flaneur" and which continues, in an impulse completely contrary to that taken in the Baudelaire book but quite compatible with that of "The Demonic Berlin": " 'My Cousin's Corner Window' is his [this type's] testament. And hence Hoffmann's great success in France, where one understood this type particularly well" (536).

For readers only familiar with Benjamin's comments in the Baudelaire essay, this statement must seem utterly puzzling, but his assessment of the novella as a physiognomical testament in "The Demonic Berlin" provides the necessary context: The flaneur needs to be a practiced physiognomist, even though his penetrating gaze may turn up unanswerable mysteries in the crowds of the modern city—the narrator of Poe's "The Man of the Crowd" after all classifies most of the people he observes quite adroitly and securely, before his art of inductive physiognomic reasoning is baffled by the unreadable figure who gives the story its name. The flaneur may ultimately desire to lose himself in the labyrinth of the city, to fall into a trancelike reverie induced by the surrounding crowds, but he can only do so because of his keen eye and his skill in the art of observation, and a physiognomical trigger lies at the origin of the flaneur's experience. "The phantasmagoria of the flaneur:" notes Benjamin in the *Arcades Project,* "reading the profession, the origin, the character in the faces" (540).

It would of course be a misunderstanding, as Benjamin points out only a few entries later, to believe that the flaneur's goal is physiognomical study as an end in itself. He is not walking the streets in an attempt to settle people's identities and to determine their characters from clues in their behavior and outward appearance. Rather, he seeks the phantasmagoria in which he can lose himself, the ghostly and ephemeral show of projected images that is the outcome of physiognomical efforts on the streets of the city, where all attempts at reading lead to unstable visions and to hallucinations not unlike those induced by hashish. The physiognomy of the crowds is the flaneur's drug of choice.[3] There is hence ultimately nothing surprising in seeing "a course in physiognomical seeing" as a flaneur's testament, even though its main protagonist may seem an anti-flaneur, paralyzed and confined to his apartment, surveying the streets from his perch high above the crowds, and who cannot join them even if he wanted to. Telescope in hand, he can still enjoy the spectacle of the crowd even though he is unable to immerse himself in it, and Hoffmann's novella, while it indeed does not portray the crowds on the thoroughfares of a high-capitalist metropolis, is for that reason neither provincial nor backward looking.[4]

At this point, a précis of *My Cousin's Corner Window* will be helpful: The protagonists of the novella are two cousins. The younger of the two is the first-person narrator of the text, who commands the relatively brief opening and closing frame narrative, and who pays an unexpected visit to his older cousin, a dying writer, who, much like Hoffmann at the time he composed the novella, is paralyzed, wheelchair bound, and unable to leave his apartment. This apartment overlooks the *Gendarmenmarkt,* from where the older cousin enjoys the same view Hoffmann himself cherished from his own corner window of his apartment in the *Taubengasse* 31 ii, corner *Charlottenstrasse.*[5] We learn from the narrator in the opening frame that his older cousin has become a recluse of late, refusing to see any visitors, having fallen into a deep depression because his illness not only paralyzes his body but also disrupts his creative process. The "evil demon of the illness," as the older cousin puts it, has blocked the crucial path from inward conception and invention to outward expression on which the writer depends for his craft. The cousin is not only physically unable to write; as soon as he begins to formulate his thoughts in an attempt to externalize his inner vision, these thoughts immediately disintegrate and vanish into thin air. In utter despair, the older cousin told the narrator in their last encounter that he has given up on the creative life altogether and has decided to shut himself off in the inwardness of his spirit like a hermit in his cell: "Cousin, it's over with me!...I give up the productive creative life, which emerges from within myself, shaped into outward form, befriending the world.—My spirit withdraws into its cell!" (597–98). Unable to befriend the internal and external worlds, subjective vision and objective reality, the cousin had ended all outside contact. The narrator is hence quite surprised when, crossing the *Gendarmenmarkt* on the day the events of the novella take place, he sees his cousin quite happily and contentedly sitting at his corner window, smoking a pipe. He makes his way up to his apartment, is granted entry, and his older cousin tells him that, while his illness is as destructive as ever, his window, or rather the view it affords, has given him solace. "But this window is my solace, here again I have understood life anew in all its colorful variety, and I feel befriended with its ceaseless activity. Come, cousin, look outside!" (599).

The bulk of the novella then unfolds as a dialogue between the two cousins, in which the older cousin, who now commands the narrative scene, attempts to communicate to the narrator the revelations of the view from his window affords and to teach him "at least the first principles [Primizien] of the art of seeing" (600). The cousin's art of seeing necessitates a glass, either a telescope as most commentators presume, or an opera glass, as Benjamin has it, which allows the two cousins to focus in on various people or groups of people on the market square below them. Using the visual clues available to them, the cousins then develop hypotheses and probable narratives about the figures they observe, producing a sequence of narrative vignettes, inspired by the work of William Hogarth, Daniel Chodowiecki, and Jacques Callot, artists and engravers dear to Hoffmann, all of whom are mentioned by the older cousin on the opening pages of the dialogue. In short, as Benjamin points out in "The Demonic Berlin," the younger cousin receives a lesson in the popular eighteenth-century art of physiognomy, and the two cousins produce narrative and visual order, if one of a highly complex kind, from the—at least for the narrator—initially impenetrable and potentially disorienting spectacle of the dense crowd below them.⁶

* * *

Hoping to counter Benjamin's disparaging remarks in the Baudelaire essay about *My Cousin's Corner Window* and the perspective of its eponymous older cousin, critics like David Darby and Robert McFarland have attempted to recuperate Hoffmann's novella for the aesthetics of a modern urban sensibility by questioning the identification of the older cousin's views with those of Hoffmann himself, a position taken by Benjamin and many subsequent readers of the novella, and by locating the modernity of Hoffmann's text in the figure of the narrator. From Darby's and McFarland's perspective, the older cousin and his exercises in physiognomy are ultimately a caricature of an obsolete aesthetics, while the younger cousin, who is seen in the middle of the crowd at the beginning of the novella and who will return to it at the end, is seen to represent an opening toward an emergent modern sensibility and an as of yet uncertain aesthetic future.

Traditional criticism can identify many pointers in the text that seem to invite an understanding of the older cousin as an autobiographical figure: his illness, his dress (a Warsaw dressing gown and a red cap, as Hoffmann portrayed himself several times in drawings and sketches), the location of his apartment, his admiration for Callot, Hogarth and Chodowiecki, as well as the fact that he compares himself to the painter in Hoffmann's story "King Arthur's Court" ("Der Artushof"). Hoffmann, however, was too fond of the play with narrative illusion for one to take such equations without the necessary dose of ironic distancing, for which the doubling of the cousins and the splitting of narrative authority is undoubtedly intended.⁷ And there are, as Darby points out, also several significant differences between the older cousin and Hoffmann himself. Hoffmann's illness, no matter how debilitating, never kept him from writing, even if he had to resort to dictation in the final months of his life. The older cousin, Darby acknowledges, voices several aesthetic positions that were important for Hoffmann at various stages of his career, but they are tinged with irony, given the distancing produced by the fact that the reader receives them through the narrative voice of the younger cousin. This doubling of perspectives produces a radical indeterminacy that subtly undermines the older cousin's seeming aesthetic authority.

To locate a newly emergent aesthetic perspective in the perspective of the narrator, both Darby and McFarland again take their cue from Benjamin, Darby in particular from a footnote in Benjamin's Baudelaire essay, which comments on the narrator's initial reaction to viewing the marketplace from his cousin's window. One's evaluation of the younger cousin's initial description of the crowd below him will indeed be pivotal to the understanding of the dialogue that follows, and it is worth presenting it here one more time in its entirety:

> The view was indeed strange and surprising. The whole market seemed to be a single crowded mass of people so that one had to believe that an apple tossed into it could never fall to the ground. The greatest variety of colors glowed in the sunshine, in very small patches that is, I had the impression of a large tulip field, blown by the wind in rippling waves, and I was forced to admit that the view was pretty nice, but, in the long run, quite tiring, and that in excitable people it might cause a slight dizziness resembling the not unpleasant delirium of impending dream. In this I sought the pleasure the corner window afforded my cousin and told him so quite frankly. (599)

In the footnote taken up by Darby, Benjamin implicitly locates a later nineteenth-century impressionist aesthetics in Hoffmann's description of the narrator's perception, which after all turns the mass of people into a moving ensemble of tiny patches of light and color. In dialogue with Benjamin, Darby makes an explicit claim for an impressionist mode of seeing in the passage and consequently locates the narrator rather than his cousin as the bearer of Hoffmann's intimation of a modern aesthetics. The narrator, Darby claims, ultimately does not learn anything from his cousin, since their didactic dialogue only seems to suggest, rather, he is merely humoring an ailing relative, whose outdated views he does not hold in particularly high esteem. When all is said and done, he, like Hoffmann in his better days, returns to the streets of Berlin to immerse himself in the crowds. The cousin's imminent death is hence not meant to mirror Hoffmann's own, but is rather emblematic of the death of a worldview no longer adequate to grasp the emerging realities of nineteenth-century industrialized urbanity.

Darby and McFarland are undoubtedly correct in insisting that the perspectives of both cousins need to be taken into account in any interpretation of Hoffmann's text and that an overly simplistic equation of the older cousin's views, which are compromised in strategic moments of the novella, with Hoffmann's own is bound to lead to misreadings. But to locate a potential modern urban perspective exclusively in the figure of the narrator, let alone to turn him into a flaneur in the Baudelairean and Benjaminean sense, as McFarland suggests, seems equally hasty. Already a close look at the narrator's description of the market scene and his reactions to it might give one pause in this respect. To begin with, the underlying metaphor of the tulip field the narrator chooses for the crowd on the marketplace is problematic in this context, for it evokes connotations that are not compatible with the unpredictable, ever-changing, and ultimately mysterious urban experience the flaneur enjoys. What could be more emblematic of the Enlightenment view of nature as an object to be controlled and readied for aesthetic consumption than the tulip field, orderly rows of plants, imported and disconnected from their original "exotic" locations and crossbred, cultivated and sold for the enjoyment of affluent European consumers? Nothing could be further from the deeply unsettling experience the narrator of Poe's "The Man of the Crowd" makes in the streets of London than the narrator's reassuring view of the Berlin crowd below him as a colorful and pleasingly moving field of tulips, who will be forever unable to move from their appointed places.[8] If the older cousin's perspective is disqualified because of his use of outdated eighteenth-century models of observation, with which he attempts to bring order to a disorienting urban experience—the *Biedermeier* nostalgia for by-gone certainties Benjamin condemns—the younger cousin's position is equally affected, for the metaphor he employs insinuates a similar predisposition for Enlightenment order and control. Whatever is already modern about the crowd on the *Gendarmenmarkt,* the younger cousin does not yet perceive it either.

Nor does he take any pleasure in what he sees or express any curiosity for it, two traits that are the precondition for a characterization of the narrator as a potential flaneur. "Pretty nice" ("recht artig") is the most he can bring himself to say about the spectacle his cousin presents to him, and studying it at length, he is sure, must be "quite tiring." True, "excitable people" might experience dizziness and the "not unpleasant delirium of impending dream," but it is quite clear that the narrator does not count himself among such people, so that one can only conclude that for him a longer viewing of the crowd might prove soporific. Contrary to McFarland's assertions, the narrator neither experiences this sense of dizziness and delirium when seeing the crowd (although he may be familiar with such hypnagogic experiences from the moments preceding sleep); he merely predicates it to "excitable people" such as his cousin, whose interest in the view he tries to explain. Nor is he "drawn to the urban spectacle and the intoxicating experiences offered by the city," as would be the nineteenth- and twentieth-century flaneurs following in his wake (McFarland 113–14). Quite the contrary, if it were not for the older cousin, the above-quoted paragraph would be the last glimpse of the *Gendarmenmarkt* the story could afford us, for the younger cousin is initially not particularly interested in the scene and would not have deemed it worthy a closer look.

Both McFarland and Darby quote from Baudelaire's crucial essay on Constantin Guys, "The Painter of Modern Life," to illustrate the aesthetic predisposition of the flaneur, which Baudelaire finds embodied in Guys in exemplary fashion:

> For the perfect flaneur, for the passionate observer it is an immense joy to establish one's domicile of choice in number, in the undulating, in movement, in the fugitive and the infinite. To be outside of oneself and yet to feel everywhere at home; to see the world, to be at the center of the world and to stay hidden to the world, these are some of the smallest pleasures of these independent, passionate and impartial spirits that language can only clumsily define.... One can also compare him to a mirror as immense as this crowd, to a kaleidoscope endowed with consciousness, which, with each of its movements, represents the multiple life and the moving grace of all elements of life. It's an *I* insatiable for the *Not-I*, which, in each instant, renders it and expresses it in images more alive than life itself, always unstable and fugitive. (*Baudelaire* 464)

Yet, the only trait in this description that fits Hoffmann's narrator is the latter's ability to establish his domicile in the crowd should he desire to do so. The novella does not suggest that he possesses any of the artistic qualities attributed to the flaneur by Baudelaire, and it seems appropriate to add the sentence immediately following, in which Baudelaire reports Guys to have commented in conversation that "every man who is not overwhelmed by one of those sorrows of a nature too positive not to absorb all mental faculties, and *who gets bored in the bosom of the multitude,* is an idiot! an idiot! and I despise him!" (464). To see the multitude from above is certainly not the same as to be immersed in it, but a true flaneur would no doubt have found the view afforded to the narrator from the cousin's corner window equally fascinating. There is also no indication on the opening pages of the novella that the younger cousin experiences any such overwhelming emotions or pleasures in the crowd as he makes his way across the *Gendarmenmarkt.* If anybody has the eyes and the kaleidoscopic consciousness of a flaneur in Hoffmann's story, it is indeed the older cousin, who alone is able to extract the multitude of stories—the phantasmagoria—hidden in the narrator's "tulip field." Clearly, he cannot become a flaneur, he cannot leave his apartment to join the crowd and experience its electrifying and intoxicating flow, and he does express positions, as Darby and McFarland rightfully remark, that portray him as out of touch with his surroundings, but he alone has both the physiognomical talent and the passion for observing the crowd that can make a flaneur. If the narrator indeed leaves his apartment at the end of the novella to return to the street as a potential flaneur, he does so thanks to the interaction with his cousin. The emerging esthete of the nineteenth-century urban experience depends on a trained eye and on practices of seeing that, while about to be radically transformed, are far from obsolete. The opening both Darby and McFarland perceive can hence not be exclusively located in the figure of the narrator but must rather be seen as emerging from the dialogue between both protagonists, while the modernity intimated in the novella's art of seeing lies on a narrative meta-level that transcends the perspectives of both the narrator and his "worthy lame cousin."

An Eye that Truly Sees

There are other reasons, too, to be cautious about a wholesale dismissal of the older cousin and his art of seeing. For the older cousin's conviction that the writer, if he or she is to deserve the name, must first of all be a keen observer is most emphatically also Hoffmann's own. In terms of poetics, the dialogue between the two cousins is clearly designed to illuminate processes of perception, the interplay of observation and imagination, seeing, reading, and writing, and as such it is also a comment on the creative process itself. Reflections on the processes of seeing and of vision are central to Hoffmann's work, in which little is more important than the ability to distinguish the lies of mechanical optical illusions, and be they those of a consciousness-consuming occult magic enveloping the mind's eye, from the real revelations of the truly felt and the truly alive. Hoffmann's humor and his satirical wit are ultimately optical instruments, meant to open the reader's eye to the ridiculousness of those who would force others to live by the rules of their own ignorance. They are instruments that cut through all the layers of artificial social custom and convention that stand in the way of a life of creative integrity. When the narrator admits that the only benefit he can imagine his cousin might derive from the view from his window to be the pleasant delirium the sight of a great crowd might induce, the cousin responds: "Cousin, cousin! Now I see that not even the smallest spark of writerly talent glows within you. You lack the first requirement to ever follow in the footsteps of your worthy lame cousin; namely, an eye that truly sees" (600). Little could be more important to Hoffmann than such an eye, and this assertion, the cousin's ironized self-importance notwithstanding, should give one pause in any assessment of the art the cousin professes to teach.

The novella's obvious focus on processes of seeing has led several critics to turn to an open "Letter to the Publisher," published by Hoffmann in the Fall of 1820 in the journal for which *My Cousin's Corner Window* was written and in which the novella was first published serially from

April 23 to May 4, 1822: Johann Daniel Symanski's new Berlin journal, *Der Zuschauer*, was inspired, as the title makes clear, by Addison and Steele's *Spectator*. The opening passage of Hoffmann's public response to Symanski's request for collaboration, in its development of a spectatorial poetics easily suggests itself as a theoretical reflection to accompany the novella it seems to anticipate when Hoffmann closes his letter by saying that "there is already something going round in my head, which probably will soon see the light of day for you" (*Nachlese* 102). Showing himself, as Benjamin assumes, to be "the type of the flaneur," Hoffmann here unequivocally presents watching, looking, and creative observation as his "favorite past-time":

> You ask me, most worthy sir!, for my collaboration with a journal that you plan to publish under the title, "*der Zuschauer*." I will happily fulfill your wish, particularly since the well-chosen title reminds me of my favorite past-time. For you probably already know how much I like to watch (zuschauen) and to look at (anschauen) and then express in black and white what I have just perceived in lively fashion (recht lebendig erschaut). (99)

Several critics, as Ulrich Stadler points out, refer to this passage as proof that Hoffmann effected a turn toward poetic realism in *My Cousin's Corner Window*, and that the novella, with its extensive observation of an everyday market scene, marks a shift in Hoffman's aesthetic priorities at the end of his life (Stadler 500). But the carefully chosen verb "erschaut," which, in contrast to the passively receptive "zuschauen" and "anschauen," denotes an active and productive process of creative inner vision that is at odds with such a position. The observations as such are not what are to be expressed and communicated in an effort to produce the rhetorical effects of aesthetic realism. Rather, they only serve as the raw material for an inner vision, which alone merits writerly communication. In and of themselves, they are only the first step in the process of perception and only as fuel for the creative process do they produce something alive that merits to be expressed "in black and white."[9] If observation does not lead to imaginative vision, no writing will (or rather: should) follow. As the subsequent passage makes quite clear, Hoffmann is here simply reaffirming his much-discussed Serapiontic principle developed in the frame narrative of his third and last story collection, *The Serapion Brothers*. In the next sentence, clearly meant to qualify the opening paragraph, Hoffmann presents the essence of this poetic principle one more time: "I think, after all, that one could not talk about anything but about what has arisen in perfect shape in one's interiority, in such a way that the people to whom one talks can perceive it in equally lively fashion (*Nachlese* 99–100). Hoffmann then remarks himself, tongue in cheek, that this principle was first presented in a book familiar to him, *The Serapion Brothers*, and he declares that he will stay faithful to it despite the criticism expressed by some reviewers:

> I think meanwhile, since the inner eyes, whose vision determines poetic perception, are situated in the head just as much as the understanding, that Saint Serapion, when he posited the principle according to which one can only bring *that* to light alive and truthfully, which one perceived internally in just this fashion, always presupposed the unchanging, faithful marital bond in which both understanding and imagination must remain if anything decent is to be the outcome. I stick to this principle! (100)

Keeping this poetic principle in mind is helpful in several ways for a discussion of *My Cousin's Corner Window*. First of all, it illuminates the breakdown of the older cousin's creative processes, which is ultimately due to a crisis of written communication. His inner poetic perceptions, the narrator tells us, are still as vivid as ever and can be transmitted orally, but they dissolve as soon as he attempts to express them in writing:

> [T]he most severe illness could not stop the rapid wheels of imagination, which continued to work within him, constantly producing something new. So it was that he told me all kinds of charming stories he had invented, despite the manyfold pain he suffered. But the path which the thought had to follow in order to take shape on paper had been blocked by the evil demon of the illness. (*Späte Werke* 597)

This crisis of writing causes the older cousin to become a recluse and to "give up the productive creative life, which emerges from within myself, shaped into outward form, befriending the world" (598). The cousin here again echoes, albeit in negative form, the Serapiontic directive as it is formulated by Lothar, one of the Serapion brothers:

> Everybody should examine well, if he indeed truly saw what he endeavors to pronounce, before he dares to make it heard. At the very least everybody should strive quite seriously to capture well the image that had arisen internally in all its figures, colors, lights and shadows, and then, when he feels quite inspired by it, to carry the representation into outer life. (*Serapion Brothers* 55)

David Darby suggests that "it is tempting to see the paralysis of the Vetter as a writer...as resulting from a creative impasse precipitated by the collision of his enlightenment-driven vision, his Serapiontic narrative practice, and the development of a new post-Napoleonic social context" (284). Other than Hoffmann, who skillfully combines all three stylistic approaches, the cousin, one could then assume following Darby's suggestion, is no longer able to communicate with a reading public whose social realities have become incompatible with his creative vision, an alienating disconnect that drives him to despair. In writing that he can no longer "befriend" the inner and the outer world, he can hence no longer heal the inherent doubleness or duplicity, which Lothar pronounces in *The Serapion Brothers* to be the fundamental condition of human existence. "There is an inner world and the mental power to see it in complete clarity, in the most perfect brilliance of the most active life, but it is our earthly inheritance that precisely the outer world into which we are nestled works as the lever that puts this power in motion" (54). The creative vision, set in motion by the outer world, must be communicated in writing if the identity of the writer is to be preserved, and Hoffmann's novella must effect such a return to writing if the "demon" of the cousin's illness is to be overcome.

It is hence no accident that his window and the view of the marketplace it affords become the "lever" through which the cousin is once again "befriended" with the outside world, and that the narrator's writing of the story is made possible through a dialog between the two cousins about the art of seeing. These narrative devices, focused on and in the motif of the window, allow for a reconciliation of the cousin's orality and the written medium through which his vision needs to be communicated. The window, as the transparent screen interposed between the seer and the seen, becomes the surface on which the preconditions for any act of seeing are made visible, on which they are written. It highlights the processes of representation that make all perception possible while simultaneously putting any direct access to an objective reality out of reach. In this sense, any act of seeing is an act of writing and vice versa, while the narrative device of the window makes the connection of both processes visible. Written communication, which cannot naively attempt to imitate the structures of oral communication, thus becomes most transparent and communicates most effectively when it includes a reflection on the processes of representation themselves, and writing is self-reflexive by nature. The modernity of Hoffmann's novella lies in its self-reflexive treatment of processes of seeing and writing, an art of seeing that is transmitted using the vehicle of eighteenth-century physiognomy the two cousins employ.

Gerhard Neumann articulates this structural feature of Hoffmann's novella most emphatically and places the text squarely in the long history of Western reflection on processes of representation developed in the extensive catalogue of window scenes in Western literature, philosophy, and art history. In the basic scenario of the novella—two characters in dialog about a scene they observe through a window—Neumann argues Hoffmann quotes something like an "originary scene of European cultural history," the view through an opening that simultaneously marks the distinction between an inside and an outside, and which consequently opens up the space of perception in which a dialogue between a self and an other can take place (224). And this originary view, one might add in support of Neumann's position, quite literally opens on a scene, for the backdrop for the market scenes the two cousins describe and decode—visible, remembered, and imaginary—is the theater, the *Schauspielhaus*, about which the reader of the story is reminded in strategic moments of the narrative. The cousin's corner window is also the fourth wall of the traditional proscenium stage, itself a picture frame that opens up on an imaginary reality, and Hoffmann, in his narrative creation of physiognomic scenes, their description, interpretation and invention, indeed dramatizes processes of seeing as both observation and creation. For Neumann, the protagonist of this drama is the process of perception (Wahrnehmung) itself, and the "genre pictures" the novella presents become for him distinctive experiments in perception (Wahrnehmungsexperimente), in which the modernist potential of Hoffmann's text is located (230; 236). From this perspective, the novella's realism and its modernism consist not so much in what it represents but rather in its reflection on representation itself. Rather than giving us an objective reality formed by realist convention, *My Cousin's Corner Window* offers a view of the processes through which a self constructs its world in dialogue with an other. In presenting an art of seeing, it writes writing.

Such self-reflexive strategies are already implicit in Hoffmann's Serapiontic principle itself, which takes account, as Walter Müller-Seidel points out, of the inescapable intertextuality of all writing and of the fact that its mimesis is always already the mimesis of preceding texts (*Serapion Brothers* 1005). The Serapiontic exhortation always to ground one's writing in a clearly perceived inner vision is meant first and foremost as a check against the mere mechanical copying and repetition of other texts. It recognizes that originality in the literary marketplace can only lie in the creative recombination of one's sources since texts always already interpose between us and our perception of the world. In the frame narrative of the *Serapion Brothers*, the literary friends indeed comment on precisely this phenomenon when they ridicule critics who track down a writer's sources in order to then accuse him of mere copying, with no understanding of the fact that the creative act lies precisely in the original appropriation of sources, not in an impossible *creatio ex nihilo* (*Serapion Brothers* 531).

Hoffmann's texts make no attempt to hide this fact and present themselves quite self-consciously as born of other texts. *My Cousin's Corner Window* is no exception. When the narrator likens his cousin to the seventeenth-century French writer Paul Scarron at the beginning of the novella, he alerts the reader to the text that Hoffmann's novella reinvents, Karl Friedrich Kretschmann's *Scarron at the Window* (*Scarron am Fenster*), published serially from 1798 to 1799, a story that would in all likelihood by now have been thoroughly forgotten had it not been for Hoffmann's creative remaking. Just as much as the view from his own window overlooking the *Gendarmenmarkt*, Kretschmann's tale of the paralyzed Scarron, looking out on the Parisian *Tuileries* becomes the pretext for Hoffmann's novella, which presents an utterly different scene as it moves the action from seventeenth-century Paris to early nineteenth-century Berlin, while changing the subjects of observation from noblemen and -women at the Parisian court to members of the bourgeoisie and the lower social classes in the Prussian capital.[10] *My Cousin's Corner Window,* which produces a view that differs widely from Scarron's as rendered by Kretschmann, is unmistakably Hoffmann's creation, but it is equally unmistakably mediated through other texts, including the prominent visual intertexts of Hogarth's, Callot's, and Chodowiecki's prints and drawings, so that the novella by no means presents itself as an unmediated view of a directly observable *Gendarmenmarkt*.

In fact, the originality of Hoffmann's narrative can also be seen to lie precisely in his creative use of his visual sources, as Günter Oesterle has convincingly demonstrated. Hogarth, Chodowiecki, and Callot, Oesterle reminds us, can be seen as representatives of specific styles in German eighteenth-century art criticism, styles analogous to Jean Paul's classification (in *Pre-School of Aesthetics*) of the novels of world literature into an Italian, Dutch, and a German school. In this context, Oesterle points out, Hogarth's prosaic didactic satire and Callot's unbridled fantastic style become emblematic of enlightenment and romantic perspectives, an aesthetic distinction indeed employed by Jean Paul himself in his preface to Hoffmann's first story collection, *Fantastic Pieces in the Manner of Callot*. Oesterle shows that the mixing and combining of the literary equivalents of the styles of all three artists in Hoffmann's text—with Chodowiecki representing a moderate and humorous German style—can ultimately be read as a poetic statement. From this perspective, Hoffmann's free recombination of all three styles in *My Cousin's Corner Window* constitutes more than a mere exercise in ekphrastic technique, let alone a reactionary commitment to by-gone artistic conventions, but rather lets another metanarrative emerge from the story: In developing an art of seeing that encompasses, combines, and transcends the didactic, the satirical, and the humorous, as well as both an enlightenment and a romantic aesthetics, Hoffmann's text hovers in a narrative distance of potentiality above all of them (Oesterle 105–09).[11] The novella's physiognomical vision is thus free of any specific instrumentalization of physiognomical perspective and allows its readers to sharpen their eyes on an aesthetic meta-level.

In fact, the text presents physiognomical observation precisely as the combination of understanding and imagination Hoffmann had advocated in the open letter to the publisher of *Der Zuschauer,* for the two cousins develop narratives that are clearly marked as hypotheses—imaginative constructions that are nevertheless arrived at through rational processes of induction and deduction. They may not be true, but they are nevertheless internally consistent and eminently believable. "Not a word may be true of everything that you've deduced here, dear cousin," the narrator remarks after the cousin develops a hypothesis about the interaction of two market women with a young girl, "but as I look at these women, thanks to your lively presentation, it all seems so plausible, that I have to believe in it, whether I want to or not" (602). These processes of creative observation are ultimately no different from the processes of ratiocination Poe describes in his Dupin stories, and the flaneur and the detective, as Benjamin points out, share the same physiognomical origins. This affinity, rooted in the uncanny potential of the urban crowd, can now lead us—again via Benjamin—to the vision of the people of Berlin that is presented in Hoffmann's text.

Moral Peace in Public Places

The immediate context for Benjamin's brief discussion of *My Cousin's Corner Window* in "The Paris of the Second Empire in Baudelaire" is precisely his attempt to develop a connection between the flaneur and the detective and to trace the origin of the detective story to the increasingly uncanny experience of the anonymity of the great crowds in the modern nineteenth-century city. Benjamin sees two basic responses to the uneasiness these crowds produce in the Paris of the 1840s: On the one hand the efforts on the part of the state to police its people and to impose order on the growing urban chaos in the form of more efficient registration of citizens, the counting and numbering of houses for more reliable tracing of residents, and through increased censorship in the volatile years leading up to the bourgeois revolution of 1848. On the other hand, Benjamin notes the popularity of the *physiologies,* guidebooks for reading the faces of the city, which were published in great numbers in the 1840s, and which provided the reassuring illusion that everybody could easily acquire the ability to read the only seemingly overwhelming urban spectacle surrounding them. By reducing the complexity of what could actually be seen, heard, and perceived, the *physiologies* thus pretend to give the bourgeois citizen the semiotic tools to decipher the undecipherable. Benjamin sees such soothing mass publications as working hand in hand with a reactionary regime in its effort to contain potential unrest in the unpredictable gatherings of people in the modern city, and he concurs with the thesis of the German Marxist scholar Eduard Fuchs, who places the increased censorship of the "September laws" of 1836, which effectively destroyed the genre of political caricature and visual satire, at the origin of the *physiologies'* flood of vapid and reassuring, apolitical publications (*Baudelaire* 538). The *physiologies,* Benjamin claims, while living on the literary credit of their eighteenth-century physiognomical precursors, lack any of the latter's artistic seriousness. Purporting to provide their readers with a semiotic code for their daily life in the city, they must refrain from encouraging or enabling any real empirical observation in order to spare their audience the unsettling experience of Poe's "Man of the Crowd" and to avoid opening their eyes to the dangers of the city the *physiologies'* "art of seeing" is meant precisely to hide.

Returning to *My Cousin's Corner Window* in this context must have predisposed Benjamin unfavorably to Hoffmann's novella, in which the two cousins can observe the "tulip field" of the *Gendarmenmarkt* without any sense of vertigo. The glass the two cousins are using—be it a telescope or an opera glass—can be employed without dangers to their sanity, and no sandman, no Coppola, no Coppelius arrives among the market women and the bourgeois housewives stocking up for their kitchen pantries to induce the younger cousin to jump headlong to his death from his vantage point high above the crowd. The people on the square remain orderly, the cousin's window seat is quite safe, and Hoffmann's text begins to resemble a Berlin *physiologie* more than a physiognomical testament. One must assume that this is the reason why Benjamin now defines the cousin's "art of seeing" as "the ability to derive pleasure from living images, which the *Biedermeier* also pursues usually. Edifying mottos provide their interpretation" (629). If the cousin is perceived as a *physiologue* rather than as a physiognomist, his art will become a provincial and ultimately a reactionary undertaking.[12] Strikingly, Benjamin's characterization of his art of seeing is now diametrically opposed to the definition he provides for the flaneur's in the *Arcades Project,* in which he notes that "[t]he category of illustrative seeing is foundational for the flaneur. He writes...his reverie as a text accompanying the images" (528). The physiognomist will treat the visible as a text to be read, as so many signs to be decoded, but where the flaneur takes this impulse as the starting point for his own reverie or phantasmagoria, producing a text that is as labyrinthine as the streets of the city he walks, the *physiologue* will insist that the process of reading is finite and can be brought to a close, that meanings are stable and that clear lessons and morals can be derived from what is to be seen. As he surveys a market square that is bounded on all sides, producing a series of vignettes with the help of the narrator that suggest readability even though they do not claim a totality of vision, the older cousin becomes an ambiguous figure.[13] The obvious pleasure he takes in watching the crowd while spinning tales from the visual clues at hand are the prerogatives for the flaneur's urban sensibility, while the world he sees and creates is nevertheless still that of a clearly delimited provincial town.

The unfairness of Benjamin's comparison of Hoffmann's novella with Poe's story has often been remarked upon—Hoffmann writes in the early 1820s, not the 1840s, and Berlin is at the time still a relative backwater in comparison to Paris and London—but such factual defenses are ultimately insufficient to dispel the charge implicit in Benjamin's assessment. What vision of Berlin does the novella provide, if it is not that of "a series of little genre pictures" meant to assuage the discomfort of bourgeois readers? Does Hoffmann's text, beyond its metanarrative engagement of matters of seeing, writing, perception, and representation, have something to say about Berlin as a city that might make it unfit for the "edification" of the readers of Symanski's *Der Zuschauer*?

An attempt to answer such questions can begin with the fact that Hoffmann's novella was written in a repressive climate of strict censorship and increasing governmental control and policing of the Berlin citizenry quite similar to the one Benjamin describes for the Paris of the 1840s. During the era of post-Napoleonic restoration, Prussia had issued its own "September laws" in the infamous Carlsbad Decrees of 1819, and the Prussian state was quite serious in seeing its biggest city as a potential hotbed of subversive political activity. The assassination of the writer August von Kotzebue by the radical student Karl Ludwig Sand in 1819 provided the necessary justification for repressive legislation, which made the politically engaged student fraternities illegal, greatly increased censorship throughout the German confederation, and severely restricted academic freedoms. The Prussian state and its people coexisted most uneasily in the capital, where "demagogues" were suspected of instigating popular uprisings, leading to the so-called Demagogenverfolgungen, the increasingly paranoid persecution of Berlin citizens by the city's formidable police force. Hoffmann not only passively observed these persecutions as a resident, as a judge and employee of the state he was directly, if very grudgingly, involved in their unfolding. In October 1819, Hoffmann was appointed to a juridical commission instituted to "investigate liaisons for purposes of high treason and other dangerous activities" ("Immediat-Untersuchungskommission zur Ermittlung hochverräterischer Verbindungen und anderer gefährlicher Umtriebe"), an appointment he greatly resented. In a letter to his close friend Theodor Gottlieb Hippel on June 24, 1820, Hoffmann characterizes the work of the commission as a "web of unholy arbitrary despotism, blatant disregard of all laws, and personal animosity" (Schnapp 263). He concedes that the state needed to step in to regulate the excesses of "some young swirlyheads" and presents Sand's assassination of Kotzebue as a despicable act born of fanaticism, but the current laws, he tells Hippel, rather than being directed at actions, unjustly target individual convictions.

Hoffmann, however, does not merely write to his friends about the abuses of power legalized by the Carlsbad decrees and in full display on the immediate-commission, he uses his considerable juridical talent to combat them to the best of his ability. The purpose of the commission had clearly been to rubber-stamp the arrests made by the Berlin police, but Hoffmann, in his carefully and diligently crafted legal positions and opinion papers, won over the other members of the commission, which ordered the release of several wrongfully imprisoned "demagogues," making Hoffmann a thorn in the side of both Karl Albert von Kamptz, Berlin's chief of police, later the Prussian minister of justice, and Friedrich von Schuckmann, the Prussian minister of the interior and the police. The highest profile case in which Hoffmann became involved concerned the arrest of the eccentric "Turnvater" ("father of gymnastics"), Friedrich Ludwig Jahn.[14] Jahn, for whose chauvinistic views Hoffmann had little sympathy, had been arrested under highly dubious pretexts, and while Hoffmann was unsuccessful in bringing about his release, he made a lasting enemy in von Kamptz, whom Hoffmann forced to appear in court for testimony in a highly public confrontation. When news began to spread in Berlin in early 1822— news that quite imprudently originated with Hoffmann himself— that his next book, *Master Flea*, would include a satire of the state's repressive activities against "democrats and demagogues," von Kamptz and von Schuckmann began to investigate. The manuscript was intercepted and confiscated at Hoffmann's Frankfurt publisher, and when von Kamptz saw himself satirized in the figure of the malicious Secret Counciller Knarrpanti, the machinery of the Prussian state began its work against Hoffmann, who, far from resorting to inoffensive writing in reactionary times, had put his legal career in jeopardy. Not only von Kamptz and von Schuckmann but even King Friedrich Wilhelm III himself became involved in Hoffmann's case, and Hoffmann could not escape an official examination on his deathbed. *Master Flea* ultimately appeared in censored form shortly before Hoffmann's death and was not published as originally conceived until 1906.[15]

It is unlikely that all these political concerns were far from Hoffmann's mind when he dictated *My Cousin's Corner Window*, which was sent to Symanski for publication on April 14, 1822, and it is probably no coincidence that the first of the text's more general comments about the citizens of Berlin involves the people's relationship to the police. Here, the narrator describes the development of a fight between two women selling vegetables, who are quickly surrounded by a great number of people and who seem on the verge of coming to blows. The narrator already sees the police making its way through the crowd when an unexpected development takes place: a group of other market women intervenes, separates, and appeases the two parties, and, to the narrator's surprise, the conflict is solved peacefully without any need for police intervention. The older cousin underscores the narrator's observation by remarking that this was the only confrontation that arose on the market square during the time of their dialogue, and he informs the narrator that "even a more serious, more threatening conflict the people usually end by themselves by coming between the quarrelers and separating them" (618). He recalls an indeed much more serious incident in which a "big, ragged fellow of insolent, wild appearance" got into an argument with a passing butcher's apprentice, whom he attacked with a huge club. The butcher's apprentice in turn picked up a meat cleaver, and blood, death and the criminal court seemed imminent (618–19). Yet here, too, the people on the marketplace themselves, first and foremost the strong and powerfully built women at the fruit stands, prevent any further violence. They hold back both men and leave nothing to the police but to pick up the wild-looking "fellow," who seems to the cousin "like a freed prisoner" when the officers lead him away (619).

The law and its enforcement, these episodes suggest, lie with the people themselves, and Berlin's police force is reduced to merely completing a job the people have already carried out themselves. Consequently, the narrator ends this episode by concluding that "hence the people are indeed governed by an internal sense of the order that needs to be kept, which cannot but be beneficial to everyone" (619). The older cousin then makes a larger claim about the people of Berlin as a whole, who in his opinion have greatly improved for the better since the end of the Napoleonic occupation, an improvement for which the marketplace again provides evidence. "My observations of the market, dear cousin, have generally strengthened my opinion," he remarks toward the end of the dialogue, "that the people of Berlin have changed remarkably since that disastrous period when an insolent, presumptuous enemy overran the country and tried in vain to suppress *that* spirit, which soon sprang up again with renewed power like a spring held down in force. In *one* word: the people's manners (äußere Sittlichkeit) have improved" (619). The true spirit of the city, the cousin claims, proved irrepressible even by an occupational force and the loss of the city's autonomy. At the same time the Napoleonic wars, despite their atrocities, have also had a positive effect on the people of Berlin, who, through their exposure to European politics on a grand scale, have became more worldly, more open toward strangers, and more courteous: "The same thing has happened to the masses as that which happens to the individual who has seen many new things, has had unusual experiences, and, along with an attitude of *nil admirari*, has gained a certain ease in manners" (619). Overall, the cousin observes a desire for greater courteousness among the people, and he uses the French word "courtoisie," rather than the German "Höflichkeit" to describe it: "You will yourself observe," he tells the narrator, "even amongst lowly maids and day laborers a desire for a certain courteousness (Courtoisie), which is quite delightful" (619). Consequently, the market, which used to be "a hotbed of quarrels, fights, swindles, and theft, and no honest woman could dare to do her shopping herself without exposing herself to the greatest harrassment," is now "the graceful image of feelings of comfort and of moral peace" (620).[16]

Günther Oesterle has proposed that despite its appearance of *Biedermeier* conservatism, this assessment of the people on the marketplace constitutes a "remarkably political" statement in the repressive climate of Prussia's restorational regime, while he sees the narrator's conclusion about the people's "internal sense of the order that needs to be kept" as Hoffmann's own "implicit criticism of the authoritarian state's paternalism, spying and revolutionary fears" (Oesterle 103–4). From this perspective, Hoffmann's depiction of the harmonious interaction of various social classes on the marketplace, historically still a relative novelty, is politically motivated and presents an argument against the repressive machinery of the police state and for the continuation of Prussian reform politics. The aesthetic strategy of Hoffmann's novella with its "calculated recourse to enlightenment modes of seeing," to use Oesterle's phrase, is tied to its political positioning, and the use of physiognomical divination is meant to dispel any charges of the inscrutable revolutionary dangers hidden in the urban crowd. The "tulip field" has been socially and politically defined, and its peacefulness is meant to be read as a quiet protest against the sinister workings of a police state.

The cousin's position is by no means unproblematic, however. Benjamin for one, in another note in the *Arcades Project*, cites—next to the cousin's desire to teach the narrator the principles of the art of seeing—precisely the cousin's view of the people's improved morals since the French occupation, as well as his perception of the marketplace's development toward comfort and moral peace, as proof for the novella's "provincial character" (564). The cousin's patronizing view of the lower classes and the working poor, meanwhile, whose attempts to imitate bourgeois manners on Sunday outings strike him as "delightful," is also quite palpable. The joke of a wagoner's boy, related by the narrator to illustrate the famous Berlin humor, strikes him as "arisen from the stinking pit of deepest deprivation" (620).[17] Indeed, little could speak more strongly for a *Biedermeier* sensibility than the belief that the general adoption of a bourgeois morality will lead to the general improvement of life in the city. From this vantage point, the cousins' culminating vision of the marketplace preemptively enacts the very desires of state surveillance. As the two cousins sketch the picture of a reasonable, self-governing people who have transformed the marketplace from a place of conflict and public danger to a safe space where goods can circulate while people from various social classes mingle and interact peacefully, the resulting image also suggests a Foucauldian vision of a self-policing people, no longer in need of public displays of state power to enforce their by-now internalized compliance with the law.

Given Hoffmann's own confrontation with the Prussian police state, however, it is quite unlikely that he intended his text as an ideological instrument to aid in the control of a potentially unruly urban citizenry, while his outspoken contempt for the philistines of his time make him an improbable candidate for advocating the civilizing qualities of bourgeois morality. The older cousin is most emphatically no Kapellmeister Kreisler, the artist figure that is Hoffmann's "true" literary alter ego, and unless one assumes that Hoffmann had given in to despair when dictating the final pages of the novella, the older cousin's voice is unlikely to be unequivocally his own. Upon closer scrutiny, in fact, the bourgeois utopia of a self-regulated populace is undercut in the cousins' dialogue at the same time it is being developed, particularly in their observations about the most abject character present on the marketplace. This figure is a blind war veteran, whom the older cousin sees as a "touching image of undeserved human misery and pious resignation in God and fate" (613). When the narrator voices his surprise over the fact that this former soldier is begging, even though war veterans are well provided for, his cousin informs him that such trust in Prussia's system of social security is misplaced. The blind beggar, he tells him, is the servant of one of the market women, whose baskets full of wares he carries to the market each morning, staggering under their weight like a beast of burden. He is verbally and physically abused by his mistress regularly, and the cousin suspects that even the money he has made begging is taken from him come evening. The cousin overtly sentimentalizes the blind beggar, whose "inner eye" he believes—in a case of projection that clearly illustrates the limits of his own perspicacity—"strives already to view the eternal light shining toward him from the beyond, promising solace, hope, and bliss" (614).[18] But despite the cousin's edifying projections, the figure of the former soldier, reduced to abject poverty and complete dependency, nevertheless stands in stark contrast to the bourgeois citizens who thrive in the city he helped to liberate, and it reveals that despite its outward peacefulness, all is not well on the marketplace.

In an extended exercise in physiognomical observation the blind beggar then serves as a semiotic touchstone for the two cousins, who attempt to discern the moral disposition of the passing citizens from the way they give him charity. In this sequence of observations only the poorer Berliners pass muster and give generously, while the richer citizens expose their miserliness and ulterior motives in the very act of giving. After the moral callousness of the more affluent citizens frequenting the market place is brought to light the older cousin concludes: "The blind man's deathly pale face, his emaciated body, his ragged clothing suggest that his situation is quite miserable, and an active philanthropist should really investigate this relationship more closely" (616). Active philanthropists the two cousins surely are not, however, and the narrator immediately changes the topic as their dialogue moves on to the next vignette. Ultimately, the cousins' exchange leads the reader to question the quality of the "moral peace" the older cousin sees displayed in the market square: What good is bourgeois courtoisie, if it can both hide and leave unaddressed the blatant inequities the cousins' observations reveal?

Such inequities are particularly palpable when one compares the blind soldier's fate to that of the first figure the two cousins observe, a "somewhat strangely dressed person," whom the narrator, because of her face, her whole appearance, and the "bright yellow cloth wrapped around her head in the French manner like a turban" readily identifies as French—"probably somebody who stayed behind after the last war to feather her nest here," as he surmises (600). The narrator is complimented on this guess by his cousin, who wagers that her husband "makes a good living thanks to a branch of French industry," which allows his wife to generously fill her shopping basket. Clearly the backlash against the former occupiers has done nothing to disrupt the economic ties that make life comfortable for those who know how to work them, and Hoffmann's narrative is not uncritical of the bourgeois opulence one can perceive on the market square. Exposed despite the cousin's optimistic views, the complexities of post-Napoleonic Berlin society remain visible, and the provincialism Benjamin detects in the older cousin's remarks need not be Hoffmann's, who may have hoped for a less sentimentalizing reaction on the part of his readers to the figure of an abused, blind war veteran begging amidst the opulence of a marketplace that can only become "a graceful image of comfort and moral peace" if the suffering that made and makes that comfort possible is overlooked.[19]

And there are other, if less prominent, scenes in the cousins' dialogue, which suggest that the vision the older cousin develops at the end of their exchange has its blind spots, and that his optimistic conception of the market must ultimately hide what both cousins have described but *not* truly seen. One might think for example of the two old market women, described at the beginning of the dialogue, whose smiles the narrator overtly describes as "demonic" and whom he sees gesticulating with "thin skeleton arms" (602). The older cousin informs the narrator that usually no love is lost between those two neighbors on the marketplace and that only the misfortune of a young girl he observed a few minutes ago had brought them as closely together as they can be seen at the moment. The girl, whose outward appearance signaled both her poverty, as well as her modesty and shame to the older cousin, had desired to buy a white scarf, but ultimately did not have enough money in her purse to cover the price that had been agreed upon after some haggling. As the girl turned away, deeply ashamed and with tears in her eyes, the old woman took back the scarf with a scornful and derisive laugh. The two women are now so deep in conversation, the older cousin surmises, because "the other satan" knows the little girl and can tell the sad story of a family fallen into poverty, "a scandalous chronicle of thoughtlessness, possibly even of crime" (602). In quite realistic guise, the demonic and the satanic here appear on the marketplace as the prosaic everyday enjoyment of innocent misfortune and melodramatic gossip. The complete lack of empathy the older cousin's description of the two old women unveils hardly provides the basis for lasting "moral peace."

And the first person to give alms to the blind soldier is an elegant lady in expensive costume, wearing a hat "in the latest fashion," who exposes, to the narrator's horror, "a blood-red, and in addition quite masculine-looking fist" as she pulls off with some difficulty the white kid glove on her right hand. For a brief moment the uncanny does surface quite powerfully in the middle of this "genre picture," and the lady's blood-red fist, accompanied by the narrator's shriek of "heaven help!" reduces the glittering surface of bourgeois elegance and wealth to what it is—a mere illusion. We hear no story about this probably syphilitic "child of depravity" as the older cousin calls her, even though the narrator points to the "peculiar" contents of her shopping basket and is clearly desirous to find out more. The older cousin quickly silences him ("Quiet, quiet, cousin, enough of the rose-red!"), and the reader is led to understand that whatever story is hidden here is not one the older cousin would want to tell (613). The tale of the "rose-red," we are left to conclude, cannot be told, because it would—just like the uncanny—explode the vision of the peaceful marketplace the older cousin desires to uphold.

The perspective from which such discrepancies and blind spots can become visible, and from which the fantastic, the demonic, and the uncanny repopulate the marketplace despite their seeming absence, is again located in the ironic distance of a metanarrative position that remains just outside both the older cousin's and the narrator's field of vision. Its critical as well as its aesthetic potential is no less "real" for being unidentified with the text's characters, while it is certain to remain undetected and unassailable by the censor's prosaic eye. In that sense it may well be the position of a self-policed citizen, but it is not that of a citizen who abides by the law.

Notes

1. All translations from the German and the French in this chapter are mine.
2. Rather ironically, it is Heinrich Heine, one of Hoffmann's great admirers, who serves as proof for Benjamin, that "other physiognomists of the big city" could very well detect the uncanny and the dreadful in the urban experience even of Berlin (629). Benjamin knows Heine as a fellow admirer of Hoffmann, and in "The Demonic Berlin" he also references the former, quoting him there as a fellow connoisseur of Hoffmann's art: " 'The devil,' Heinrich Heine has said about Hoffmann's writings, 'cannot write such devilish stuff' " (88). If Heine can see the uncanny in the streets of Berlin in the 1840s, he does so in part, as Benjamin knows, because his vision has been sharpened by Hoffmann's writings twenty years earlier.
3. "The phantasmagoria has been extracted from nature" is Baudelaire's résumé of the artistic process leading to the paintings and drawings of Constantin Guys, the artist-flaneur who is the subject of his essay "The Painter of Modern Life" (466). This process begins with what Baudelaire calls "child-like perception," close and penetrating

physiognomical observation without predetermined goals or categories, a state of pure but nevertheless analytical visual alertness that furnishes the artist's memory with all the specific detail that will later be recomposed, reclassified, and remade in the phantasmagoria that is the work of art.
4. Not coincidentally, the impetus behind Benjamin's *Arcades Project* itself is also physiognomical, as Rolf Tiedemann remarks in his introduction. Like the physiognomist, who desires to arrive at the invisible and the "inner" through inductive reasoning based on physical outward detail, Benjamin desires to uncover the "signature" of the nineteenth century in the signs—the imprint—left behind in the cultural artifacts of early industrialism (29). Pouring over book after book in the *Bibliothèque Nationale* in Paris, Benjamin himself is something of a stationary flaneur, the *Arcades Project* his very own labyrinth of an unseen city.
5. In a well-known drawing, included in a letter to his publisher, Kunz, in Bamberg from July 18, 1815, Hoffmann sketched the floor plan of his new apartment and his view of the *Gendarmenmarkt* and the architectural monuments that frame the square: the *Schauspielhaus*, today called the *Konzerthaus*, where Hoffmann' s opera *Undine* would have its triumphant premiere a year later, the French and the German cathedral and the adjacent streets, as well as a self-portrait in the window seat, smoking a pipe with his close friend, the actor Ludwig Devrient. Hoffmann's drawing is much more explicitly "hoffmannesque" than the verbal depictions of the scene in *My Cousin's Corner Window*: fantastical, literary, and historical characters populate the streets and buildings, a monkey is perched atop the *Schauspielhaus*, which takes center stage, with a lion and an ostrich close by, while the courthouse, the *Kammergericht*, Hoffmann's daily workplace, is barely visible in the distance, a tiny building in the upper right-hand corner.
6. For the roots of the cousin's art of seeing in Georg Christoph Lichtenberg's pathognomy, see Stadler, 507. Lichtenberg sharply distinguishes his own practice of pathognomy—"a semiotics of affect or a knowledge of the natural signs of thoughts and emotions (Gemütsbewegungen) in all their gradations and mixtures" from a conception of physiognomy, particularly as practiced by Johann Kaspar Lavater and his adherents, which claims to be able to determine a person's character ("the constitution of the mind and heart") from their physical appearance (Lichtenberg 372). For a discussion of Lichtenberg's conflicted relationship to physiognomical practices of reading, see also Blumenberg, 199–213. A discussion of the physiognomy in the art of Hogarth, Callot, and Chodowiecki can be found in Oesterle.
7. Some of Hoffmann's most elaborate play with the treacherous distinctions between reality and fiction and the figures of narrator, character, and author can be found in his story "The Secrets," in which the narrator introduces a character named E. T. A. Hoffmann, Hff. for short, the same shorthand often employed by Hoffmann himself. Hff., under pressure to submit a sequel to his story "The Errancies," is overjoyed

to receive a letter from one of the characters in this earlier story, which leads him to said character's address. When Hff. follows the lead, however, in hopes of gaining material for his new piece, he is shocked to encounter, not the character he expects, but rather his own double, wearing the familiar dressing gown and red cap, smoking Hoffmann's favorite Turkish pipe. Hoffmann greatly enjoyed wreaking this kind of havoc with narrative convention, with his unfinished novel *The Life and Opinions of Tomcat Murr* providing the best-known example, and the boundaries of the self and the real, between narrators and narration, are never easily established in his texts.

8. As such, the narrator's metaphor is diametrically opposed to the analogy, discussed by Benjamin, between the city and the North American wilderness commonly employed in French texts of the 1840s to highlight the dangers of life in the metropolis. Where Paris is made to resemble a forest full of unknown dangers, the narrator's *Gendarmenmarkt* is a park in which the exotic is already safely circumscribed and made familiar (Benjamin, *Baudelaire* 541–44).

9. Fundamentally, Hoffmann's rendition of the creative process is hence not so different from the one Baudelaire sketches in "The Painter of Modern Life." See note 3.

10. The structural similarities between both texts, as well as the crucial differences Hoffmann effects are described in detail in Stadler, 502–4. Günther Oesterle also presents a discussion of the relation of Hoffmann's text to Kretschmann's and of the other intertexts that inform the novella.

11. For a discussion of the novella's complex physiognomical, or pathognomical, "staging" of Hogarthian, Chodowieckian, and Callotian perspectives, see also Jörn Steigerwald's *Die fantastische Bildlichkeit der Stadt*.

12. In one of his notes for the *Arcades Project* Benjamin already presents the cousin's attempt to teach the principles of the art of seeing as a sign of the novella's provincialism: "In regards to the provincial character of 'My Cousin's Corner Window': the cousin wants to teach his visitor 'the principles of the art of seeing'" (565).

13. For an analysis of the narrative structures of Hoffmann's text with an eye to the techniques employed in the early nineteenth-century panorama to reach a totality of vision, see Eicher. See also Stadler, 509.

14. During the Napoleonic occupation, Jahn had established Prussia's first gymnastics ground on the *Hasenheide* in Berlin. The open-air gymnastics exercises performed there were meant to further the fitness of a patriotic populace preparing to overthrow their French oppressors, and Jahn and his followers were active in the Anti-Napoleonic resistance. Among Jahn's more outlandish propositions was the proposal to create an artificial "desert" in which German citizens would fight wild beasts to increase their manly vigor. For Hoffmann's extensive legal opinion in defense of Jahn, which does not attempt to hide Jahn's eccentricities, see vol. 6 of *Sämtliche Werke*.

15. For a detailed presentation of Hoffmann's embroilment with the Prussian state over his role in the "Demagogenverfolgungen" and the publication of *Master Flea*, including Hoffmann's official defense of the text's satirical passages, see Wulf Segebrecht's notes in *Späte Werke*, 899–913, as well as Friedrich Schnapp's contextualizing comments to the letters from and to Hoffmann over the time of the "Master Flea affair" (Schnapp 346–71).

16. The cousin anticipates a rejection of such views from "enthusiastic rigorists, hyperpatriotic ascetics," who "grimly attack the improved manners of the people, as they are of the opinion that with this polishing of manners the people' s character (das Volkstümliche) is also polished away and lost" (620). He here has in mind the excessive patriotism of the student organizations and in particular of the followers of "Turnvater" Jahn, whose efforts to cleanse and purify the German body (politic) as well as the German language Hoffmann himself seized every chance to ridicule. In "The Bridal Choice," one of the stories collected in *The Serapion Brothers*, for example, Hoffmann' s narrator performs a tongue-in-cheek act of self-censorship, letting one of the characters smoke a "Tabaksröhrlein," a "little tobacco roll," "as the purists would like the cigar to be called." In the first printing of the text, Hoffmann had included an even more direct attack on Jahn, warning his readers through the narrator that anybody using foreign terms is in danger "to be exercised to the ground by some professor of gymnastics" (550; 1082). Hoffmann would vigorously defend Jahn against unjust persecution by the state, but he most emphatically did not subscribe to the latter's political views.

Hoffmann' s text most certainly aims a barb at the potent force of chauvinistic nationalism in post-Napoleonic Prussia, and as if to spite such "rigorists" and "purists," the two cousins in fact quite happily employ French terms throughout their dialogue, which had of course long become part of German usage over the course of the eighteenth century. Not everything French is to be rejected, nor a long history of French presence in Berlin to be denied, recent Napoleonic imperialism notwithstanding, the cousin implies, while tolerance and courtesy, he insists, cannot possibly be harmful to the national character: "I for my part am firmly and thoroughly convinced that a people who treat both the local and the foreigner not with coarseness or scornful disdain but with courtesy (höflicher Sitte), cannot possibly lose its character in doing so" (619). Indeed, the very setting of Hoffmann' s novella highlights the fact that Berlin could not be conceived as a purely Prussian or German city, for the *Gendarmenmarkt* is the historical heart of French, Huguenot Berlin. Before it became the *Gendarmenmarkt* in reference to the cavalry regiment that had its main station and stables nearby from 1736 to 1773, the square had been the *Friedrichstädter Markt*, the main square of *Friedrichstadt*, the Berlin neighborhood where the French huguenots, who had come to the city in the first half of the eighteenth century, seeking protection from religious persecution, had mainly taken residence. The huguenots, whose immigration was actively encouraged by the Prussian state, became an important presence in Berlin, influencing the city's economy, culture and language—the word *Gendarm* itself is of course of French origin, derived from the French *gent d' armes* (armed man), and the very name of the *Gendarmenmarkt* speaks to the ways in which French and German culture are intertwined in Berlin. This relationship is symbolized most explicitly by the German and the French cathedral that frame the square on the left and the right, and which, although only the German cathedral is briefly mentioned in passing at the end of Hoffmann' s narrative, loom large just outside the field of vision the cousins share with the reader. The two cathedrals were built in the early eighteenth century to commemorate and consolidate the ties between the huguenot and the lutheran protestant communities in Berlin, and Hoffmann may be making a subtle argument for conciliation by alluding to French presence and Berlin' s historic French heritage in his novella. The comparison of the older cousin with the French comic writer Scarron, as well as the hypotheses about the figure on the market square who is read equally plausibly as a German drawing instructor and a French pastry chef strikingly repeat such French-German doublings within the narrative.

17. The cousin's social conservatism is also obvious in an earlier remark, when he criticizes a recent custom—"even" among "higher employees of the state"—to send their daughters to shop on the market to gain practical experience in running a household. He can see no benefit that might justify the dangers inherent in exposing young bourgeois women to the "lowest kind of people" and their dirty jokes and loose talk, not to speak of the possible encounters with lovelorn young men (604).

18. In a footnote to "On Several Motives in Baudelaire" Benjamin presents the older cousin's characterization of the beggar as a prominent example of the "edifying" quality of his art of seeing and contrasts it with the final line of Baudelaire's poem "Les Aveugles" ("What do they look for in heaven, all these blind ones?"), a *Tableau Parisien* that offers no hint of religious consolation (629).

19. Hoffmann' s unsparing if placative "Vision on the Battlefield near Dresden" of 1814, which depicts Napoleon being dragged to eternal damnation by an avenging dragon, also presents explicit and gruesome depictions of the dead and dying soldiers on the battlefield, which Hoffmann had seen in 1813. The text makes it clear that he was no stranger to the atrocities of war and the brutalities that brought the blinded soldier to his present state on the marketplace. See *Nachlese*, 28–31.

8

Renzo in Milan

Ernesto Livorni

Introduction

Alessandro Manzoni's novel *The Betrothed* was in many respects a novelty in the panorama of the Romantic historical novel.[1] Written in the first half of the nineteenth century (three editions appeared between 1821 and 1840), the novel is the only one Manzoni ever wrote and, more importantly perhaps, one of the first novels, if not the first, that places a peasant as the hero of the entire work. To be sure, as the title of the first edition (*Fermo e Lucia*) suggests, the heroes are both the peasant Renzo and his fiancée Lucia, but it becomes quite apparent from the hero's first appearance in the novel that the narrator thoroughly enjoys the opportunities the main character offers for general remarks on the embarrassing aspects of the human soul. Furthermore, Manzoni takes advantage of those episodes to make political statements revealing of the ideology of the writer, converted to Catholicism in 1810.[2]

Among the adventures that Renzo and Lucia unwillingly experience from the beginning of the novel all the way to the end, the two sequences of chapters in Milan accompany Renzo as he lives in the city only one day in each sequence of chapters.[3] In the first sequence (from the end of Chapter 11 to the end of Chapter 17), Renzo is in Milan looking for shelter in the convent fra Cristoforo recommended, but instead the hero gets distracted and even drawn into the riots taking place in Milan on the very day he arrives in the city. In the second sequence (from the last paragraph of Chapter 33 to the end of Chapter 36), Renzo is looking for Lucia at the time of the plague, when he finally finds her in the lazaretto and he is able to be reunited with her forever. There are several reasons that the city of Milan plays an important role in the development of the story and of the character of Renzo. However, I would argue that the most compelling value of Milan is in allowing Manzoni to craft the intersection between the history of the Thirty Years War and the story of the betrothed; that is, between collective history destined to come down to posterity condensed in the names of a few individuals of power and the individual story of characters who would otherwise be destined to anonymity.[4] Against the backdrop of this intersection, the first Milan sequence reveals once and for all the ineptitude of the male character in his naïve and vain attempts at solving problems on his own. Instead, the second Milan sequence presents a savvier hero negotiating the lazaretto, now that he himself has survived the plague, and searching for his beloved Lucia by employing the lessons learned through his previous experience in the city. However, the second sequence is also the one in which the reunion of Renzo and Lucia is granted by Providence, the true moving force of the story, and more crucially, of history, according to Manzoni's understanding of political and historical process through the philosophies of Antonio Rosmini and his pupil Vincenzo Gioberti. It is also true that the second sequence in Milan relies heavily on the historical accounts of the period: Manzoni does not even try to hide his own adoption of the works by Ripamonti and Tadino (Chapter 31). As we know, Manzoni extrapolated his own historiographical research that became the independent book *Storia della Colonna Infame*.[5]

The first sequence of chapters taking place in Milan is just as long as the initial sequence in which Renzo is in action to ensure that he and Lucia will have their wedding (Chapters 3–8). Manzoni, however, is keenly interested in the chapters in which the story evolves in Milan because those chapters place Renzo in the midst of historical events. This is an ironic interest on the part of the author because the hero of the novel cannot possibly understand those events, not only when he first enters the city, but indeed even when he leaves it. By the time Renzo leaves the city of Milan in Chapter 17, the reader discovers that the hero has learned nothing about the general, collective, and political situation in which he had found himself involved, despite his statements in the last pages of the novel about the lessons he has learned in all his adventures. In fact, those statements confirm that Renzo's knowledge is limited to a very circumscribed private learning experience. What Renzo learns works, if and when it works, only on the individual (indeed individualistic and selfish) level. At the end of the first sequence in Milan, Renzo is still the peasant he was when he entered the city; he is still absolutely cut off from the course of history and, in particular, he has no possibility of gaining any awareness, let alone consciousness, of the historical process and its mechanisms. The narrator, however, at the beginning of both sequences, cleverly elaborates in detail in a few chapters (12 and 31–32) the historical and economic reasons that led the population of Milan to organize the riots and the mobbing of the bakeries in the first sequence, and the historical and economic reasons that caused the spreading of the plague in the second sequence.[6] The two sequences also offer the opportunity to observe two different sides of Renzo. In the first sequence, Renzo's ineptitude is apparent in actions and words until he manages to get out of the city. In the second sequence, however, he at least reunites with Lucia, after he has reconciled himself with the world through prayer and forgiveness.

This is an evident strategy that Manzoni adopts to erect a distance between the reader and the hero. As long as Renzo moves in his natural environment, the countryside in which he grew up and worked and in which he met Lucia and planned on marrying her and living out his days contentedly, his actions can be understood according to a rational and logical strategy. But in Milan, Renzo is caught in a bigger game. When he arrives in that city, the narrator has just explained the rules of that bigger game for the benefit of the reader, but those rules remain totally alien to the male protagonist. This ironic situation already places the hero in a disadvantageous position for he is doomed to fail in his already simple mission: he is required only to present himself to a convent with a letter of reference fra Cristoforo wrote on his behalf. However, Renzo moves in the streets of Milan unable to understand what is really happening in the city, so that he succumbs to shady figures and finds himself first drunk and then arrested.

Milan as a City: The Cathedral Square

In both sequences, Milan as a city always appears in the background, with very few places that are used as landmarks, and often in ironic contrast between the topography of the city in 1628 and the implicit allusion to the changes that have occurred since then. More importantly, Milan as a city is a place of perdition, one in which the naïve peasant Renzo becomes prey of collective forces that are just as blind as he is before the movement of history. This is to Manzoni the terrifying face of the infernal dimension of the city: one does not necessarily get lost because of lack of familiarity with the plane geometry of the city; rather, one gets lost because of ignorance and an inability to interpret the action of one's fellow citizens.

In fact, there are only a few actual places that are indicated in Milan. This is for two reasons. On the one hand, Manzoni wants the reader to be as disoriented as the hero: to this end the only reference that is obvious to both reader and hero is that of the Cathedral of Milan, which was then (both in 1628 and in the first half of the nineteenth century, when Manzoni wrote the novel) and is even now the most obvious, and today touristic, attraction. On the other hand, Manzoni takes the opportunity to point out sites that have changed since the time in which the facts narrated take place, sometimes even alluding to the historical events that brought the changes visible to the citizens and visitors of Milan at Manzoni's time, and at least in some cases, even to those who have lived or visited that city since then. To appreciate the writer's strategies in this respect, it is necessary to consider the references to the Cathedral and the few other places Manzoni deliberately specifies in their location.

The Duomo is first seen through the eyes of Renzo as he is approaching the city of Milan toward the end of Chapter 11:

> Renzo, salito per un di que' valichi sul terreno più elevato, vide quella gran macchina del duomo sola sul piano, come se, non di mezzo a una città, ma sorgesse in un deserto; e si fermò su due piedi, dimenticando tutti i suoi guai, a contemplare anche da lontano quell'ottava meraviglia, di cui aveva tanto sentito parlare sin da bambino. (222)
>
> As Renzo climbed up one of those paths to a higher level, he caught sight of the vast mass of the cathedral standing up alone out of the plain, as if it had been built not in a city but in the middle of the desert. He stood quite still, forgetting all his troubles, and gazed at the prospect, distant as it was, of that eighth wonder of the world, which he had so often heard of ever since he was a child. (Penman 224)

Immediately after seeing the Cathedral, Renzo turns back to look at the mountains from whence he came and among which he recognizes "il suo Resegone" (222) "his own Resegone" (225). The contrast could not be sharper, since the mountain is accompanied by the possessive adjective, which conveys the affection of the beholder, and defining "con voce lombarda, il Resegone" (9) "by the Lombard-sounding name of Resegone" (25), as the reader learns in the very first paragraph of the novel. More importantly, Renzo sees the Cathedral not only as "quell'ottava meraviglia" ("the eighth wonder of the world," which seems to anticipate the glamorous descriptions of tourist brochures), but also and primarily as "quella gran macchina del duomo sola sul piano" ("the vast mass of the cathedral standing up alone out of the plain"; literally translated, Manzoni's image alludes to a Baroque metaphor, since he literally calls the Cathedral "that great machinery of the cathedral"). The image is supposed to convey Renzo's surprise and wonder before the spectacle; but the loneliness of the building, as though it were "in un deserto" ("in the middle of the desert") is already implicitly telling the reader, through the words Manzoni uses to report Renzo's amazement, something crucial about that city. It is a desert, it is indeed an infernal place, in which people arrive thinking that there they will find what they are looking for (after all, Renzo carries a letter from fra Cristoforo that is supposed to take care of his situation), only to find that they wander as though indeed in a desert. The only way out of this desert is to retreat to the countryside.

The same striking appearance of the Cathedral is remarked upon when Renzo glimpses it as he finally enters Milan. In fact, our peasant reaches that site by following one man who, in turn, was following others:[7]

> Tutti questi s'incamminavano dalla stessa parte, e a un luogo donvenuto, si vedeva.—Cos'è quest'altra storia?—pensò di nuovo Renzo; e andò dietro a uno che, fatto un fascio d'assi spezzate e di schegge, se lo mise in ispalla, avviandosi, come gli altri, per la strada che costeggia il fianco settentrionale del duomo, e ha preso nome dagli scalini che c'erano, e da poco in qua non ci son più. La voglia d'osservar gli avvenimenti non potè fare che il montanaro, quando gli si scoprì davanti la gran mole, non si soffermasse a guardare in su, con la bocca aperta. Studiò poi il passo, per raggiunger colui che aveva preso come per guida; voltò il canto, diede un'occhiata anche alla facciata del duomo, rustica allora in gran parte e ben lontana dal compimento; e sempre dietro a colui, che andava verso il mezzo della piazza. La gente era più fitta quanto più s'andava avanti, ma al portatore gli si faceva largo; egli fendeva l'onda del popolo, e Renzo, standogli sempre attaccato, arrivò anche lui al centro della folla. (242)

> "What's this again, then?" thought Renzo. He noticed a man make up a bundle of broken planks and splintered wood, swing it on to his shoulder and walk off in the same direction as the others. Renzo decided to follow him. The man went along the road which passes the north side of the cathedral, and is now called after the steps that used to be there, but were removed a short time ago. Keen as he was to find out what was happening, the young Hillman could not help stopping when the great edifice appeared before him, and looking up at it with open mouth. Then he quickened his pace, to catch up with the man he had chosen as his guide. He turned the corner and glanced up at the façade of the cathedral, which was still to a large extent in a rough and unfinished state at that time, and went on again, still following the other man, who was heading for the centre of the square. The crowd got thicker as he went on, but it made way for the man with the load. He cut his way through the mass of people, and Renzo, still in his wake, arrived with him at the centre of the mob. (Penman 243)

Renzo follows an anonymous man quite by chance: there is no rationale behind the peasant's decision, and he is unable to understand even the simple actions of the man "che aveva preso come per guida." Manzoni aptly and ironically calls Renzo "il montanaro" as to highlight his role as outsider. It is not by chance that the great façade of the cathedral witnesses the contrasting movements of the two men in the scene: one of them goes about his business and the other, Renzo, caught in a moment of astonished surprise, halts in order to look at the beauty of the edifice "con la bocca aperta" before such monumental architecture. Manzoni also takes this opportunity to point out how the cathedral appeared then in the early seventeenth century, with steps that "da poco in qua non ci son più," even though the name given to the northern side of the cathedral still recalls those destroyed steps. By the same token, as the readers follow Renzo's movements in turn following those of the anonymous man with a bundle of wood, they are informed about the unfinished condition of the façade.[8]

However, the most remarkable event that takes place in this paragraph is Renzo's approaching "il mezzo della piazza" without being aware of being there. In that last sentence, Manzoni observes that "La gente era più fitta," while Renzo "fendeva l'onda del popolo" until "arrivò anche lui al centro della folla." In other words, in describing the gathering of human beings at the center of the square, the writer employs three different terms: his description moves from the neutral representation of "gente" to the already metaphorical "onda del popolo" to the final derogatory definition of "mob." As we shall see, the image of the wave metaphor opens possibilities that the writer will exploit as he turns to storm images.

The First Sequence in Milan

The metaphor "onda del popolo" invites us to consider how Manzoni approaches the description of the historical and political situation in Milan at the time of Renzo's arrival. The author purports to keep a realistic and objective view of the overall picture in which the hero inadvertently enters, but the author himself exposes his bias in specific metaphors employed to describe the power of the mob: the one aforementioned is just one more instance of a long sequence that invades Chapters 12 and 13, the chapters in which there is a historical introduction to the causes of the shortage of goods, especially of bread, and the assault at the Bakery of the Crutches. This is all before we follow Renzo joining the crowd and acting and speaking, as we shall see, in ways that end up meaning the opposite of the hero's good intentions.

The true protagonist of these two chapters is the multitude, to use one of the terms, perhaps the most neutral one, which Manzoni employs to describe the public in the city of Milan at the time of Renzo's arrival.[9] The fact that the people involved in the riots are neither "popolo," nor class, but indeed "moltitudine," "gente," and "folla," (sometimes even "massa," "turba," "marmaglia") at best, is indicative of the social and political interpretation that the author is tacitly and implicitly proposing. Behind these terms there is indeed the political and ideological agenda Manzoni had held throughout the Risorgimento in Italy, first during the evening meetings at his own house with intellectuals and patriots and then, after the unification of Italy, as a deputy in the Italian parliament. Perhaps the most striking proof of Manzoni's position can be found in the short pamphlet he wrote right after the unification of Italy in 1860: *La Rivoluzione Francese del 1789 e la rivoluzione italiana del 1859. Saggio comparativo.*[10] Even though Manzoni wrote this pamphlet about twenty years after publishing the final edition of *The Betrothed*, it is a pamphlet that clarifies Manzoni's political engagement in the Risorgimento much more than his active role as representative in the Parliament of the Kingdom of Italy, which he kept until he died in 1873. According to Manzoni, the Italian Revolution was more effective than the French Revolution because it did not require the violent intervention to grant freedom. Instead, a government actually brought freedom itself to the citizens and protected it for them. In other words, Manzoni favored a revolution from above, so to speak, rather than one that started as a grassroots movement. By the same token, in the chapters in which Renzo reaches Milan, the people involved in the riots cannot be endorsed in their protest against the high prices of bread and flour. Although the Spanish authorities are presented in their full hypocrisy, the narrator does not spare the people of Milan from implicit criticism hidden in the unfolding of a pervasive metaphor.

Quite interesting from a stylistic and rhetorical standpoint is the reiterated use of the complex metaphor of the rain storm. This is even more intriguing when one keeps in mind the role the rain has in Chapter 37 in washing the pestilence away. At that point, in the next to the last chapter of the novel, the literal representation of the rain cleanses the scene and allows for a resolution, a happy ending of the novel itself. Instead, in the chapters of the first sequence in Milan, the rain appears as a storm metaphor and it starts as soon as the narrator finishes the overall presentation of the historical and economic background that has led to the unstable situation in Milan:

> La sera avanti questo giorno in cui Renzo arrivò in Milano, le strade e le piazza brulicavano d'uomini, che trasportati da una rabbia comune,

> predominati da un pensiero comune, conoscenti o estranei, si riunivano in crocchi, senza essersi dati l'intesa, quasi senza avvedersene, come gocciole sparse sullo stesso pendìo. Ogni discorso accresceva la persuasione e la passione degli uditori, come di colui che l'aveva proferito. Tra i tanti appassionati, c'eran pure alcuni più di sangue freddo, i quali stavano osservando con molto piacere, che l'acqua s'andava intorbidando; e s'ingegnavano d'intorbidarla di più , con que' ragionamenti, e con quelle storie che i furbi sanno comporre, e che gli animi alterati sanno credere; e si proponevano di non lasciarla posare, quell'acqua, senza farci un po' di pesca. (234)
>
> The evening before Renzo reached Milan, the city's streets and squares had been swarming with men. Possessed by a common anger and dominated by a common thought, all of them, whether they knew each other or not, began to form into groups. They joined forces without any prearrangement, almost without being aware that they were doing so, like drops of water coming together as they run down the same slope. Every speech that was made increased the conviction and the passion both of the listeners and the speakers.
>
> Amid all those enthusiasts, there were some cooler heads, who were very pleased to see the muddy water stirred up, and did their best to stir it up still further. They put forward arguments and stories of a kind that the cunning can always invent and the hot-headed will always believe. They had no intention of letting the troubled waters settle again without doing a little fishing in them. (Penman 235)

The first sentence already presents those men in a mildly derogatory metaphor, since they are caught in an action usually associated with the movement of insects, quite often as different as bees and worms. In fact, in this respect, if the possible allusion to worms is self-explanatory, the probable one to bees stresses the ironic use of the term, as the bees would move actively and constructively, whereas the men in the scene are "Trasportati da una rabbia comune, predominati da un pensiero comune:" they have no control over their own actions and they are acting irrationally because, one may infer, of their angry state of mind. It is at this point that the simile of the "gocciole sparse" opens up a variety of possibilities that the writer starts exploiting immediately in this very paragraph while he focuses on some shady figures waiting for the right moment to fish in "the muddy water." The metaphorical reference to water is quite common in these pages, and it is always associated with the movement of the crowd. It is telling that Chapter 11 ends with exactly these images with the metaphorical verb here considered and the water metaphor, still loosely presented: "Attraversò la piazzetta, si portò sull'orlo della strada, e si fermò, cone le braccia incrociate sul petto, a guardare a sinistra, verso l'interno della città, dove il brulichìo era più folto e più rumoroso. Il vortice attrasse lo spettatore." ("He traversed the square, and stood at the side of the road, with his arms crossed, looking over to the left, towards the centre of the city, where the murmur of the crowd was loudest and most concentrated. The trouble-centre began to attract the listener.") (226–27; Penman 230). The maelstrom attracts Renzo whose will is subjugated to the power of the mass movement that he senses and witnesses.

The movement of the crowd is described with water metaphors as occurs in the episode of the mobbing of the Bakery of the Crutches: "Ma quelli che vedevan la faccia del dicitore, e sentivan le sue parole, quand'anche avessero voluto ubbidire, dite un poco in che maniera avrebber potuto, spinti com'erano, e incalzati da quelli di dietro, spinti anch'essi da altri, come flutti da flutti, via via fino all'estremità della folla, che andava sempre crescendo." ("But even those who could see the speaker's face and hear his words—even if they had wanted to obey him—how could they do what he said? They were being pushed and trampled by the people just behind them, who in turn were being pushed by others, wave on wave, back to the edge of the crowd, which was still growing.") (236–37, Penman 237). The "folla" is transformed into a sea of "flutti," and this imagery supports several metaphors in the pages of this and the next chapter. When at last the crowd cannot be contained anymore, "la porta fu sfondata, l'inferriate svelte; e il torrente penetrò per tutti i varchi." ("The door was broken in, the bars over the windows were torn down, and the human flood poured in at every gap.") (238, Penman 239).[11]

The storm metaphor is the founding metaphor of the chapters in which Renzo is in Milan and witnesses and unwillingly takes part in the riots. Such metaphor starts appearing discreetly in the mobbing of the Bakery of the Crutches, when the captain's words are lost "nella tempesta di grida" ("in the tempestuous clamour") (238, Penman 239). Later on, in the description of this scene, an anonymous participant in the mobbing recalls the stones launched against the captain himself, "pietre di questa fatta, che venivan giù come la grandine" ("Stones this big, coming down like hail!") (241, Penman 242).

Manzoni employs the storm metaphor to portray the dangers of the city and it is into this treacherous landscape that he leads the unsuspecting Renzo. At this point Renzo is inserted again into the picture with telling words: "[. . .] s'avviava, senza saperlo, proprio al luogo centrale del tumulto" ("Though he did not know it, he was heading for the very centre of the storm.") (239, Penman 241).

Needless to say, the storm images get even denser in the next two chapters especially in the initial paragraphs of the two following chapters. In fact, as the crowd moves to the commissioner's house, his servants hurry to secure all the entrances to the house:

> [...] I servitori ne hanno appena tanto che basti per chiuder la porta. Metton la stanga, metton puntelli, corrono a chiuder le finestre, come quando si vede venire avanti un tempo nero, e s'aspetta la grandine, da un momento all'altro. L'urlìo crescente, scendendo dall'altro come un tuono, rimbomba nel vuoto cortile; ogni buco della casa ne rintrona: e di mezzo al vasto e confuso strepito, si senton forti e fitti colpi di pietre alla porta. (245)
>
> [...] The servants hardly had time to shut the doors, which they rapidly bolted and barred. Then they ran to shut the windows, as people do when the sky goes very black and a hailstorm is expected from one moment to another.
>
> The howling outside grew louder and louder. In the courtyard it seemed to be coming down from the sky, like the sound of thunder; and every room and hollow space in the building resounded with it. (Penman 247)

The arrival of the protesters is compared to that of "un tempo nero," the noise they make to "un tuono," ever more threatening as courtyard and house are left empty. It is that emptiness that makes the protesters' presence ever more ominous. One should not be misled by the nature comparison: Manzoni is emphasizing the impossibility of controlling natural phenomena, such as a hailstorm and even lighting (of which the thunder is the sound effect). After all, in the seventeenth century the lightning-rod had not been invented yet, and the invention was quite recent even at Manzoni's time.

The same image returns when the protesters start leaving the commissioner's house. Groups of people form and they will soon see Renzo as one of the protagonists while he delivers a speech that is memorable both for the character's inability to relate to the situation and for the narrator's ironic enjoyment of putting him in ever more difficult situations.[12] In the meantime, these groups are again compared to natural phenomena through storm metaphors: "[...] era come quella nuvolaglia che talvolta rimane sparsa, e gira per l'azzurro del cielo, dopo una burrasca; e fa dire a chi guarda in su: questo tempo non è rimesso bene." ("[...] it was like the clouds which sometimes remain scattered across the sky after a storm, traveling across the blue background, so that we look up at them and say: 'It hasn't really cleared up yet.'") (263, Penman 264).

The impact of the storm metaphor is twofold. First, the metaphor describes the dangerous elements that cause the storm and that point out how unpredictable the movements and the thoughts of the mob may be, erratic as drops of water and yet all leading to a common ground, although not necessarily to a common goal, let alone a collective idea. Then, the storm metaphor presents the effects upon the storm's victim, Renzo, who is introduced in Milan just when the reader has been informed and will keep receiving information that is instead denied to the hero.

Let us consider the description of the turmoil in Milan. Manzoni puts no trust in the people, which are in fact presented as "moltitudine" ("multitude," "mob," "crowd"), "folla" ("all," "crowd," "mob"), "gente" ("crowd," "poor," "rabble," "people," "mob," "brutes," "folk," "everyone"), "massa" ("mass," "in general"), "calca" ("crowd"), even "marmaglia" ("rabble") and "turba" ("crowd"). The rare employment of the term "popolo" ("people," "multitude," "mob") is not to be understood in that ideological sense of the term that was very familiar to the author, educated in the first years of the nineteenth century at the Parisian salons of the last ideologues, and that in the first half of the nineteenth century became the referential term for the socialist and Marxist ideologies.[13]

The other operation of the storm metaphor concerns Renzo, as it reveals Manzoni's strategy of sharing information about the events taking place in Milan with the readers, while keeping the main character unaware of the meaning and consequences of those events. As a man from the countryside newly arrived to the city, Renzo is doomed to play the role of the ignoramus. But Manzoni stresses this role by enjoying Renzo's gullible attitude from the time the hero starts talking to the crowd: his speech is supposed to be in striking contrast with the double truth that comes out of the Grand Chancellor Antonio Ferrer. In fact, the Spanish authority utters sentences in two languages, Italian out loud to the crowd and Spanish under his breath, thereby affirming his power through his control over the people through the language they speak and his loyalty to his occupying country through his own native language (253–62, Penman 255–63). Instead, Renzo naively addresses a group of people spontaneously gathered around him and talks about his own misfortunes in such an enigmatic way that he is, on the one hand, mistook for a leader of the riots and, on the other, recognized for the fool he is (264–67, Penman 265–68). After putting his trust in an unknown man who leads him to an inn for some food and a place to sleep, Renzo ends up getting drunk and talking too much (267–80, Penman 269–80).[14] The next morning, he finds himself arrested (281–97, Penman 281–98). He is finally forced to be resourceful, and he takes advantage of the fact that a crowd can be manipulated: as he is taken to prison through the streets of Milan, he manages to convince the people around him that he is being arrested for having participated in the riots the previous day, which incites the people to free him. The adventures in the city have taught Renzo deception and he takes advantage of it, and thanks to the mistrust he now holds for the words of the others, he finds his way out of the city. The subsequently more discreet and savvier attitude Renzo displays first at the cottage just outside Milan and then at the inn in Gorgonzola allows us to appreciate the lesson the hero learned while spending just one day in Milan (303–15, Penman 304–15). Only once he is away from the city, after reaching the Adda River at night and getting ready to spend the night in the woods on the banks of the river, Renzo finds a moment to pray. He is convinced that, having skipped the prayers the night before because of his drunkenness, he received the right punishment for that behavior when he was arrested in the morning (322–25, Penman 319–23).

Milan as a City: The Lazaretto

Renzo returns to Milan at the end of Chapter 33, and he remains in that city until the end of Chapter 36 when he leaves after reuniting with Lucia. Whereas the first time Renzo had been sent to Milan by fra Cristoforo with a letter, this time Renzo makes the decision himself and goes on his own, "prendendo per sua stella polare il duomo; e dopo un brevissimo cammino, venne a sbucar sotto le mura di Milano, tra porta Orientale e porta Nuova, e molto vicino a questa" ("using the cathedral as his guiding star. After a very short walk, he came face to face with the city wall, between the East Gate and the New Gate, which was not far away" (628, Penman 626). This time Renzo is much more confident, and he puts himself right away in the hands of Providence, so to speak, as he lets the building of the cathedral guide him so that he can orient himself in the city not only physically, but also morally. In fact, as soon as he enters the city, Manzoni points out crosses that he sees along the way, and Renzo himself cannot see beyond those religious symbols:

> La strada che Renzo aveva presa, andava allora, come adesso, diritta fino al canale detto il *Naviglio*: i lati erano siepi o muri d'orti, chiese e conventi, e poche case. In cima a questa streada, e nel mezzo di quella che costeggia il canale, c'era una colonna, con una croce detta la croce di sant'Eusebio. E per quanto Renzo guardasse innanzi non vedeva altro che quella croce. (631)
>
> The road which Renzo had taken led straight to the canal called the Naviglio, as it does today. On either side were garden walls or hedges, and churches and monasteries; there were not many houses. At the

junction of this road with the one that ran along the bank of the canal there was a column, with a cross dedicated to St. Eusebius. And, however hard Renzo looked along the road in front of him, there was nothing to be seen except that cross. (Penman 629)

Once again, while specifying which streets Renzo is taking, Manzoni also points out that the topography has not changed since then: the acknowledgment becomes even stronger when one thinks of the presence of the cross, from which Renzo cannot take his eyes. However, this is not the only cross that he encounters, as there is another one just on the next street that Manzoni points out: "Arrivato al ponte, voltò senza esitare, a sinistra, nella strada di san Marco, parendogli, a ragione, che dovesse condurre verso l'interno della città." ("When he reached the bridge, he at once turned to the right, into St. Mark's Street, which he rightly thought would take him towards the centre of the city.") (632; Penman 631). Renzo can orient himself in the city; he has the right sense about it. Still, he acts sensibly and rightly when he encounters a starving woman with children and offers her some bread he is carrying. At this point, he remembers the loaves of bread he had found in the street on the day of the riots: "A Renzo intanto gli vennero in mente que' pani che aveva trovato vicino alla croce, nell'altra sua entrata in Milano, e pensava:—ecco: è una restituzione, e forse meglio che se gli avessi restituiti al proprio padrone; perchè qui è veramente un'opera di misericordia" ("Meanwhile he began to think about those other loaves, which he had found at the foot of the Cross of St. Denis, when he had come to Milan for the first time. 'You could say I'm returning that first lot of bread,' he thought, 'and it's better than if I'd returned it to its proper owner, for this is a real work of mercy.'") (633, Penman 631–32).

When Renzo resumes his journey, he goes through places that seem to be familiar to him and, more importantly, to the readers, as Manzoni does not indulge anymore in any other specification than the name of the squares, streets, and quarters. Thus, Renzo reaches "Piazza san Marco" ("St. Mark's Square") where he sees "l'abbominevole macchina della tortura" ("the abominable instrument of torture") (634, Penman 632) and "pregava intanto per quei morti sconosciuti" ("was praying for the souls of those unknown dead") (635, Penman 633); then, "vide a destra il ponte Marcellino; prese di lì, e riuscì in Borgo Novo" ("he saw the Marcellino Bridge to his right, crossed it and came out into the Borgo Nuovo") (635, Penman 633). It is no wonder that at this point, after seeing Renzo pray and receive the right information from a priest about don Ferrante's house, where he hopes to find Lucia, Manzoni offers a sentence that seems to picture the hero's feelings toward the city: "Quale città! E cos'era mai, al paragone, quello ch'era stata l'anno avanti, per cagion della fame!" ("And what a city it was! The state to which the famine had reduced Milan the year before was nothing to this") (636, Penman 635). The city was and is in dire straights, but it is the visitor who has in the meantime changed and is able to reflect and compare.

Renzo enters an even more miserable section of the city in the immediately following paragraph: the narrator marks it by signals that are getting by now familiar to the hero and to the readers: "Renzo s'abbatteva appunto a passare per una delle parti più squallide e più desolate: quella crociata di strade si chiamava il *carrobio* di porta Nuova. (C'era allora una croce nel mezzo, e, dirimpetto ad essa, accanto a dove ora è san Francesco di Paola, una vecchia chiesa col titolo di Sant'Anastasia.)" ("Renzo's way happened to take him through one of the most squalid and desolate areas, around the crossroad known as the Carrobio of the New Gate. [There was a cross in the middle of it then, and opposite the cross, next to the site where the church of St. Francis of Paola now stands, was an old church dedicated to St. Anastasia."]) (636, Penman 635). The parenthetical specification is actually more telling than its syntactic structure would like the readers to believe. Manzoni notes the difference in the landscape then and at the time in which he writes; more importantly, he again points out that there was a cross at the crossroad, highlighting the symbolic reference even in the terminology he employs. It is at this point that Renzo enters the truly hellish part of the city as he gets closer to the lazaretto. After witnessing a mother delivering her dead daughter Cecilia to the *monatti*, "vide da una parte una moltitudine confusa che s'avanzava" ("he saw a confused multitude advancing") (642, Penman 641).

Once he finds out that Lucia is not at don Ferrante's house, in order not to be confused for an anointer, and worried for his beloved, who, he is told, has gotten the plague, Renzo jumps on one of the carts of the *monatti*, protected by the fact that he had already survived the plague.[15] This gesture earns him the admiration of the *monatti* themselves and an advantageous position thanks to which he can better look for Lucia. In fact, this is how Renzo reaches the lazaretto, where the narrator explicitly states his loss of interest for descriptions that are not relevant but to the hero: "Questo spettacolo, noi non ci proponiam certo di descriverlo a parte a parte, nè il lettore lo desidera; solo, seguendo il nostro giovine nel suo penoso giro, ci fermeremo alle sue fermate, e di ciò che gli toccò di vedere diremo quanto sia necessario a raccontar ciò che fece, e ciò che gli seguì." ("We do not propose to offer a complete and detailed description of that sight, nor would the reader wish it. But we shall follow Renzo as he makes his painful round of the place, and shall stop where he stops. Of the sights that he saw, we shall relate enough to explain what he did, and what came of it.") (651, Penman 650). This time, such a statement means that the city is no longer relevant to the adventures of the hero. Whereas in Renzo's first journey through Milan the city was essential to the growth of the character, in this second trip Milan is at this point superfluous, as the lazaretto has become the city within the city in which the young peasant hopes to find his beloved.

It is in the context of the lazaretto that the storm images return, but this time the storm is a literal one: "Ogni tanto, tra mezzo al ronzìo continuo di quella confusa moltitudine, si sentiva un borbottar di tuoni, profondo, come tronco, irresoluto; nè, tendendo l'orecchio, avreste saputo distinguere da che parte venisse; o avreste potuto crederlo un correr lontano di carri, che si fermassero improvvisamente." ("Every so often, amid the continual murmur of that confused multitude, the threatening voice of the thunder could be heard in deep, broken, hesitant rumbling tones. The listener could not tell from which direction it came, and might have taken it for the sound of carts being driven along some distant road with many sudden stops.") (653, Penman 651). The narrator elaborates further by alluding to both the present time and the weather, while still employing storm references: "Era uno [...] di que' tempi forieri della burrasca" ("It was [...] the sort of weather that goes before a storm.") (653, Penman 652). The events succeed rapidly: Renzo encounters fra Cristoforo, forgives the agonizing don Rodrigo who is dying in the lazaretto, and reunites at last with Lucia. It is at this point that another reference to the stormy weather is offered: "Il tempo s'era andato sempre più rabbuiando, e annunziava ormai certa e poco lontana la burrasca." ("The sky meanwhile had continued to darken, and there could be no doubt now that the storm would soon break.") (678, Penman 680). The last words of this chapter still refer to the "burrasca imminente" ("the coming storm") (683, Penman 685), which indeed is the true protagonist of the beginning of the next chapter: "Appena infatti ebbe Renzo passata la soglia del lazzeretto e preso a diritta, per ritrovar la viottola di dov'era sboccato la mattina sotto le mura, principiò come una grandine di goccioloni radi e impetuosi, che, battendo e risaltando sulla strada bianca e arida, sollevavano un minuto polverìo" ("Renzo passed through the gates of the lazaretto and turned to the right to look for the path which had brought him through the fields to the city walls that morning. No sooner had he begun to do so than a few big drops began to fall, looking almost like hailstones, as they struck and bounced along the dry, white surface of the road, each kicking up a minute cloud of dust.") (684, Penman 686). As the narrator joyfully adds in the next paragraph, "quella gioia portava via il contagio" ("The rain literally washed the pestilence away.") Thus, there are at least two considerations that need to be made. On the one hand, Renzo is truly the hero who is now looking for the right path so that he can trace back his steps. According to a dynamics of anabasis and katabasis, showing once again his control over the situation, as though he had accomplished his mission, one may say that he has reached the center of that labyrinth that is the lazaretto and has found Lucia thanks not only to his own resourcefulness, but also to the help of Providence (the crosses along the way, the acts of mercy, and the prayers all help Renzo to succeed).[16] On the other hand, the metaphorical storm of the first visit to Milan becomes the liberating literal storm that, as an event that acts as the hand of Providence, puts a closure to the pestilence and to the betrothed's misfortunes and separation.

Conclusion

Through the recounting of the adventures of Renzo in Milan, Manzoni expresses his implicit opinion about the city, its social organization, and the political activities that take place in it. Manzoni has an ambivalent approach to the topic. On the one hand, with the pretense of objectivity, he takes his distance from the protagonist of the novel, as the narrator observes the character getting involved in less than appealing and compromised situations. On the other, the depiction of the riots is such that the reader cannot but sense the narrator's disapproval of the events that lead the people to a protest of what is felt as exploitation through the fluctuation of the price of bread. The city appears, then, in its basic forms, in the following aspects: it is a labyrinth in which the protagonist (a peasant from the countryside in Lombardy) gets lost; it is the place of the kind of deception the people of the city perpetrate against the more naive people of the countryside; it is the horror that the economic system of the city itself produces and provokes when the exploited people rebel. Finally, the city's characteristics are a foil to the freedom that the protagonist enjoys after leaving the city. It is this sense of freedom that Manzoni also reconciles with a return to a reasonable attitude as well as to a merciful one, in accordance with his providential understanding of history. Furthermore, it is this sense of freedom that confirms that the city is a trap, indeed a prison to honest people like Renzo. Manzoni aims at depicting the city as a hellish place that threatens the virtues of the male protagonist and contrasts with the more idyllic countryside, a place more conducive to contemplation and reflection.

NOTES

1. Quotations are from the following edition: *I Promessi Sposi*. Florence: Nuova Italia, 1974. Quotations from the Penman translation are from the following edition: *The Betrothed*. Trans. Bruce Penman. London: Penguin, 1972. Quotations will be accompanied by the page numbers of both the novel and its translation in parentheses in the text.
2. For a general appreciation of the question, see at least Augusto Simonini, *L'ideologia di Alessandro Manzoni*, Ravenna: Longo, 1978.
3. The sequences of chapters in which the two betrothed are actually separated have invited critics to talk about the "Storia di Renzo," which would be the chapters of Renzo in Milan during the first sequence, and the "Storia di Lucia:" see Angelo Marchese, "Il Bildungsroman di Renzo. Punto di vista e senso del racconto," *L'enigma Manzoni. La spiritualità e l'arte di uno scrittore «negativo»*, Rome: Bulzoni, 1994, 275–310; Sergio Pautasso, *I promessi sposi. Appunti e ipotesi di lettura*, Milan: Arcipelago, 1988. For readings of specific chapters, see also Giovanni Getto, *Letture manzoniane*, Florence: Sansoni, 1964.
4. In the vast critical bibliography on the topic, see at least Clareece Godt, "From History to Story: Manzoni and the Chroniclers of Milano," *The Reasonable Romantic: Essays on Alessandro Manzoni*, Ed. Sante Matteo and Larry H. Peer, New York: Lang, 1986, 179–94.
5. Among several editions, see *Storia della Colonna Infame*, Milan: Bompiani, 1985. For the Penman translation, see *The Column of Infamy*, Trans. Kenelm Foster and Jane Grigson, London: Oxford UP, 1964. See at least Francesco Di Ciaccia, "La peste nella *Colonna Infame*," *La parola e il silenzio. Peste carestia ed eros nel romanzo manzoniano*, Pisa: Giardini, 1987, 101–98.
6. Regarding the chapters of the riots in Milan, see at least Remo Fasani, "I fatti di Milano," *Saggio sui* Promessi sposi, Florence: Le Monnier, 1952, 106–25; Enzo Noè Girardi, "Il tumulto di San Martino (Cap. XIII)," *Manzoni «reazionario.» Cinque saggi sui Promessi Sposi*, Bologna: Cappelli, 1966, 15–31; Clareece G. Godt, "Self-Reflecting Episodes: The St. Martin's Day Riots and the Famine," *The Mobile Spectacle: Variable Perspective in Manzoni's* I Promessi Sposi, New York: Lang, 1998, 33–64; Umberto Mariani, "La visuale di Renzo: l'avventura in città," "La visuale di Renzo: le estreme conseguenze," *Per un Manzoni più vero*, Turin: SEI ,1996; Giovanni Negri, "Fra i tumulti per il rincaro del pane," *Sui* Promessi sposi *di Alessandro Manzoni*, Milan: Scuola Tipografica Salesiana, 1903, 27–53; Elena Parrini, "La Storia per la storia (PS, cap.XII)," "Dalla narrazione alla storia (PS capps.XXXI–XXXII)," *La narrazione della storia nei* Promessi Sposi, Florence: Le Lettere, 1996, 61–115, 179–219.
7. The square of the cathedral remains a point of reference on other occasions as well: in fact, it is present in almost all the chapters in which Renzo is in Milan. At the beginning of Chapter 14, after his speech to the people there gathered and before going toward the inn where he

spends the night, Renzo gives appointment to his audience for the next day "sulla piazza del duomo" ("in the Cathedral Square") (267, Penman 268). The next morning, after being arrested, Renzo asks, "Passeremo dalla piazza del duomo?" ("Shall we be passing the Cathedral Square?") (Penman 292). When he finally runs away from the guards, he asks for directions for Bergamo and he is sent again to the "piazza del duomo," while looking for the East Gate. The paragraph describing Renzo in the Cathedral Square is quite telling, as it is narrated in the present tense:

> Renzo arriva sulla piazza del duomo; l'attraversa, passa accanto a un mucchio di cenere e di carboni spenti, e riconosce gli avanzi del falò di cui era stato spettatore il giorno avanti; costeggia gli scalini del duomo, rivede il forno delle grucce, mezzo smantellato, e guardato da soldati; e tira diritto per la strada da cui era venuto insieme con la folla; arriva al convento de' cappuccino; dà un'occhiata a quella piazza e alla porta della chiesa, e dice tra sè, sospirando:—m'aveva però dato un buon parere quel frate di ieri: che stessi in chiesa a aspettare, e a fare un po' di bene. (300)

> Renzo reached the Cathedral Square, and went across it, passing a heap of charcoal and ashes in which he recognized the remains of the fire he had seen burning so brightly the day before. He passed close by the cathedral steps, saw the Bakery of the Crutches again, half dismantled and guarded by soldiers, and went straight on down the streets up which he had come with the mob. He reached the Capuchin monastery, and glanced at the doors of the church that stood in the little square. "Well," he said to himself with a sigh, "that friar yesterday gave me a very sound piece of advice when he told me to go and wait in the church, where I could do some good while I was waiting." (Penman 301)

The paragraph is useful to see how Renzo's day in Milan begins and ends in the Cathedral Square, but at the end of his journey in the city he starts learning from his mistakes. As he had been cautious in asking for directions to get out of Milan, so in the square he reflects on what he did wrong, on what he should have done the previous day. The contrast between the sanctity of the monastery, in which Renzo could have done some good or at least could have preserved himself, and the hellish dimension of the city, where he is certainly at a loss and at the mercy of slicker people than he is, is quite striking.

8. A similar strategy Manzoni uses in describing other locations in Milan. In a long paragraph he first describes the lazaretto, to which we shall return later, and then a column: "Lì c'era una colonna, con sopra una croce, detta di San Dionigi" (223, Penman 226). The readers are supposed to understand that that column is not there anymore. Near the column Renzo finds a loaf of bread, which first invites him to think that he has reached a wonderful place, but then turns out to be the first hint of his lack of awareness or grasp on the reality surrounding him. The reference to the column and the bread aptly returns when Renzo is just outside Milan: the bread he receives in the cottage invites the

writer to implicitly browse in Renzo's thoughts, while he considers that bread "un pane ben diverso da quello che aveva trovato, il giorno avanti, appiè della croce di san Dionigi" ("a piece of bread—it was very different in quality from the loaf he had found by the Cross of St. Denis the day before") (304, Penman 305). At the end of Chapter 12, a statue of Philip II is mentioned; however, Manzoni ironically refers to its being renamed as the statue of Marcus Brutus in 1797 when the Jacobins ruled in the Lombard city before being destroyed in 1799 when in fact the Jacobins did not rule anymore (243–44, Penman 244–45).

9. Regarding studies of the multitude in the novel, see at least Severino Monticone, "La psicologia della folla," *Nella miniera dei Promessi Sposi,* Turin: SEI, 1965, 220–32; Reto Roedel, "La folla nei *Promessi Sposi,*" *Note manzoniane,* Turin: Chiantore, 1934, 5–104.

10. Manzoni started working on this pamphlet several times and left it unpublished. It is available in *La Rivoluzione Francese del 1789 e la rivoluzione italiana del 1859. Dell'indipendenza dell'Italia,* Milan: Centro Nazionale Studi Manzoniani, 2000, which is volume 15 of the *Edizione Nazionale ed Europea delle Opere di Alessandro Manzoni.*

11. Such metaphors may be grouped according to river and sea images. The sea images focus on the wave metaphor: besides the reference to "l'onda del popolo" already observed when Renzo enters the Cathedral Square (242, Penman 243), the same image returns at the commissioner's house, just before the arrival of the Grand Chancellor Antonio Ferrer: "I portatori, all'una e all'altra cima, e di qua e di là della macchina, urtati, scompigliati, divisi dalla calca, andavano a onde." ("It was carried by a man at each end and others on either side; they were pushed, jostled, and separated from each other by the crowd, so that their advance was slow and irregular.") (249, Penman 251). In fact, even when Ferrer arrives, the people around him are described with the same image: "Renzo, che, facendo un po' da battistrada, un po' da scorta, era arrivato con la carrozza, potè collocarsi in una di quelle due frontiere di benevoli, che facevano, nello stesso tempo, ala alla carrozza e argine alle due onde prementi di popolo." ("Between clearing the way and acting as escort, Renzo reached the door at the same time as the carriage, and was able to take his place in one of the two lines of men of good-will who were flanking the carriage and holding back the two surging divisions of the mob.") (257, Penman 259). One notices, parenthetically, that here the image returns to describe the crowd just as it did in chapter 12. But there are also those metaphors that may be called the river metaphors and that are distributed in the same chapter pages: therefore, to describe the violent impetus of the mobbing of the Bakery of the Crutches, Manzoni writes: "Più d'uno fu conciato male; due ragazzi vi rimasero morti. Il furore accrebbe le forze della moltitudinee: la porta fu sfondata, l'inferriate svelte; e il torrente penetrò per tutti i varchi." ("A number of people were hurt; two boys were actually killed. Rage gave new strength to the multitude. The door was

broken in, the bars over the windows were torn down, and the human flood poured in at every gap.") (238, Penman 239). Toward the end of this episode and of the chapter, Renzo is observed as he barely moves surrounded by the action: "Renzo rimaneva indietro, non movendosi quasi, se non quanto era strascinato dal torrente" "Renzo held back, only moving when he was carried along by the human torrent" (243, Penman 244). As though those occurrences were not enough, at the beginning of the next chapter Manzoni insiststhat "Renzo, questa volta, si trovava nel forte del tumulto, non già portatovi dalla piena, ma cacciatovisi deliberatamente." ("This time Renzo was in the thick of it. He had not been carried there by the movement of the crowd, but had thrust his way into the centre of things deliberately.") (246, Penman 248). The "piena" to which Manzoni alludes is the overflow of the river, in its literal sense, and of the crowd, in its metaphorical sense: both are dangerous and out of control states.

12. Regarding this particular ironic strategy, see the section on Renzo in Luisa Manfreda, *Figure dell'ironia nei* Promessi Sposi. *Il ruolo doppio a rovescio dei personaggi*, Pesaro: Metauro, 2006, 115–46.

13. These are all the occurrences of the terms in question in the novel: "moltitudine" ("multitude," "mob," "crowd") (230–31; 238; 243–244; 252; 255; 258; Penman 232–33; 239; 245; 254; 256; 259); "folla" ("all," "crowd," "mob") (235; 237–39; 242; 244; 245; 247–50; 253; 257; 259; 263–64; 297; 300; Penman 236; 237; 240; 243; 245; 247; 249; 251–52; 255; 259; 261; 264–65; 297–98); "gente" ("crowd," "poor," "rabble," "people," "mob," "brutes," "folk," "everyone") (236; 238–39; 241–43; 247–48; 250; 252; 256; 258; 262–63; 265; 269; 275; 289; 297; 306; 309; 311–12; 314; 318; 323; Penman 237; 239–40; 242–44; 249; 252–53; 257; 259; 263–64; 266; 269; 275; 289; 297; 307; 310; 311–14; 318; 322); "massa" ("mass," "in general") (251; 256; Penman 253; 257), "calca" ("crowd") (243; 260; Penman 245; 262); "marmaglia" ("rabble") (244; Penman 245); "turba" ("crowd") (244; 247; Penman 246; 248); "popolo" ("people," "multitude," "mob") (231–33; 242; 257; 260; Penman 233; 235; 243; 259; 262). Regarding some of these terms, see at least Vincenzo Di Benedetto, "Parte seconda: Lo spazio della gente," *Guida ai* Promessi sposi, Milan: Rizzoli, 1999, 175–296.

14. Regarding the episode of Renzo in the inn, see at least Maria Corti, "Con Manzoni all'osteria della Luna Piena," *Leggere* I promessi sposi. *Analisi semiotiche*, Ed. Giovanni Manetti, Milan: Bompiani, 1989, 35–49; Enzo Noè Girardi, "Renzo agl'Inferi," *Manzoni «reazionario.» Cinque saggi sui* Promessi Sposi, Bologna: Cappelli, 1966, 43–60; Ezio Raimondi, "L'osteria della retorica," *La dissimulazione romanzesca. Antropologia manzoniana*, Bologna: Il Mulino, 2004, 81–110; Giovanni Negri, "Dall'osteria della luna piena a quella di Gorgonzola," *Sui* Promessi sposi *di Alessandro Manzoni*, Parte II, 55–89.

15. Regarding the plague in Manzoni's novel, see at least Giusi Baldissone, "Il vuoto in biblioteca: Alessandro Manzoni e la peste," *Prospettive sui*

Promessi sposi, Ed. Giorgio Barberi Squarotti, Turin: Tirrenia, 1991, 77–93; Francesco Di Ciaccia, "La peste nei *Promessi Sposi*," in *La parola e il silenzio*. *Peste carestia ed eros nel romanzo manzoniano*, Pisa: Giardini, 1987, 13–100; Remo Fasani, "La carestia e la storia della peste," "I quadri della peste," *Saggio sui* Promessi sposi, Florence: Le Monnier, 1952, 149–65; 182–94; Enzo Noè Girardi, "Renzo, la peste e i cvronisti milanesi del Seicento," in *Omaggio ad Alessandro Manzoni nel bicentenario della nascita*, Ed. Giuseppe Catanzaro, Francesco Santucci, and Salvatore Vivona, Assisi: Accademia Properziana del Subasio, 1986, 299–316; Michele Mazzitelli, *La peste. Nel centenario de* I promessi sposi *(1840–1940)*, Presentazione di Antonino Anile, Tredici tavole fuori testo, Apuania Carrara: Bassani, 1940; Corrado Muscarà, *Il dolore nei* Promessi Sposi, Rome: Bardi, 1950, 75–123.

16. See at least Giovanni Negri, "I pentimenti di Renzo e la sua fede nella Provvidenza," *Sui* Promessi sposi *di Alessandro Manzoni*, Parte II, 91–107.

9

ROME ABOVE ROME: NIKOLAI GOGOL'S ROMANTIC VISION OF THE ETERNAL CITY

Tatiana V. Barnett

On Nikolai Gogol's (1809–1852) bicentennial, celebrated last year, a recurring discussion was brought once again about the nature of his art and whether he belongs at all to the European Romantic movement. Romanticism in Russia is different than the European mainstream both in its aesthetics and in its chronological outline, extended beyond the 1840s. Given the title the "father of Russian realism," generally because of his major epic poem *The Dead Souls*, Nikolai Gogol, however, marked a strong Romantic presence in the early folklore gothic of his Ukrainian novellas, in the grotesque metamorphosis of his "Petersburg stories" (*The Nose* and *The Overcoat*), and in the passionately heroic ethos of the *Taras Bulba*. Gogol belonged to the literary generation of the 1830–40s, when the romantic dichotomy of *dream and reality* was painfully breaking into *a dream* and *a reality*. The very core of Gogol's art evolves from this experience of the broken harmony of Heaven and Earth, which brings to life his preoccupation with forms of evil in its attempts to substitute itself for the true and the beautiful, to endanger human identity, to see the world picture falling into fragments, and to show the partial mocking wholeness. Metaphysical horror, underlying his work, points to a personal crisis of no earthly nature, and, eventually, through his later years, Gogol, like Chateaubriand, turns to mysticism involving a deep religious quest.

Rome had been his place of cultural refuge since March 1837, after the storm of both success and severe criticism of *The Inspector General*, which followed the premier of the play in St. Petersburg (1836). A European trip—Hamburg, Geneva, Paris, on the way to Italy—instead of alleviating his spirit, only intensified the unrest and fatigue from the emotional emptiness of the contemporary cities. An unpredictable setback—the outbreak of cholera in Italy—forced him to stay in Paris for several months. Paris seemed very disquieting to him: "here everything is politics.... You stop on the street to clean your boots and they jam a magazine into your hands," he wrote on January 5, 1837 in a letter to N. Prokopovitch, and he begged for "oblivion" (*Letters* 65, 67). In the tumult of the "political" capital, quite surprisingly, his work on "another leviathan," the epic poem/novel *The Dead Souls* proceeded with a good tempo. As it did in Rome, where Gogol settled in the beginning of spring, and where his spirit had revived. He appeared to be an urban author: he always worked better in a city. Pushkin's habit of writing in the countryside seemed unknown to him. Separation from homeland, however painful, offsets a writer with a better focus, a wider panorama. In a letter to P. A. Pletnev on March 17, 1842 he confided, "Besides, contained in my very nature is the ability to imagine a world graphically only when I have moved far away from it. That is why I can write about Russia only in Rome" (*Letters* 111).

Gogol was the first among the Russian authors to open up a metaphysical perspective on the national artistic subject from afar, culturally distancing the new literature from the European influence. After Gogol's epic *The Dead Souls*, which he accomplished living in Rome, other major Russian literary masterpieces, like Fyodor Dostoevsky's *The Idiot*, and also many of Ivan Turgenev's works, were born in the European exile. Nostalgia became a quintessential Russian phenomenon. Nevertheless, Rome and Italy offered Gogol a refuge from urban and social distress—an unbroken continuity, a living past. In a letter to M. P. Balabina on September 5, 1839 (Vienna) he wrote,

> Now imagine that God in great mercy on that man...threw him...into a paradise where unbearable mental reproaches do not torment him, where peace embraced his soul, peace as clear as the sky which now surrounded him and about which he had dreams in the north during his poetic visions, where in place of that tempestuous fountain of poetry striving every minute to burst from his breast,...he saw poetry not in himself, but around himself....People, cities, nations, relations and everything that crushes, agitates and torments people has disappeared from before me. (*Letters* 82–83)

Rome drew a dividing line in Gogol's life: one epoch ended, and another began. The news of the death of Alexander Pushkin, his mentor and friend, put Nikolai Gogol into an "inexpressible melancholy": "All the pleasure of my life, all my highest pleasure disappeared together with him" he wrote in a letter to P. A. Pletnev on 28 March 1837 (*Letters* 67). The divination of Pushkin had an existential value to Gogol: he transposed, in a way, his transcendental self into his friend's creative persona. The best of Gogol's creations, *The Dead Souls* and *The Inspector General*, developed from the two vagabond plots suggested by Alexander Pushkin—the inheritance that Gogol cared for till the last days of his life. The task of completing the second part of *The Dead Souls*—a sublime monomania of Gogol's later years—to a certain extent, was carried as an inner pledge of honor. Quite likely this feeling of immense loss affected Gogol's decision to return; instead, he chose to stay longer in a self-imposed literary Roman exile.

The new stage of life began for him under the sign of triple separation—from his homeland, from his friends, and from his transcendental self. Rome marked for him a period of transition in search for a metaphysical ground. As anything, it was not a steady process; it had all its falls and rises: from 1837 to 1842 Nikolai Gogol completed some of his literary gems, both in prose and in comedy (*The Overcoat, Rome, Marriage*), revised several pieces from *The Arabesques*, published out of his extensive correspondence the volume of *Selected Passages from Correspondence with Friends* (1843).

Nikolai Gogol had never planned to settle down in Italy permanently, but it turned out that, along with his in-between European travel and occasional trips to Russia, the chronological span of his Italian, or, rather, "expatriate" period made ten years. The writer's return to Russia in 1848 was followed by a tragic chain of events: the burning of a sequel for *The Dead Souls*, then an early death of the author in 1852. The illustrious beginning of the Italian period had a poignant sequence, continually sliding into the torment of an artist renouncing literature under the influence of an overwhelming religious conversion.

The Italian period of Gogol's life received the most comprehensive and detailed coverage in *La "Meravigliosa," Roma di Gogol* (2002), the book by an Italian scholar Rita Guiliani awarded the Nikolai Gogol's Prize (Russia, 2009). In Ukrainian criticism, the book by A. Balabko described the Italian years of *"Signore Nikkolo"* (2006); among the forums dedicated to this period, the most representative seems to be the international conference *Gogol I Italia* (Moscow, 2002). All sources recount Nikolai Gogol's fascination with Italy, his enthusiastic travel, his plunge into the natural beauty and artistic splendor of the

Mediterranean. The Southern climate had its healing effect, and in a while he could submit himself to an aesthetic pursuit of eternal beauty, to creative freedom, and to the camaraderie of the émigré artistic community. In a short time, he became the best guide to his visitors in Rome, showing the amazing sites he explored by himself, as recalled by Gogol's friend and companion of his Italian years, Alexandra Osipovna Smirnova:

> Nobody knew Rome better; such a cicerone has never been since and cannot be. There wasn't an Italian historian or a chronicler that he did not read, no Latin writer that he didn't know; everything that belonged to the historical progress of art...that he didn't know about and in some special way animated for him the entire life of this country which excited his young imagination...in whose soul he clearly saw Russia. (qtd. in Fokin 277)

It is quite interesting that Gogol's first literary work was a poem, *An Ode to Italy* (1829). Gogol's artistic sense in Italy was pleased in every aspect. His natural versatility as an actor, a playwright, and a painter was nurtured in bliss, as were his musical and intellectual cravings.

THE ANNUNCIATION

In Rome Gogol became a friend of a group of Russian artists—Alexander Ivanov and others—who were mostly pensioners of the Russian Imperial Academy of Arts (St. Petersburg), devoted to the study of the Italian masterpieces. The revivalist nature of their aesthetics was typical for the nineteenth-century sporadic classical *renaissances* that arrived as an answer to pragmatic social advance in Europe. They emerged in various national movements, like the Austrian-German "Nazareners" living for some time in Rome (they supposedly influenced the Russian artistic commune), or the Romantics—the mid-century English *Pre-Raphaelites*. Near-monastic concentration, convergence of new content with the classical form, and sensual richness of expression combined with the idealistic restraint from contemporary reality were the key principles of their aesthetics. Alexander Ivanov, the leading figure among the academicians, spent almost twenty years in an ascetic devotion to finish his only gigantic canvas, *The Appearance of Christ before the People* (1837–57), toiling to perfection in every detail. Companionship with such altruists of genius makes it easier to understand Gogol's perfectionism and his solitary concentration on one work (DS), a project worthy of Dante. Bringing God to Earth, in an artistic sense, is an attempt at *creation*, and creation is always *One*.

The Russian painters in Rome could be described as the "Raphaelites," since they insisted on permeating the formal restrictions of neoclassicism with revitalization from the Italian Renaissance. The synthetic collaboration of North and South, a lifelong dream of Madame de Staël, looked possible for the Russian community. The only thing is that the classical form prevailed in their practices, while the psychological dynamics of "passions" and the idea of organic unity belonged to contemporaneity. In the essay on *The Last Day of Pompeii* from *The Arabesques*, Gogol refers to Karl Brullov's well-known neoclassical painting as an example of such unity. The true *Raphaelite* ideal would be far from exalted expressions, focused on harmony and the Feminine Divine.

Nikolai Gogol, as a passionate supporter of this group of artists, was sincerely sharing with them the Raphaelite ideal. It is known that one of Gogol's few private possessions was a copy of God the Father's head from the *Annunciation*, by Raphael (Oddi Altar, 1503), which he received as a gift from his fellow painter I. S. Shapovalov. The image of God the Father in a distance over the arched colonnade amazingly reminds one of the faces and expressions of saints in the Russian icons. The spatial clarity of its composition with the two symmetrical figures—Mary and Gabriel on the Holy Doors, creates a scene open to the view equally from within and without. This composition resembles the *Annunciation* by Pietro Perugino (Durante Altarpiece), which Gogol refers to in the *Nevsky Prospect*: the forest-like colonnade, only the figure of Mary in the center. The serene landscape in the background of Raphael's painting, with some suggestion of the Russian humility, merges with the temple inside. In the same way the vision of Andrei's house against the misty Russian landscape fuses with the Italian church colonnade in the final scene of Andrei Tarkovsky's film *Nostalgia* (1983). Raphael's *Annunciation* gives a key to the spatial reconciliation of the nostalgic theme (convergence of the earthly home with the heavenly home, motherland with the land of artistic soul, North with South, nature with art) as perceived by both Russian artists, divided by almost a century and a half. The nostalgic theme links with the theme of longing for the preordained unity of the human spirit, which resolves or transcends in death, both in Nikolai Gogol and in Andrei Tarkovsky.

The motif of "annunciation" appears implicit or explicit in some of his works. Obviously, the name of his heroine in *Rome*, Annunziata, is a derivative from the Italian *Annunciazione*—"annunciation." It has an essentially feminine aspect, as the Angel Gabriel announced the news of the holy incarnation to Mary. But in its symbolic form or as a reminiscence it can be read as "the beginning of a new age," the Divine

Feminine revealed. The title of the fragment may imply that some kind of new transformative experience had to be pronounced by this work in progress. In this respect, the implementation of the annunciation motif in a reverse reality grotesque takes a specific turn. Gogol's short story *The Nose* is written almost at the same time as *Rome*, a fact which Nabokov mocked in his ironic remark that Gogol "was especially nose-conscious when living in Italy" (122). The action takes place on Annunciation Day (24th and 25th of March), when the collegiate assessor Mayor Kovalev finds out that his nose disappears and walks as a persona in the streets of St. Petersburg. The nose steals the identity of his owner and even triumphs over the owner in a social distinction, while Kovalev is completely stripped of his humanity, emptied of himself. At the Annunciation Day service at the Kazansky Cathedral, Mayor Kovalev finds his double standing in on a prayer among the officials and has a queer feeling of himself as a "shadow" of his nose, who continues acting, who appears and disappears, exposing qualities of Khlestakov. Thus, one ordinary clerk of a rather earthly nature and character, through the separation from his facial "buffoon" feature (nose), splits into two shadows. Gogol's fantastic talent is in his ability to show the broken wholeness (or "holiness") of a literary subject as an inevitable emptying of substance deprived of spirit. Evidently influenced by Chamisso, with his *Peter Schlemhl* in particular, Gogol goes much further in social satire; there is also a deliberateness of a parody in his usage of Chamisso's story.

The Romantic duality in Gogol's work goes to its extreme, denies itself; it seems that the contrasts have no more common ground to reconcile—it is either the realm of pure ideal or the earthly hell. But in his writings after 1837 an important change can be noticed, which consists in an attempt to bring the broken unity together. Even Mayor Kovalev goes through the redemptive circumstances: the return of the nose and the identity restored holds a promise for him. Vladimir Nabokov in *Nikolai Gogol* (1944) wrote,

> in Gogol's books the real plots are behind the obvious ones.... His stories only mimic stories with plots. It is like a rare moth that departs from a moth-like appearance to mimic the superficial pattern of a structurally quite different thing—some popular butterfly. (152)

The theme that appears under the submotif of "annunciation" in the idyllic settings of *Rome* and the reverse reality of *The Nose* can be associated *only* by their formal features, especially by the *spatial disintegration restored*. Spatiality is the mode of Gogol's imaginative world. Time tends to spring forth, like a figurine of the music box, only to come back to the original position, as in a story of the *overcoat*, the *nose*, and so on. The same material of substantial importance, like the notion of "emptiness," may become "everything" or "nothing," positive or negative infinitude. The empty space was essential in Raphael—the habitation of the unspoken, of the spirit. The empty space has always been functional in the antireality of Gogol's creations. The notion of emptiness gives a spatial freedom to the substance of art—to the imagery. Gogol creates through the synthetic language and creates the new language; he transcends through the word. His style cannot be imitated. Vassily Rosanov, the Russian philosopher, in his *essay Genius of Form*, compared Gogol to "the sun in a drop of water" (236), writing that the sun "was his genius, incomparable, magnificent" (236).

Annunziata and the *Arabesques*

The impressions he received from Rome formed a core for Gogol's new work—a novel, or novella, titled *Annunziata* after the name of its heroine, an Italian beauty and a symbol of Italian art. A fragment of it survived under the title of *Rome*, which was included in the second revised edition of the *Arabesques* for the third volume of the collection of Gogol's writings. The first edition of the *Arabesques* (1835) consisted of three Petersburg novellas and a number of essays on history and the arts from different time related to the author's subject. The second edition (1842) included four more stories (*Rome, The Nose, The Overcoat,* and *The Carriage*) written during Gogol's European sojourn: the outline of the book also changed, the novellas becoming more integrated and linked to each other by common themes, symbols, and imagery. The geometrical form of the "arabesque," born in the oriental decorative panels repeating the symbolic pattern and by that expanding the infinite original heavenly design, played a similar role in Gogol's book. He inserted the recurring themes inside and outside the stories in multifold dreams or repetitive images. According to I. A. Vinogradov, the second edition brought the "Petersburg" theme into a universal context, "an inseparable part of Gogol's reflection on the world and national history" (212). He points out the cyclic composition of the volume,[1] beginning with the *Nevsky Prospect* and concluding with *Rome*, which polarizes the two imperial cities—St. Petersburg and Rome, North and South, present and past, actual and ideal.

Negative reality clashes with romantic subjectivity in the works of the Petersburg cycle: the demonic force unleashes through impossible events in some sort of a trial. *The Nevsky Prospect* opens up with the theme of the feminine divine ideal lost: the timid artist Piskarev, who bears "in his soul sparks of feeling ready on the right occasion to burst into flame" (253) follows a beauty he met by chance in a leisurely crowd at Nevsky Prospect. He finds out that she is a courtesan, and his broken fantasy cannot be restored; Gogol describes a series of the artist's dreams recapturing the ideal, a series of his attempts to solve the mystery, ending in a suicide. The hero's story doubles—as it always happens in the misty, unreal Petersburg of Gogol, a city of shadows—with Piskarev's partner who is engaged in a parallel pursuit of a young German woman, the wife of a tinsmith. The light-haired beauty brings the officer to the German quarters of the city, which ends in a tedious parody of German romanticism. The tinsmith Schiller, the cobbler Hoffmann, and their drinking companion Kuntz (*Art*) are literally engaged in a fight that throws the lover out of the house to the city street. The parody is, at the same time, a sad grimace that might have thrived from the author's awareness of the mutiny of "poshlust,"[2] or mediocrity, where greatness can be transgressed, where the poet Schiller can turn into a tinsmith. This novella is unusually packed with female personages: they sit in crowded rooms and appear on the stairways, so that the protagonist, artist Piskarev, has difficulty finding the sparkle of his ideal in this endless puzzle of women. Michael Vaiskopf in his book *Gogol's Plots* indicates that the plot of the search for the feminine ideal in this story is reminiscent of the Sophia principle of the older Gnostics, with the female descending from the divine into an earthly condition, but with the hope for her future redemption.[3] Like sparkles of light, the Sophia nature is scattered in the world, and the artist's search takes him to the corners of the vicious, low life and spiritual and mundane danger.

In the beginning of the story both friends go after two different women, a light blonde and a dark-haired beauty; the latter reminds the artist of an incarnated ideal from the Italian Renaissance world, "a perfect Perugino Bianca" (251) (the Adoration of the Magi, Oratory of Santa Maria del Bianchi, Cittià della Pieve, 1504). In the painting of Perugino, the worship of Virgin Mary by a crowd of people, stretching all around from a distance away, becomes an antithesis to the vision of a beautiful woman, a stranger lost in the crowded chaos, that appears in the *Nevsky Prospect*, where only the artist singles out the beautiful face. This episode establishes a concealed link to the adoration of the feminine soul of Rome that opens the last, Italian novella of the *Arabesques*. Not only the *Nevsky Prospect*, but other stories in the *Arabesques* (especially *The Portrait*), allude to the feminine ideal as it can be found in the cradle of art, Italy of the Renaissance times.

The *Annunziata* story (*Rome*), written possibly by 1839, was published for the first time against Gogol's will by the Russian editor

Michael Pogodin in the third issue of the conservative *Moskovite* Journal (1842). This fragment describes one day in the life of the city at the time of the carnival through the eyes of the protagonist, an Italian Count who comes to Rome after several years of study in Paris. Fascinated with the beauty of Annunziata, the young man would like to meet her; he arranges a follow-up meeting with a local servant named Peppo, but it never happens since, at the panoramic sight of Rome other thoughts come to the protagonist, transcending what he is seeing, so that the hero suddenly changes his mind, declining a search for a beauty. As a counterstory to *Nevsky Prospect*, *Rome* reduces the theme of "following beauty," which has lost it significance at the revelation of the ideal, by the appearance of Annunziata.

The protagonist's short biography, which reminds one vaguely of Stendhal's Fabrizio in the *Chartreuse de Parme* (1839), is described by Gogol in a lively, condensed, and emotional manner. The collection of G. Danilevsky has a copy of the *Chartreuse de Parme* that belonged to Gogol, so it can be assumed that he knew the novel, but mostly the influence of Stendhal came from *Histoire de la Peinture en Italie* (1817), and *Rome, Naples et Florence* (1826), which was extremely popular with the Romantics. Stendhal and Gogol were staying in Italy during the same period in the '30s and both shared a fascination with the plastic forms and sensuousness of Italian art and a discontent with those who saw Paris as the symbol of the contemporary city rather than Rome, the "eternal city." In Stendhal's essay *On Love* (*De L' Amour*, 1822), the birth of love on the map of its "crystallization" is illustrated in the French "gallant" tradition as a route from a carefree Bologna across the Apennines to Rome, the latter being an emblem of "perfect love," which obviously originated in a stereotyped palindrome ROME—AMOR. Amorous sensation was characteristic of Nikolai Gogol's affection toward Italy; as he wrote to his friend, the poet V. A. Zhukovsky, upon leaving Switzerland and anticipating Rome on October 30, 1837:

> If you knew with what joy I abandoned Switzerland and flew to my dear soul, *my beauty—Italy. She is mine*! No one in the world will take her from me! (*Letters* 72)

With an overwhelming exaltation he pictures a symbolic, feminine image of Italy in the opening page of *Rome* in a portrait of Annunziata as she is seen by the count. She appears at a glare of lightning with tremor and a "flood of sparkle" in her black eyes (166)[4]—a vision of an antique Goddess, a Juno or a Diana. Her momentary manifestation is immediately cast in Paros marble by some invisible hand. Now she is a statue, by a turn of her snowy face coming to life, rotating to show the perfection of her lines "from shoulders to the antique breathing leg" (166). Now she is a picture, and as she strolls to the fountain with a jug on her head, she engenders the picture wherever she goes—to the galleries under the trees or to the square with the singing silver fountains.

Such is the Allegory of Art in its historic revelation to mankind—first *sculpture* of the old classical times, when religion was based on "the god-like beauty of women" (*Hanz* 25), then *painting* with its mysterious embrace that "crashes through the frontiers of the sensitive world" (*Hanz* 26), and finally *music* that turns people to God. Annunziata reveals herself in direct, step-by-step accordance with Nikolai Gogol's description of the three sister Muses from his short essay on "Sculpture, Painting and Music" in the *Arabesques,* except for the allegory of music, which Gogol endows with a subjective Romantic meaning.[5] Based on Herder's aesthetics, he describes the features of classical sculpture in the land of the "gracious mythology" as (1) *capturing a momentary phenomenon,* that reminds a woman looking in a glass, in Annunziata suggested by the turning of the figure; (2) *white, milky surface,* as Venus born of sea-foam, "comfort and voluptuousness"; (3) expressing *rapid movements*—Annunziata is like a "supple panther"; and (4) spirituality "swallowed by *sensuality.*" As the author proceeds to painting, he emphasizes the role of this form of art in the expansion of the sphere of beautiful that crosses the borders of the "worldly phenomena." Later, Annunziata dressed in royal purple, steps down into the crowd, changing the surroundings by her mere presence—the atmosphere of the countryside, the distant landscape, the arrangement of the city crowd; everything harmonizes in an all-embracing picture. In painting, and art is not just a matter of form, says Gogol, "the spiritual involuntarily permeates everything" (*Hanz* 27) in what he describes as an "embrace": "Nor does she *embrace* mankind alone—her limits are wider: she *embraces* the entire world; all things of beauty which surround Man are in her power" (*Hanz* 27; italics mine).

An animated setting only highlights the beauty's reign; the sounds of the fountain, the voices of the townswomen, and the brass of her own voice (brass has the sun quality) add the musical atmosphere to the scene. Joining a celebration in the "dark woody gallery," which stretches from Albano to Castel Gandolfo, relocates Annunziata into a series of brightly colored genre paintings of the Italian school; into a perspective of the painting itself. It corresponds, too, with the imaginative reasoning of the essay: "There flash, as in a cloudy mist, long galleries, where from the ancient gilt frames you are displayed as alive but darkened by the passage of inexorable time" (*Hanz* 26).

A passing procession of the costumed young men, the women in white headbands sitting on donkeys with half-closed eyes, a presence of an occasional bystander, an Englishman in a spotted mackintosh—all are displayed in the interplay of shadow and light, which are signs of temporality. From the darkened deepness of the gallery Annunziata comes into view "all shining, all in glitter" (167)—the passage of time only attenuates the presence of the ideal. Nikolai Gogol's aesthetics is centered around an impact of beauty on the soul of an observer. S. Shambinago, a scholar of the old Russian school, and author of the book *The Trilogy of Romanticism (N. V. Gogol)*, directly stated that "Gogol considered his creations the pictures, and himself—a painter"(45),[6] though the book holds the concept of the influence of the Spanish painter Francisco Goya on Gogol's style. The entire idea of ultimate communicativeness of the ideal, penetration of the content of beautiful, its restorative quality, conveys a Romantic attribute to the overall traditional three-part European art form division of Gogol's aesthetics. In the opening passage of *Rome*, the author accentuates the eyes of Annunziata (Gogol uses the poetic Russian word "ochi"), when he writes that she glances "eyes into eyes," and that her radiant face is a "wonderful celebration [that] soars off her face to everybody" (167). If this is a Sophia manifestation, it is the aspect of light and creativity that is engaged in a shining prolonged scene. The fiery glance inspires an artist with a "Van Dyke beard" (possible prototype—a painter Alexander Ivanov) to stay longer than anybody at her sight; elevates an enthusiast; but only love can admit this ultimate "celebration." This need of an "irresistible" response is being answered by the young count, a Byronic type, who keeps watching her every "word, movement and the movement of her thought"(167), who "is bringing in his black eyes" (167) as if in a holy sacrifice.

At this point the passage ends, giving way to a story of the young man's life. There is a certain incongruity in the shift of the plot, when a totally visionary scene, a large-scale allegory, develops into a disconnected from it chapter of a nineteenth-century *Bildungsroman*. Andrei Bely, in his work *Gogol's Artistry* (1934), separates Gogol's "linear style" from a "painterly" style. The story of the young count's childhood and youth, his life in Paris, is written in the linear style, while both visions—of the beginning (Annunziata) and the end (Rome)—are made in the painterly one. The image of Annunziata is wrapped in so many layers of allegory, symbolism, abounding connotations, visual effects, and verbal virtuosity that she breaks out of the context. She is a Corinne's chant, a "portrait" of transformative power, opposed to the demonic portrayal of a mysterious stranger in Gogol's novella *The Portrait*, one of the "Petersburg" cycle. It tells a story of a painter by the name of Chartkov who fell under the spell of the satanic eyes from the picture he bought at an auction, successfully acquired fame and money through this pact with the Devil, and eventually lost his creativity and became a hater of art, buying masterpieces just for the pleasure of destroying them. Gogol makes clear that the work of art is neither an imitation, nor a style; the source of creativity is in the utmost communicability of the ideal (as the demon has the power of transmission). The fashionable artist's commercialization is perceived by Nikolai Gogol not as a mere transgression, but as a complete fall. Gogol's ideal is absolute: "As creation is higher than destruction;...so is a lofty artistic creation higher than anything that exists in the world" (391). By the end of the story, a redemptive act is carried out by the original painter of the horrifying "eyes," who, after years of monastic life, accomplishes the *Nativity* icon. *Rome* balances in the *Arabesques* the diabolic theme of the disintegration of an artist by portraying the sublime "eyes," the "fire" of inspiration. In Gogol's early work the *Woman* (1830), a fictionalized treatise on aesthetics, the monologue of a philosopher Plato expounds the thoughts on women to a young student Telecles, betrayed by his beloved Alcinoe. In an explication of the art of painting in platonic terms, there is a peculiar conception of the feminine: "While a painting is still incorporeal and is still being created, turning about in the head of the artist—that is woman; when it turns into matter and becomes tangible—that is man" (*Hanz* 97).

The inversion that Gogol uses here can be recognized in Dante's *Purgatorio* and *Paradiso*, where a woman inspires the poet, also everywhere, according to Daniel Andreev, "in the spheres of ultimate creativity"(262).[7] That is why the famous Gogol's "lyrical digressions" in the *Dead Souls* convey such unimaginable beauty, and are the expressions of this mystery, breaking out of this world to indescribable spheres. The eye imagery connects Gogol's destiny to the feminine soul of Russia: "Russia! What do you want from me? What is that unattainable and mysterious bond between us? Why do you gaze on me so? And why has everything about you turned eyes of great expectation upon me?" (239).

In the novel this type of inner connectedness has no root in the direct narrative as well; the space (vast lands of Russia, endless roads)[8] and movement store the archetype, connect to metahistory. It is the third type of time relation—not linear, not cyclic, but a movement "above," or out of this world, on the "high road." Time or timelessness, elusiveness of contemporary civilization or inheritance of great art and culture—the young man in *Rome* has to make his choice. The dilemma he faces is given through the experience of the two cities— Paris and Rome.

Paris and Rome

Paris strikes him with the atmosphere of novelty and lightness, the first sight pleasing and quieting. The "fluttering sounds" of the language itself, their "sliding rustle," seemed to him elevated, free of the "convulsive movements" characteristic of the Southern nations (170). Women were of the same fluttering type, aerial creatures, "with the fire in their eyes, and the light, almost unpronounced speech" (170). They inhabited the lucid windows of the shops, "as if the austere appearance of a man would have been improper," as a "dark spot behind the solid glass" (170). This is not an angelic lightness, but its substitute, a condition of displacement, of cultural deracination. Instead of the "dark woody galleries" in Rome covering a colorful crowd of any age and any province, in Paris he comes across the covered street crossings with their glass ceilings that let the glitter of the street lights fall through on the multitude of mostly young people. The "clear transparent lower floors of the buildings, made completely of plate glass" (170) were reversing visually the earthly order, where the heavy stone part of the house is supposed to be a base to a lighter construction, that of glass. In the world of Gogol, with its mythological and folklore dualities of up and down, earth and heaven, such inversions in the status of things play a great role. Reversing the natural order is something "devilish" and is always the influence of the negative forces. The eerie night scene, when "all that magical mound" of a city is flared up in a "magical gas light," triggers Gogol's specific spatial imagery, emptying of the inner space, a false disclosure:

> all buildings became transparent, shining fiercely from beneath; the windows and the glass of the shops, it seemed, disappeared, vanished altogether, and everything that was laid inside them, was staying in the middle of the street, unguarded, sparkling and reflected by the mirrors in a deepening of the room. (171)

Although the young count exclaims, *"Ma quest'? una cosa divina!"* he cannot stop yawning at all the exciting scenes of the city life. Gogol in his extended description of the everyday routine of his hero—from a morning cup of thick coffee with the reading of colossal magazines to the night performances—uses a persistent anaphora, "he was yawrning." The count "was yawning" at the sight of all kinds of shop windows—with the elf-like salesgirls, chocolate machines, and gastronomic curiosities. He was yawning in front of the book display, where like the "spiders, darkening on the elephant paper" (172), were seen the bold black vignettes, "thrown in the heat of a moment," with strange hieroglyphic letters. The "spider" simile estranges the object, the book acquires an unusual shape, and its content is omitted—spiders mostly dwell in the abandoned corners. Nikolai Gogol's "gothic story" animation adds to the picture of the emptiness of the city, or, rather, "emptying" of it by the author.

Earlier, in a description of the count's first impression of Paris, he was stunned by the chaotic swirl of its features, its architectural disarray, and the "endless mixed crowd of golden letters climbing upon the walls, windows, on the roofs and even on the pipes" (170). The golden spider invasion of the huge letters, trying to take over the silent areas—intrusive but meaningless—points to the character of a contemporary city as a nonreadable space. In a way, it is a noncommutative space, too, despite the everyday "maelstrom throwing sparkles of news, enlightenment, fashion, exquisite taste, petty but strong laws, from which even their opponents cannot be torn away" (170).

Apart from the thin, contracted Italian newspapers, still thriving on political anecdotes almost "from the times of Thermopiles and the Persian king Darius," the French journals, volumes of massive reading, were piling dispute upon dispute. Each hardly noticeable move and action of the ministries was growing into a movement at a great scale, threatening world calamities and even revolutions. When the young count leaves his literary seclusion in the morning, only Paris can efface the overdose of information out of his memory. After this heavy reading, all the "glimmer fluttering around, and dotted movement" (171) of the city looked like some "delicate flowers, running up the edge of the abyss" (171–72). Lightness prevails altogether; anything sober, heavy, earthy is subdued, and the heavier is the resistance, the quicker is the escape: "In one instant he would resettle into the street, all of him" (172) to be taken by the passing wave of idle walking. Daily contrasts of "carefree gaping and restless awakening, an easy eye work and a hard brain work" (173) do not allow a busy city dweller a chance for a balanced personal development, or, at least for an hour of "practical living." The influence of "bookish, typographically subsisted politics" (174) upon a man turns one into a phantom in this "empire of words instead of deeds" (174).

The city literally creates psychological "gaps" that might obscure individual talent, integrity, or understanding. In contemporary metropolis, New York or Chicago, the word *GAP* made its way to the heart of the public areas—accidental letters, of their own wish, had shaped an urban symbol. Lack of continuity defines the city, which displays "disordered roofs," a "density of chimneys," "non-architectural masses of buildings pulled together, plastered with the crowded scraps of the storefronts," and the "ugliness of the bare split side walls" (170). Strange impression, created by the sight of "bare side walls" in-between the blocks of high rising buildings: it results in a familiar feeling of a "gap," or a spatial discord. The protagonist cannot "collect himself" as he walks along the streets that are "peppered with all kind of people," "crisscrossed by the omnibus' tracks" (170). Everything is grotesquely multiplied in a swift progression—"an amassment of diligences," "millions" of theater posters.

Gogol draws an expressionistic picture of the modern city in its daily dynamic performance, fleeing masquerade, and deceptive variety of forms and activities. In this respect he goes beyond his time, differs from his contemporaries, and captures the attention of the European modernists of the early twentieth century, like Franz Kafka or Andrei Bely (*Petersburg*). His technique, based on exploration of the phenomenon of "emptiness," connected to the idea of the disintegration of the human self and the human environment, is more innovative than his variations on the classical ideal. A historic Paris or Petersburg has always had much to offer to any devotee of art and architecture and has always possessed mysterious features inspiring the poets. Nikolai Gogol deliberately or spontaneously abstracted himself from their exterior appeal, as a subjective artist and a romantic. When Hegel mentioned in his *Lectures on Aesthetics* (1835) that "the material of Romantic art...is extremely limited" (6), he meant internalization of the literary purpose and device, which implies that nature in its "divine attributes..., as well as the universal process of nature" has all lost its "value with respect to the representation and content of the Absolute" (6). The city, with all its topography, landmarks, body, and style began to lose its tangible forms in Romantic representation. In that case, why is the description of Rome's contrast to Paris in Gogol's novella so tangible, so corporeal? What is *roma*ntic in his Rome? In Gogol's view, Rome evokes every feature of the classical ideal, nature with its "divine attributes," untouched by the course of time. But as a thing from the past, it is also limited in its material, to a certain extent; therefore, Gogol's romantic effort toward representation of Rome requires a magical spell to bring spirits back to life. Andre Bely, a Russian symbolist, in the best investigation of the language of Gogol, pointed in *Rome* to the recurring usage of the words "shining," 'brilliance," and "sparkle," and other words referring to the imagery of "light": "All of *Rome* is made of the superlative degree of empty categories of light, flame, magnificence, luxury, and unconveyable solemnities" (256).

The aspect of light and flame is not an "empty" category, though it can be used, as in some Paris scenes, to the effect of emptying the content. It is an attribute of creation, of revealing itself intelligence—*gnosis*. A seemingly intrusive repetition of endless epithets and metaphors of light in the text's graphic display creates a radiant, living, and eloquent picture in the mind of a reader—in the manner of the impressionist painting when the whole impression is shaped of the intermingling short strokes of paint. Light in a subdued cityscape of Paris surfaces the entire picture: it has a "glimmering," "sparkling," "glistening" quality, more often a reflection than a substance. Numerous mirrors, glass windows, and polished surfaces reproduce its seductive shine. It is mostly used for the interiors, and at nighttime it enhances the transparency of things. In the spin of the city, light can break into the sky like the fountain of sparkles (170), but only twice Gogol uses the "fire" aspect of it—the "fiery answer" (170) in the eyes of women and the threat of revolution that might "blaze up" any moment (171). In a depiction of Rome nothing shrouds the shine of light: it is "flooding." The epithets sound stronger, changing into "blazing," "fiery," and "sparkling." The young hero's eyes are the "throwers of fire," and Annunziata is "a woman—lightning" with a "sparkling laugh."

On his return to Rome the count meets Annunziata in the midst of carnival, when the attention of the procession switches to a celebration of the "dead poet," as somebody walks forward, carrying a giant puppet with a "tailed" sonnet (*sonetto, colla, coda*) attached in the shape of a kite (possibly an allusion to Francesco Berni, the Italian poet).[9] Annunziata (here the *Aphrodite Pandemos*) appears between the dead poet and the living one (it is hard to believe that the count's vocation is not poetry) to inspire the latter. At this culmination of the story, she displays her ultimate power of the goddess—"she is the sun," the total beauty. "Everything that was scattered and is glistening singly in the beauties of the world, here all that came together" (191); her shine "blinded" the spectator. In totality of expression, Gogol makes the crowd to "convert into One artist" (191). As an "initiation" into the carnival, at some moment the count is accidentally powdered with the white flour, and, thus, "white as snow, even his eyelashes white" (192), he runs back to his room. This is very probably an allusion to Psalms 51:7, "wash me, and I will be whiter than snow," which is referring to King David's adultery with Bathsheba, thus bringing into the scene of the adoration of Annunziata a new meaning of personal guilt and the need for repentance. This possible guilt could be for the idolization of Beauty—something that Gogol seemed to repent in his years of religious conversion. In this scene Annunziata feels "embarrassed" for a moment and does not meet the count's eyes.

Gogol's formalistic experiment is almost nonhuman in his efforts to create a portrait of the city using image, word, sound, color, line, and movement. Both the Paris and Rome of Gogol are not the cities of a travelogue or a diary, not a mere setting for a story; they have their own expression, aura, and "intention." There is something "above" these cities—their historical predestination, their formative presence, and their collective consciousness. Madam de Staël wrote on Rome: "The city has still spells, into which we require initiations. It is not simply an assemblage of dwelling, it is a chronicle of the world, represented by figurative emblems" (20).

Paris—a European capital of new times—and Rome—the center of the old Europe. Gogol measures up to their capacity to be an emblem of the "whole." Not quite a new Babylon versus Jerusalem, not quite a "reality" versus "utopia"; they represent two poles of cultural composition, metaphysics of the whole. Gogol's famous palindrome of the word *Rome* in Russian orthographic from *РИМ* to *МИР* (*Rome* to *World*) illustrates it better than anything. Scholars find that Gogol uses the similar paradigm of the "city-world" in the title of his second collection of stories, *Mirgorod*, which plays on the Russian word *gorod*—"a town or a city" (Vyrolajnen).

In Gogol's subjective narrative the time pattern of the cities does not follow the stereotypic antithesis of the linear/cyclic; fragmentation of lifestyle in Paris obliterates the direction, and the time "lapses." Gogol writes ironically about living in the heart of Europe, where, simply walking, "you are rising higher, you feel yourself the member of a great world association" (173–74)! In so-called venues of intellectual life the count found only novelty instead—"everywhere bright episodes, and no solemn, magnificent flow of the whole" (174–75); the entire nation is "a shining vignette, and not a picture of a great master" (175). Despite the brilliant diversity of the European "progress," there is no progress in count's inner development. After four years in Paris, the hero feels emptiness and boredom; he makes a decision to escape to Italy.

The first "beautiful station" on his way to Rome was Genoa, the "first kiss of Italy," where he prayed for the first time—"prayed that Italy had accepted him..., that he had joy in his soul, and that this prayer, apparently, was the best" (177). As on the route of love, described by Stendhal, he crossed the Apennines in the same blissful state of mind and arrived in Rome. He settled down in the ancient estate of his ancestors, cut every tie to a local society, became a foreigner in his own land, and began finally *seeing* the city. "Not like a foreigner devoted only to Titus Livius and Tacitus..., no, he found all equally beautiful" (179): the ancient, the middle, and the new world. In the manner remarkable to Gogol's searching eye, the "non-glistening" city starts "moving forward" out of the maze of dark and narrow side streets. With the awakening of the soul, the stone masses come to life: the ruins, "stirring from under the dark architrave"; "a quivering market"; a fountain, "splashing the water upon itself." He loved the fusion of the old and the new, "those features of a peopled capital and a desert together" (180). The "cyclic" time of Rome, as a favorable climate, advances the young count's personal growth and the development of his artistic taste; it also launches his religious quest. Any change in him happens in a nonforced way, spontaneously, generated by closeness of the inimitable and innumerable masterpieces. He compares the "contemptible luxury" of the modern Europe to the architectural creations of Bramante, Borromini, Sangallo, and the galleries opening the power brush of Raphael and Michelangelo. He thought that the commercial world had to pay the price for abandoning the Beauty to pessimistic, cold, mercantile speculations, for an early bluntness of feelings: "The icons were taken out of the shrine, and the shrine is not a shrine: a dwelling of bats and evil spirits" (181).

The count explores the city in a circular (secular) manner, cycle by cycle, layer by layer—its antiquities, nature, history and chronicles, the people and customs, to reach the "wholeness" of understanding and sensation, to reach the meaning of what is called the "eternal Rome." His search is for the *immortality* wrapped in the eternal sleep of the city, traced in the "burials of antiquities," in the masterpieces of art. He carefully observes the advantages of this "drowning in time" in a friendly and generous disposition of the citizens, absence of despair in the eyes, undying aesthetic feeling, as if everything, including their religion, stayed for the only purpose—so that "in the quiet would be preserved its proud humandom" (189). This state of immortality is sustained by the "religion of the heart" and "religion of beauty" more than by any clerical guidance. In the light of this devotion, almost everything in Rome can easily be turned into a "shrine": even the food keeper's shop at the marketplace—the *Sorochinskaya Fair*—rebuilds itself into a classic cathedral, while still shining with naïve folk decorations, as on Easter Day in a Ukrainian Church. Gogol in the complex architectonics of his narrative selects three points holding the picture together: (1) a view from the "Vatican window," (2) a view on the fields from Roman Campagna, and (3) the panorama from the heights of Janiculum. Each epitomizes correspondingly history, nature, and the creation of a "total city." The emotional center, or heart of the Roman walks is put on view in the verbal landscape that fascinates the count in Roman Campania—the fields of blooming "golden" yellow flowers intermixed with the wild red poppies, in the splendor of their color reviving the picture of the spring steppe in Ukraine. They "end by Rome himself," merging nature and the city as if they grew together due to the fantasy of their creator. He describes a structural landscape, with the view open to the four cardinal points, each a picture of its own. He finds himself literally in the "heart" of Rome—perhaps, in the "heart" of the world—standing in the golden-red flowers, which are also the center of a four-sided natural cross. As the city is unfolding itself, it embraces more and more "worlds" of the nostalgic author's self—the naturalness and southern splendor of Ukraine, the endlessness of Russia, the majesty of St. Petersburg. Above the "seven hills" one can sense a projection of Russia as a "New Jerusalem." Later Nikolai Gogol writes to a friend, as recorded in the *Selected Passages from Correspondence with Friends*, that the "will of God [was] shown in the choice of the family of Romanov" (59). The palindrome hidden in name of *Romanov*—"Roma Nuova," the new Rome, alludes to the prophetic Orthodox concept of the "three Romes," Russia being the last of them.

Rome is so far free of the theological and political overtones that will occupy Gogol through the 1840s. It is a love song to the world, his personal "vita nuova" rather than "Roma nuova,"—an attempt to reconcile the discord, to stretch the soul, to touch the heavens. In stages, the narrator identifies with the protagonist, and the story of Gogol's "soul journey" in exile receives a detailed inner account. The center of this novella is the search for the artist's identity, probably misplaced in exile and confused by the European experience. There are two difficult points in this quest: first, the relation to the absolute ideal that the contemporary world identifies with the past (the Feminine Divine of the Italian Renaissance); second, identification with his own land that Europe perceives as archaic and dormant.

This crisis is shared by both an author and the protagonist that correlate with the common Destiny of their native land. With his characteristic high amplitude of emotion, the narrator of *Rome* is torn between the picture of "the end of times" and a revolt of feeling anticipating future liberation. The picture of "emptiness" in place if Italy loses its greatness he expresses in the images of the "dried out river," "shallowness," a "beautifully dying Venice" with her "charred eyes," a "speechless Ferrara." Only music, in his opinion, remains to continue the great tradition, which spreads around the world in its "wailing sounds." The third Muse of the three finally arrives in the text of *Rome*, to complete the cycle of art.

Gogol was interested in the present life of Italy no less than in the history and antiquities. He discovered the flavor of the Italian satire in the dialectal poetry of the nineteenth century, the artistic value of the *commedia dell'arte* for the contemporary literature and theater. Under the disguise of his Roman adventures and the strangeness of a foreign land, Nikolai Gogol was able, in a situation of a terrible repression of thought under Nikolai I, to express his innermost concern about the situation in Russia, his despair and his hopes.

The Feminine Principle is embodied in the image of Annunziata. She appears three times to the hero, the last time at the carnival in

Corso, where she shows the sign of her closeness to the crowd, to the people of Rome. She is changing along with the young man's growing awareness of her, getting more spiritualized; she leaves the pedestal, her meaning is sacred. She appears at the time of the evening mass, at *Ave Maria*. The allegory of music is written into this scene, though in the low plane of the narrative—musicians with a huge masquerade violin cross the way in front of her passage, as the count tries to approach Annunziata. The count makes an appeal for bringing the ideal, the worship of beauty into the world. He makes an allusion to Mark 4:26, comparing Annunziata to a lamp that should not be hidden:

> Will the architect build the temple in a narrow side street?...Was the lamp lighted, as the heavenly teacher said, just to conceal it and put it under the table? No, the lamp was lighted so that it could stand on the table, so that everybody could see it. (193)

Gogol launched the search for the transformative power of the Feminine Ideal in Russian literature, "lighted the lamp" and made the longing for the Divine Feminine a major attribute of the Russian psyche—something that would recur in the poetry of Alexander Blok, the writings of Dostoevsky, and the philosophy of V. Solovyev and A. Rosanov.

This ideal is unattainable; therefore, in the last scene of *Rome* any attempts by the count to meet Annunziata are vain, and, though he arranges for a meeting with the help of a servant by the name of Beppo, he has to break away with his dream. The name *Beppo* alludes to the name of the satirical poet Giovanni Belli, Gogol's friend, who introduced him to the carnival culture of Italy. The depiction of carnival in Corso makes a strong argument in the Romantic dispute of Gogol's art. The emotional, subjective, allegorical texture of his writing is especially apparent when compared to Charles Dickens's realistic and, in its own way, beautiful travelogue, *Pictures from Italy* (1846). Charles Dickens visited Rome in 1844 and wrote his impressions just three years after Gogol's *Rome* came out of print. To continue the literary references, Gogol's text also contains a hidden allusion to Byron's poem *Beppo* (1817), with a crisscross theme of the carnival (Venetian in Byron) and an abrupt, "open" ending. Considering that Byron was an idol of the Russian Romantics, it is quite possible that Gogol used the abrupt plot in deference to Byron's poem:

> My pen is at the bottom of a page,
> Which being finish'd, here the story end.
> 'Tis to be wish'd it had been sooner done,
> But stories somehow lengthen when begun. (*Beppo* XCIX, 5–6)

Coming back to the story of the young Romantic hero, the arrangement to see Annunziata is interrupted by the count's sudden change of mind at the sight of the Roman panorama from the heights of Janiculum. The exciting panorama spreads before him, like a wonderful musical orchestration, and for the first time he perceives the city in its "wholeness." In an instant vision of the Eternal City, the hero puts behind him the bohemian life of Paris, the expectation of an amorous acquaintance, and the carnival clamor. He reaches the ultimate focus of his artistic vision that goes beyond the visible. The moment of epiphany, a sudden illumination of the hero, concludes the fragment. It is difficult to say where the hero transcends his experience, as the ambiguity of this silent scene does not give a final answer. The final passage suggests that the hero has come to terms with the world, and goes beyond, "having forgotten himself, and the beauty of Annunziata, and the mysterious destiny of his people, well, and everything that is in the world" (200).

This understanding of the grand silent finale in *Rome* changes the nature of its genre: it is no longer a "fragment," but an open-ended novella that employs the technique of "a vision," where a seemingly overcrowded exposition is balanced by a prolonged glance of the last scene.

Notes

1. Vinogradov suggests the reader view the *Arabesques* as a cycle of novellas, in the following sequence: *Nevsky Prospect—The Nose—The Portrait—The Overcoat—The Carriage—The Diary of a Madman—Rome* (213).
2. The term "poshlust" was made popular by Vladimir Nabokov. He used it in his book *Nikolai Gogol* (1944). It means, "certain false values for the detection of which no particular shrewdness is required" (64).
3. I note also the presence of Sophia symbolism in Gogol's *Arabesques* novellas.
4. All translations from *Rome* are my own as there are no published English translations. It was translated from the *Collected Works of N. V. Gogol* 166–200.
5. In Gogol's essay "Sculpture, Painting and Music," the music represents the art of the new time, and for that reason the Allegory of Art in Annunziata, being a classical figure, does not refer to music, except for the sounds of natural environment. Hearing music, according to him, is converted into "a wailing of illness, as if the only desire gripping the soul is to tear itself of one's body" (*Hanz* 28).
6. At the turn of the twentieth century, Sergei Shambinago, a scholar of the old Russian critical school, supported a very unpopular concept in Russia of the Romantic nature of Nikolai Gogol's work. V. Zenkovsky in the early twentieth century was the major supporter of the Romantic

theory. Among the contemporary scholars, I. V. Kartasheva has written about Gogol's Romantic tendencies (Карташева И. В. *Гоголь и Романтизм*. Калинин, 1978).

7. Daniel Andreev, a Russian esoteric philosopher, is the author of the famous book *The Rose of the World*, written in the 1950s and published in 1991. He wrote about a mystical and universal sense of the Eternal Feminity.
8. The image of the road in Gogol's works, its symbolic and structural importance, has been investigated deeply in Russian criticism by Y. Mann, A. Ivanitsky, and others.
9. Francesco Berni was an Italian poet-satirist of the early sixteenth century. The scene with a "dead poet" may possibly refer to him, as he was the only one of the poets in Italy to write the "tailed sonnets."

Part III

London

10

WORDSWORTH'S INVIGORATING HELL: LONDON IN BOOK 7 OF *THE PRELUDE* (1805)

Eugene Stelzig

I

We are accustomed to think of Wordsworth, to cite the opening of Percy Shelley's sonnet dedicated to him, as the "Poet of Nature," one to whom, as Wordsworth recalls in *The Prelude,* "The earth / And common face of Nature spake…/ Rememberable things" (1: 614–16).[1] The poet who spent his childhood and adolescence amidst the beautiful scenery of the English Lake District returned at the age of thirty to settle there permanently (in Grasmere) at the end of 1800. Wordsworth, however, is also the occasional poet of the city, and, as Nicola Trott reminds us, "the man who is popularly regarded as an unbudgeable Grasmere fixture…spends a surprising amount of time away from home. The confirmed ruralist is also an avid metropolitan, making regular sorties to London throughout his life," visiting it for the last time in 1847, three years before his death (15).

Although Wordsworth the "avid metropolitan" enjoyed his visits to London, seeing friends like Charles Lamb and Henry Crabb Robinson who lived there, the *poet* Wordsworth tends to script the city according to the Romantic valorizing of the rural over the urban. Thus in *Michael* (1800), Luke, sent away to work for a relative to earn the money to pay off a loan, "in the dissolute city gave himself / To evil courses: ignominy and shame / Fell on him, so that he was driven at last / To seek a hiding-place beyond he seas" (453–56). The "city" here is not even minimally described, but it is signaled as the place of the fall from a prelapsarian pastoral state—although one admittedly threatened by modern economic forces (the loan Michael had cosigned, and whose forfeiture threatens him with the loss of his land). When Wordsworth does describe the city in positive terms—most famously so in the "Composed Upon Westminster Bridge, September 3, 1802" sonnet—the radiant beauty the poet beholds is of the city at its *most* natural and *least* city-like moment: in the early morning, when "the very houses are asleep; / And all that mighty heart is lying still" (13–14). In what amounts to a visionary "spot of time," the poet experiences a revelation of the dormant city in a state of suspended animation:

> Dull would he be of soul who could pass by
> A sight so touching in its majesty:
> The City now doth like a garment wear
> The beauty of the morning; silent, bare,
> Ships, towers, domes, theatres, and temples lie
> Open unto the fields, and to the sky;
> All bright and glittering in the smokeless air. (2–8)

The romantic metaphor of the city's "beauty" as a "garment" also suggests concealment, though what the routine or daily appearance of a London stripped of its glorious morning garb might be is not a thought the poem invites us to entertain. However, it is one he will elaborate in considerable detail in his autobiography in blank verse, *The Prelude*.

If the Westminster Bridge sonnet is Wordsworth's most famous short and romanticizing visual take on London, another that is just as strikingly beautiful but relatively unknown because Wordsworth left it in manuscript, is his vision of St. Paul's cathedral in the winter of 1808 (printed in Gill 332–33). As he wrote in a letter of April 8, 1808, he had left his friend Coleridge early on a Sunday morning and was walking "entirely occupied with my own thoughts, when, looking up, I saw before me the avenue of Fleet Street, silent, empty, and pure white, with a sprinkling of new-fallen snow, not a cart or Carriage to obstruct the view, no noise, only a few soundless and dusky foot passengers here and there." In the distance he sees "the huge and majestic form of St Paul's, solemnized by a thin veil of falling snow" (*Letters* 209). Staying close to this prose description, Wordsworth turned this experience into a majestic blank-verse "spot of time:"

> It chanced
> That while I thus was pacing, I raised up
> My heavy eyes and instantly beheld,

> Saw at a glance in that familiar spot
> A visionary scene—a length of street
> Laid open in its morning quietness,
> Deep, hollow, unobstructed, vacant, smooth,
> And white with winter's purest white, as fair,
> As fresh and spotless as he ever sheds
> On fields or mountains. Moving Form was none
> Save here and there a shadowy Passenger
> Slow, shadowy, silent, dusky, and beyond
> And high above this winding length of street,
> This moveless and unpeopled avenue,
> Pure, silent, solemn, beautiful, was seen
> The huge majestic Temple of St Paul
> In awful sequestration, through a veil,
> Through its own sacred veil of falling snow. ("St Paul's," 11–28)

As in the Westminster Bridge sonnet, Wordsworth here witnesses a "visionary scene" of London at its most poetic, least familiar, and city-like, and most *natural*. There is of course also a touch of the Sublime in both poems—in that "mighty heart...lying still" and the "sacred veil of falling snow"—that is a gift of "Imagination's holy power" (9) in a revelatory moment of entranced witnessing.

II

"Composed Upon Westminster Bridge" and "St Paul's" are highly romanticized impressions of London that provide a striking visual and even painterly framing of a depopulated and almost immobile city through the elements of nature. Wordsworth's most extended and detailed description of London in Book 7 of *The Prelude*, however, is in a very different register or key, one more in keeping with the negative characterization in his "Preface to *Lyrical Ballads*" (1802) of "the encreasing [sic] accumulation of men in cities, where the uniformity of their occupations produces a craving for extraordinary incident, which the rapid communication of intelligence hourly gratifies" (Gill 599). Wordsworth's portrayal of London in *Prelude* 7 is also based on an extensive experience of the city, a protracted encounter both literal and imaginative.

After taking his degree at Cambridge in January 1791, Wordsworth, at loose ends as to what to do with his life, "pitched [his] vagrant tent," as he puts it in *The Prelude*, "among / The unfenced regions of society" (7: 60–62). He spent the next four months—to continue with the geographic metaphor—in a "wide waste" (76). That "waste" was not some remote and sparsely populated location such as the wilds of North America or the depths of the Sahara (the latter figures only in the apocalyptic Arab-Quixote dream in Book 5 of *The Prelude*), but the teeming metropolis of London. Thus negatively characterized as a "waste" at the beginning of his account of his protracted stay in the capital, by the end of Book 7 London is epitomized as a monstrous site of "blank confusion...To the whole swarm of its inhabitants" save for "a Straggler here and there" (696–99). To one of these stragglers, the improvident but visionary young poet, the great city finds its demonic embodiment in St. Bartholomew Fair, held annually at Smithfield, whose luridly vivid description forms the rhetorical climax of the poet's account of his stay in London. St. Bartholomew is an unholy spectacle "that lays...The whole creative powers of man asleep" (653–55): It is "a hell / For eyes and ears," an "anarchy and din / Barbarian and infernal" (659–62). Wordsworth's antipathy to the infernal urban spectacle and his disgust with the outrageous festivities are presented with a gusto that makes the description of it a satirical tour de force.

The negative presentation of the city of London in Book 7 of *The Prelude* is part of a larger and well-known literary typecasting, Romantic *and* Modern, that scripts the city as a site of extreme alienation and even a kind of necropolis. It runs through English literature from at least the later eighteenth century—the famous "black'ning Church" and "Marriage hearse" of Blake's "London"—through the Victorian period (e.g., Dickens's novels) to the early twentieth century and T. S. Eliot's "Unreal City" in *The Waste Land* (by way of Dante and Baudelaire): "A crowd flowed over London Bridge, so many, / I had not thought death had undone so many" (ll. 60, 62–63). D. H. Lawrence in *Women in Love* (written during World War I) takes this negative characterization of London to an apocalyptic level when he has his fictional neo-Romantic and Zarathustran alter ego, Birkin, confessing to his travel companion on the train to the city, the industrial magnate Gerald Crich, "I always feel doomed when the train is running into London. I feel such despair, so hopeless, as if it were the end of the world: Don't you feel like one of the damned?...It is real death (54)." But paradoxically, this urban site of death, alienation, and despair also proves highly invigorating to the artistic imagination, because the setting of the city elicits such a powerful response—as we see, for instance, in Birkin's unconventional relations in London with the avant garde art crowd, where this unlikely school inspector demonstrates his acute aesthetic appreciation of an exotic African statuette, a woman in the physical extremity of childbearing, not as the artifact of a primitive culture but as an "art" because this "totem" is "pure culture in sensation…it is so sensual as to be final, supreme" (72).

The same kind of finality, but in a very different context and key, is also projected with the rhetorical overkill of Wordsworth's St. Barholomew finale of Book 7, in which his extended satiric and carnivalesque depiction of London shows a similar pattern of the urban site of alienation stimulating the imagination and making the writer's creative juices flow: the poet's vehement condemnation of the metropolis as a horrific spectacle of "motley imagery" and a "Babel din"(151, 157) elicits from him a powerful imaginative response that makes his impressionistic portrait of London—a composite not only of his four post-Cambridge months there, but later visits also—the most vividly descriptive book of his blank verse life narrative as well as, in the words of Ken Johnston, "one of the most exciting representations of the energy of urban life in English literature" (247). What is more, Wordsworth's vivid account of his extended stay in the capital offers up an energizing and indeed attractively *cosmopolitan* portrait of the city even within the poet's overt and self-righteous rhetoric of condemnation. Like De Quincey's illustrations of the dire consequences of opium-taking with his hallucinatory account of his nightmares ("The Pains of Opium" *Confessions of an English Opium Eater*), which make the effects of the drug sound imaginatively appealing, Wordsworth's indictment of the "hell" of London makes for a riveting and ultimately highly attractive depiction of the great metropolis whose culture and street life the young poet obviously observed with a *flaneur*'s relish. Even the satiric condemnation of the grotesque entertainments of Bartholomew fair points to this relish: to quote Johnston again, "he presents the fair's wild hodgepodge of novelties as ostensibly destructive of 'the whole creative powers of man'…but the verbal energy of his description belies his thesis" (262).

Wordsworth's suggestion that London is the infernal city is underpinned on two occasions with allusions to Milton's hell: the "thickening hubbub" (7: 227) of its streets echoes the "universal hubbub wilde" (*Paradise Lost*, 2: 951) of Chaos encountered by Satan, and the "All out-o'-th'-way, far-fetched, perverted things"(7: 688) on display at St. Bartholomew fair harks back to hell, "Where all life dies, death lives, and Nature breeds, / Perverse, all monstrous, all prodigious things, / Abominable, inutterable" (*Paradise Lost*, 2: 624–25). Yet the rising action of the poet's condemnation of the spectacle that is the city and that culminates in the St. Bartholomew set piece is countered by a sense of amazement and even wonder at the theatrical variety of the urban scenery that strikes his attentive eye as he wanders its streets. Wordsworth's highly descriptive and dramatic rendering of his impressions of London is multilayered and ambivalent. Indeed, the poet's description of London is precariously balanced between admiration and condemnation, with the former (admiration) setting the tone for the earlier sequences of the book, and the latter (condemnation) foregrounded in its later sections. Another way to characterize Wordsworth's complex ambivalence to the city is that underneath the posture of the outraged poet-prophet and the sophisticated Juvenalian satirist—among Wordsworth's Juvenilia there is an "Imitation of Juvenal"—there is also the open-mouthed and wide-eyed country boy on his first extended visit to or stay in the dazzling capital.

The stand-in for Wordsworth the Lake District boy is the "Cripple" and fellow schoolboy mentioned near the beginning of Book 7 "whom chance / Summoned from school to London—fortunate / And envied Traveller!" (95–96). For the boy Wordsworth the London of his imagination was indeed an enchanted location, as he illustrates with a finely elaborated romantic and geographic conceit:

> There was a time when whatsoe'er is feigned
> Of airy Palaces and Gardens built
> By Genii of Romance, or hath in grave
> Authentic history been set forth of Rome,
> Alcairo, Babylon, or Persepolis,
> Or given upon report by Pilgrim-Friars
> Of golden Cities ten months' journey deep
> Among Tartarean Wilds, fell short, far short,
> Of that which I in simpleness believed
> And thought of London; held me by a chain
> Less strong of wonder and obscure delight. (81–91)

The adult writing of his impressions of London combines, as it were, the simpleness of the enchanted boy dreaming of the city, and the sophistication of the disenchanted writer who has lived in the city and who vehemently condemns yet grudgingly admires its dazzling, frivolous, and ultimately corrupt exhibitions in the spheres of politics (parliamentary debates he witnessed), religion (the sermon by the young preacher), the theater (the prostitute with her child), and the teeming and variegated life of its streets.

These urban spectacles are condemned in a mounting crescendo of indignation, but also with considerable zest and bravura in a powerful series of satiric and descriptive pastiches that show Wordsworth for once as the poet of the city as much as the poet of nature—even if he uses the norm of nature or the natural as his ethical touchstone for condemning what he ultimately judges to be unnatural in the extreme.

But it is precisely the perceived unnaturalness of the city that stimulates his imagination and draws it out of its hiding places and that makes for the impressively sustained satirical rhetoric of the latter portions of his account of his "Residence in London."

Though at the outset of Book 7 Wordsworth epitomizes London as a "waste," as we have seen, once he begins to describe his lengthy, leisurely, and apparently aimless walks through its streets—his pedestrian route has been beautifully reconstructed in Ken Johnston's biography of the young Wordsworth (248–61)—what strikes him most is the sheer proliferation of the bewildering variety of life all around him, an overwhelming spectacle that fascinates him as the perambulator and observer ab extra. There is so much to take in, such an indiscriminate and accumulating mass or welter of impressions of the metropolitan beehive (my metaphor, not his), that the young poet without a job or even an agenda beyond perambulation, is willing to simply soak them in like a sponge—and the author writing about these impressions in the first half of Book 7 roughly a decade later is willing to pile on the descriptive details of the vertiginous urban scenery without passing an immediate and categorically negative judgment. It is only in the second half of Book 7 that the poet writing about his impressions has decided that the indiscriminate hodgepodge that is the bustling life of London is not only too much—but that that too much needs to be unequivocally condemned as a modern inferno. In thus finally denouncing and dismissing the city, the poet allows the moralist in him to overwhelm the admiring spectator—but that wide-eyed spectator in turn has been the precursor and indeed the precondition for the moralist and his heavy artillery.

As Wordsworth begins "copying the impression [of London] from the memory" (146), he is at once amazed, dazzled, bewildered, and exhausted by its vastness and variety:

> The endless stream of men and moving things,
> From hour to hour the illimitable walk
> Still among the streets with clouds and sky above,
> The wealth, the bustle, and the eagerness,
> The glittering Chariots with their pampered Steeds,
> Stalls, Barrows, Porters; midway in the Street
> The Scavenger, who begs with hat in hand,
> The labouring Hackney Coaches, the rash speed
> Of Coaches traveling far, whirled on with horn
> Loud blowing, and the sturdy Drayman's Team,
> Ascending from some alley along the Thames
> And striking right across the crowded Strand
> Till the fore-horse veer round with punctual skill:
> Here, there, and everywhere, a weary throng,

> The comers and goers face to face,
> Face after face...(158–73)

The specular and theatrical aspect fascinates him—

> a raree-show is here
> With Children gathered round, another Street
> Presents a company of dancing Dogs,
> Or Dromedary, with an antic pair
> Of Monkies on his back, a minstrel Band
> Of Savoyards, or, single and alone,
> An English Ballad-singer (190–196)—

as does the range of its ethnic and racial diversity, captured in a nonsatirical catalogue culminating in a line of striking chiaroscuro:

> See...
> The Italian, with his Frame of Images
> Upon his head; with Basket at his waist
> The Jew; the stately and slow-moving Turk,
> With freight of slippers piled beneath his arm.
> Briefly, we find...
> Among the crowd, conspicuous less or more
> As we proceed, all specimens of man
> Through all the colours which the sun bestows,
> And every character of form and face;
> The Swede, the Russian; from the genial South,
> The Frenchman and the Spaniard; from remote
> America, the Hunter-Indian; Moors
> Malays, Lascars, the Tartar and Chinese,
> And Negro Ladies in white muslin gowns. (228–43)

The "Spectacles / Within doors" (245–46)—the huge panorama paintings of famous European locations and the rude theatrical entertainments at "Half-rural Sadler's Wells" (289) also fascinate the poet—especially the latter (with its mixture of music and pantomime) where he "Saw Singers, Rope-dancers, Giants and Dwarfs, / Clowns, Conjurors, Posture-masters, Harlequins / Amid the uproar of the rabblement, / Perform their feats" (294–97).

His description of these crude amusements registers a naïve enjoyment until he interpolates the story of the seduction of Mary "the Maid of Buttermere" staged there and segues from that to the spectacle of the young prostitute at the theater (with the "painted bloom" of her make-up) whose beautiful infant boy, placed on the refreshment "board" at intermission, is "a sort of alien scattered from the clouds" surrounded by "dissolute men / And shameless women" (370–87). For Wordsworth, the theater is both a fascinating source of amusement *and* corruption—as it has been for moralists before him, from Augustine to Rousseau, who see in such urban spectacles, no matter how attractive and diverting, a great danger to public morality. Wordsworth frankly acknowledges his attraction to theatrical performances, "which then were my delight... / Life then was new, / The senses easily pleased; the lustres, lights / The carving and the gilding, paint and glare, / And all the mean upholstery of the place, / Wanted not animation in my sight: / Far less the living Figures on the Stage" (438–45).

The story of Mary Robinson ("the Maid of Buttermere") and "the lovely boy" (396) at the play intermission are both versions in different ways of the corruption of innocence in or by the city and thus also thematically linked with the fate of Michael's son Luke. Wordsworth's interpolation of the former refers back not to his stay in London in 1790, but to events more than a decade later when an adventurer posing as a member of Parliament married the Lake District innkeeper's beautiful daughter in October 1802 (although he was already married and had several children). The following April the story was put on the stage in London (at Sadler's Wells) "as an operatic piece in rhyme" (de Selincourt 564), *Edward and Susan or the Beauty of Buttermere*—albeit with a happy end (Mary marries a former sweetheart). For Wordsworth, however, Mary's story is tragic, a version of the archetypal "Gretchen" scenario of the seduction of an innocent young woman caught in the snares of a manipulative and worldly man (as we still see it in the mid-nineteenth century in Steerforth's elopement with and abandonment of Little Em'ly in Dickens's *David Copperfield*): "the Spoiler came, 'a bold bad Man' / To God unfaithful, Children, Wife, and Home, / And wooed the artless Daughter of the Hills, / And wedded her, in cruel mockery / of love and marriage bonds" (323–27). The intensity of Wordsworth's imaginative identification with the fate of Mary Robinson may have biographical sources too remote for my topic,[2] but it is certainly also a function of childhood innocence done in by worldly corruption:

> This memorial Verse
> Comes from the Poet's heart, and is her due.
> For we were nursed, as almost might be said,
> On the same mountains, Children at one time,
> Must haply often on the self-same day
> Have from our several dwellings gone abroad
> To gather daffodils on Coker's Stream. (340–46)

Wordsworth cannot put the story of Mary retailed on the London stage out of his mind even as he seeks to resume his narrative thread (London). The fact that he envisions her innocence restored in and by the natural setting of the Lake District reinforces the corrupt city/innocent nature binary of Book 7:

> Thy image rose again,
> Mary of Buttermere! She lives in peace
> Upon the spot where she was born and reared;
> Without contamination does she live
> In quietness, without anxiety:
> Beside the mountain-Chapel sleeps in earth
> Her new-born Infant, fearless as a lamb
> That thither comes from some unsheltered place
> To rest beneath the little rock-like Pile
> When storms are blowing. Happy are they both,
> Mother and Child! (350–60)

The living mother and the dead child are united in this idyllic setting, and the suggestion is that the child is better off dead, because its innocence is preserved. It has been saved from the corruption of the world and Luke's fate in the city.

Mary's dead child links up in Wordsworth's extended digression on the theater with the prostitute's boy, who in an act of intense imaginative identification is also envisioned in a state of eternal childhood, "as if embalmed / By Nature"—a variant of the poetic image of the dead Lucy in "Three years she grew." Wordsworth imagines the boy

> Through some special privilege,
> Stopped at the growth he had; destined to live,
> To be, to have been, come, and go, a Child
> And nothing more, no partner in the years
> That bear us forward to distress and guilt,
> Pain and abasement; beauty in such excess
> Adorned him in that miserable place.
> So have I thought of him a thousand times,
> And seldom otherwise. But perhaps,
> Mary! may now have lived till he could look
> With envy on thy nameless Babe that sleeps
> Beside the mountain Chapel undisturbed. (400–412)

The rhetorical excess of "a thousand times" signals the intensity of Wordsworth's imaginative investment in the idealized image of the child embalmed by Nature and reveals the poet in his Holden Caulfield mode, seeking to preserve the innocence of children by sealing them in that condition and keeping them, like the Catcher in the Rye, from falling into adulthood (with childhood linked with Nature, and adulthood with the city).

III

It is Wordsworth's lengthy and digressive take on the theater (281–412) and its sophisticated combination of innocent amusement, artifice, and corruption that constitutes the fulcrum or tipping point that shifts his characterization of London into a predominantly negative and denunciatory mode. This is also where he begins to take a satiric turn, "from entertainments that are such / Professedly, to others titled higher" (517–18): the parliamentary debates, with famous orators like William Pitt the Younger ("Words follow words, sense seems to follow sense; / What memory and what logic!—till the Strain / Transcendent, superhuman as it is, / Grows tedious even in a young man's ear" [540–43]), and the sermon by the vain young preacher, a "pretty Shepherd" and "comely bachelor, / Fresh from the toilette of two hours" whose affected and ostentatious preaching ("Of rapt irradiation exquisite") "Leads up and down his captivated flock" (547–66). These theatrical performances of state and church are given as specimens of the sophisticated corruption of urban culture, now condemned in a Juvenalian outburst: "Folly, vice, / Extravagance in gesture, mien, and dress, / And all the strife of singularity, / Lies to the ear, and lies to every sense— / Of these, and of the living shapes they wear / There is no end" (572–77).

Wordsworth's characterization of London is nothing if not complexly ambivalent, however, as I have argued, and before launching into his final satiric denunciation, he interpolates the famous "blind Beggar," who in the poet's imagination is inflated into an apocalyptic image of the cognitive and even metaphysical limits of human understanding, with the label the Beggar wears on his chest turned into "a type / Or emblem of the utmost that we know/ Both of ourselves and of the universe" (618–20). While the Beggar fits into the negative stereotype of London as a figure of human alienation and immiseration, "His fixed face and sightless eyes" upon which the poet looks "as if admonished from another world" (622–23) add up to an arresting moment of stark sublimity that threatens to catapult Wordsworth right out of his account of the city. As Hartman has suggested, like the famous Crossing of the Alps "spot of time" in *Prelude* 6, the Beggar "causes a quasi-apocalyptic feeling of reversal turning the mind around or into itself" and threatens Wordsworth with "the engulfing solipsism of Imagination" (242).

To force himself back from "such structures as the mind / Builds for itself," Wordsworth turns back to "full-formed" London scenes that "take, with small internal help, / Possession of the faculties" (625–28). And he also defamiliarizes and poeticizes the city by depicting it at night

> When the great tide of human life stands still,
> The business of the day to come unborn,
> Of that gone by, locked up as in a grave;
> The calmness, beauty, of the spectacle,
> Sky, stillness, moonshine, empty streets, and sounds
> Unfrequented as in deserts... (631–36)

The vision of the deserted city forms a stark contrast to the whirl and swirl of its frenetic daytime life, and if the moonlit night brings out the poetry of London in a manner similar to the Westminster Bridge sonnet and the "St. Paul's" blank verse fragment, the few stragglers and even the weather suggest a pervasive alienation as well:

> at late hours
> Of winter evenings when unwholesome rains
> Are falling hard, with people yet astir,
> The feeble salutation from the voice
> Of some unhappy Woman now and then
> [is] Heard as we pass; when no one looks about,
> Nothing is listened to. (636–42)[3]

As a powerful satirical and dramatic foil to the city deserted, the "annual Festival" of St. Bartholomew is presented as an instance of "times when half the city shall break out / Full of one passion, vengeance, rage or fear" replete with "Mobs, riots, or rejoicings" (646–52). Wordsworth describes the festivities of the Fair as a nightmare "Monstrous in colour, motion, shape, sight, and sound" (662) with manic glee by way of a grotesque and vividly descriptive catalogue:

> Chattering monkeys dangling from their poles,
> And children whirling in their roundabouts;
> With those that stretch the neck, and strain the eyes,
> And crack the voice in rivalship, the crowd
> Inviting; with buffoons against buffoons
> Grimacing, writhing, screaming; him who grinds
> The hurdy-gurdy, at the fiddle weaves;
> Rattles the salt box, thumps the kettle drum,
> And him who at the trumpet puffs his cheeks,
> The silver-collared Negro with his timbrel,
> Equestrians, Tumblers, Women, Girls, and Boys,

> Blue-breeched, pink-vested, and with towering plumes.
> —All moveables of wonder from all parts
> Are here, Albinos, painted Indians, Dwarfs,
> The Horse of Knowledge, and the learned Pig,
> The Stone-eater, the Man who swallows fire,
> Giants, Ventriloquists, the Invisible Girl,
> The Bust that speaks and moves its goggling eyes. (668–85)

This grotesque inventory—carnivalesque and Fellini-esque—with its vivid details of sight and sound and its many action verbs, is as powerful a blank verse passage as Wordsworth ever penned. And even though he condemns this extraordinary spectacle as a "Parliament of Monsters" (692), the climactic rhetoric of denunciation he deploys also suggests the power of attraction this spectacle held for the young poet that the moralizing rhetoric is designed to overwhelm or repress:

> Oh blank confusion! and type not false
> Of what the mighty City is itself
> To all, except for a Straggler here and there,
> To the whole swarm of its inhabitants;
> An undistinguishable world of men,
> The slaves unrespited of low pursuits,
> Living amid the same perpetual flow
> Of trivial objects, melted and reduced
> To one identity by differences
> That have no law, no meaning, and no end;
> Oppression under which even highest minds
> Must labour, whence the strongest are not free. (696–707)

Though Wordsworth was to make repeated visits to London throughout his long life after his extended stay there as a young man, the rhetoric of Book 7 suggests that the only way to avoid such "Oppression" is to leave the city behind altogether. However, if Nature is the antidote to the "blank confusion" and hellish corruption of the urban center, then the child of nature, the poet Wordsworth, can bring to his stay in the metropolis a mindset that can safeguard him in his innocence like the London prostitute's divine child "who walked with hair unsinged / Amid the fiery furnace." In what I have argued elsewhere is "a unique kind of romantic Gestalt psychology" (Stelzig 147), Wordsworth suggests that because of his early "education" in and by natural scenery, he can maintain his cognitive and psychic integrity in the city even in the face of its theatrical monstrosities:

> The mountain's outline and its steady form
> Gives a pure grandeur, and its presence shapes

> The measure and the prospect of the soul
> To majesty: such virtue have the forms
> Perennial of the ancient hills; nor less
> The changeful language of their countenances
> Gives movement to the thoughts, and multitude,
> With order and relation. (723–30)

The poet in the urban inferno is still the child of Nature and is thus able to keep his balance in "that vast receptacle:"

> The Spirit of Nature was upon me here,
> The Soul of Beauty and enduring life
> Was present as a habit, and diffused,
> Through meagre lines and colours, and the press
> Of self-destroying, transitory things,
> Composure and ennobling harmony. (736–41)

We recognize in this "natural" Gestalt psychology a distinctive Wordsworthian version of what Jerome McGann has famously epitomized as the Romantic ideology. However, if even "highest minds" are not entirely immune to the centrifugal or distracting and disintegrative pressures of these urban spectacles, the rest of us not so privileged should feel no guilt in enjoying such entertainments. No doubt the young Wordsworth felt no guilt as he made his leisurely way through the streets of the capital at the end of the eighteenth century—streets with sights and sounds not altogether dissimilar to those that literally millions of tourists are taking in every year more than two centuries later in the great global metropolis that is London, and for which many of us would die and think we had gone to heaven if we could spend four months there exploring its vast cultural and theatrical riches.

Notes

1. All quotations from and citations of *The Prelude* are of the 1805 version in Gill's (*Oxford Authors*) edition and will be given by book and line number(s). All other quotations of Wordsworth's poetry are also from the Gill edition.
2. Wordsworth's imaginative identification with the story of Mary Robinson "the Maid of Buttermere" may also be a function—or a displaced version?—of his guilt at having made pregnant and then abandoned his French lover, Annette Vallon.
3. Wordsworth's complex ambivalence about London is reflected in the fact that elsewhere in *The Prelude* he can also give an idyllic glimpse of humans in "the vast Metropolis" (8: 747) that stand in stark contrast to the figures of the blind Beggar and the prostitute's child at the theater.

In Book 8, written before Book 7, he offers a scene of a working-class male "sitting in an open Square" with "a sickly Babe / Upon his knee, whom he had thither brought / For sunshine, and to breathe the fresher air." It is revealing that this touching portrait of a "tender" and loving parent-child relationship in the city is correlated (in a striking mixture of literal and metaphoric description) with the elements of nature:

> He held the Child, and, bending over it
> As if he were afraid both of the sun
> And of the air which he had come to seek,
> He eyed it with unutterable love. (8. 844–59)

11

Blake's Golgonoosa: London and/as the Eternal City of Art

Mark Lussier

I. Preludium

Describing William Blake as a city poet is something of a cliché, if not a critical mainstay, in Blake studies, thereby placing him in contradistinction to the "nature" poets often positioned at the creative core of first-stage English Romanticism, and the tracks of this biographical constant (and hermeneutic constraint) lead backward from our own writing to the mid-nineteenth century construction of "Blake."[1] As Kathleen Raine phrases it, "Blake is of all English poets the supreme poet of the City, and what he wrote on his own city, London, must surely have meaning for any city...For Blake, a city is a living organism."[2] However, almost immediately, a necessary historical and biographical contextualization must ensue to position his fifty-seven-year presence in London in relation to his thirteen-year "absence" from the city proper at perhaps the most protean periods of his artistic production and for his aesthetic achievements. During that "impossible" decade described by Saree Makdisi and John Mee,[3] Catherine and William resided between 1791 and 1800 in Lambeth, not exactly far distant from London but a location requiring a walk across Westminster Bridge into Surrey on the southern side of the Thames. During the Lambeth residence, they lived in the Hercules Buildings, an aptly named home given the artistic and literary achievements that illuminated their residency therein. During the Lambeth years, Blake conceived and executed both historical (e.g., *America, A Prophecy* and

Europe, A Prophecy) and psychological illuminated books of prophecies (e.g., *The Book of Urizen* and *The Book of Ahania*), and like ligaments connecting parts of an active body, the solidifying mythic structure through which Blake sought to unify inner and outer "events" began to emerge.[4] Of course, this grand unification also assumed, for the first time, a singular textual body in the ur-epic *Vala*, (which later became *The Four Zoas*), Blake's schizoanalytic diagnosis of and prognosis for the dis/eases disturbing the mind and body of Albion.[5] Blake's ten-year stay across the Thames also brought the execution of a number of Blake's most famous paintings, including "Elohim creating Adam," "Newton," and "Nebuchadnezzar" (all amazingly dated to 1795). This is truly Herculean productivity on every aesthetic front upon which Blake resided.

Shortly before his next relocation in September 1800, Blake, in a letter to George Cumberland (July 2, 1800), comments directly on the transformations at work in the city of London and, as Laura Smith insightfully proposed in a slightly different context (her review of the most recent Tate Gallery Blake exhibition), the letter expressed a maturation in his ability to "respond to, to see, the physical city in which he lived": "It is very Extraordinary that London in so few years from a City of meer Necessaries or at [l]east a commerce of the lowest order of luxuries should have become a City of Elegance in some degree" (Erdman 706).[6] Within two months of this description, the Blakes began a less temporally extended but much more spatially distant and culturally complicated three-year residence in Felpham (1800–1803), a village on the southern coast in Sussex. The Blakes lived in a cottage provided by William Hayley, a generous yet meddlesome patron, a poor poet yet insightful critic, and the very archetype of what Blake meant by "corporeal friend [but] spiritual enemy" (as the letters written during this period make abundantly clear).[7] And yet, these years were stunningly prolific as well. During his three-year slumber, as he drolly named it, Blake imagined and executed the poem *Milton* and conceived the last epic, *Jerusalem*, while also producing numerous engravings, prints, and paintings. Of course, he also encountered a serpent in his garden, one John Scofield (of the First Royal Dragoons), and the encounter led to Blake's trial for an ultimate acquittal of high treason (predictably Scofield finds a permanent textual home in *Jerusalem* itself as "the ninth of Albion's sons").[8]

I have briefly traced this literal, actual map of where Blake lived to set it aside, since I believe this type of map leads only back to the historical London after the Felpham stay and is incapable of encapsulating the trans-shifting, multidimensional, simultaneity of perspective required to travel onward to Golgonoosa, which requires a much more comprehensive map capable of charting the geography of the imagination and which, in strikingly similar ways, pursues an "integration [of] the rational-scientific [i.e., historical] and the mythopoeic [i.e., poetic]" as "different modes of understanding."[9] The remainder of the chapter strives to take this latter approach, and I argue that the passage from historical London to visionary Golgonoosa comes only to be achieved through the deployment of principles associated with "visionary geography" (a critical step beyond the "heavenly cartography" long ago announced and pursued by Mark Schorer).[10] Of course, precisely as Anne Buttimer suggests in her sense that the human spirit infuses physical cartography, this textual pilgrimage from London (a depressingly time-bound place of relentless labor collapsing into constant disappointment) and to Golgonoosa (a psychophysical locale emitting light, enfolding space, and generating infinite aesthetic possibilities by which to gratify the creative urges of body and soul) manifests "a whole new perspective" (7) that enfolds a collective "historical record" with individual "life histories" (6–7).

II. The Absence of Visual Form

As an engraver, illustrator, painter, and printer undergoing apprenticeship in the latter half of the eighteenth century, one could certainly predict the graphic influences of William Hogarth (who died shortly after Blake's birth) and the robust print culture to emerge in his wake, although these traces tend toward a utopian presence at odds with that described by Nicholas M. Williams.[11] As well, when Blake functioned as apprentice to James Basire, "he was employed in making drawings from old building and monuments," an activity leading into Westminster Abbey but equally allowing the emerging artist to shape his aesthetic sensibilities by drawing other "Gothic churches round London" (Bentley 39; 41). This wandering through the city certainly positioned Blake to see "the Old London juxtaposed with the emerging new" aspects of the city under architectural renovation.[12] And so, what type of social dynamics defined the London that Blake traversed across his years in the city? Critics might describe a restrictive place that "sustains its stratifications only at the expense of individual fulfillment" yet equally might describe an expansive space of vibrant energy where most city locations provided "sites for watching social change and engaging in various forms of contestation."[13] The city was, as well, prone to periodic eruptions of violence, as when the twenty-two-year-old Blake witnessed the storming of the House of Lords by fourteen thousand people protesting Lord George Gordon's proposed "anti-Catholic petition" in June 1780.[14] As Blake entered his most productive decade, the 1790s, the city had become an urban space filled with "disfiguration and agony... as all of society was gradually beginning to turn into a factory," a state "already evident in London's streets" (Makdisi 106). The violence enacted on its citizens reproduced itself in an assault on the city's environment as well, for "Blake's London was an ecologically disastrous place to live," an over-populated and desperately polluted place, where "yellow fog" fouled the air and raw sewage flowed into the Thames, creating "disincentive[s] to breathing the air [and] drinking the water."[15] Indeed, Blake's description in his poem of experience, "London," hints at all these dire dimensions, where suffering is etched in faces and cries of agony accompany any passage through it, a state Blake crystallizes into one of his most provocative images of inner and outer control. The cityscape and its environment, its people, its buildings and streets, its atmosphere and rivers manifest the presence of "mind-forg'd manacles" (E 27: 8) and are thereby ideological productions of tyranny and capital run amok. The London imaged through these words evokes a cluttered and contentious cityscape whose stratified inhabitants contested for discursive presence in a multidimensional and increasingly complex cultural conglomerate defined by interactive fields of physical and semiotic forces. And yet, just as clearly, Blake loved London; indeed, he so loved the city that he transformed it through prodigious acts of imagination into Golgonoosa, the city of art, a move Peter Otto insightfully observes as the "first time [that] Los creates rather than merely reconstructs Urizen's world."[16]

The Blakean *polis* manifests contraries everywhere the ear hears and the eye sees, and the next step along the road to Golgonoosa necessitates the cultivation of and commitment to the ability to comprehend the city as a multiverse to be traversed.[17] Within this perspective, the city becomes an enriched space-time environment negotiated through intellection and imagination, operates through perceptual modes of complementarity "between generation and eternity," and provides transportation "between Golgonoosa, 'the spiritual fourfold London' [E 114] and the dirty, impoverished London" (Williams 170–71) awaiting the visionary poet and painter just outside his door any given moment.[18] Blake gives voice to this ability to articulate a visionary geography grounded on such principles—and steps well beyond the description offered earlier through his 1800 letter—after his return from Felpham, when he exudes

> I behold London, a Human awful wonder of God!
> He says: Return, Albion, return! I give myself for thee:
> My Streets are my Ideas of Imagination.

Awake Albion, awake! And let us awake up together.
My Houses are Thoughts: my inhabitants; Affections. (*Jerusalem* 38. 29–33)

London is human; its streets are veins of imaginations; its houses are abodes of contemplation, its inhabitants are flows of fellow feeling. Here one can perceive the antidote to the dis/eases described in "London" and discussed previously, and not surprisingly, given Blake's earlier diagnosis, this is a very complicated body indeed, so complicated, in fact, that the catalogs of streets that occur in *Jerusalem* later became evidence to support the circulating rumor of Blake's madness.[19]

The combination of Blake's training in the visual arts and his acutely developed imaginative attributes provided a unique cluster of talents through which to image a city with the dimensions offered by the anthropic principle in Blake's description of the city.[20] In light of the importance that scholarship has attached to the geopolitical and psychophysiological dimensions of London operative in Blake's poetic works and given his skills in the graphic arts honed by excursions made into the city, I thought a representative sampling of those visual works that represent the enigmatic and energized environment of the City of London could best serve my ends to shed light on the necessity of employing a visionary geographic method to travel from London to Golgonoosa. However, perhaps to the surprise of many, Blake offered virtually no prospective representation of the city of London in any type of work, although occasional spots can be found in his commissioned prints for other texts. (The current Blake exhibit [2009] mounted at the Morgan Library and Museum in New York includes numerous works, from pages of the illuminated books to a full copy of the Job designs, yet the only place one can gain a glimpse of London is in the background to his stunning "The Canterbury Pilgrims.")

In a poem seeming to offer an extremely intimate and profoundly insightful description of London, the short lyric of *Experience* entitled "London," the design severely constricts the eye, restricting vision to an extremely tight view of a city street. This same tendency occurs in Blake's painting of *The Penance of Jane Shore* (c. 1793), a watercolor roughly contemporaneous with *Songs of Innocence and of Experience*, whose structure squeezes numerous bodies into a crowded street scene to emphasize a claustrophobic crush of human chaos. Even in the expansive visionary text of *Jerusalem*, in which the "London" design is reiterated with greater detail (at the foot of plate 84), the major representational changes shift the direction of movement (reversing the earlier left to right) and bring the figures ("blind" man and leading child) into the light (inverting the "London" design). The figural pair emerges from the street to discover a multispired cathedral backlit by a setting sun; they do not emerge into anything that might be described as a cityscape and or be remotely identifiable as London. And yet, this plate begins with a catalog of locations ("Highgates heights & Hampsteads, to Poplar Hackney & Bow / To Islington & Paddington" [Erdman 243; 84.1–2]) that support the building of Jerusalem in "England's green and pleasant land," and the effect of word and design moves the visionary geographic mode to the foreground, since cities separated by vast spans of time and space are superimposed, to borrow an apt term from quantum physics. Thus, on this plate, "I see London blind & age-bent begging thro the streets / Of Babylon" (84.11–12), and as Georges Poulet phrases the event, we pronounce ourselves this "I" in the act of readerly reception, "on loan" as it were, to the text that "acts within [us]."[21]

III. Turning toward Golgonoosa

As might be ascertained by my last phrase, the turn toward Golgonoosa has been taken in earnest, and as Nelson Hilton notes, the very name carries within it the techniques undergirding a visionary cartographic agenda. While the specific term "remind[s] us only of Golgotha, 'the place of skulls,'" the metonymic method by which it emerges, initially individual but expansive enough to connect Jerusalem and London, expresses as well one of the main themes in the final epic.[22] The city of "Art & Manufacture," which operates through the agency of Los, first appears in *The Four Zoas* and gains discursive power through the linguistic and representational intensity apparent in *Milton*. However, in both cases, London serves as the actual foundation within the real, since the edifice is built along the banks of the Thames, and the concept "combines the quotidian reality of Blake's London, its streets, buildings, and public spaces, with the visionary New Jerusalem" to serve as its textual foundation.[23] In the initial forms of Golgonoosa, the dependence of the imagery on visionary geography is already quite pronounced, with the cosmopolitan merging with the cosmological and mythological dimensions in Blake's epic efforts. What begins as allegorical representation of "the individual poet-painter [transmutes] into the cosmic" (Damon 164). Of course, the crescendo of description occurs in *Jerusalem*, with plates eleven and twelve (the heart of Blake's description of Golgonoosa) offering some of the most exotic symbolism found in Blake's work.

Time and space rightly prohibit any exhaustive reading of these plates, yet even an extended reading cannot clarify the location of Golgonoosa. However, a short survey of its emergent features can provide a signpost on the cartographic map leading to the passage into the eternal city of art, and these are, not surprisingly, reflected in the reality of London itself: "The great City of Golgonoosa: fourfold toward the north / And toward the south fourfold, & fourfold toward the east & west / Each within other toward the four points" (*Jerusalem* 12.46–8). The "foursquare" city manifests a predictable fourfold symmetry built upon corresponding alignment with the four directions of the compass and the four planes of Blakean existence, but each one also opens onto/into the others. The only symbolism capable of even remotely imaging this last description would be wormhole theory specifically associated with "the Einstein-Rosen bridge in space-time geometry,"[24] since such conditions require tunneling through relatively flat or enfolded sheets of space-time. Visionary geography and visionary physics form implicate bonds unfolding beyond any Newtonian physicality yet manifesting portals that open onto the fourfold vision of Ezekiel or any number of other associations too numerous to recount. One approaches Golgonoosa through a radical form of metonymy as well, where the fourfold idiom occurs in both particular and general states.[25] For example, Blake's construction proposes that "and every part of the City is fourfold; & every inhabitant, fourfold. / And every pot & vessel & garment & utensil of the houses, / And every house, fourfold" (*Jerusalem* 13.21–3). This radical metonymic overdetermination gains greater complexity still when juxtaposed with the mode of transformation Blake conceives to facilitate the passage from London to Golgonoosa (and back):[26]

> The nature of infinity is this: that everything has its
> Own Vortex, and when once a traveler thro' Eternity
> Has pass'd that Vortex, he perceives it roll backward behind
> His path into a globe itself infolding like a sun
> Or like a moon, or like a universe of starry majesty
> ...Or like a human form
> Thus is the earth one infinite plane
> ....
> Thus is the heaven a vortex pass'd already, and the earth
> A vortex not yet passed by the traveler thro' Eternity. (*M* 14.21–34)

Fourfold dimensionality requires this dynamic mode of transportation to connect all metonymic locations and thereby complete the passage into the fearful symmetries that populate and thereby define Golgonoosa. The journey to Blake's vibrant multiverse is accomplished through vertical acts of perception that bridge individual beings and buildings, cities and galaxies, and accompanied by the ability to explore stratified states of consciousness. Having arrived at Golgonoosa, the last step leads through one of its four gates.

Golgonoosa's four gates are constructed through totemic and animistic associations, and the radical seriality of the cataloging of the gates approaches what can only be described as a proliferating form of symmetry that eventually provides a poetic critique of the "mathematical" sublime (a predictable position given Blake's stance against "Mathematical Proportion" in *Milton*): "sixty-four thousand Genii, guard the Eastern Gate...sixty-four thousand Gnomes, guard the Northern Gate...sixty-four thousand Nymphs guard the Western Gate,...And sixty-four thousand Fairies guard the Southern Gate" (*Jerusalem* 13. 26–29). As Thomas Weiskel argues, Blake's critical stance relative to Burkean and Kantian theories of the sublime (in both their positive and negative registers) results from his view that such polarized mental events were "not genuine contraries but two versions of the same lapse...a negation of visionary perception."[27] If such negation becomes established as perceptual boundary condition, the portals to Golgonoosa slam closed until the faculties again develop the capacity for visionary geographic sojourns of the psychophysical type, beginning in the minute and particular yet extending to the eternal and infinite.

IV. THROUGH THE GATES OF GOLGONOOSA

As Robert Essick observes, "images of cities and their buildings" best represent Losian creativity, a point of view certainly supported by the "construction of Golgonoosa," but any rational reconstruction of this metropolis quickly collapses, since "its gates expand well beyond three dimensional space to become a metaphor for the expanded senses and the multidimensional universe they perceive and in that perceiving create."[28] Imaginary geography, in other words, is always already a geography of the imagination. This multiverse only emerges, in Essick's estimation, through "Blake's mythic geography of mental states" (262), although I would extend this description further to incorporate the full spectrum of physical and psychical connections Blake employs to construct of his eternal city of art.

I would assert, from this position, that passing through a Golgonoosan gate one might enter Doris Lessing's last Martha Quest novel, *The Four-Gated City*, which overtly tropes off the visionary geographical principles discussed throughout this chapter, where London as "the physical city must be replaced by the four-gated city of imagination."[29] Passing through another gate, one could stumble into the textual geography of Dublin as pursued across the canon of James

Joyce, whose location clearly falls within the parameters established for Golgonoosa in *Jerusalem* (i.e., extending across the entirety of Great Britain).[30] Through another portal, one discerns the operations of Yeats's complex work of eternal recurrence, *A Vision,* with his edition of Blake providing symbolic and imaginary signposts for his own mode of visionary cartography. These modernist writers openly acknowledge Blake's influence but equally operate beyond any slavish dedication to him. They are equal creators and not dependent disciples, for if one truly passes into Golgonoosa, one passes out of it simultaneously (as Blake's description of the multidimensionality of its gates would suggest) and into a creativity perhaps stimulated by the attributes of the city but never bound within its limits.

Thus, other gates of Golgonoosa open onto postmodern spaces, with passage through yet another portal entering the textual space Tanelorn, a city at the heart of several science fiction series of Michael Moorcock (e.g., The Runestaff or Count Brass cycles) that temporally trans-shifts and thereby only rarely occupies a fixed space-time coordinate. Another parallel textual universe accessible from Golgonoosa would be Michael Dibdin's *Dark Spectre* and the commune located on one of the San Juan Islands off Seattle in the control of a drug-ravaged hippy who assumed the name of Los and established a dystopia inversely based on Blake's myth. Another postmodern space reachable from yet another gate would be the graphic novel *From Hell* by the artistic pair Alan Moore and Eddie Campbell, in which Jack the Ripper identifies Blake as his ghoulish inspiration and actually articulates a form of visionary geography pursued across this chapter. Golgonoosa's gates open into cinematic directions as well, whether leading to the ravaged cityscape of a Los Angeles within which replicants and blade runners clash in Ridley Scott's filmic exploration of the postmodern condition ("Blade Runner") or arriving at the frontier town of Machine in Jim Jarmusch's imaginary west in "Dead Man."

Both modern and postmodern texts catalogued here do, in fact, open onto eternity and infinity as well. However, the authors/auteurs cited in this metonymic chain of Blakean allusion, while acknowledging Blake's influence, necessarily leave the bard behind, passing him in their own passage to and through Golgonoosa. Thus, I am reminded of a well-known Buddhist proverb suggesting that should one meet the Buddha along the road (to enlightenment), one should kill him. The metonymic chain of texts just traced suggests a similar path to wisdom. In fact, this proverb might be adapted and placed over all the gates of Golgonoosa as the sole requirement for those who enter. If one meets Blake along the road to Golgonoosa, kill him; otherwise, one might arrive at his metropolis of "Art and Manufacture" but never leave it for the eternal and infinite creativity of the imagination lurking just beyond its gates.

Notes

1. All references, unless otherwise indicated, will be to David V. Erdman, ed., *The Complete Poetry and Prose of William Blake*, Garden City: Anchor, 1982, and will appear parenthetically by page number and, where necessary, by plate and line number.
2. Kathleen Raine. *Golgonooza, City of Imagination*. Ipswich: Golgonooza P, 1991. 100.
3. Saree Makdisi. *William Blake and the Impossible History of the 1790s*. Chicago: U of Chicago P, 2003. 51–53. John Mee. *Dangerous Enthusiasm: William Blake and the Culture of Radicalism in the 1790s*. Clarendon: Oxford UP, 1992. 20–33; 214–26.
4. The use of the term is designed to intersect that theorized by Alain Badiou, who in *Being and Event* (London: Continuum, 2005), reconceptualizes what is generally considered an external phenomenon by arguing that "An event…is the multiple composed of: on the one hand, elements of the site; and on the other hand, itself (the event), which requires that 'Self-belonging is thus constitutive of the event…an element of the multiple'" (506–7). This view has implications for the operation of the gates of Golgonoosa discussed deeper in the essay.
5. The term "schizoanalytic" evokes the latter stage of theoretical analysis located in Gilles Deleuze and Félix Guattari's *Anti-Oedipus: Capitalism and Schizophrenia*, Minneapolis: U of Minnesota P, 1983, 273–382.
6. Laurie Smith, "Seeing the City," *Magma Poetry* 21. <http://www.magmapoetry.com/archive/magma-21/articles.html>.
7. G. E. Bentley, Jr. *The Stranger from Paradise: A Biography of William Blake*. New Haven: Yale UP, 2001. 202–67.
8. S. Foster Damon. *A Blake Dictionary*. Boulder: Shambhala, 1979. 361.
9. Anne Buttimer. *Geography and the Human Spirit*. Baltimore: Johns Hopkins UP, 1993. 215–16.
10. *William Blake: The Politics of Vision*. New York: Vintage, 1946. 113.
11. Nicholas M. Williams. *Ideology in the Poetry of William Blake*. Cambridge: Cambridge UP, 1998. 170–71.
12. Paul Johnson. *The Birth of the Modern*. New York: HarperCollins, 1991. 453.
13. Anne Mellor. *Blake's Human Forms Divine*. Berkeley: U of California P, 1974. 55. Jeffrey Cox and Michael Gamer. Introduction. *The Broadview Anthology of Romantic Drama*. Toronto: Broadview P, 2003. xvi.
14. Michael Davis. *William Blake: A New Kind of Man*. Berkeley: U of California P, 1977. 23.

15. Stuart Peterfreund. *William Blake in a Newtonian World.* Norman: U of Oklahoma P, 1998. 170.
16. Peter Otto. *Blake's Critique of Transcendence.* Oxford: Oxford UP, 2000. 172.
17. Brian Greene. *The Elegant Universe: Superstrings, Hidden Dimensions, and the Quest for the Ultimate Theory.* New York: Vintage, 1999. 366–69.
18. Minna Doskow. *William Blake's* Jerusalem. Rutherford: Fairleigh Dickinson UP, 1982. 110.
19. Bentley 330–43.
20. Greene 368.
21. Georges Poulet. "Criticism and the Experience of Interiority." *Reader-Response Criticism.* Ed. Jane P. Tompkins. Baltimore: Johns Hopkins UP, 1980. 45.
22. Nelson Hilton. *Literal Imagination: Blake's Vision of Words.* Berkeley: U of California P, 1983. 235–56.
23. Morton Paley. *The Continuing City: William Blake's* Jerusalem. Oxford: Clarendon P, 1983. 136.
24. Walter Sullivan. *Black Holes: The Edge of Space, The End of Time.* New York: Anchor, 1979. 200.
25. Donald Ault. *Visionary Physics: Blake's Response to Newton.* Chicago: U of Chicago P, 1974. 141–60.
26. Mark Lussier. "Blake's Vortex: The Quantum Tunnel in *Milton.*" *Nineteenth-Century Contexts* 18.3 (1994): 278–91.
27. Thomas Weiskel. *The Romantic Sublime.* Baltimore: Johns Hopkins UP, 1986. 68.
28. Robert Essick. "Jerusalem and Blake's Final Works." *The Cambridge Companion to William Blake.* Ed. Morris Eaves. Cambridge: Cambridge UP, 2003. 262.
29. Susan Levin, "A Fourfold Vision: William Blake and Doris Lessing." *William Blake and the Moderns.* Ed. Robert J. Bertholf and Annette S. Levitt. Albany: SUNY P, 1982. 213.
30. Robert J. Gleckner. "Joyce's Blake: Paths of Influence." *William Blake and the Moderns.* 136–39; Paley, *The Continuing City,* 166.

12

London's Immortal Druggists: Pharmaceutical Science and Business in Romanticism

Thomas H. Schmid

In the 1821 *Confessions of an English Opium Eater*, Thomas De Quincey famously recounts his first purchase of opium from an "immortal druggist" located in London's Oxford Street, near what he calls, borrowing a phrase from Wordsworth's "Power of Music," "the *stately* Pantheon" (43; italics in text). Even more famously, De Quincey recollects that on his next visit to London the druggist had "vanished," "evanesced," or "evaporated," confirming De Quincey in his fanciful notion that the chemist had been no "sublunary druggist" but rather an ethereal dispenser of "celestial pleasures" (43). While De Quincey's particular druggist may have disappeared from Oxford Street, the Romantic-period urban landscape was populated with pharmaceutical businesses that proved more substantial and lasting. These small firms often included onsite laboratories and manufacturing facilities, in addition to their retail shops, and a number of them became famous throughout the nineteenth and twentieth centuries, evolving into such household names as Allen & Hanburys, John Bell & Croyden, and Corbyn, Stacey & Co. With these commercial houses, the period marked the historical beginnings of a modern drug industry, one that combined wholesale and retail sales with pharmaceutical research and marketing. Romantic-period druggists were often on the cutting edge of new developments in medical and chemical science; at the same time, the drive for profits led to the need for legislative regulation and oversight, which came in the latter half of the nineteenth century and continue to this day. Far from evanescing, the druggists with whom De Quincey transacted business proved to be a permanent feature of the London cityscape, and their model of combining trade, manufacturing, scientific research, and retail sales persists in the modern drug corporation and its uneasy relationship with regulatory agencies.

De Quincey's *Confessions* excepted, Romantic literary references to pharmaceutical *materia medica* largely ignore the growing number of actual businesses in which such products could be found. Wordsworth's leech-gatherer from "Resolution and Independence" trades in a product typically displayed in ornate English Delftware jars in druggists' shops at the time, but he himself is a supplier not a retailer, and the poem never follows him beyond his increasingly ill-paid toil among the Cumberland lakes. When Percy Shelley writes to Thomas Love Peacock in 1818 that the first canto of Byron's *Don Juan* seems "more like a mixture of wormwood and verdigrease [sic] than satire" (42), he makes metaphoric use of two exceedingly common druggist's products in the period—one a botanical derivative, the other a poisonous acetate of copper used in dyes and as an antifungal treatment—but has no occasion to mention where such products may be purchased. Keats, the licensed apothecary whom John Gibson Lockhart and William Maginn derided in 1820 as a "Cockney" poet "who practises poetry and pharmacy" (678n), loads his verse with references to herbal medicines, poisons, and narcotics readily available in retail shops throughout London and most nineteenth-century cities and towns, but never depicts an actual sale. Even so, the various botanicals in Keats's works—the infusions and extracts of nightshade, hemlock, bittersweet, wolfsbane, *papaver somniferum* (opium), yew-berry, and so on—not only were "included in the 1815 edition of the London *Pharmacopoeia* that Keats would have been examined on" during his licensing, as Gareth Evans has engagingly discussed, but also were prepared in the backroom laboratories of retail druggists who sold them to physicians and apothecaries as well as displaying them for sale on their own shelves (49). When Keats writes in the "Ode on Melancholy" of twisting "Wolf's-bane tight-rooted for its poisonous wine" (2), Evans stresses, he is describing accurately the standard pharmaceutical preparation of *Aconitum napellus*, the leaves of which, as with other medicinal plants, would be pressed until, as one pharmacy manual from 1810 states, "they yield their juice" (qtd. in Evans 52). Increasingly in the nineteenth century the work of such drug preparation was pursued quite profitably by an emerging class of retail druggists that gained professionalization and commercial influence apart from the apothecaries, surgeons, and physicians with whom they consulted and traded. De Quincey gives one of the few positive descriptions of these very real druggists in canonical Romantic literature, and his brief portrait attests to the new commercial presence and respectability of the druggist as a distinct class of urban professional, even as it seeks to erase the physical traces of the actual Oxford Street shop in which De Quincey made his life-changing purchase. De Quincey's account of the immortal druggist straddles the line between the real and the imaginary, establishing the materiality of the druggist and his shop on the one hand and subsequently fancying his dreamlike intangibility and impermanence. The latter fancy is, quite obviously, pure imaginative play and serves the more crucial point about the transcendent quality of the product purveyed by the druggist, the opium itself. De Quincey fully appreciates the material reality of the druggist's shop; yet the intensely pleasurable effects of opium make him unwilling in retrospect to "connect any mortal remembrances with that hour, and place, and creature, that first brought me acquainted with the drug" (43). The ethereal drug etherealizes its supplier and user, as Charles Rzepka proposed over a decade ago in *Sacramental Commodities*. In Rzepka's reading, opium for De Quincey is "*mana* to be received with gratitude and passed along with grace" and "something much more than a commodity for personal consumption" (180). In comparison with such ichor, considerations of shop location and the ontological status of the pharmacist necessarily fade. De Quincey's partial erasure of the druggist from Oxford Street also fits well with discursive readings of "drugs" in general as beyond "conceptual arrest," in Avital Ronell's phrase—as "radically nomadic parasite[s] let loose from the will of language" (51–52). In De Quincey's account both opium and the shop in which it is bought resist a stable origin or definition, as Alina Clej has discussed. In order properly to extol the celestial powers of opium, De Quincey must minimize the mundane reality of the shop in which it could be bought, literally for pennies.

Yet such shops abounded in Romantic-period London, several famous ones in Oxford Street near the Pantheon, and De Quincey very much depended on actual retail pharmacists to supply him. In the note to readers that precedes the confessions proper, he substantiates his claims to the prevalence of recreational opium eating in the city by citing the testimony of "three respectable London druggists, in widely remote quarters of London, from whom I happened lately to be purchasing small quantities of opium"(5). When he tells the story of his first purchase of opium in Oxford Street, he pinpoints the shop's location near the intersection of Oxford and Poland Streets, emphasizes the "wet and cheerless...Sunday in London," and describes the druggist himself as looking "dull and stupid, just as any mortal druggist might be expected to look on a Sunday." Finally, again for humorous effect, he reports that the druggist handed him the requested opium tincture "as any other man might do: and furthermore, out of my shilling, returned to me what seemed to be real copper halfpence, taken out of a real wooden drawer" (43). Regardless of his later fancies about the druggist's "beatific" and "immortal" nature, De Quincey sketches an ordinary business transaction, an exchange of real product for ready cash. Even his footnote on the power of evanescence as historically associated with "blood-royal, and by no means...allowed to druggists" (43n) humorously undercuts his later imaginings of the druggist's celestial status and situates him instead in the material world of Oxford Street.

De Quincey's emphasis on the respectability of the three druggists from "widely remote corners of London" reflects the growing image of druggists in the period as commonly reliable and professional, even if the apparent need for the qualifier, "respectable," implies that not all pharmacists were necessarily so. The historical record corroborates the image of respectability, however, as does a somewhat surprising reference in a novel published four years before the *Confessions*, but initially drafted sometime in the mid to late 1790s: Jane Austen's *Northanger Abbey*. Late in the novel, at the crucial moment of Catharine Morland's epiphany about her own foolish fancies and the noncriminality of the Tilneys, the narrator describes Catharine as "completely awakened"— "The visions of romance were over" (187). As Catharine continues her mortified self-criticism, she marvels at how she could have been so consumed by imaginary fears and bloody visions of spousal murder in an enlightened age: "In the central part of England there was surely some security for the existence even of a wife not beloved, in the laws of the land, and the manners of the age. Murder was not tolerated, servants were not slaves, and neither poison nor sleeping potions to be procured, like rhubarb, from every druggist" (188). Though the passage is tinged with at least potential irony in its confident assertions of the benevolence and rationality of the age, Catharine's conversion to a preference for reality over romance is partly anchored in the image of the druggist as implicitly responsible, prohibited by ethical and professional standards from selling murder weapons to customers off the street, and above all as an ordinary merchant providing common services. Lethal poisons and narcotics actually *could* be readily obtained at druggists' shops at the time, but the crucial point for the reader's understanding of Catharine's character is that she herself comes to believe in a fundamental English normalcy and respectability that include—and are indeed exemplified by—professional pharmacists.

This image of general reputability contrasts sharply with satires and caricatures of apothecaries and druggists that were still common in the period, but it more realistically represents the rising professional status and credentials of each. As Penelope Corfield discusses, the image of the apothecaries gradually shifts from one of "poison peddlers" to that of "civic worthies" during the Georgian period, and the druggists' reputation follows suit. Corfield cites an entry in *The London Tradesman* from 1747 as typical of the negative reputation apothecaries and druggists would eventually overcome: "This is the *mere* apothecary—a Creature that requires very little Brains.... There is no Branch of Business in which a Man requires less Money to set him up, than this very profitable Trade: Ten or twenty Pounds, judiciously applied, will buy Gallipots and Counters, and as many Drugs to fill them with as might poison the whole Island" (qtd. in Corfield 1; italics in text). According to Corfield a common joke in the period ran, "I felt unwell—I resolved to get better—I took medicine—I died" (2). Coleridge and Southey's anonymous *Morning Post* satire from 1799, "The Devil's Thoughts," also exemplifies the negative stereotype of the apothecary/druggist as a dealer in death:

> An apothecary on a white horse,
> Rode by on his vocation,
> And the Devil thought of his old friend
> Death, in the Revelation. (13–16)

As late as 1831, a revised version of Coleridge and Southey's poem was reissued with accompanying illustrations by Thomas Landseer, one of which depicts the apothecary. As Ruth Richardson remarks, "The picture is not pleasant." An image of the etching is included in Richardson's article for readers' reference, but her description is worth quoting at length:

> The lank apothecary sits high on his horse, inhaling snuff deeply from a pill box and looking utterly disreputable. He carries a tubular box, possibly for a stethoscope. His horse is a hack, starved, weak, and sickly, pitted with sores, barely able to carry its master. Half-concealed behind him on the saddle is a dead baby (a reference to back-street abortion?) doubtless destined for dissection, and a copy of *The Lancet*, whose title reinforces this idea.... A moribund dog convulses in the gutter. In the background a body is borne away on a stretcher; men muffle their faces from the pestilential atmosphere; a coffin-bearer follows. In the midst of this desolation, a quizzical face smirks over the nag's mane: the Devil, sniffing rosemary, approving all he sees. (646)

Landseer's grim portrait of the apothecary in 1831 seems a little outdated to Richardson, and the "association with *The Lancet*...curious, as the journal was known for its reforming stance towards medical corruption and incompetence" (646).[1] Certainly, Landseer's unflattering illustration, along with Coleridge and Southey's text, is a far cry from the benign images of druggists in De Quincey and Austen (if De Quincey's characterization of druggists in general as "dull and stupid" appears to echo the picture of the apothecary as requiring "very little Brains" in the 1747 *London Tradesman,* it also asserts their competence and reliability). Part of the source of the negative portrayals is an increasingly anachronistic equation of apothecaries—as pill peddlers, exclusively—with druggists. In fact, the two professions were becoming more and more distinct within the Romantic period, with each developing improved reputations. By Keats's time, John Gibson Lockhart can criticize the writer for being too much the apothecary, too little the poet, but his infamous 1818 review of *Endymion* still identifies the apothecary primarily with the prescription and sale of *materia medica* from a "shop": "So back to the shop, Mr. John, back to 'plasters, pills, and ointment boxes,' etc. But, for Heaven's sake, young Sangrado, be a little more sparing of extenuatives and soporifics in your practice than you have been in your poetry" (524). By 1818, apothecaries had largely abandoned the shop to the druggists, although "even towards the end of the century there were large numbers of 'dispensing doctors' " and "the Society of Apothecaries did not give up its commercial activities in retail and manufacturing pharmacy until 1922" ("History" 215). Still, by Keats's time, apothecaries and druggists had developed mostly separate technical expertise and business practices that belied the satiric stereotypes.

In presenting a predominantly realistic and appreciative portrait of druggists, De Quincey and Austen reflect the elevated economic and professional status of the pharmaceutical industry as it developed in the long nineteenth century (1780–1900) and especially in the decades between the passing of the 1815 Apothecaries Act and the formation of the Pharmaceutical Society in 1841. From the seventeenth century on, the apothecaries' and physicians' trade in pharmaceuticals and medical services had competed with an ill-defined and disparate group of retail drug purveyors, most without any formal medical training, many of them selling patent medicines of their own concoction to an unwary public. While the sale of dubious patent medicines did not wane in the nineteenth century, and, in fact, led to the first legislative drug regulation and oversight in the Pharmaceutical Act of 1868, the period laid what Andreas-Holger Maehle calls "the foundations of modern pharmacology" as a thriving manufacturing, retail, and wholesale business (1). As apothecaries pursued their own growing professionalization as medical practitioners, culminating in the educational and licensing requirements under the Apothecaries Act, the business of making and selling pharmaceutical products fell increasingly to the druggists, who could be relied upon to maintain stable manufacturing facilities and retail shops with regular business hours. In other words, the "Golden Age of the apothecary-cum-general practitioner," as Roy Porter and Dorothy Porter describe it, which "saw [the apothecary] leaping over the counter, stepping into the physician's shoes, and becoming a prescriber in his own right," also saw him of necessity neglecting the shop and spending less and less time compounding his own drugs, thereby creating a market niche for the wholesale and retail druggist. The result, according to Porter and Porter, was that druggists assumed "a crucial...role as the manufacturers and distributors of the very sinews of medicine" and became "the authentic progenitors of the pharmaceutical industry" (282). One indicator of the extent to which the druggists themselves recognized the commercial potential of their independence from the apothecaries can be inferred from the numbers of influential druggists, such as John Bell, who lobbied actively—and ultimately successfully—for the exemption of druggists from the regulatory provisions of the Apothecaries Act (Marland, "Doctor's Shop" 83). While each professional group was dependent to a degree on the other, each succeeded in achieving growth and prosperity in separate commercial domains: the apothecaries because of the Apothecaries Act, the druggists in defiance of it.

For the druggists, growth meant a proliferation of retail shops catering to the general public and anticipating the birth of today's corner drug store and drug store chain. Predictably, too, such growth was largely an urban phenomenon. According to S. W. F. Holloway, "The number of chemists and druggists increased markedly after the year 1780. From that date, not only was there an increase in the absolute number in all the urban areas of Britain but also a growth relative to the rising population and relative to the growing number other medical practitioners. Chemists and druggists rapidly became established as a new species of *homo medicus*" (82). As Louise Hill Curth summarizes the history of these developments,

> rapid industrialization and urbanization...in the nineteenth century [were] accompanied by a decline in the number of "pedlar-druggists" and an even more rapid rise in the number of chemists and druggists operating from fixed, specialist shops....Not only did the numbers of chemists' and druggists' shops expand rapidly, the largest businesses opened a number of branches and followed the grocery trade into multiple retailing. (8)

By 1841 the ratio of retail chemists and druggists to medical practitioners in Great Britain was one to two, and by the 1850s the proportion was even higher (Marland, "Doctor's Shop" 84). Hilary Marland suggests that the increase in numbers was spurred by the rapid population growth of the cities, the increasing willingness of doctors to turn pharmaceutical sales over to the druggists, and to a rapid rise in the number of drug-savvy poor and middle-class buyers who lacked the income to pay a high-priced physician and sought instead the more affordable medical advice and dispensing available at retail drug shops ("Doctor's Shop" 84). On this latter point, Judy Slinn observes that "while the services of medical practitioners were still too expensive for most working-class pockets, medicines from the pharmacists or chemist and druggist became affordable for more people" in the nineteenth century (169), and Marland notes that "by the mid-nineteenth century, the minimum fee generally charged for one visit by a general practitioner was approximately 5s" ("Doctor's Shop" 104). When De Quincey reports getting change back from his one shilling for opium, then, it can be safely assumed that he was getting the drug for less than one-fifth of the price he would have paid to see a doctor first. In self-medicating and cutting out the medical middleman, De Quincey was typical of the age: as S. W. F. Holloway explains, "Self-diagnosis and therapy were standard practice at all levels of society" and "the success of the chemist and druggist depended upon his ability to meet" the direct consumer demand for pharmaceutical products (82).

To serve the growing consumer demand and remain competitive, retail establishments, especially in market centers such as London, also greatly expanded their services and wares, the variety of which look forward to today's retail drug chains such as Boots and Superdrug in England or Walgreens and CVS in the United States. Marland observes that

> a typical chemist's shop of the nineteenth century would, in addition to a wide range of pharmaceutical preparations, stock a selection of toilet articles, tobacco, snuff, tea, coffee, herbs, and other foodstuffs, oils, candles and dyes. In some cases, the chemist combined with his pharmaceutical enterprises the activities of a grocer, bookseller, insurance agent, tea or lead merchant. ("Doctor's Shop" 87)

Marland adds specific examples of urban businesses that supplemented their pharmaceutical offerings with the sale of everything from paint, wine, and nonpharmaceutical chemicals to cosmetics, hair dyes, perfumes, spices, sauces, and so on. Many of these businesses, as Porter and Porter note, can trace continuous histories from the eighteenth through the twentieth century (284). At least one, John Bell & Co., still thrives today (under the name John Bell & Croyden) barely half a mile from the Oxford Street address where it was originally established in 1798, two blocks from the "stately Pantheon" of Wordsworth and De Quincey fame.

The Pantheon actually proved more "evanescent," to use De Quincey's term, than its neighboring drug store. John Bell & Co. has enjoyed continuous growth and diversification since its founding, but public entertainments in the Pantheon had already ceased seven years before De Quincey invoked its name in 1821; in 1867, having long been extensively remodeled and converted into a bazaar, the Pantheon was acquired by a wine merchant; in 1938, the building was demolished to make way for a major branch of Marks and Spencer, the department store, which still welcomes customers through its entrances at 173 Oxford Street and around the corner on Poland Street. The only reminder of the Pantheon's once stately presence at Oxford and Poland streets is the nickname for the Marks and Spencer branch: "the Pantheon Store." In contrast, John Bell's druggist shop at 338 Oxford Street (later renumbered 225) survived in that location for 114 years until the firm, now merged with Croyden and Co., moved in 1912 to its present location on Wigmore Street, just eight blocks away. The current establishment continues to grow and adapt, offering extensive online and instore drug prescriptions, health, beauty and bath products, vitamin supplements, athletic and fitness products, as well as a broad range of consultation and clinical services, and the firm has held the Royal Warrant as Pharmacists to Her Majesty Queen Elizabeth II continuously since 1958. But its roots in John Bell's Oxford Street shop are still highlighted on the company website; and even the Croyden pharmaceutical company with which John Bell & Co. merged in 1908 was itself originally an offshoot of John Bell & Co., Charles Croyden having served as an assistant in the Bell firm before founding his own business in 1832 at the Wigmore Street location.

John Bell and his son Jacob, who helped build and eventually run the business as sole proprietor upon his father's death in 1849, exemplify the new professional, scientific, and entrepreneurial model that defined the Romantic period pharmaceutical business. Like most druggists in the period (Marland, "Medical" 439), John Bell lived over his shop at 338 Oxford Street, and Jacob was born there. John Bell was instrumental in gaining druggists' professional recognition and independence from the apothecaries in 1815, and Jacob was a founding and lifelong board member—and for several terms president—of the new professional and research organization for druggists, the Pharmaceutical Society, in 1841; a staggering thirteen of the society's original board members had also at one time or another been employed by John Bell & Co. Jacob Bell founded and edited *The Pharmaceutical Journal* in 1841, the first technical trade journal to serve the profession, and he encouraged company employees to attend lectures on chemistry and medicine at the Pharmaceutical Society's School of Pharmacy. Bell was instrumental in lobbying for legislation in 1852 to regulate the pharmaceutical industry and articulated a view of the diagnostic and healing functions of the druggist as necessarily limited, writing in 1844 that

> [the druggist] may be quite competent to administer an aperient draught... [but] would not be justified in undertaking to manage a case of enteritis. He may be competent to prepare a rhubarb mixture, and calculate the dose with which he may relieve a patient whose bowels are slightly relaxed; but if he attempt to cure dysentery, cholera, or nephritis, he may do more harm than good. (qtd. in Crellin, "Revisiting" 60)

Bell strictly enforced standards for the manufacture and compounding of prescriptions according to the London *Pharmacopoeia* and maintained, like his father, an onsite laboratory that produced all the shop's pharmaceuticals and guaranteed consistency and purity to both retail and wholesale customers. J. K. Crellin notes that the "better" shops in the period "were equipped with quite elaborate laboratories," and he singles out the one at John Bell & Co. as a particularly famous example ("History" 218). John Bell's laboratory even became the subject of a well-known and widely distributed mezzotint of a watercolor by William Henry Hunt, called "The Shop Boy" and published by J. G. Murray in 1842. Dianne Macleod describes the engraving as "an unusual example of the genre painting in the service of commerce in that it captures a characteristic moment in the daily life of laboratory assistants with the obsessive attention to detail that is the hallmark of Hunt's style." Attention to detail was also the hallmark of the laboratory work itself at John Bell & Co., and Hunt's painting is often cited as a representative image, Macleod stresses, of the compounding and manufacturing side of pharmacy in the early to mid-nineteenth century (76). Mohr and Redwood's influential *Practical Pharmacy* of 1849 included descriptions of the type of in-house laboratory represented at Bell & Co., and Crellin notes that the *Pharmaceutical Journal* "enthusiastically recommended" the book "to the young chemist about to open a shop" ("History" 218).

John Bell & Co. represents only one example among many of successful wholesale, retail, and research pharmacies that defined De Quincey's age and provided a lasting model for today's pharmaceutical corporations and retail chains. Allen & Hanburys, founded by

Silvanus Bevan in Plough Court in 1715, just across the river from Guy's Hospital, also exemplifies an unusually successful and enduring business, one focused as much on scientific research as on product sales. According to Porter and Porter, "the bulk of the Plough Court trade lay in drug manufacture and distribution, though a retail department was retained" and "the business, in Quaker hands, had a reputation for high standards of purity and fair dealing: the drugs, it was explained, were genuine rather than cheap" (285). William Allen, who joined Plough Court pharmacy in 1792 and took over the business three years later, became a cofounder of the Pharmaceutical Society in 1841, served as its first president, lectured at Guy's Hospital and held fellowships in both the Linnaean and Royal Societies. Like Bell & Co., Allen & Hanburys maintained its own laboratories and warehouses and avidly sought to improve the scientific knowledge of pharmaceuticals. Daniel Hanbury, for instance, who worked in the business from 1857 to 1870, published a seminal scientific textbook designed to solidify the knowledge of botanical-based medicines. The firm he worked for at least indirectly underwrote the decades of research that led to publication, and it enjoyed continuous commercial growth throughout the nineteenth and twentieth centuries, eventually being acquired by pharmaceutical giant, GlaxoSmithKline, in 1958, which still lists Allen & Hanburys as a "group" company on the corporate website.

There are many more examples of such firms. Corbyn, Stacey & Co. began in the mid-eighteenth century and its founder, Thomas Corbyn, could be said to have pioneered the first use of drug samples to increase sales. According to Porter and Porter, "Corbyn's technique was to dispatch, unasked, a chestful of drugs, probably about £50 worth. He would suggest to the recipients that they do business on a sale-or-return basis, and asked them to distribute the drugs, parcelled up into appropriate quantities, to local medical practitioners" (291). Corbyn Stacey incidentally also acquired an established druggist's shop in Oxford Street in the 1870s, operated in the De Quincey years by W. H. Bucklee. The firm as a whole remained continuously in business from 1743 until 1927 and in the eighteenth century developed large scale manufacturing capabilities:

> [Corbyn's] warehouse stock book or inventory, dated December 1761, runs to 2,500 different items of materia medica, which were stored in extraordinarily large quantities—he held 276 pounds of senna and 806 of magnesia alba for example. Corbyn also made up his drugs in impressively large batches: the recipes not infrequently require ingredients by the hundred-weight. Thus, that for bark extract begins with instructions to digest 150 pounds of bark with 90 gallons of spirit; similarly,

the recipe books envisage making up tartar emetic to 365 pounds. (Porter and Porter 288)

Such large quantities of raw material and final product fed the growing eighteenth- and nineteenth-century demand for retail and wholesale pharmaceuticals, measured partly, in Corbyn's case, by accounting records for annual orders, numbering in the hundreds, from "the most fashionable metropolitan [medical] practitioners," manufacturing chemists and provincial practitioners (Porter and Porter 290).

As Porter and Porter stress, firms such as Corbyn's, John Bell & Co., and Allen & Hanbury's were, from a business standpoint, "big by any standards"—and tremendously profitable (284). Hilary Marland observes that many druggists in the period enjoyed a "wealth and high social standing" that not only resulted from the growing professionalization of the trade but also set the druggists apart from other "fringe" or "para-medical" groups in Georgian and Regency society ("Medical" 416). Professionalization and profitability went hand in hand, as

> the leading pharmacists saw themselves not as mere shopkeepers retailing goods at competitive prices but as skilled practitioners selling their services. The public relied upon their knowledge and skill in manufacture, compounding, and dispensing. Their specialist knowledge was required to provide the basis for determining their purity and freshness, for recommending them for their efficacy in treating illness, for furnishing advice on their dosage and mode of administration, and for warning of their dangers. (Holloway 86-87)

Those dangers, the public's trust, and the immense profits at stake for pharmaceutical entrepreneurs all contributed to what the pharmacists themselves saw as the need for restrictions and regulations on individual businesses and substances in an era when, as Holloway paraphrases one writer from 1854, "Pennyworths of poison...were handed across the counter as nonchalantly as cakes of soap" (86). Out of this tension between profitability and the need for public safety, the Pharmaceutical Society of 1841 and the various pharmacy and poison bills of the 1850s and 1860s were born—and influential druggists such as Jacob Bell had an active and defining hand in each. In Holloway's fascinating account, nineteenth-century druggists succeeded in shaping drug legislation in much the same way that the pharmaceutical industry influences policy today. The goal of the Pharmaceutical Society, formed by successful businessmen like Bell, was explicitly "to become the regulatory authority for pharmacy in Britain" (86), and the *Pharmaceutical Journal* argued in 1857-58 that "if Pharmacy is to advance and prosper in [England], it must be under the fostering care and management of the Pharmaceutical body. If any science, art, or profession is to be well governed, it must be entrusted to its own members"; "'The security of the public,' argued Jacob Bell, 'would be better effected by an attention to the intelligence and qualification of the vendor than by any arbitrary regulations'" (qtd. in Holloway 91; 94). Regulation did come, but it was largely dictated by the pharmacy industry itself and left the state little control over that industry. The tension between the entrepreneurial freedom of the individual and government regulation in the nineteenth-century drug industry exemplifies a final, and profound, way in which the business model for pharmacy in the period persists today and the way in which, as Porter and Porter conclude, "The making and marketing of drugs provided the commodity upon which the modern business of medicine was founded" (295).

Thomas De Quincey was, among many other things, a consumer of that commodity, both a beneficiary and a victim of pharmaceutical modernity. His *Confessions* record, among many other things, the traces of that modernity. Alina Clej has proposed that "intoxication" functions as the most prominent discursive trope of modernity in De Quincey's *Confessions,* furnishing "a means both of breaking the modern subject's resistance (to modernity) and of preserving this resistance by the constant displacement and reconfiguration of experience that occurs in opium dreams" (13–14). For Clej, the "perfect emblem" of such displacement is the narrative of the disappearing druggist, through which "any definite memory of the past is volatilized, and the origin of things—like that of De Quincey's confession itself—melts into a haze" (62). Equally important to the foundations of De Quincey's confessions, displacements, and dreams, however, is not just the opium but the shops in which it was sold. As De Quincey's narrative of addiction makes clear, the druggist disappears only in the sense that his shop front remains an all-too common feature of the London streets, iterated along Oxford Street alone, near the Pantheon, in the going concerns of W. H. Bucklee, Peter Squire, and John Bell,[2] and replicated beyond Oxford Street in numerous locations throughout the city; the particular druggist matters little when each could be more or less equally relied upon to provide the same variety and quality of pharmaceutical merchandise. If not immortal, these businesses proved to have remarkable staying power. In both celebrating and dismissing them, De Quincey creates not only a narrative of modern displacement, but also a Romantic engagement with the urban ordinary, a world of real copper halfpence and real wooden drawers.

Notes

I wish to thank Larry H. Peer and the International Conference on Romanticism for the opportunity to share my work in this volume of essays: it is a great honor to be included among so many fine scholars; thank you also to Joshua Wilner for his able organization of the 2009 ICR conference in New York; warmest thanks to Marilyn Gaull for including the first version of this paper on her panel at the 2009 ICR.

1. For a thorough discussion of the role of *The Lancet* in combating "quackery" in medical and pharmaceutical practice in the 1820s, see Roy Porter, *Health for Sale*, Ch. 8, especially 221–25.
2. For alphabetical listings of historical addresses for all druggists mentioned in this chapter, see Richmond, Stevenson, and Turton.

13

Wordsworth's "Illustrated Books and Newspapers" and Media of the City

Peter J. Manning

I

Wordsworth's 1846 sonnet "Illustrated Books and Newspapers" has gained notoriety as the prize exhibition, in the words of Gillen D'Arcy Wood, of the resistance of "the literary elite" to "the cultural influence of new visual media":

> Discourse was deemed Man's noblest attribute,
> And written words the glory of his hand;
> Then followed Printing with enlarged command
> For thought—dominion vast and absolute
> For spreading truth, and making love expand.
> Now prose and verse sunk into disrepute
> Must lacquey a dumb Art that best can suit
> The taste of this once-intellectual Land.
> A backward movement surely have we here,
> For manhood—back to childhood; for the age—
> Back towards caverned life's first rude career.
> Avaunt this vile abuse of pictured page!
> Must eyes be all in all, the tongue and ear
> Nothing? Heaven keep us from a lower stage!

"For Romantic writers," Wood continues, the illustrated book "symbolized the spread of an infantilizing visual medium" (173). Yet as

Peter Simonsen replies, Wood's judgment is "too simple," in light of Wordsworth's suggestion in 1836 to Edward Moxon, his publisher, that illustrations be added to his poems (*LY* 3: 318)—the *Poems* of 1815 had already contained engravings by Sir George Beaumont—and the appearance in 1843 of an amply decorated *Select Pieces*, reprinted by Moxon with Wordsworth's encouragement in 1847.

The seeming intransigence of the sonnet nonetheless asks an explanation beyond the usual invocation of Wordsworth's conservatism. The pioneering illustrated newspaper was the *Illustrated London News*, which Herbert Ingram began to produce in May 1842. As the prospectus for "No. 1 of A NEW WEEKLY JOURNAL," of which Ingram and the engraver and publisher Henry Vizetelly distributed a million copies, had declared in March 1842, the newspaper was not as "dumb" or hostile to "prose" as Wordsworth's denunciation might lead one to believe:

> Entitled The ILLUSTRATED LONDON NEWS, Price Sixpence. Containing Thirty Engravings Every Week of the Most Interesting Events of the Day, in Addition to Forty-Eight Columns of News. Engagements have been made with Artists of Ability in Every Important Town in England and in Paris and other places on the Continent.

If the illustrations were the chief attraction of the new paper, the forty-eight columns of closely printed letterpress, three columns to a page, were not trivial. Frederick William Naylor Bayley, the paper's first editor, maintained in his address to the British Public on the front page of the first issue that "Art—as now fostered...has, in fact, become the bride of literature," and he affirmed that the paper would "associate its principle with a purity of tone that may secure and hold fast for our journal the fearless patronage of families; to seek in all things to uphold the cause of public morality,...and to withhold from society no point that its literature can furnish or its art adorn."

The statement reveals the mixed feelings that the paper's reliance on illustration inspired even among its own staff: association with the image raised the specter of mere sensationalism, to be counterbalanced by such high-minded pronouncements as this one. Yet the first issue was undeniably sensational: two pages of pictures of the Fancy Dress Ball given by Queen Victoria at Buckingham Palace only two days before publication, and a front-page illustration, produced by enhancing an existing print borrowed from the British Museum, of a disastrous fire at Hamburg of which news had reached London only on May 10. Other stories included a Dreadful Railway Accident near Paris, an Awful Steamboat Explosion in America, War in Afghanistan, and Cases Heard at the Central Criminal Court.

This hodgepodge of topical news from around the world, of accidents, entertainments, and crimes, suggests that the target of the sonnet, the supersession of "Discourse" by the "dumb Art" of illustration points to deeper discontents. Wordsworth's asperity was no doubt sharpened by his unhappy experience more than a decade earlier of publishing in the *Keepsake,* in which letterpress was deliberately subordinated to the plates of which the annual boasted.[5] The visual seems less offensive per se than the miscellaneous nature of the news the paper collects. As for William Cowper and George Crabbe before him "the news" challenges the poet's capacity to absorb and assimilate.[6] Despite the title of the sonnet I want to suggest that the illustrated book is not at issue, nor is the image the primary target, at least not in the way a first reading of the sonnet suggests. For Wordsworth, as his commentary years before on his sonnet "With ships the sea was sprinkled" makes clear, the mind needs a single point of reference from which to organize and calm the pressure of an influx of impressions:

> [W]ho is there that has not felt that the mind can have no rest among a multiplicity of objects, of which it cannot either make out one whole, or from which it cannot single out one individual, whereupon may be concentrated the attention divided or distracted by a multitude? After a certain time we must either select one image or object, which must put out of view the rest wholly, or must subordinate them to itself while it stands forth as a Head.[7]

In his poem "The Newspaper" of 1785 George Crabbe had already declared "Newspapers enemies to Literature" and denounced their "vapid sheets" (49):

> A daily swarm, that banish every Muse,
> Come flying forth, and mortals call them NEWS:
> For these, unread, the noblest volumes lie;
> For these, in sheets unsoil'd, the Muses die; (25–28)

William Cowper, in Book IV of *The Task* of the same year, is more detailed about the experience of reading the jumble of news and advertisements that characterized the newspapers:

> Cataracts of declamation thunder here, There forests of no meaning spread the page In which all comprehension wanders lost; 75While fields of pleasantry amuse us there, With merry descants on a nation's woes. The rest appears a wilderness of strange But gay confusion, roses for the cheeks And lilies for the brows of faded age, Teeth for the toothless, ringlets for the bald, Heaven, earth, and ocean plunder'd of

their sweets, Nectareous essences, Olympian dews, Sermons and city feasts and favourite airs, Æthereal journeys, submarine exploits, 85And Katterfelto with his hair on end At his own wonders, wondering for his bread. (*The Task*, Book IV, "The Winter Evening")[8]

Cowper, sitting by his fire sipping tea, is enabled to contemplate the bustle of the world without being overwhelmed by it, fulfilling the desire "[t]o see the stir / Of the great Babel and not feel the crowd, / To hear the roar she sends through all her gates / At a safe distance" (89–92). He preserves his "uninjured ear" (93) by "sitting and surveying thus at ease / The globe and its concerns" (94–95) in a verse that refigures the competing particulars of the newspaper—with the exception of the egregious Katterfelto[9]—into familiar type-narratives and satires. By this strategy Cowper, far from being overwhelmed, seems to himself "advanced / To some secure and more than mortal height, / That liberates and exempts me from them all" (95–97). From this secure vantage, the globe "turns submitted to my view, turns round / With all its generations; I behold / The tumult and am still" (98–100). Cowper presents himself "at home" (119) both in his cottage and in the world the newspaper enables him to draw into himself.

In contrast Wordsworth in the sonnet conquers the rush of news by repressing the contents of the news entirely: there are no particulars in the poem. That it is heterogeneity rather than the visual itself that oppresses him connects the denunciation of the sonnet to another dimension as well: not just the spatial form of the image but also the insistent chronological return of the newspaper, its perpetually renewed presence, its ever repeated presentation of disconnected *faits divers*. "Illustrated Books and Newspapers" takes up again the cultural criticism of the Preface to *Lyrical Ballads* decades before:

> [A] multitude of causes, unknown to former times, are now acting with a combined force to blunt the discriminating powers of the mind, and unfitting it for all voluntary exertion to reduce it to a state of almost savage torpor. The most effective of these causes are the great national events which are daily taking place, and the encreasing [*sic*] accumulation of men in cities, where the uniformity of their occupations produces a craving for extraordinary incident, which the rapid communication of intelligence hourly gratifies.[10]

The "thirst after outrageous stimulation" he had then condemned announced itself with greater force in a mass circulation national illustrated newspaper: by the end of 1842 the circulation of the *Illustrated London News* had grown to sixty thousand copies a week.

For Wordsworth the combined effect of frequency and heterogeneity is to crowd out the space of "discourse."

At issue here, as the *OED* definitions disclose, is a tension in the meaning of discourse itself. Etymologically "discourse" derives from a. F. *discours*, ad. L. *discurs-us* "running to and fro, conversation, discourse" (after *cours*: L. *cursus*) and is connected to such meanings as "onward course; process or succession of time, events, actions, etc.; = COURSE." The *OED* characterizes this meaning as obsolete, but so it does a second meaning which we may assume was pertinent for Wordsworth, classically trained and saturated in Milton as he was: "'The act of the understanding, by which it passes from premises to consequences' [as Johnson's Dictionary had it,] reasoning, thought, ratiocination; the faculty of reasoning, reason, rationality." The tension between "running to and fro"—heterogeneity—and the organizing process of reason underlies Wordsworth's denunciation of the scattering effect of the newspapers. The *OED* gives as the currently prevailing sense "a spoken or written treatment of a subject, in which it is handled or discussed at length; a dissertation, treatise, homily, sermon, or the like." This weaker definition is also threatened by the newspaper as Wordsworth saw it. The sonnet speaks repeatedly in terms of extension: "enlarged command," "dominion vast," "spreading truth," "making love expand." The proprietors of the *Illustrated London News* might well have claimed that it was just such enlargement that they sought to promote through mass circulation; Wordsworth, on the other hand, understood such terms not primarily in terms of readership but in terms of intellectual comprehension, a comprehension impossible when multiple topics and illustrations were crammed into sixteen pages, to be succeeded the following week by a new array of topics and images. As Wordsworth continues explaining the logic of his sonnet to Lady Beaumont in the letter just quoted he develops a characteristic opposition:

> "Joyously it showed," this continued till that feeling may be supposed to have passed away, and a kind of comparative listlessness or apathy to have succeeded, as at this line, "Some veering up and down, one knew not why." All at once, while I am in this state, comes forth an object, an individual, and my mind, sleepy and unfixed, is awakened and fastened in a moment.

The ships "Veering up and down" in the sonnet, like the "running to and fro" of newspaper discourses, produces not mental activity for Wordsworth but a "sleepy and unfixed" mind or, in the sharper words of the Preface to *Lyrical Ballads*, "savage torpor." He there lamented that "the literature and theatrical exhibitions of the country have conformed themselves" to the "craving for extraordinary incident" fueled by modern "life and manners." What the *Illustrated London News* apprehends as stimulation, Wordsworth senses as distraction.[11]

II

There is some irony in Wordsworth's having chosen the sonnet form to vent his dismay at illustrated newspapers, because the brevity of the sonnet made it seem to contemporaries the privileged genre for the impatient readers of an accelerating age. And it may also seem self-contradicting that Wordsworth should have placed his protest against miscellaneousness in the category of Miscellaneous Sonnets, as he did when he first published "Illustrated Books and Newspapers" in 1846. Before addressing these issues I should like to turn back to an earlier incident which may have contributed to Wordsworth's animosity toward the *Illustrated London News,* while at the same time suggesting that his scorn had causes not merely personal.

On the death of Robert Southey in 1843 Wordsworth was offered, and prevailed upon to accept, the Laureateship. The *Illustrated London News* covered this event in its issue of April 15, 1843, accompanying the article with a portrait (figure 13.1): "Here, reader, is his likeness."

Frances Blanshard describes the "portrait" (in scare quotation marks) as "a miserable woodcut from no known original, indeed not resembling any that we do know.... though recalling portraits of Milton"; a resemblance she clinches by also reproducing the frontispiece portrait of Jonathan Richardson's *Explanatory Notes and Remarks on Milton's Paradise Lost* (1734) (figure 13.2).[12]

The *Illustrated London News* was probably drawn to "the Richardson head of Milton" by the discussion of it in Thomas De Quincey's recent essays on Wordsworth in *Tait's Edinburgh Magazine* (1839):

> Judge of my astonishment when, in this portrait of Milton, I saw a likeness nearly perfect of Wordsworth, better by much than any which I have seen, of those expressly painted for himself. The likeness is tolerably preserved in that by Carruthers, in which one of the little Rydal waterfalls, &c., composes a background;[13] yet this is much inferior, as a mere portrait of Wordsworth, to the Richardson head of Milton; and this, I believe is the last which represents Wordsworth in the vigour of his power.[14]

Seeking an image for their article, the editors of the *Illustrated London News* appear to have grafted a crudely modified version of the long-locked head of Milton from Richardson onto a torso in nineteenth-century dress, adding an enfeebling cane (which appears in no other

Figure 13.1 The new poet Laureate.

Source: All figures used are courtesy of the Division of Rare and Manuscript Collections, Cornell University Library.

portrait of Wordsworth). As Blanshard notes, many readers of the newspaper might have seen Wordsworth in person; many readers might have known the Watt engraving of the Pickersgill portrait that appeared in the 1836 edition of Wordsworth's poems, and again in the issues of 1840, 1841, 1842, and 1843. Well might the poet have felt, in the words of the sonnet, that the travesty constituted a "vile abuse of pictured page!" *Illustrated Books and Newspapers* could not have been what the editors hoped when in their article they urged Wordsworth to

> give us some offerings in honour of his new station, even if they be confined within the sweet circle of the sonnet—such sonnet as he could so gloriously celebrate and so exquisitely write. Who does not remember the fine confirmation of his power in that walk of poetic inspiration?

If this speculation is correct, the aggravation of having been misrepresented in a widely circulated portrait would have been magnified by

Figure 13.2 Jonathan Richardson, frontispiece, *Explanatory Notes and Remarks on Milton's Paradise Lost* (London: np, 1734).

its occasion. "*Tait's*," Grevel Lindop observes, "was a cheap magazine and an organ of Radicalism."¹⁵ Worse: Wordsworth regarded De Quincey's gossipy essays as an unforgivable violation of personal confidence. Henry Crabb Robinson remembered: "I was with Words. one day when the advertisement of one of his [De Quincey's] papers was read. He said with great earnestness: 'I beg that no friend of mine will ever tell me a word of the contents of these papers' & I dare say he was substantially obeyed."¹⁶

For De Quincey to have converted experiences based on friendship into salable articles for a journal was to drag the dignified poet into the commercial culture of personality and celebrity that he claimed to abhor; put less idealistically, it transferred control of his image from his own productions to another. The fraudulent "likeness" in the *Illustrated London News* was a literal repetition of the affront of De Quincey and *Tait's*.

The pique is not merely personal, but points to the divergent views on the nature of truth held by the poet and the periodicals. The address on the first page of the first issue of the *Illustrated London News* declared: "The public will have henceforth under their glance, and within their grasp, the very form and presence of events as they transpire, in all their substantial reality, and with evidence visible as well as circumstantial." "Vigorous illustration" was held up less as an appealing innovation than as a monitor of reality more faithful than discourse: "if the pen be ever led into fallacious argument, the pencil must at least be oracular with the spirit of truth."¹⁷ "Evidence visible" formed a crucial part of the mission of the *Illustrated London News* to become an object of reference and of the historical record: as Toni Weller has noted, the *Illustrated London News* "gave away 'monthly wrappers'... in which to bind issues, as well as 'a title page and index' at the end of each year to organize and structure the information contained within its pages."¹⁸ The oversize bound biannual volumes in which the newspaper is now often found in libraries are an apt marker of the aspiration of the *Illustrated London News* to rise from the ephemera of the week to permanence, from newspaper to book.¹⁹ Such episodes as the tinkered plate of Hamburg in the first issue, not a picture of the fire at Hamburg but of Hamburg with fire added, or a "likeness" of Wordsworth cobbled from a portrait of Milton, a representation of which the falsity many readers of the newspaper would immediately perceive, thus called the veracity of "evidence visible" into question, and the integrity of the newspaper with it. More: De Quincey's comparison of Wordsworth to Milton signifies not only a literal (and fortuitous) physical resemblance, but also insinuates a claim that De Quincey, despite his disappointment in Wordsworth the man, affirmed: that Wordsworth is a poet in the line of Milton, a claim at once on genealogy and on merit. To construe "likeness" as a matter of image alone is to raise a doubt whether the editors of the *Illustrated London News* knew how to *read*, in the sense that Wordsworth would have understood the term. From this perspective his question "Must eyes be all in all, the tongue and ear / Nothing?" looks less hyperbolical.

III

To place "Illustrated Books and Newspapers" under the catch-all heading of Miscellaneous Sonnets as Wordsworth did in 1846 would not suggest that position in a sequence will matter much to its interpretation and effect, were it not that all his life he was scrupulous about the organization of his poems. As he wrote to Henry Crabb Robinson while preparing the 1827 collected edition

> Miscellaneous poems ought not to be jumbled together at *random*—were this done with mine the passage from one to another would often be insupportably offensive; but in my judgement the only thing of much importance in arrangement is that one poem should shade off happily into another—and the contrasts where they occur be clear of all harshness or abruptness—[20]

Wordsworth followed "Illustrated Books and Newspapers" with the forceful contrast of "To Lucca Giordano," making clear that it is the threat to philosophic contemplation that generates his anxiety, rather than the "dumb Art" of the visual itself:

> Giordano, verily thy Pencil's skill
> Hath here portrayed with nature's happiest grace
> The fair Endymion couched on Latmos-hill;
> And Dian gazing on the Shepherd's face
> In rapture,—yet suspending her embrace,
> As not unconscious with what power the thrill
> Of her most timid touch his sleep would chase,
> And, with his sleep, that beauty calm and still.
> O may this work have found its last retreat
> Here in a Mountain-bard's secure abode,
> One to whom, yet a School-boy, Cynthia showed
> A face of love which he in love would greet,
> Fixed, by her smile, upon some rocky seat;
> Or lured along where green-wood paths he trod.

Rydal Mount, 1846 Wordsworth recounted his acquisition of the painting to William Boxall, who had painted his portrait in 1831 and decades later became Director of the National Gallery:

I don't know whether you are acquainted with the works of Lucca Giordano—he is a clever painter. My son picked up at Lucca three large Pictures of his which now hang in my staircase, which they exactly fill. One is Vulcan presenting to Venus the armour he has forged for Aneas, the other Diana hanging over Endymion on Mount Latmos, and the third, a scene from Ariosto or Tasso, of a Lady bending over her dead lover, who has been slain. These pictures cost John but little on the spot and I shall take care that he does not lose by the Purchase. They have cost me a good deal putting into order etc.[21]

The provenance gave the picture a personal connection to the poet; its location made it a familiar daily presence, a constant of domestic routine as opposed to the ever varying, ever the same newspaper.

The mythological framework of the sonnet brings a transhistorical value that is the antipodes of the quotidian matter of the newspaper, and the contrast between this poem and the previous one runs deeper still. "Dian gazing on the Shepherd's face / In rapture,—yet suspending her embrace" (4–5) is paradigmatic of absorbed contemplation, the suspension the opposite of the ships "veering up and down" of "With ships the sea was sprinkled" or the "running to and fro" of the confusion of newspaper articles. Dian's gaze is focused attention, the heightened "fasten[ing]" of the mind that produces the paradox of "calm and still" (8) mental activity. Dian gazes on Endymion as Wordsworth gazes on the portrait in its accustomed location, a parallel that equally models the kind of reading Wordsworth seeks for his poem.

Yet readers who are not familiar with the seventeenth-century Neapolitan Baroque painter are likely to be surprised by the brilliant coloring and theatrical composition of Giordano's work. *Diana and Endymion* by Giordano in the National Gallery, Washington, shows Diana with one nipple bare looming over the sleeping shepherd, the brilliant blue of her cape paralleling the brilliant red of his, setting off the pale flesh tones and the chiaroscuro of the background.[22] The sestet surprisingly substitutes the youthful Wordsworth for Endymion: through the stability of the image the seventy-six year old "Mountainbard" recovers a glimpse of his past self, moving the poem from the indoors of a "secure abode" (10) with a hint nonetheless of impending death in its figuration as a "last retreat" (9) to the pastoral pleasures of remembered "green-wood paths" (14). This unexpected pairing of the object of erotic desire with the elderly, philosophic "Mountain-bard" who emphasizes his current state by appending the date to his text seems to me not without wit. As he narrates it the picture preserves the older poet's narcissistic image of himself: the young Wordsworth has revived through the tableau of intimacy he formed with Cynthia: "A face of love which he in love would greet" (11). The "unfixed" mind of Wordsworth's commentary on "With ships the sea was sprinkled" is replaced with the erotic potential of "Fixed, by her smile" (13), and even the overtones of danger in "lured" (14) reassert the affectional energies of the aged poet laureate, and his physical motion too: the poem ends with the image of his walking along the forest paths.

The mediation of art, visual and verbal, invests the mythological figure of Endymion with personal significance, restoring the passionate youth to be found outdoors amid "rocky seat[s]" and "green-wood paths" rather than in Rydal Mount, already for decades an object of pilgrimage. The picture connects the poet both with his past self and with the next generation, the son who gave it to him. It counters the transient and distracting images of "Illustrated Books and Newspapers" with a stable and personally charged image providing the secure shelter that memory alone does not; the object is not lost, but present to be encountered anew each day. Stepping from "Illustrated Books and Newspapers" to the ekphrastic "To Lucca Giordano" one feels the difference in conceptions of the image and of reading: in the second poem reading is a vital exchange between the image, which completes itself in the responsiveness of the viewer/writer, and the writer who finds his inward likeness in the image of Dian and Endymion.[23]

For the edition of 1850 Wordsworth relocated "Illustrated Books and Newspapers" to the category of Poems of Sentiment and Reflection, a grouping that includes such meditative works as "The Two April Mornings" and "The Fountain: A Conversation," as well as the "Ode to Duty" and the "Ode to Lycoris," and placed it between the four linked sonnets that comprise "Personal Talk" and "To the Spade of a Friend" juxtapositions that underscore the values of the sonnet.[24] "Personal Talk" reads like a crystallization of Cowper's ingathering gestures:

> Now stir the fire, and close the shutters fast,
> Let fall the curtains, wheel the sofa round,
> And while the bubbling and loud-hissing urn
> Throws up a steamy column, and the cups
> That cheer but not inebriate, wait on each,
> So let us welcome peaceful evening in. (*The Task*, Book IV, 436–41)

As Kevis Goodman argues in the essay already cited, Cowper's "loopholes of retreat" are not an isolating withdrawal—he is reading the newspaper—but the portals through which he looks out on the world from a position of security. Wordsworth's withdrawal is more daringly privative; so far from hiding the perils of withdrawal, he foregrounds them. Recalling the etymological origin that suggests a counterplot in "Illustrated Books and Newspapers"—or perhaps one should say, "anticipating," since that sonnet now follows *Personal Talk*—he declares that to "such discourse" as the mere "personal talk" of "friends...neighbours...chance-acquaintance" (3–9) he prefers "silence long, / Long, barren silence" (9–10). The repetition of "silence" seems to mark constancy, of the condition itself and of Wordsworth's commitment to it, as a matter of desire and ethics both. In a figure that crosses from discourse to image Wordsworth confesses that "These all wear out of me, like Forms, with chalk / Painted on rich men's floors, for one feast-night" (7–8). The figure joins trivia to transience: rejecting the "fits of sprightly malice" that those he stigmatizes as the "tribe" of "Our daily world's true Worldlings" claim "but bribe / The languid mind into activity" (17–22) enables concentration and a countervailing intellectual adventurousness: "Wings have we,—and as far as we can go / We may find pleasure" (29–30). The address in the first issue of the *Illustrated London News* had proclaimed: "Here we make our bow, determined to keep continually before the eye of the world a living and moving panorama of all its activities and influences." Against the moving and distracting world *Personal Talk* celebrates "The Poets" (53): "Dreams, books, are each a world; and books, we know / Are a substantial world" (33–34).

The contrast between book and newspaper enforced by the sequence acquires further character in the instances Wordsworth gives of the books in which he finds "personal themes, a plenteous store":

> Matter wherein right voluble I am,
> To which I listen with a ready ear;
> Two shall be named, pre-eminently dear,—
> The gentle Lady married to the Moor;
> And heavenly Una with her milk-white Lamb. (37–42)

(Note that the silence is filled by speaking books to which the now "voluble" reader "listen[s].") In singling out Shakespeare's Desdemona and Spenser's Una, figures of embattled virtue, Wordsworth juxtaposes the active outward-looking perspective of the *Illustrated London News* to a feminized contemplativeness. The citation of Desdemona in this context is particularly striking, because it is Othello's misconstruction of the handkerchief that Iago offers him as the "ocular proof" (*Othello* III.iii.357) he demands of his wife's infidelity that destroys them both. "Illustrated Books and Newspapers" in its shifting contexts embodies a cardinal distinction in the modes of nineteenth-century literacy, the distinction between extensive reading, a wide but shallow familiarity with a great variety of materials, and intensive reading, the concentrated return to a small number of cherished texts. At issue in the sonnet and its frames is the question whether the truth of the age is to be represented through "ocular proof," "evidence visible," or acts of sympathetic identification and sustained inwardness. In their own ways both poet and newspaper strove to record and comprehend their age.

In forecasting his vocation in the *Prelude* Wordsworth pledged himself to "making verse / Deal boldly with substantial things" (*1850*, 13: 234–35). In Wordsworth's lexicon "substantial" stands against "change": a newspaper devoted only to picturing whatever is timely and topical this week sinks the visual into a "vile abuse" of the "pictured page" and destroys the contemplativeness of "this once-intellectual Land." Hence the importance to him of arranging the succession of even his miscellaneous sonnets to overcome any hint of mere momentaneity, integrating an individual text into a longer sequence. How much he distrusted "rapid communication," to recur to the language of the Preface to *Lyrical Ballads*, can be seen in a late letter to Henry Crabb Robinson: "How comes it that you write to us so seldom, now that Postage is nothing [the uniform penny post had been introduced in January 1840]. Letters are sure to be impoverished by the change, and if they do not come oftener, the gain will be a *loss*, and a grievous one too."[25] Robinson relied upon his long friendship with Wordsworth to reply frankly, teasingly turning the poet's own words on him:

> The answer is an obvious one, and you will give me credit for being quite sincere when I make it. It is but seldom that I dare to think that I have anything to say that is worth your reading....Formerly, and even now in a slight degree, I used to be checked, both in writing and in talk, by the recollection of the four sonnets, so beautiful, and yet beginning so alarmingly—
> > I am not one who much or oft delight
> > To season my fireside with personal talk....
> > Now, after all, a letter—a genuine letter—is but personal talk.[26]

Much as the "fireside" (2) and the "kettle" (14) of *Personal Talk* recall the inviting coziness of Cowper, and much as Robinson trusts that he has earned the privilege of entering Wordsworth's sanctuary, it is easy to share his sense that Wordsworth's scorn for the topical was "alarming," the egotistical sublime at its most self-enclosed and self-satisfied.

IV

On the back page of its issue of April 27, 1850, the *Illustrated London News* announced the death of Wordsworth on April 23 (figure 13.3).

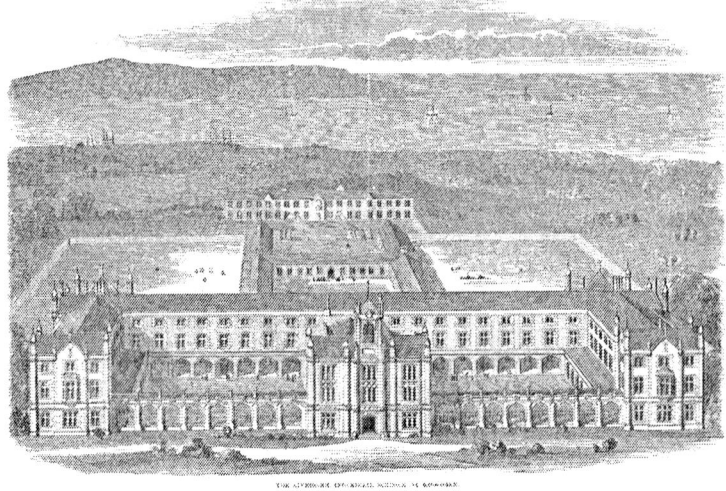

Figure 13.3 *Illustrated London News*, 27 April 1850.

The brief obituary on page 296 is subordinate to a "View of the picturesque retreat of the lamented poet, at Rydal Mount," complete with gardeners scything the grounds at the rear of the house, which occupies the top center of the page.[27] The article ends with a cross-reference: "A portrait of Wordsworth appeared in No. 50 of our Journal." However spurious this particular portrait, the gesture, as Weller points out, typifies the ambition of the newspaper to achieve documentary status. The only other article on the page concerns The Liverpool Industrial Schools, which opened in May 1845 in an attempt to offset a growing "juvenile pauperism" in the city. The institution currently housed 1,123 poor children, offering basic, religious, and vocational education at an "annual cost to the parish" of "£10,483 1s. 9d." At the bottom of the page and spreading all across it is an engraving of the massive building, its wings extending well beyond the scene of Rydal Mount above it, just as the text of the article far exceeds that of the obituary of the poet, wrapping around and framing the image of his home. The fortuitous conjunction of this example of Victorian social engineering with an obituary for the poet of an often solitary childhood in nature, "Fostered alike by beauty and by fear" (*1850 Prelude*, 1: 307), open to the interplay of accident and providence, and recuperating error by the retrospective power of interpretation, might seem exactly the sort of jumble against which Wordsworth inveighs in "Illustrated Books and Newspapers." This unremarked contrast uncannily repeats the temporal coincidence in No. 50 that placed the summary of a bill on national education next to the announcement that Wordsworth, who had declared to his patron Sir George Beaumont "Every great Poet is a Teacher: I wish to be considered as a teacher, or as nothing," had received the laureateship (see figure 13.1).[28] The juxtapositions may also be seen as an unintended but luminous paradigm of the significant Victorian cultural debate that the sonnet and the newspaper enact, which we may read without succumbing either to Wordsworth's vilification of illustrated books and newspapers or of the prevailing contempt for the conservatism of his old age.

Notes

Research for this chapter was begun in a year as a Fellow of the Obermann Center for Advanced Studies at the University of Iowa. I owe more than I can here acknowledge to the Director of the Center, Jay Semel, the colleagues with whom I shared my time there, and the resources of the university.

1. Wordsworth's sonnets quoted from *Last Poems, 1821–1850*.

2. Simonsen 30–31; see also 174. Simonsen cites (193 n. 41) the suggestion of Mark L. Reed that the sonnet might have been "kindled partly by this collection of his own poetry" (71), but Reed's account seems to me to support a contrary interpretation. The 1843 publication by James Burns had not been fairly authorized by Wordsworth, but when Moxon brought out a legitimate revision in 1847 with still more vignettes Wordsworth took two dozen copies for himself; a new printing followed in 1854. The total number of copies ran to seven thousand, and Wordsworth and his heirs earned more than £375 from the venture.
3. "The Early History of *The Illustrated London News*." Weedy: *Illustrated London News* website. See Weedy.
4. Bailey 208; 211.
5. Manning in Jordan and Patten 44–73.
6. On Crabbe's protest against the "variety of dissociating articles which are huddled together in our Daily Papers" (*Poetical Works* 2:111) see Ellison. Her nuanced distinction between the responses of Crabbe and Cowper to the newspapers should be read with Goodman.
7. Letter of May 21, 1807. *MY* 148.
8. All quotations of *The Task* from vol. 9 of *Works*.
9. Gustavus Katterfelto was a Prussian quack doctor and conjurer who took advertisements in the newspapers headed "Wonders! Wonders! Wonders!"
10. Preface to *Lyrical Ballads* 249.
11. The description in the *Prelude* of Bartholomew Fair is the *locus classicus* of this anxiety in Wordsworth: "Oh, blank confusion! true epitome / Of what the mighty City is herself, / To thousands upon thousands of her Sons, / Living amid the same perpetual whirl / Of trivial objects, melted and reduced / To one identity, by differences / That have no law, no meaning, and no end" (*1850*, 7: 722–28).
12. The *Illustrated London News* article appears on 259 of the issue of April 15, 1843. I quote from Blanshard 93; she reproduces the two images as Plates 24b and 19b; I have sought out the original publications. In her caption to 19b Blanshard cites De Quincey, but without quotation or commentary.
13. Reproduced as Plate 5 in Blanshard.
14. De Quincey 140–41.
15. Lindop 305.
16. Quoted in Jordan 346.
17. For a careful reading of this program see Sinnema.
18. Weller 203.
19. On the genre crossing of the *Illustrated London News* see Houfe:
    Its format was entirely that of the newspaper and yet its appearance in two cloth-bound volumes at the end of the year, blind-stamped decoration at the corners, gilded cypher in the middle, gave it an air of permanence. This was not something to be discarded like a newspaper, but kept on the table in view of visitors,

to be pored over like an album. There was much of the album in these volumes. (71–72)
20. Letter of April 6, 1826. *LY* 1: 440.
21. Letter of May 21, 1846. *LY* 4: 781.
22. For the image see: <http://www.nga.gov/fcgi-bin/timage_f?object=72078&image=18524&c=>. The annotated catalog drily notes "For which no on bid" (Munby 55). There is a Giordano of *Venus Giving Arms to Aeneas* at the Museum of Fine Arts, Boston; see: <http://www.mfa.org/collections/search_art.asp?coll_keywords=luca+giordano&submit.x=8&submit.y=13.> It is intriguing to speculate that the paintings in these American collections might once have been Wordsworth's, but the matter is tangled. At the auction of Wordsworth's library in July 1859 following the death of the poet's wife the last item of the second day was a "fine gallery picture...a capital specimen of the Neapolitan School, by one of its most consummate Masters—Lucca Giordano," *Vulcan presenting to Venus the armour for Mars*, which I take as a misdescription of *Venus Giving Arms to Aeneas*. The catalog dryly notes "For which no one bid" (Munby). The paintings are no longer at Rydal Mount, and neither Marian Elkington, the curator, nor Jeff Cowton, curator of The Wordsworth Trust at Dove Cottage (which never held the paintings) knows of their whereabouts. Anne Halpern of the Department of Curatorial Records, National Gallery of Art, Washington, D. C., and Victoria Reed, Monica S. Sadler Assistant Curator for Provenance, Museum of Fine Arts, Boston, have been extraordinarily generous in pursuing the possible connections between the holdings of their institutions and Wordsworth, but so far no links have been established. There are gaps in the provenance; Giordano was a prolific painter who produced multiple versions of these subjects; attributions shift. Perhaps this chapter will reach someone with the missing information.
23. Cf. Shackford, who argues that Wordsworth distinguished between "mere illustrators who lure readers away from 'discourse,' intellectual activity, and exchange of ideas" and "the power of creative visualization, so essential in intelligent appreciation" (71).
24. I have written on *To the Spade of a Friend* in *Reading Romantics* 244–54.
25. Letter of March 16, 1840. *LY* 4:49.
26. Henry Crabb Robinson 1: 224–25.
27. The image is briefly discussed by Samantha Matthews 155.
28. Letter of February 20, 1808. *MY* 1:195.

14

Babylon and Jerusalem on the Old Kent Road

Tim Fulford

> *There never was any age or any country so favourable to the success of imposture and the growth of superstition, as this very age and this very England*
>
> —Robert Southey, Letters from England (1807)[1]

One of the most extraordinary features of the late eighteenth and early nineteenth centuries—those years of commercialization and urbanization, utilitarianism and political economy—was the prevalence of prophecy: Londoners of both genders and all classes—respectable Anglican clergymen, members of Parliament, veteran scientists, servant girls from the West Country, half-pay navy officers, artisan engravers—proclaimed their conviction that God was about to end the world and remake it, bringing about a millennium of love and peace in which the redeemed would live with Christ on earth. The Swedenborgians attracted hundreds to their New Jerusalem Church; Richard Brothers was followed by thousands when he envisioned London's destruction and remaking in apocalyptic fire; Joanna Southcott's supporters numbered in the hundreds of thousands, believing she was pregnant with the returning Messiah. But while historians of religion have attributed prophets' popularity to the failings of the established church,[2] and historians of radicalism have related it to the French Revolution,[3] there was also another cause—London itself, and the new and bewildering kinds of social experience it produced, which rendered some of its inhabitants desperate to imagine themselves into a better, more human way of life.

In this chapter I want to ask what some of these prophecies had in common and what they had to do with the experience of London, the world's largest and most commercial city. I shall ask a further question too: what happened to them? The eruption of prophecy, I shall suggest, was in fact the end of something, the last great flowering of the practice of interpreting current events through the framework of Old Testament scripture. Ultimately, for most Britons such prophecy failed to encompass the new urban conditions within a convincing structure of meaning, failed, that is, adequately to understand the city. It was De Quincey, I will show, who diagnosed this failure, making himself an embodiment of the city's perversion of the capacity for redemptive vision. In the process he foresaw a decisive shift, an inaugural moment of modernity—the secularization of prophecy in the poetic imagination and the flight of that poetic imagination to the countryside.[4] De Quincey, in other words, anticipated, and suggested the cause of, a division between country and city and poetry and prose that would dominate the next two hundred years of British culture.

The overwhelming nature of the new urban conditions is attested by the German visitor G. C. Lichtenberg, describing his first experience of London in the 1770s:

> Imagine a street about as wide as the Weender in Göttingen, but, taking it altogether, about six times as long. On both sides tall houses with plate-glass windows. The lower floors consist of shops and seem to be made entirely of glass; many thousand candles light up silverware, engravings, books, clocks, pewter, paintings, women's finery, modish and otherwise, gold, precious stones, steel-work, and endless coffee-rooms and lottery offices. The street looked as though it were illuminated for some festivity...a porter runs you down, crying "By your leave," when you are lying on the ground. In the middle of the street roll chaises, carriages and drays in an unending stream. Above this din and the hum and clatter of thousands of tongues and feet one hears the chimes from church clocks, the bells of the postmen, the organs, fiddles, hurdy-gurdies, and tambourines of English mountebanks, and the cries of those who sell hot and cold viands in the open street corners. Then you will see a bonfire of shavings flaring up as high as the upper floors of the houses in a circle of merrily shouting beggar-boys, sailors and rogues. Suddenly a man whose handkerchief has been stolen will cry "Stop thief," and everyone will begin running and pushing and many of them not with any desire of catching the thief, but of prigging for themselves, perhaps, a watch or purse. Before you know where you are, a pretty, nicely dressed miss will take you by the hand....Then there is

an accident forty paces from you.... Suddenly you will, perhaps, hear a shout from a hundred throats, as if a fire had broken out, a house fallen down... I have said nothing about the ballad singers who, forming circles at every corner, dam the stream of humanity which stops to listen and steal.[5]

By the 1780s London was no like other place on earth. It was the most crowded, dirtiest, poorest city, but also the brightest, wealthiest, and most alluring. Its streets were a new world, a dense intermingling of people, goods, signs, and shops. As a middle-class person, you had your ears deafened by balladeers, your hand held by whores, your pockets fingered by thieves. The signs of rank—cleanliness, nice clothes—made you a target to be sold to or stolen from. And so the street became a rite of passage for newcomers, a symbol of entry into a metropolitan maelstrom,[6] where everything, even the people were for sale.

The new urban experience challenged people to make sense of a city where individual identity was threatened by the sheer mass of people and where commodities were king. It was because London's teeming population and relentless commercialism undermined human connection that it seemed both frightening and alienating—one thinks of Blake, showing the human results of the "chartered" (capitalized/incorporated[7]) city in the soldier's blood and the harlot's curse.[8] Or Wordsworth, writing "my mind did at this spectacle turn round / As with the might of waters" (*Prelude* [1805] 7: 615–16)[9] when he saw the horrifying sight of the blind beggar with a paper pinned to his chest, his only sign of who he was. Wordsworth diagnosed an increasing alienation and corruption owing to "the encreasing [*sic*] accumulation of men in cities, where the uniformity of their occupations produces a craving for extraordinary incident which the rapid communication of intelligence hourly gratifies."[10] This excessive rapidity led to an addiction to "gross and violent stimulants," an overstimulation that required higher and higher doses of the trivial to be satisfied: living in the city was akin to drug-dependency,[11] corrupting taste: "The invaluable works of our elder writers, I had almost said the works of Shakespeare and Milton, are driven into neglect by frantic novels, sickly and stupid German Tragedies, and deluges of idle and extravagant stories in verse."[12] Thus corrupt, the urban crowds seemed diseased and infectious—"pestilential masses of ignorant population."[13]

Wordsworth's alarm was not new: it was in the 1780s that William Cowper first delineated the new capitalism and its effects on the metropolis, now enriched by the profits of empire. Cowper detected corruption beneath the city's glittering surfaces, and reached for an old trope to indict it:

> where has commerce such a mart,
> So rich, so throng'd, so drain'd, and so supplied,
> As London, opulent, enlarg'd and still
> Increasing London? Babylon of old
> Not more the glory of the earth, than she
> A more accomplish'd world's chief glory now.[14]

Cowper's biblical London had a topical cause: London seemed the new Babylon because its wealth stemmed in great measure from the Oriental colonies which had, since Lord Clive's conquests in India, been pouring money into the coffers of the East India Company. According to Cowper, this Oriental wealth was responsible for a rise in consumption not only of goods but also of other people. Orientalism fostered a capitalism that was as morally and politically dangerous as it was all-pervasive. "Hast thou," Cowper asked his nation,

> though suckled at fair Freedom's breast,
> Exported slavery to the conquer'd East,
> Pull'd down the tyrants India served with dread,
> And raised thyself, a greater, in their stead?
> Gone thither arm'd and hungry, return'd full,
> Fed from the richest veins of the Mogul,
> A despot big with power obtained by rapine and by stealth?
> With Asiatic vices stored thy mind,
> But left their virtues and thine own behind,
> And, having truck'd thy soul, brought home the fee
> To tempt the poor to sell himself to thee? (*Expostulation*, 365–75)[15]

Appalled by imperial greed, Cowper left London for rural retirement, as Wordsworth also did—satirizing it, and all it stood for, from a moral distance. But he also chose to interpret it in terms provided by millenarian prophecy. London was Babylon—a city of sin whose existence indicated the Lord's displeasure, heralding a coming apocalypse in which it would be destroyed, and the world remade.

Cowper was but the first of many: millenarian prophecy sprang up all over town in the last decades of the eighteenth century and first of the nineteenth. Joseph Priestley announced that the violence of the French Revolutionary war was fulfilling Daniel's prophecies that a fifth monarchy, ruled by the Son of Man, would shortly supersede all others. By 1804 Southcott was offering her followers visions of the New Jerusalem shortly to dawn when she, the "woman clothed with the sun" had given birth to a "man child, who was to rule all nations."[16] Bishop Joseph Horsley, meanwhile, prophesied that the French Revolution was the Antichrist; its rise heralded "a dissolution of the whole fabric of the external world."[17] And G. S. Faber, Fellow of Lincoln College Oxford, claimed that Britain would alone be saved like "a column in the midst of the surrounding ruins [w]hile mighty empires totter to their base, and while Antichrist advances with rapid strides to his predicted sovereignty over the inslaved [*sic*] kings."[18] A pattern emerged: the more socially disadvantaged the prophet, the more, therefore, they spoke from the city's crowded alleys, courts and garrets, the more Britain, and, at its center, London, was seen as a sinful sign of God's wrath. Thus William Bryan and John Wright, two poor artisans who in 1789 traveled to Avignon to join the society of prophets there, expected the divine destruction of the capital city, since "here is the time in which God will break the laws made by the children of the earth. Here is the time wherein he will reprove the science of men, and here is the time of his justice. This is the time that we must believe all those who announce the new reign of the Lord."[19] Both men became followers of the "King of the Hebrews," Richard Brothers, who in 1795 declared London to be the "SPIRITUAL BABYLON" of Revelation 18: it would be destroyed in retribution for its commercialism, whereby all things, even human beings, were for sale: "Beasts, Sheep, and Horses, ... *and Slaves*, and *Souls of Men*."[20] George III, as monarch of Babylon, would be struck down by the Lord and die unless he gave up his throne. By 1800 Brothers's prophecies were echoing in Ireland, where Francis Dobbs, who had encountered the Swedenborgians and Avignonians in London, predicted that the Apocalypse would destroy the present fabric of the world: Europe's Babylonish capitals would be replaced by a New Jerusalem.

> And lo! Her palaces and temples rise,
> In true magnificence. In polish'd marble,
> Exquisitely wrought, the diff'rent orders
> Are with the justest taste dispos'd—Her lofty spires
> The Streets adorn—and strictest symmetry
> In all her buildings is display'd. What'er
> Babylon, of old renown'd, or later Rome—
> Or Paris, or London, now can boast—is here
> So far excell'd, as not to be compar'd.[21]

It was because London seemed at once so powerful and so dreadful in its reduction of everything to an item for sale, that it demanded the biblical metaphor of Babylon—it was uncategorizable in normal terms. Thus the Scottish moralist Robert Mudie, writing in 1825, termed the city "the Great Babylon" because it presented an "unthreadable labyrinth," producing a "total insignificance of single persons and single objects."[22] The figure of Babylon also gave London's endless dizzying parade, so overwhelming in its relentless trivialization and commodification, meaning where it seemed meaningless. The city became an example of sin, set aside for God's wrath. There was a divine plan to its alienating chaos. And paradoxically, it was because it was categorizable as Babylon that it was possible, and necessary, to make it Jerusalem: so appalling was its destruction of authenticity that it was necessary to transform it to its opposite to reassert the human values that would otherwise be denied. Its assault on human sympathy and therefore on the imagination—encapsulated by Wordsworth's "The *face* of every one / That passes by me is a *mystery*" and Blake's "mark in every face I meet / *Marks* of weakness, *marks* of woe"[23]—demanded, of those who felt it, a reassertion, an alternative London, created by the imagination, in which meaning, value, and justice recolonize the streets, shops, and squares. Within the framework of biblical prophecy, however, this imagination often took literal and material form: many of the visionaries were sure that a coming apocalypse would see London replaced by a real millennial city, a new, rectilinear, and salubrious Jerusalem of spacious squares and symmetrical buildings. They transformed the teeming chaos of Babylon into neoclassical order in an effort to delineate a redeemed polis in which laws, ethics, and human relationships are right and true. They exercised, that is to say, their architectural imagination in order to prophesy the setting-in-stone of a society again governed by the sympathy and empathy that present-day "chartered" London had eroded. In 1801 Brothers, for instance, set out a detailed architectural plan of the New Jerusalem in which he tried to unite the visions of Ezekiel with modern town planning: his city is all garden squares, good ventilation, and Corinthian columns—

> The garden of Eden, or rather in English the Lord's garden, is a square of 6912 feet each side, the one to the north, the other to the south, the third to the east, the fourth to the west. Each side has three gates, in all twelve, one gate in the centre of each side, and one in each quarter: the four centre gates are to be shut, the six working days of the week, and the eight quarter gates to be kept open; but on the sabbath and every public holiday, all the twelve gates are to be opened. All people, poor and rich, foreigner and native, who are in a cleanly dress, are always to have free liberty to walk or sit in the garden.[24]

"Free liberty" is built into the cityscape, but only on public holidays: Brothers's Jerusalem will not be a Godwinian overturning of private property so much as an ordered alleviation of the commercial culture in which wealth allowed one to own—and exclude others from—the Lord's earth. Jerusalem, it turns out, is rather like the new area of London then being named after the reformist Whig magnates who called themselves "friends of the people:" as in Bloomsbury's Bedford and Russell Squares, symmetry of design and a hint of the pastoral characterize the redeemed city, replacing the dense, crowded, crooked narrow streets of the medieval town.

As John Barrell has shown, imagination was a politicized issue in the mid-1790s, as a repressive government, alarmed that agitators would bring about a revolution akin to that occurring in France, arrested radicals on a charge of "imagining the king's death."[25] Imagination became, in the ministry's eyes, a reason to try radicals for treason whether or not any action had been taken to kill the monarch. Convinced that the images he saw in dreams and visions—including the death of George III—would come about, Brothers was now a prospective traitor because he had faith in his own imagination. In 1795 he was arrested and interrogated by the Privy Council, which was much more interested in his vision of the king's demise than in that of the New Jerusalem. It was time for visionaries to be careful about what, and how, they imagined.

As Morton D. Paley pointed out in 1973,[26] the Jerusalem of Brothers was rather similar to that of Blake, who also saw "London blind & age-bent begging thro the Streets / Of Babylon, led by a child"[27] and imagined the redeemed city as an architectural superimposition on the sinful one, a new Eden where all had access to green fields:

> The fields from Islington to Marybone,
> To Primrose Hill and Saint Johns Wood:
> Were builded over with pillars of gold,
> And there Jerusalem's pillars stood.[28]

The difference between Blake's poetic imagination and the literal imaginations of Brothers, Southcott, and Bryan is that Blake knew his visionary city was symbolic of the liberation of human imagination from the repression that flourished in the real city—an alternative, mental reality in which "the stones are pity, and the bricks, well-wrought affections / Enamel'd with love & kindness & the tiles engraven gold."[29] Designed to make people question what they thought was true—to bring about "mental fight"—Blake's Jerusalem was similar to Coleridge's Xanadu, of which he says "I would build that dome in air."[30] The reality of imagination's vision is mental—a castle in the air—but no less valid and no less communal, when shared through words and images, than was the material city that the millenarian prophet envisioned. Brothers was certain the city of dreams would take material form: he made ready to lead his followers east toward the holy land, to build the New Jerusalem there. He got as far as a madhouse, where, confined on the orders of the Privy Council, which had decided his imagination was deluded rather than traitorous, he continued to publish intricate descriptions of the free and open Jerusalem he was sure he would one day build.

It was not until 1815, after the collapse of Brothers's following, after disappointment of Joanna Southcott's failure to give birth to the returning Shiloh and her subsequent death, and after the end of the Napoleonic War, that prophecy began to wane. It did not, however, die, for one of its causes—London's Babylonish nature—still existed. The city still seemed to many a wen of human exploitation and alienation as well as a commercial powerhouse at the center of empire. Thus the painter John Martin exhibited his vast canvases *The Fall of Babylon* (1819) and *Belshazzar's Feast* (1820) portraying the city as a vast array of classical architecture in the face of which its people were reduced to insignificance. But it was easier to imagine it as Babylon on the eve of destruction than transformed as the New Jerusalem. The *London Magazine* published "The Bricks of the Modern Babylon"—an article foreseeing the new architecture of Regent Street in terminal decay: "Its skin will peel off, like the bark of a rotten tree, and the hide will hang in rags and tatters about the rotting carcass."[31] Martin also offered no millenarian visions of the remade city but published, instead, a series of detailed practical plans for the gradual amelioration of London's sewage collection and fresh water provision.[32] These plans involved hiding the necessary tunnels and pipes under arrays of neoclassical buildings: Martin's imagination was visual and architectural, but he envisaged change occurring by the adoption of empirical measures, the case for which had been made by rational argument.

Martin's pictures of Babylon and schemes for improvement were not alone. From 1820s onward, much of prophecy's imaginative energy was displaced into discourses that accepted their own fictional and symbolic status, offering their imaginative visions as rational or emotional responses to the city rather than as divinely or biblically given. One such was Thomas De Quincey's *Confessions of an English Opium Eater*—a vision of the city as hell. Published in the September and October 1821 numbers of the *London Magazine*, the *Confessions* became the most popular contribution to a periodical that aimed to convey a view of "the very 'image, form, and pressure' of that '*mighty heart*' whose vast pulsations circulate life, strength, and spirits, throughout this great Empire."[33] Elsewhere in the October number, Charles Lamb described his city dreams as pleasurable experiences, as if to present London life as a delightful as well as civilizing influence on the mind. De Quincey, however, stands out against this urban and urbane context: he not only imagines London as a labyrinth of "Babylonian confusion,"[34] but also makes the city resonate with biblical symbols of guilt, sin, and punishment.

It is his experience of having been a runaway child sleeping rough that first brings De Quincey into contact with the grim London experienced by the socially disadvantaged. He uses the street-child he met then, the lost child-prostitute Ann, as a Magdalen figure of the city's commodification of bodies—and of his inability to remedy the process. He lost Ann in the teeming crowds and could never again find her to restore her tainted innocence. Seared by this experience, he configures London as a place of alienation, destruction that he is unable to redeem, not least because of its effects on his own body and mind: "the calamities of my novitiate in London," he writes "had struck root so deeply in my bodily constitution, that afterwards they shot up and flourished afresh, and grew into a noxious umbrage that has over-shadowed and darkened my later years."[35] Led by his pain into addiction to London's principal Oriental commodity and source of wealth—opium—he dreams of the city presided over by the biblical and Miltonic figure of Sin, the "stony hearted stepmother" of Oxford Street, who forbids redemption and consumes her own children. For De Quincey, vision is experienced as constraint, for it is the unwilled eruption, in the forms of dreams, of an imagination already malformed by drug addiction. His opium dreams offer a theater that is the visionary and the prophetic shrunk and subjectivized, an avowed internalization of the city, which is replayed in symbolic form in the head. They diagnose urban experience as alienation, dependence, and loss of identity and are at the same time symptoms of it—involuntary hauntings.[36] Thus he writes that his dreams "haunted me so much, that I feared lest some dropsical state or tendency of the brain might thus be making itself... *objective*; and that the sentient organ might be projecting itself as its own object" (69). Here he offers himself as an en-mind-ment as well as embodiment of addiction: his imagination as well as his brain is diseased by opium and by the city where he buys his opium—its most lucrative commodity. He is, he implies, thoroughly commodified.

Unable to redeem the city in his own imagination, De Quincey still wants, like the millenarians, to build an imaginary London, a symbolic city that can repair, for those who dream it or read his dream-narratives, the real London. Precisely because he recognizes himself as a guilty embodiment of the perverse pleasures and pains of the city of capital/capital city, his aim is to convert addiction and alienation to redemption and forgiveness. But he cannot do this by himself or of his own volition. Instead, his New Jerusalem was someone else's—the vision of a poet-prophet who was critical of London and its culture. That poet-prophet was Wordsworth, whose still-unpublished *Prelude* rejection of London's dazzling but ultimately degrading allure De Quincey was one of the few to have heard.

Wordsworth appears in *The Confessions of an English Opium Eater* when De Quincey, attempting to find a language adequate to the description of his strange, haunting, opium dreams of city architecture, quotes from *The Excursion:*

> From a great modern poet I cite the part of a passage which describes, as an appearance actually beheld in the clouds, what in many, of its circumstances I saw frequently in sleep:—
>
>> The appearance, instantaneously disclosed,
>> Was of a mighty city—boldly say
>> A wilderness of building, sinking far
>> And self-withdrawn into a wondrous depth.
>> Far sinking into splendour without end!
>> Fabric it seem'd of diamond and of gold,
>> With alabaster domes and silver spires,
>> And blazing terrace upon terrace, high
>> Uplifted; here, serene pavilions bright,
>> In avenues disposed; there towers begirt
>> With battlements that on their restless fronts
>> Bore stars—illumination of all gems!
>> By earthly nature had the effect been wrought
>> Upon the dark materials of the storm
>> Now pacified; on them, and on the coves,
>> And mountain-steeps and summits whereunto
>> The vapours had receded—taking there
>> Their station under a cerulean sky.
>
> The sublime circumstance—"that on their *restless* fronts bore stars"—might have been copied from my own architectural dreams, so often did it occur. (69)

In its original context in *The Excursion* the poetic passage is offered as a modern equivalent to biblical prophecy: the buildings seen in the clouds are "such as by Hebrew Prophets were beheld / In vision"[37] and the whole passage echoes Ezekiel's vision of a heavenly city. Nevertheless, it is the capacity to see visions, rather than the biblical truth of the visions themselves, that excites the poet—and De Quincey too, as his comment indicates. "[R]estless fronts bore stars" is the phrase in the passage that points up the seer's awareness that the buildings he visualizes are actually fluttering shapes in the night sky—creations of his imagination but not about to become miraculously existent material realities. The phrase ensures that the vision is offered as a demonstration of imagination's power to conjure something from nothing, rather than a divinely communicated reality. It is therefore an internalization and secularization of prophecy. In *The Prelude* Wordsworth denominates himself a "prophet of nature" (13: 442), one whose poetic imagination is so fostered by the rural world that he can see beyond its material form into its spiritual life (and that of the people who live in it), as Ezekiel and Isaiah once did. But he does not offer to predict the future: he does not, unlike Ezekiel and Daniel, or for that matter Dobbs and Brothers, literally believe in the advent of the millennium. Rather, he seeks to inherit the role that, according to the revisionist accounts of the biblical scholars Robert Lowth and Johann Michaelis,[38] the Hebrew prophets played—the role of expressing the spiritual yearnings and needs of their people in the language available to them in that place and time. They were proto-poets, rather than passive receptors of God's dictated word. And as such Wordsworth makes himself their heir.

A significant element in De Quincey's citation of Wordsworth's passage is its apparent individuality: he terms the Jerusalem vision Wordsworth's own. Yet this is not quite accurate, for in its original context the passage is that of individual who speaks, as De Quincey was unable to do, from a rural community. It is a rural vision of a heavenly city, seen not by the poet in his own person but by the character whom he calls the Solitary—a man who has retreated from the disappointments of revolutionary politics to a self-isolated life of contemplation in one of the Lake District's loneliest valleys. The Solitary experiences the vision alone, when he steps aside, rapt by what only he sees, from the party bearing home from the fells the body of an old man (a fellow tenant of the Solitary's rural cottage) who has been lulled by hypothermia into a state of semiconsciousness after becoming lost in a snowstorm. The old man is left enraptured by his near-death experience of mountain exposure but it is the Solitary, an educated fellow who knows his Ezekiel and Revelation, who turns fellside rapture into a verbal prophecy that aligns his own experience with biblical visions. And, as a further displacement, the poet then tells out the Solitary's vision in the poem called *The Excursion*: there's a chain of substitutions through which dumb rapture becomes more and more articulate, so that Wordsworth's metrical blank-verse rendition of the New Jerusalem becomes the most sophisticated version of a condition that begins with the silent rustic. The Solitary's vision and, by self-referential implication, Wordsworth's own poetry, become an articulation—a telling out in prophetic words—of what the inarticulate rustic feels but cannot/does not say. As such, they are both personal and solitary (a formulation of a lonely insight) and communal (derived from and a displacement of others' solitary responses to the fells), as if Wordsworth is dramatizing the contradictory affiliations of his own muse to, on one hand, the rural community and, on the other, to separate solitary encounters with landscape. Here, then, Wordsworth identifies visionary power as something both intensely personal and derived from the experience of a community that maintains traditional ways of interacting with nature. If he turns prophecy into imagination, religious vision into poetic scene, he nevertheless does not turn it into a power vouchsafed to himself only. Nevertheless, he confidently places himself at the apex of all those who live in harmony with nature, assuming the authority to speak what they know but cannot say. Also, of course, he takes vision outside the city: for Wordsworth the New Jerusalem cannot be imagined in London but only in the parts of the countryside still immune from the commodifying processes of capitalism and corrupting mass culture of urban life.

The function of the passage in the *Confessions* is complex: by quoting it De Quincey supplements his prose with another's poetry and describes his dream in another's words. This is a different process from Wordsworth's own: whereas the poet, at the articulate end of a chain of substitutions of which the dumb rustic is the beginning, positions himself as the spokesman for a community of which he is part, De Quincey imports another writer's words. If Wordsworth's vision is both his own and that of a community, De Quincey, borrowing it for his own text, can speak neither by himself nor for others. The redemptive holy city is never wholly his own: his dreams defer to another's poem. Moreover, Wordsworth's vision comes from out of town, from the countryside, rather than the city in which De Quincey is stuck. Here there is a deference to the rural and communal as the location for redemptive vision that still more apparent in a passage in which De Quincey identifies the Wordsworthian Lakes as a region of spirituality he cannot discover in London:

> Amongst these attractions that drew me so strongly to the Lakes, here had also by that time arisen in this lovely region the deep deep magnet (as to me only in all this world it then was) of William Wordsworth. Inevitably this close connexion of the poetry which most of all had moved me with the particular region and scenery that most of all had fastened upon my affections, and led captive my imagination, was calculated, under ordinary circumstances, to impress upon my fluctuating deliberations a summary and decisive bias. But the very depth of the impressions which had been made upon me, either as regarded the poetry or the scenery, was too solemn and (unaffectedly I may say it) too spiritual, to clothe itself in, any hasty or chance movement as at all

adequately expressing its strength, or reflecting its hallowed character. If you, reader, were a devout Mahometan, throwing gazes of mystical awe daily towards Mecca, or were a Christian devotee looking with the same rapt adoration to St. Peter's at Rome, or to El Kodah, the Holy City of Jerusalem (so called even amongst the Arabs, who hate both Christian and Jews) how painfully would it jar upon your sensibilities if some friend, sweeping past you upon a high road, with a train (according to the circumstances) of dromedaries or of wheel carriages, should suddenly pull up, and say, "Come, old fellow, jump up alongside of me; I'm off for the Red Sea, and here's a spare dromedary," or "Off for Rome, and here's a well-cushioned barouche." Seasonable and convenient it might happen that the invitation were; but still it would shock you that a journey which, with or without your consent, could not but assume the character eventually of a saintly pilgrimage, should arise and take its initial movement upon a casual summons, or upon a vulgar opening of momentary convenience. In the present case, under no circumstances should I have dreamed of presenting myself to Wordsworth. The principle of "veneration" (to speak phrenologically) was by many degrees too strong in me for any such overture on my part. (147)

The Bible again: De Quincey's holy land is Cumbria because it is there that Wordsworth prophesies, demonstrating the capacity of the poetic imagination to form spiritual visions when nourished by nature. The Lakes offer what London cannot, a ground on which redemptive vision can flourish because humanity has not been alienated from itself by city life. All at sea in the capital, De Quincey has already yearned to escape thence: "during my first mournful abode in London," he says, "my consolation was (if such it could be thought) to gaze from Oxford Street up every avenue in succession which pierces northwards through the heart of Marylebone to the field and the woods; for *that* said I, travelling with my eyes up the long vistas which lay part in light and part in shade—'*that* is the road to the north and, therefore, to Grasmere'... 'and if I had the wings of a dove, *that* way I would fly for rest'" (40). Here the allusion to the dove positions Grasmere as Ararat, a haven for overwhelmed exiles, and De Quincey as an arkite refugee from God's destruction of sinful cities. Grasmere is a biblical promised land.

If Grasmere is the promised land, London is Babylon—a Babylon that De Quincey, without Wordsworth's aid, cannot transform to the New Jerusalem. It is after Wordsworth's *Excursion* vision that he relates his own Jerusalem dream in the Lake District. From Grasmere churchyard he sees

> The domes and cupolas of a great city—an image or faint abstraction, caught perhaps in childhood from some picture of Jerusalem. And not

a bow-shot from me, upon a stone, and shaded by Judean palms, there sat a woman; and I looked; and it was—Ann! She fixed her eyes upon me earnestly; and I said to her at length: "So then I have found you at last." (73)

It is in a Wordsworthian mountain vision that he refinds the lost innocent; only after this rural redemption does he finally dream of being "in Oxford Street, walking again with Ann" and thus repairing his urban alienation and guilt. But the dream slips away; visions of "the caves of hell" and Milton's "incestuous mother" return; he slips back into tormented addiction (74).

De Quincey is not Blake, not even Brothers, Dobbs, or Edward Irving, the charismatic preacher who began to draw large London congregations to his millennial church in the 1820s. He cannot redeem the city, much as he wants to, so great is the burden of guilt that it, and the opium habit it sponsors, lays upon him. This not least because it has its sinful pleasures as well as pains: the city and the drug (the city as drug) produce a theater in which De Quincey vicariously experiences delights, whether as a solitary walker in London's night-time streets, or as an opium dreamer. And so, stimulated by and addicted to the city's pleasures and pains, a solitary and damaged product of its culture, he imports Wordsworth's rural vision of the heavenly city to substitute for a redeeming vision and an imaginative community that neither he, nor anyone else for whom he could speak in London, can form. He does, however, claim, having quoted Wordsworth's vision and thus made his dreams secondary to it, that it is secondary to his own—it "might have been copied from my own architectural dreams." But this is a brief and half-hearted gesture, an attempt to prioritize the redeeming power of his own imagination that he cannot sustain. Ultimately the register of biblical prophecy is lost to De Quincey's city-self; it is available only as a poetic import from the sole remaining land in which he can imagine the purity necessary for a healthy imagination to exist—the uncorrupted Lake District. It will not be formulated in his own London-based prose, and he cannot aspire to the transcendence possible for Wordsworth in the medium of verse. Nor, he imagines, can anyone else: De Quincey undermines prophetic London, doubting the ability of the city-dweller to generate visions of renewal as well as hell, for to be a city-dweller is to be vitiated by alienation, abjection, and guilt while such visions demand what he terms "power." By the same token, he identifies poetic imagination as the medium for redemptive vision, terming "power" the defining characteristic of true literature and deriving it from a heightened language that is to be found in verse rather than in the prose that befits urban life.³⁹ To illustrate this language De Quincey adduces the poetry of Wordsworth and Milton, declaring of the latter (in a phrase borrowed from Wordsworth's discussion of poetic imagination) that it acts as "a vital agent on the human mind."⁴⁰

Prose-writer rather than poet, buying-in words and substances from outside, De Quincey presents, for the first time in history, a self-portrait of the artist as commodity, a product of the city culture that he and Wordsworth bemoaned. He is a commodity, too, because his dreams, his very words, are formed from those he has absorbed from others—from Wordsworth's mountain visions and from Coleridge's anecdotes (as when his symbol of the artist doomed to repeat himself without ever escaping from the prison of his imagination turns out to be a Piranesi print that Coleridge had described to him). Unlike Wordsworth, he has no rural sanctuary and is unable of his own free will to see visions: his dreams, fuelled by opium, are involuntary and internal—the dark inverts of Wordsworth's fellside epiphanies and Blake's city-prophecies. They are Romanticism's perverted urban other, the doppelganger of the rural, lyric imagination.⁴¹ Racked by dreams he cannot control, De Quincey appears as a new phenomenon, the perverse guide—in prose—to a self crippled by the city experience that speaks through him but that he cannot transcend. And of course this phenomenon—the alienated hollow man in romantic agony—would be enormously powerful, through Baudelaire, Poe, Stevenson, Conan Doyle, Conrad, and Eliot and into today's popular culture, partly as a result of De Quincey's direct influence.⁴²

Crippled by and addicted to the city, De Quincey could not be Blake and imagine its renewal from within: neither poetic imagination nor the prophetic tradition of millenarian religion would succeed in redeeming urban experience. And in this he was, ironically enough, prophetic: his borrowed Jerusalem signaled a pivotal moment in the history of culture, for it revealed a split between the rural and the urban that would not be overcome—effectively the retreat of poetic vision from the city (a retreat that the next two hundred years of English lyric poetry would follow as it sought transcendence and visionary insight but found them among the cliffs, hills, and hedges rather than on the streets). The causes of this development were seen clearly by De Quincey's successor as commentator on the psyche of London—Mudie—when he noted that

> the very ignorance and consequent indifference which each has toward all whom he meets, together with the politeness which is necessary to render a heartless society bearable, throw the gates of experiences as wide as any man can wish; and thus, though London may not be the

place in which one may best study the poetry of one species, it is the one in which to study the prose.[43]

Urban dwellers were prosaic: they were bombarded with new experiences but lacked deeper relationships. Poetry, the medium for such relationships, was lost to London: as it largely gave up its traditional narrative function and concentrated on briefer lyrical forms,[44] it would henceforth be the worldly, disenchanted, satirical prose of the novel that would envision the pleasures and pains of London. And what the novel saw there was, more often than not, a city of dreadful night.[45] As for poetry, from then onward Jerusalem would be imagined in the rural fringes, in Tintagel, in Dorset, in Adlestrop, in Little Gidding, and in Fern Hill: it would no longer be seen in Paddington or St. Pancras and along the Old Kent Road.

Notes

I am grateful to Julia S. Carlson, David Higgins, Elizabeth A. Nieman, Morton D. Paley, and Joshua Wilner for their helpful advice on drafts of this chapter.

1. Robert Southey. *Letters from England.* Ed. Jack Simmons. London: Cresset, 1951. 443.
2. See, for example, Robert Hole, *Pulpits, Politics and Public Order in England, 1760–1832*, Cambridge, Cambridge UP, 1989; W. H. Oliver, *Prophets and Millennialists: The Uses of Biblical Prophecy in England from the 1790s to the 1840s*, Auckland: Oxford UP, 1978; J. F. C. Harrison, *The Second Coming: Popular Millenarianism 1780–1850*, New Brunswick: Rutgers, 1979.
3. For millenarianism as a displacement of social and political grievances see E. P. Thompson, *The Making of the English Working Class*, London: Gollancz, 1963. The culture of the artisan classes in London, though not the urban experience of London as such, is considered in the account of millenarian radicalism given by Iain McCalman, *Radical Underworld: Prophets, Revolutionaries and Pornographers in London, 1795–1840*, Cambridge: Cambridge UP, 1988. See also Jon Mee, *Dangerous Enthusiasm: William Blake and the Culture of Radicalism in the 1790s*, Oxford: Oxford UP, 1992; and David Worrall, *Radical Culture: Discourse, Resistance and Surveillance, 1790–1820*, London: Harvester, 1992.
4. On the "lyricisation" of poetry in the nineteenth century and since, see the discussion in Virginia Jackson, *Dickinson's Misery: A Theory of Lyric Reading*, Princeton: Princeton UP, 2005, 7–15.
5. Georg Christoph Lichtenberg. *Lichtenberg's Visits to England as Described in his Letters and Diaries.* Oxford: Clarendon, 1938. 63–65.
6. As De Quincey puts it in "The Nation of London," *Autobiographical Sketches, The Works of Thomas De Quincey*, vol. 19.

7. On the meaning of "chartered" to the radical Blake and Wordsworth, see Robert N. Essick, "William Blake, Thomas Paine, and Biblical Revolution," *Studies in Romanticism* 30 (1991): 189–212. Also Morton D. Paley, *Apocalypse and Millennium in English Romantic Poetry*, Oxford: Clarendon, 1999, 176.
8. "London." *Songs of Innocence and Experience*. Ed. Andrew Lincoln. Princeton: Princeton UP, 1998. Plate 46.
9. *The Prelude: A Parallel Text*. Ed. J. C. Maxwell. Harmondsworth: Penguin, 1971.
10. Preface to *Lyrical Ballads* (1800). *Prose Works*. Ed. W. J. B. Owen and Jane Worthington Smyser. 3 vols. Oxford: Oxford UP, 1974. 1: 128.
11. On Wordsworth's theory of stimulation and its medicinal origins in the opium-therapy of John Brown, see Gavin Budge, "The Post-Darwinian Poetics of William Wordsworth: 'Excitement without the Application of Gross and Violent Stimulants,'" *British Journal for Eighteenth-Century Studies* 30.2 (2007): 279–308.
12. Preface to *Lyrical Ballads*. *Prose Works* 1: 128.
13. Wordsworth's letter to C. Cookson, June 4, 1812. *The Letters of William and Dorothy Wordsworth. Vol. 3. The Middle Years, Part 2, 1812–1820*. Ed. Ernest de Selincourt. Rev. Mary Moorman and Alan G. Hill. Oxford: Clarendon, 1970.
14. *The Task. The Poems of William Cowper*. Ed. John D. Baird and Charles Ryskamp. Vol 2. 3 vols. Oxford: Oxford UP, 1980–95. 1: 715–24.
15. *Expostulation. The Poems of William Cowper*. Vol. 1. 365–75.
16. Revelation 12:1, 5. See Joanna Southcott, *Song of Moses and the Lamb*, London, 1804; and *A Continuation of the Prophecies*, Exeter, 1802.
17. *Critical Dissertation on the Eighteenth Chapter of Isaiah* (1799). Quoted in Oliver, 52.
18. G. S. Faber. "Letters to the Author of Antichrist in the French Convention." Quoted in Oliver, 61.
19. Southey details their prophesying in *Letters from England*, 422.
20. *A Revealed Knowledge of the Prophecies and the Times*. London, 1795. 1: 47–48.
21. The trigger for Dobbs's apocalyptic prophecy was the forthcoming Act of Union between Britain and Ireland which, as a member of the Irish parliament, he resisted. "Poem on the Millennium" *Memoirs of Francis Dobbs*. Dublin, 1800. Quoted in Morton D. Paley, *The Continuing City: William Blake's Jerusalem*, Oxford: Clarendon, 1983, 163.
22. *Babylon the Great: A Dissection and Demonstration of Men and Things in the British Capital*. 2 vols. Philadelphia: Carey, 1825. 2: 293 (labyrinth). 1: 49 (insignificance).
23. *Prelude* (1805) 7: 596–97. "London" Plate 46.
24. *A Description of Jerusalem*. London, 1801. 40.
25. *Imagining the King's Death: Figurative Treason, Fantasies of Regicide 1793–1796*. Oxford: Oxford UP, 2000.
26. "William Blake, the Prince of the Hebrews, and the Woman Clothed with the Sun." *William Blake; Essays in Honour of Sir Geoffrey* Keynes.

Ed. Morton D. Paley and Michael Phillips. Oxford: Clarendon, 1973. 274–75.
27. *Jerusalem: The Emanation of the Giant Albion.* Ed. Morton D. Paley. Princeton: Princeton UP, 1998. Lines 11–12 of plate 84.
28. *Jerusalem.* Lines 1–4 of plate 27.
29. *Jerusalem.* Lines 31–32 of plate 12.
30. "Kubla Khan." *The Poetical Works of S. T. Coleridge.* Ed. E. H. Coleridge. 2 vols. Oxford: Oxford UP, 1912. 1: 46.
31. Sep. 1825, 75.
32. On John Martin see William Feaver, *The Art of John Martin*, Oxford: Clarendon, 1975. Gregory Dart considers Martin's painting and improvement schemes in the context of London in "On Great and Little Things: Cockney Art in the 1820s," *Romanticism* 14.2 (2008): 149–67.
33. John Scott's Prospectus to *The London Magazine* (Jan.–Jun. 1820, iv), alluding to the sonnet "Composed upon Westminster Bridge," in which Wordsworth portrays the city at dawn, unclogged by people or pollution, as the height of beauty—a portrayal very different from that made in *The Prelude* (an as-then still unpublished text that De Quincey knew and Scott did not). I am grateful to David Higgins for drawing my attention to this reference.
34. The phrase comes from his later *Autobiographical Sketches*, chapter VII "The Nation of London," in *The Works of Thomas De Quincey*, vol. XIX.
35. My text is that of the 1821 *London Magazine* as given in *The Works of Thomas De Quincey.* Vol. 2. *The Confessions of an English Opium Eater 1821–1856.* Ed. Grevel Lindop. London: Pickering, 2000. 39–40.
36. On the involuntary nature of De Quincey's dreams as a critical deconstruction of Coleridge's idealism, see Nigel Leask, *British Romantic Writers and the East: Anxieties of Empire*, Cambridge: Cambridge UP, 1992, 223.
37. *The Excursion.* Ed. Sally Bushell, James A. Butler, and Michael C. Jaye. Ithaca: Cornell UP. 2: 869–86. See the perceptive reading by Joshua Wilner, "The Stewed Muse of Prose: Wordsworth, De Quincey, Baudelaire," *Feeding on Infinity: Readings in the Romantic Rhetoric of Internalisation*, Baltimore: Johns Hopkins UP, 2000, 68–77.
38. On Lowth's and Michaelis's redefinition of prophecy and inspiration see Stephen Prickett, *Words and* The Word*: Language, Poetics and Biblical Interpretation* (Cambridge: Cambridge UP, 1986), chapter 3.
39. On De Quincey's new definition, dividing literature from other kinds of writing on the basis of its ability to communicate power, see Jonathan Bate, "The Literature of Power: Coleridge and De Quincey," *Coleridge's Visionary Languages: Essays in Honour of J. B. Beer*, Ed. Tim Fulford and Morton D. Paley, Cambridge: Brewer, 1993, 137–50.
40. De Quincey's phrase is derived from Wordsworth's 1815 characterization of the poet (quoted in Bate, "The Literature of Power," 145).
41. On the lyric imagination as the product of rural Romanticism see Geoffrey Hartman, "Wordsworth, Inscriptions, and Romantic Nature

Poetry," *Beyond Formalism*, New Haven: Yale UP, 1970. Also M. H. Abrams, *Natural Supernaturalism: Tradition and Revolution in Romantic Literature*, New York: Norton, 1971.

42. De Quincey influenced Baudelaire, who imported the vision of the city seen in the clouds into his *Petits poems en prose*, having translated De Quincey's *Confessions*. On this, see Wilner, "The Stewed Muse."
43. Mudie, *Babylon the Great*, 1: 77.
44. A tendency enshrined and perpetuated by Francis Turner Palgrave's anthology *A Golden Treasury of English Songs and Lyrics* (1861–91), the enormous influence of which lasted into the second half of the twentieth century.
45. James Thomson's 1874 poem *City of Dreadful Night* found no redemption in London, configuring it as a benighted city of the lost:

> O melancholy Brothers, dark, dark, dark!
> O battling in black floods without an ark!
> O spectral wanderers of unholy Night!
> My soul hath bled for you these sunless years,
> With bitter blood-drops running down like tears:
> Oh dark, dark, dark, withdrawn from joy and light. (710–15)

The Poetical Works. Ed. Bertram Dobell. Vol. 1. 2 vols. London: Reeves, 1895.

Works Cited

Abrams, M. H. *The Mirror and the Lamp: Romantic Theory and the Critical Tradition*. Oxford: Oxford UP, 1953.
———. *Natural Supernaturalism: Tradition and Revolution in Romantic Literature*. New York: Norton, 1971.
Altick, Richard. *The Shows of London*. Cambridge: Harvard UP, 1978.
Andreev, Daniel. *Roza Mira*. Moscow: Mir Uranii, 2005.
Andrieux, Maurice. *Daily Life in Venice in the Time of Casanova*. Trans. Mary Fitton. New York: Praeger, 1969.
Arnold, Dennis. "Music at the Mendicanti in the Eighteenth Century." *Music and Letters* 65 (1984): 345–56.
Ault, Donald. *Visionary Physics: Blake's Response to Newton*. Chicago: U of Chicago P, 1974.
Austen, Jane. *Emma*. Ed. James Kinsley. Oxford: Oxford UP, 1980.
———. *Mansfield Park*. Ed. James Kinsley. Oxford: Oxford UP, 1980.
———. *Northanger Abbey*. Ed. Marilyn Butler. London: Penguin, 2003.
Babbit, Irving. *Rousseau and Romanticism*. New York: Houghton, 1919.
Bacon, Francis. *The New Atlantis*. New York: Dodo Press, 2006.
Badiou, Alain. *Being and Event*. London: Continuum, 2005.
Bailey, Isabel. *Herbert Ingram Esq. MP*. Boston: Kay, 1996.
Balabko, Oleksandr. *Syn'ior Nikolo i Syn'ior Mikele: Rym Hoholia I Kapri Koisiubynskoho*. Kiev: Fakt, 2006.
Baldick, Chris, ed. *The Oxford Book of Gothic Tales*. 1993. Oxford: Oxford UP, 2001.
Baldissone, Giusi. "Il vuoto in biblioteca: Alessandro Manzoni e la peste." *Prospettive sui* Promessi sposi. Ed. Giorgio Barberi Squarotti. Turin: Tirrenia, 1991. 77–93.
Barker-Benfield, G. J. *The Culture of Sensibility: Sex and Society in Eighteenth-Century Britain*. Chicago: U of Chicago P, 1992.
Barrell, John. *The Idea of Landscape and the Sense of Place*. Cambridge: Cambridge UP, 1972.
———. *Imagining the King's Death: Figurative Treason, Fantasies of Regicide 1793–1796*. Oxford: Oxford UP, 2000.
Bate, Jonathan. "The Literature of Power: Coleridge and De Quincey." *Coleridge's Visionary Languages: Essays in Honour of J. B. Beer*. Ed. Tim Fulford and Morton D. Paley. Cambridge: Brewer, 1993. 137–50.
———. *The Song of the Earth*. Cambridge, MA: Harvard UP. 2000.

Baudelaire, Charles. *Curiosités esthétiques L'Art Romantique et autres Œuvres critiques.* Ed. Henri Lemaitre. Paris: Garnier, 1990.

Beddoes, Thomas. *Hygëia: or, Essays Moral and Medical on the Causes Affecting the Personal State of our Middling and Affluent Classes.* 3 vols. Bristol: R. Phillips, 1802.

Bell Wakefield, Priscilla. *Reflections on the Present Condition of the Female Sex; with Suggestions for its Improvement.* 1798. *The Longman Anthology of British Literature.* Ed. Susan Wolfson and Peter Manning. Vol. 2A. New York: Pearson, 2006. 328–31.

Bely, Andrei. *Gogol's Artistry.* Trans. Christopher Colbarth. Evanston: Northwestern UP, 2009.

Benjamin, Walter. *Charles Baudelaire. Ein Lyriker im Zeitalter des Hochkapitalismus. Gesammelte Schriften.* Ed. Rolf Tiedemann and Hermann Schweppenhäuser. Vol. 1.2. Frankfurt: Suhrkamp, 1991. 509–690.

———. "Das Dämonische Berlin." *Gesammelte Schriften.* Ed. Rolf Tiedemann and Hermann Schweppenhäuser. Vol. 7.1. Frankfurt: Suhrkamp, 1989. 86–92.

———. "E. T. A. Hoffmann und Oskar Panizza." *Gesammelte Schriften.* Ed. Rolf Tiedemann and Hermann Schweppenhäuser. Vol. 2.2. Frankfurt: Suhrkamp, 1989. 641–48.

———. *Das Passagen-Werk.* Ed. Rolf Tiedemann. Vol. 1. Frankfurt: Suhrkamp, 1983.

———. "Short History of Photography." Trans. Phil Patton. *Artforum* (Feb. 1977): 46–51.

Bentley, G. E., Jr. *The Stranger from Paradise: A Biography of William Blake.* New Haven: Yale UP, 2001.

Bergson, Henri. *Matter and Memory.* Trans. N. M. Paul and W. S. Palmer. New York: Zone, 1991.

Bhabha, Homi K. *The Location of Culture.* London: Routledge, 1994.

Birkhead, Edith. *The Tale of Terror: A Study of the Gothic Romance.* London: Constable, 1921.

Black, Jeremy. *Italy and the Grand Tour.* New Haven: Yale UP, 2003.

Blake, William. *The Complete Poetry and Prose of William Blake.* Ed. David V. Erdman. Garden City: Anchor, 1982.

———. "London." *Songs of Innocence and Experience.* Ed. Andrew Lincoln. Princeton: Princeton UP, 1998.

———. *Jerusalem: The Emanation of the Giant Albion.* Ed. Morton D. Paley. Princeton: Princeton UP, 1998.

Blakey, Dorothy. *Minerva Press 1790–1830.* London: Oxford UP, 1939.

Blanshard, Frances. *Portraits of Wordsworth.* London: Allen, 1959.

Blumenberg, Hans. *Die Lesbarkeit der Welt.* Frankfurt: Suhrkamp, 1993.

"The Bricks of the Modern Bablyon." *London Magazine* Sep. 1825: 75.

Brothers, Richard. *A Description of Jerusalem.* London, 1801.

———. *A Revealed Knowledge of the Prophecies and the Times.* London, 1795.

Bruno, Alfredo. Ed. *Il Giocodell'Amore: Le cortigiane di Venecia dal Trecento al Settecento, Cataolgo della mostra.* Milan: Berenice. 1990.

Budge, Gavin. "The Post-Darwinian Poetics of William Wordsworth: 'Excitement without the Application of Gross and Violent Stimulants,'" *British Journal for Eighteenth-Century Studies* 30.2 (2007): 279–308.

Burney, Frances. *Evelina*. Ed. Edward Bloom. Oxford: Oxford UP, 1982.

———. *Evelina, or The History of a Young Lady's Entrance into the World*. 1778. Ed. Edward A. Bloom. Oxford: Oxford UP, 2002.

Buttimer, Anne. *Geography and the Human Spirit*. Baltimore: Johns Hopkins UP, 1993.

Byron, George Gordon. "Beppo." <http://en.wikisource.org/wiki/Beppo_(Lord_Byron)>.

Cassirer, Ernst. *Rousseau, Kant, Goethe*. Princeton: Princeton UP, 1945.

Cavell, Stanley. *The Claim of Reason*. Oxford: Oxford UP, 1979.

———. *In Quest of the Ordinary: Lines of Skepticism and Romanticism*. Chicago: U of Chicago P, 1988.

Chandler, James and Kevin Gilmartin. *Romantic Metropolis: The Urban Scene of British Culture, 1780–1840*. Cambridge: Cambridge UP, 2005.

Clej, Alina. *A Genealogy of the Modern Self: Thomas De Quincey and the Intoxication of Writing*. Stanford: Stanford UP, 1995.

Coleridge, Samuel Taylor. *Biographia Literaria*. 1817. New York: Leavitt, 1834.

———. *Biographia Literaria*. Ed. James Engell and W. Jackson Bate. 2 vols. Princeton: Princeton UP, 1983.

———. "Kubla Khan." *The Poetical Works of S. T. Coleridge*. Ed. E. H. Coleridge. 2 vols. Oxford: Oxford UP, 1912.

Coleridge, Samuel Taylor, and Robert Southey. "The Devil's Thoughts." *Morning Post and Gazetteer*. Sep. 6, 1799. *Romantic Circles*. University of Maryland, n.d. Web. Dec. 21, 2009. <http://www.rc.umd.edu/editions/shelley/devil/devil.stc1799.html>.

Constable, M. V. "The Venetian '*Figlie del coro*': Their Environment and Achievement." *Music and Letters* 63 (1982): 181–212.

Corfield, Penelope J. "From Poison Peddlers to Civic Worthies: The Reputation of the Apothecaries in Georgian England." *Social History of Medicine* 22.1 (2009): 1–21.

Corti, Maria. "Con Manzoni all'osteria della Luna Piena." *Leggere* I promessi sposi. *Analisi semiotiche*. Ed. Giovanni Manetti. Milan: Bompiani, 1989. 35–49.

Cowper, William. *Expostulation: The Poems of William Cowper*. Ed. John D. Baird and Charles Ryskamp. Vol. 1. 3 vols. Oxford: Oxford UP.

———. *The Task: The Poems of William Cowper*. Ed. John D. Baird and Charles Ryskamp. Vol. 2. 3 vols. Oxford: Oxford UP, 1980–95.

———. *The Works of William Cowper*. 15 vols. London: Baldwin, 1835–37.

Cox, Jeffrey N. and Michael Gamer. *The Broadview Anthology of Romantic Drama*. Toronto: Broadview P, 2003.

Cox, Philip. *Reading Adaptations: Novels and Verse Narratives on the Stage, 1790–1840*. Manchester: Manchester UP, 2000.

Crabbe, George. *The Poetical Works of the Rev. George Crabbe: with his letters and journals, and his life*. 8 vols. London: Murray, 1834.

Crellin, J. K. "Pharmaceutical History and its Sources in the Wellcome Collections." *Medical History* 11.3 (1967): 215-27.

———. "Revisiting Counter Practice amid Pharmacy and Medical Reform in Nineteenth-Century Britain." *Pharmaceutical Historian* 30.3 (2000): 44-49. *Apothecaries and the Drug Trade: Essays in Celebration of the Work of David L. Cowen*. Madison: American Institute of the History of Pharmacy, 2001. 57-72.

Curth, Louise Hill, ed. Introduction. *From Physick to Pharmacology: Five Hundred Years of British Drug Retailing*. Aldershot: Ashgate, 2006.

Damon, S. Foster. *A Blake Dictionary*. Boulder: Shambhala, 1979.

Darby, David. "The Unfettered Eye: Glimpsing Modernity from E. T. A. Hoffmann's Corner Window." *Deutsche Vierteljahrsschrift für Literaturwissenschaft und Geistesgeschichte* 77.2 (2003): 274-94.

Dart, Gregory. "On Great and Little Things: Cockney Art in the 1820s." *Romanticism* 14.2 (2008): 149-67.

Davis, Michael. *William Blake: A New Kind of Man*. Berkeley: U of California P, 1977.

Davydov, Aleksei. *Dusha Gogolia*. Moscow: Novyi Khronograf. 2008.

de Certeau, Michel. *Heterologies: Discourse on the Other*. Trans. Brian Massumi. Minneapolis: U of Minnesota P, 1986.

———. *The Writing of History*. Trans. Tom Conley. New York: Columbia UP, 1988.

DeCook, Travis. "The Ark and Immediate Revelation in Francis Bacon's *New Atlantis*." *Studies in Philology* 105:1 (2008): 103-22.

de Man, Paul. *The Rhetoric of Romanticism*. New York: Columbia UP, 1984.

De Quincey, Thomas. *The Confessions of an English Opium Eater 1821-1856*. *The Works of Thomas De Quincey*. Ed. Grevel Lindop. Vol. 2. London: Pickering, 2000.

———. *Confessions of an English Opium Eater and Other Writings*. Ed. Barry Milligan. London: Penguin, 2003.

———. "The Nation of London." *Autobiographical Sketches*. *The Works of Thomas De Quincey*. Ed. Grevel Lindop. Vol. 19. London: Pickering, 2000.

———. *Recollections of the Lakes and the Lake Poets*. Ed. David Wright. Harmondsworth: Penguin, 1970.

De Staël, Madame. *Corinne, or Italy*. Philadelphia: Carey, 1836.

Deleuze, Gilles, and Félix Guattari. *Anti-Oedipus: Capitalism and Schizophrenia*. Minneapolis: U of Minnesota P, 1983.

Di Benedetto, Vincenzo. "Parte seconda: Lo spazio della gente." *Guida ai Promessi sposi*. Milan: Rizzoli, 1999. 175-296.

Di Ciaccia, Francesco. "La peste nei *Promessi Sposi*." *La parola e il silenzio. Peste carestia ed eros nel romanzo manzoniano*. Pisa: Giardini, 1987. 13-100.

———. "La peste nella *Colonna Infame*." *La parola e il silenzio. Peste carestia ed eros nel romanzo manzoniano*. Pisa: Giardini, 1987. 101-98.

Dickens, Charles. *Pictures from Italy*. Ed. David Paroissien. New York: Coward, 1974.

Doskow, Minna. *William Blake's* Jerusalem. Rutherford: Fairleigh Dickinson UP, 1982.
Duncan, Ian (with Leith Davis and Janet Sorensen). Introduction. *Scotland and the Borders of Romanticism.* Cambridge: Cambridge UP, 2004. 1–19.
Eicher, Thomas. "'Mit einem Blick das ganze Panorama des grandiosen Platzes.' Panoramatische Strukturen in *Des Vetters Eckfenster* von E. T. A. Hoffmann." *Poetica. Zeitschrift für Sprach- und Literaturwissenschaft.* 25.3–4 (1993): 360–77.
Eliot, T. S. *The Waste Land and Other Poems.* New York: Harcourt, 1958.
Ellison, Julie. "News, Blues, and Cowper's Busy World," *Modern Language Quarterly* 62 (2001): 219–37.
Essick, Robert N. "Jerusalem and Blake's Final Works." *The Cambridge Companion to William Blake.* Ed. Morris Eaves. Cambridge: Cambridge UP, 2003.
———. "William Blake, Thomas Paine, and Biblical Revolution." *Studies in Romanticism* 30 (1991): 189–212.
Evans, Gareth. "Poison Wine—John Keats and the Botanic Pharmacy." *Keats-Shelley Review* 16 (2002): 31–55.
Fasani, Remo. "La carestia e la storia della peste" "I quadri della peste." *Saggio sui* Promessi sposi. Florence: Le Monnier, 1952. 149–65; 182–94.
———. "I fatti di Milano." *Saggio sui* Promessi sposi. Florence: Le Monnier, 1952. 106–25.
Feaver, William. *The Art of John Martin.* Oxford: Clarendon, 1975.
Ferguson, Frances. *Solitude and the Sublime: Romanticism and the Aesthetics of Individuation.* New York: Routledge, 1992.
Fleming, James. *Fixing the Sky: The Checkered History of Weather and Climate Control.* New York: Columbia UP, 2010.
Foucault, Michel. *Madness and Civilization: A History of Insanity in the Age of Reason.* Trans. Richard Howard. New York: Pantheon, 1965.
Frank, Frederick. *The First Gothics: A Critical Guide to the English Gothic Novel.* New York: Garland, 1987.
Frazier, Melissa. *Frames of Imagination. Gogol's Arabesques.* New York: Lang, 2000.
Fulford, Tim; Lee, Debbie; Kitson, Peter J. *Literature, Science and Exploration in the Romantic Era: Bodies of Knowledge.* Cambridge: Cambridge UP, 2004.
Gallaway, W. F. "The Conservative Attitude toward Fiction, 1770–1830." *PMLA* 55 (1940): 104–59.
Galperin, William H. *The Historical Austen.* Philadelphia: U of Pennsylvania P, 2003.
———. *The Return of the Visible in British Romanticism.* Baltimore: Johns Hopkins UP, 1993.
Galt, John. *The Apostate. The New British Theatre. A Selection of Original Dramas, not yet acted; Some of which have been Offered for Representation but not accepted with Critical Remarks from the Editor.* 4 vols. London: Colburn, 1814–15.

Galt, John. *The Canadas: As They At Present Commend Themselves to The Enterprise Of Emigrants, Colonists, And Capitalists*. London: Wilson, 1832.

———. *Letters from the Levant: Containing Views of the State of Society, Manners, Opinions, and Commerce, in Greece and Several of the Islands of the Archipelago*. London: Cadell and Davies, 1813.

Garcia, Jose Maria Rodriguez. "Patterns of Conversion in Francis Bacon's *New Atlantis*." *Lit: Literature Interpretation Theory*, 17: 2 (2006): 179–211.

Gaull, Marilyn. *English Romanticism: The Human Context*. New York: Norton, 1998.

Getto, Giovanni. *Letture manzoniane*. Florence: Sansoni, 1964.

Girardi, Enzo Noè. "Renzo agl'Inferi." *Manzoni «reazionario.» Cinque saggi sui* Promessi Sposi. Bologna: Cappelli, 1966. 43–60.

———. "Renzo, la peste e i cvronisti milanesi del Seicento," *Omaggio ad Alessandro Manzoni nel bicentenario della nascita*. Ed. Giuseppe Catanzaro, Francesco Santucci, and Salvatore Vivona. Assisi: Accademia Properziana del Subasio, 1986. 299–316.

———. "Il tumulto di San Martino." *Manzoni «reazionario.» Cinque saggi sui* Promessi Sposi. Bologna: Cappelli, 1966. 15–31.

Gleckner, Robert J. "Joyce's Blake: Paths of Influence." *William Blake and the Moderns*. Ed. Robert J. Bertholf and Annette S. Levitt. Albany: SUNY P, 1982. 136–39.

Godt, Clareece. "From History to Story: Manzoni and the Chroniclers of Milano." *The Reasonable Romantic: Essays on Alessandro Manzoni*. Ed. Sante Matteo and Larry H. Peer. New York: Lang, 1986. 179–94.

———. "Self-Reflecting Episodes: The St. Martin's Day Riots and the Famine." *The Mobile Spectacle: Variable Perspective in Manzoni's* I Promessi Sposi. New York: Lang, 1998. 33–64.

Gogol' bez Gliantsa. Proekt Pavla Fokina. St. Petersburg: Amfora. 2008.

Gogol' i Italia: Materialy Mezdunarodno i Konferentsii "Nikolai Vasil'evich Gogol': 2002, Rome (Italy). Moscow: RGGU. 2004.

Gogol, Nikolai. *Arabesques*. Trans. Alex Tullock. Ann Arbor: Ardis, 1982.

———. *The Collected Tales*. Trans. Richard Pervear and Larissa Volokhonsky. New York: Vintage, 1999.

———. *Dead Souls*. Ed. George Gibian. Trans. George Reavey. New York: Norton, 1985.

———. "*Hanz Kuechelgarten*," "*Leaving the Theater" and Other Works*. Trans. Ronald Meyer. Ann Arbor: Ardis, 1990.

———. *Letters of Nikolai Gogol*. Ed. Carl R. Proffer. Ann Arbor: U of Michigan P, 1967.

———. *Selected Passages from Correspondence with Friends*. Trans. Jesse Zeldin. Nashville: Vanderbilt UP, 1969.

Gogol', Nikolai Vasil'evich. "Rim." *Sobranie Sochinenii*, 3. Moscow: Russkaia Kniga. 1994. 166–200.

Golinski, Jan. *Making Natural Knowledge: Constructivism and the History and Science*. Cambridge: Cambridge UP, 1998.

Goodman, Kevis. "The Loophole in the Retreat: The Culture of News and the Early Life of Romantic Self-Consciousness," *South Atlantic Quarterly*

102 (2003): 25–52, revised in Chapter 3 of her *Georgic Modernity and British Romanticism*. Cambridge: Cambridge UP, 2004.

Gordon, Ian A. *John Galt: The Life of a Writer*. Toronto: U of Toronto P, 1972.

Greene, Brian. *The Elegant Universe: Superstrings, Hidden Dimensions, and the Quest for the Ultimate Theory*. New York: Vintage, 1999.

Grinnell, George. "Thomas Beddoes and the Physiology of Romantic Medicine." *Studies in Romanticism* 45:2 (2006): 223–50.

"GSK Group Companies." GlaxoSmithKline, Dec. 11, 2009. Web. Dec. 27, 2009. <http://www.gsk.com/>.

Guéhenno, Jean. *Jean-Jacques Rousseau*. Trans. John Weightman and Doreen Weightman. New York: Columbia UP, 1962.

Guiliani, Rita. *La "Meravigliosa," Roma di Gogol*. Rome: Studium, 2002.

Guillory, John. *Cultural Capital: The Problem of Literary Canon Formation*. Chicago: U of Chicago P, 1993.

Hahn, Daniel. *The Tower Menagerie: The Amazing 600 Year History of the Royal Collection of Wild and Ferocious Beasts Kept in the Tower of London*. New York: Penguin, 2003.

Harootunian, Harry. "The Historical Present." *Critical Inquiry* 33 (2007): 471–94.

Harrison, J. F. C. *The Second Coming: Popular Millenarianism 1780–1850*. New Brunswick: Rutgers, 1979.

Hartman, Geoffrey H. "Wordsworth, Inscriptions, and Romantic Nature Poetry." *Beyond Formalism*. New Haven: Yale UP, 1970.

———. *Wordsworth's Poetry 1787–1814*. New Haven: Yale UP, 1964.

Haworth, H. E. "Romantic Female Writers and the Critics." *Texas Studies in Literature and Language* 17 (1976): 725–36.

Hegel, Friedrich. *Lectures on Aesthetics*. Ed. B. Bosanquet and W. M. Bryant, 1905. <http://www.hkshp.org/wclassic/hegel-aesthetics.htm>.

Heidegger, Martin. *Being and Time*. Trans. John Macquarrie and Edward Robinson. New York: Harper, 1962.

Herbold, Sarah. "Well-placed Reflections: (Post) Modern Woman as Symptom of (Post) Modern Man." *Signs* 21.1 (1995): 94–106.

Hertz, Neil. *The End of the Line: Essays on Psychoanalysis and the Sublime*. Baltimore: Johns Hopkins UP, 1985.

Hibbert, Christopher. *Venice: The Biography of a City*. New York: Norton, 1989.

Hilton, Nelson. *Literal Imagination: Blake's Vision of Words*. Berkeley: U of California P, 1983.

Hoeveler, Diane Long. "Gothic Riffs: Secularizing the Uncanny in the European Imaginary, 1780–1820." Columbus: Ohio State UP, 2010.

Hoffmann, E. T. A. *Nachlese*. Ed. Friedrich Schnapp. München: Winkler, 1981.

———. *Sämtliche Werke in sechs Bänden*. Ed. Wulf Segebrecht and Hartmut Steinecke. 7 vols. Frankfurt: Deutscher Klassiker Verlag, 1985.

———. *Die Serapions-Brüder*. Ed. Wulf Segebrecht. München: Winkler, 1976.

Hoffmann, E. T. A. *Des Vetters Eckfenster. Späte Werke.* Ed. Wulf Segebrecht. München: Winkler, 1979. 595–623.
Holcroft, Thomas. *The Life of Thomas Holcroft: Written by Himself.* London: Constable and Company. 1925.
Hole, Robert. *Pulpits, Politics and Public Order in England, 1760–1832.* Cambridge, Cambridge UP, 1989.
Holloway, S. W. F. "The Regulation of the Supply of Drugs in Britain before 1868." Porter. 77–96.
Holmes, Richard. *The Age of Wonder: How the Romantic Generation Discovered the Beauty and Terror of Science.* New York: Pantheon Books, 2008.
Houfe, Simon. *The Dictionary of 19th Century British Book Illustrators and Caricaturists.* Woodbridge, Suffolk: Antique Collectors Club, 1978.
Houston, Chloe. "'An Idea For a Principality'? Encountering the East in Bacon's *New Atlantis.*" *Seventeenth Century* 21:1 (2006): 22–32.
Hume, David. *An Inquiry Concerning Human Understanding.* New York: Bobbs-Merrill, 1955.
Hume, Robert. "The Economics of Culture in London, 1660–1740." *Huntington Library Quarterly* 69 (2006): 487–535.
Inchbald, Elizabeth. *A Simple Story.* 1791. Ed. Anna Lott. Peterborough: Broadview, 2007.
Inkster, Ian. "Advocates and Audience: Aspects of Popular Astronomy in England, 1750–1850." *Journal of the British Astronomical Association* 92:3 (1982): 199–223.
Irving, Sarah. "'In a Pure Soil': Colonial Anxieties in the Work of Francis Bacon." *History of European Ideas* 32:3 (2006): 249–62.
Ivanitskii, A. I. *Gogol': Morfologiia Zemli I Vlasti.* Moscow: RGGU, 2000.
Jackson, Virginia. *Dickinson's Misery: A Theory of Lyric Reading.* Princeton: Princeton UP, 2005.
Jacobs, Edward. *Accidental Migrations: An Archaeology of Gothic Discourse.* Lewisburg: Bucknell UP, 2000.
Jalobeanu, Dana. "Bacon's Brotherhood and Its Classical Sources: Producing and Communicating Knowledge in the Project of the Great Instauration." *Intersections: Yearbook for Early Modern Studies* 11 (2008): 197–230.
James, Louis. *Fiction for the Working Man: 1830–1850.* London: Oxford UP, 1963.
"John Bell & Croyden." John Bell & Croyden, Ltd., 2009. Web. Dec. 23, 2009. <http://www.johnbellcroyden.co.uk>.
Johnson, Paul. *The Birth of the Modern.* New York: HarperCollins, 1991.
Johnston, Kenneth R. *The Hidden Wordsworth: Poet Lover Rebel Spy.* New York: Norton, 1998.
Jordan, John E. *De Quincey to Wordsworth.* Berkeley: U of California P, 1963.
Jowitt, Claire. "'Books will speak plain'? Colonialism, Jewishness, and Politics in Bacon's *New Atlantis.*" *Francis Bacon's* New Atlantis: *New Interdisciplinary Essays.* Ed. Bronwen Price. Manchester: Manchester UP, 2002. 129–55.

Kant, Immanuel. *Anthropology from a Pragmatic Point of View*. Trans. Robert Louden. Cambridge: Cambridge UP, 2006.
———. "Conjectural Beginning of Human History." *Perpetual Peace and Other Essays*. Trans. Ted Humphrey. Indianapolis: Hackett, 1983.
———. *Critique of the Power of Judgment*. Trans. Paul Guyer and Eric Matthews. Cambridge: Cambridge UP, 2000.
———. *Groundwork of the Metaphysics of Morals*. Trans. Mary Gregor. Cambridge: Cambridge UP, 1998.
———. *Lectures on Ethics*. Trans. Peter Heath. Cambridge: Cambridge UP, 1997.
Kateb, George. "Technology and Philosophy" *Social Science Research* 64:3 (1997). 1241.
Keats, John. "Ode on Melancholy." *Complete Poems*. Ed. Jack Stillinger. Cambridge: Belknap P of Harvard UP, 1982. 283–84.
Kelly, Gary. "Fiction and the Working Classes." *The Cambridge Companion to Fiction in the Romantic Period*. Ed. Richard Maxwell and Katie Trumpener. Cambridge: Cambridge UP, 2008. 207–33.
———. Introduction. *Varieties of Female Gothic*. Vol. 2. *Street Gothic: Female Gothic Chapbooks*. Ed. Kelly. London: Pickering, 2002. i–xxv.
Koch, Angela. "'The Absolute Horror of Horrors' Revised: A Bibliographical Checklist of Early–Nineteenth–Century Gothic Bluebooks." *Cardiff Corvey: Reading the Romantic Text* 9 (2002): n.p. Web.
———. "Gothic Bluebooks in the Princely Library of Corvey and Beyond." *Cardiff Corvey: Reading the Romantic Text* 9 (2002): n.p. Web.
Korsgaard, Christine. *Creating the Kingdom of Ends*. Cambridge: Harvard UP, 1996.
Lawrence, D. H. *Women in Love*. New York: Viking, 1972.
Leask, Nigel. *British Romantic Writers and the East: Anxieties of Empire*. Cambridge: Cambridge UP, 1992.
Leavis, F. R. and Denys Thompson. *Culture and Environment: The Training of Critical Awareness*. London: Chatto. 1993.
Lefebvre, Henri, *Critique of Everyday Life*. Trans. John Moore and Gregory Elliott. 3 vols. London: Verso, 2005.
Levey, Michael. *Painting in Eighteenth Century Venice*. London: Phaidon, 1959.
Levin, Susan. "A Fourfold Vision: William Blake and Doris Lessing." *William Blake and the Moderns*. Ed. Robert J. Bertholf and Annette S. Levitt. Albany: SUNY P, 1982.
Lichtenberg, Georg Christoph. *Lichtenberg's Visits to England as Described in His Letters and Diaries*. Oxford: Clarendon, 1938.
———. "Über Physiognomik." *Werke in einem Band*. Ed. Peter Plett. Hamburg: Hoffmann, 1967. 369–409.
Lindop, Grevil. *The Opium-Eater: A Life of Thomas De Quincey*. London: Dent, 1981.
Lockhart, John Gibson. "Cockney School of Poetry No. IV." *Blackwood's Edinburgh Magazine* Aug. 1818: 519–24.

Lockhart, John Gibson, and William Maginn. "The Building of the Palace of the Lamp." *Blackwood's Edinburgh Magazine* Sep. 1820: 675–79.

Lussier, Mark. "Blake's Vortex: The Quantum Tunnel in *Milton*." *Nineteenth-Century Contexts* 18.3 (1994): 278–91.

Macleod, Dianne Sachko. "Homosociality and Middle-Class Identity in Early Victorian Patronage of the Arts." *Gender, Civic Culture and Consumerism: Middle Class Identity in Britain, 1840–1900.* Ed. Alan J. Kidd and David Nicholls. Manchester: Manchester UP, 1999. 65–80.

Maehle, Andreas-Holger. *Drugs on Trial: Experimental Pharmacology and Therapeutic Innovation in the Eighteenth Century.* Amsterdam: Rodopi, 1999.

Makdisi, Saree. *William Blake and the Impossible History of the 1790s.* Chicago: U of Chicago P, 2003.

Manfreda, Luisa. *Figure dell'ironia nei* Promessi Sposi. *Il ruolo doppio a rovescio dei personaggi.* Pesaro: Metauro, 2006. 115–46.

Manning, Peter J. *Reading Romantics.* New York: Oxford UP, 1990.

———. "Wordsworth in the *Keepsake*, 1829," *Literature in the Marketplace.* Ed. John O. Jordan and Robert L. Patten. Cambridge: Cambridge UP, 1995.

Manzoni, Alessandro. *The Betrothed.* Trans. Bruce Penman. London: Penguin, 1972.

———. *The Column of Infamy.* Trans. Kenelm Foster and Jane Grigson. London: Oxford UP, 1964.

———. *I Promessi Sposi.* Florence: Nuova Italia, 1974.

———. *La Rivoluzione Francese del 1789 e la rivoluzione italiana del 1859. Dell'indipendenza dell'Italia.* Vol. 15. *Edizione Nazionale ed Europea delle Opere di Alessandro Manzoni.* Milan: Centro Nazionale Studi Manzoniani, 2000.

———. *Storia della Colonna Infame.* Milan: Bompiani, 1985.

Marchese, Angelo. "Il Bildungsroman di Renzo. Punto di vista e senso del racconto." *L'engima Manzoni. La spiritualità e l'arte di uno scrittore «negativo».* Rome: Bulzoni, 1994.

Mariani, Umberto. "La visuale di Renzo: l'avventura in città," "La visuale di Renzo: le estreme conseguenze." *Per un Manzoni più vero.* Turin: SEI, 1996.

Marland, Hilary. "The 'Doctor's Shop': The Rise of the Chemist and Druggist in Nineteenth-Century Manufacturing Districts." *From Physick to Pharmacology: Five Hundred Years of British Drug Retailing.* Ed. Louise Hill Curth. Aldershot: Ashgate, 2006. 79–104.

———. "The Medical Activities of Mid-Nineteenth-Century Chemists and Druggists, with Special Reference to Wakefield and Huddersfield." *Medical History* 31.4 (1987): 415–39.

Matthews, Samantha. *Poetical Remains: Poets' Graves, Bodies, and Books in the Nineteenth Century.* Oxford: Oxford UP, 2004.

Mayo, Robert D. "Gothic Romance in the Magazines." *PMLA* 65 (1950): 762–89.

———. "The Gothic Short Story in the Magazines." *Modern Language Review* 37 (1942): 448–54.
Mazzitelli, Michele. *La peste. Nel centenario de* I promessi sposi *(1840–1940)*. Presentazione di Antonino Anile. Tredici tavole fuori testo. Apuania Carrara: Bassani, 1940.
McCalman, Iain. *Radical Underworld: Prophets, Revolutionaries and Pornographers in London, 1795–1840*. Cambridge: Cambridge UP, 1988.
McFarland, Robert. "Ein Auge, welches (Un)wirklich(es) schaut. *Des Vetters Eckfenster* und E. T. A. Hoffmanns Ansichten von Berlin." *E. T. A. Hoffmann Jahrbuch* 13 (2005): 98–116.
McKusick, James C. *Green Writing: Romanticism and Ecology*. New York: St. Martin's P, 2000.
McWhir, Ann. "The Gothic Transgression of Disbelief: Walpole, Radcliffe, and Lewis." *Gothic Fictions: Prohibition/Transgression*. Ed. Kenneth W. Graham. New York: AMS, 1989. 29–48.
Mee, John. *Dangerous Enthusiasm: William Blake and the Culture of Radicalism in the 1790s*. Clarendon: Oxford UP, 1992.
Mellor, Anne. *Blake's Human Forms Divine*. Berkeley: U of California P, 1974.
Merezhkovsky D. S. *Gogol and the Devil*. Letchworth: Prideau, 1976.
Merling, Michael. "The Brothers Guardi." *The Glory of Venice: Art in the Eighteenth Century*. New Haven: Yale UP, 1994.
Milton, John. *Paradise Lost. Poetical Works*. Ed. Helen Darbishire. Vol. 1. Oxford: Oxford UP, 1962.
Molmenti, Pompeo. "The Decadence." *Venice: Its Individual Growth from the Earliest Beginnings to the Fall of the Republic*. Trans. Horatio Brown. London: Murray, 1880.
Monnier, Philippe. *Venice in the Eighteenth Century*. Trans. Monnier. London: Chatto, 1907.
Montesquieu, Charles-Louis. *Voyages de Montesquieu*. Ed. Albert de Montesquieu. Bordeaux: Gounouilhou, 1894.
Monticone, Severino. "La psicologia della folla." *Nella miniera dei Promessi Sposi*. Turin: SEI, 1965. 220–32.
Moody, Jane. *Illegitimate Theatre in Long, 1770–1840*. Cambridge: Cambridge UP, 2000.
Morassi, Antonio. *Antonio e Francesco Guardi*. 2 vols. Venice: Alfieri, 1973.
Morus, Iwan Rhys. *Frankenstein's Children: Electricity, Exhibition, and Experiment in Early-Nineteenth Century London*. Princeton: Princeton UP, 1998.
Mudge, Bradford K. "The Man with Two Brains: Gothic Novels, Popular Culture, Literary History." *PMLA* 107 (1992): 92–104.
Mudie, Robert. *Babylon the Great: A Dissection and Demonstration of Men and Things in the British Capital*. 2 vols. Philadelphia: Carey, 1825.
Munby, A. N. L. *Sale Catalogues of Libraries of Eminent Persons*, vol. 9, *Poets and Men of Letters*. Ed. Roy Park. London: Mansell, 1974.
Muscarà, Corrado. *Il dolore nei* Promessi Sposi. Rome: Bardi, 1950.
Nabokov, Vladimir. *Nikolai Gogol*. New York: New Directions, 1961.

Negri, Giovanni. "Dall'osteria della luna piena a quella di Gorgonzola." *Sui Promessi sposi di Alessandro Manzoni*. Parte II. Milan: Scuola Tipografica Salesiana, 1903. 55–89.

———. "Fra i tumulti per il rincaro del pane," *Sui Promessi sposi di Alessandro Manzoni*. Milan: Scuola Tipografica Salesiana, 1903. 27–53.

———. "I pentimenti di Renzo e la sua fede nella Provvidenza." *Sui Promessi sposi di Alessandro Manzoni*. Parte II. Milan: Scuola Tipografica Salesiana, 1903. 91–107.

Neumann, Gerhard. "Ausblicke. E. T. A. Hoffmann's letzte Erzählung *Des Vetters Eckfenster*." 'Hoffmanneske Geschichte' Zu einer Literaturwissenschaft als Kulturwissenschaft. Ed. Gerhard Neumann. Würzburg: Königshausen, 2005.

Nuzzo, Angelica. *Ideal Embodiment: Kant's Theory of Sensibility*. Bloomington: Indiana UP, 2008.

O'Connor, Ralph. *The Earth on Show: Fossils and the Poetics of Popular Science, 1802–1856*. Chicago: U of Chicago P, 2007.

O'Quinn, Daniel. *Staging Governance: Theatrical Imperialism, 1770–1800*. Baltimore: Johns Hopkins UP, 2005.

O'Rourke, James. *Sex, Lies and Autobiography*. Charlottesville: U of Virginia P, 2006.

Oesterle, Günter. "E. T. A. Hoffmann: *Des Vetters Eckfenster*. Zur Historisierung ästhetischer Wahrnehmung oder Der kalkulierte romantische Rückgriff auf Sehmuster der Aufklärung." *Der Deutschunterricht* 39.1 (1987): 84–110.

Oliver, W. H. *Prophets and Millenialists: The Uses of Biblical Prophecy in England from the 1790s to the 1840s*. Auckland: Oxford UP, 1978.

Olson, Roberta and Pasachoff, Jay M. *Fire in the Sky: Comets, Meteors, the Decisive Centuries, in British Art and Science*. Cambridge: Cambridge P, 1998.

Otto, Peter. *Blake's Critique of Transcendence*. Oxford: Oxford UP, 2000.

Paley, Morton D. *Apocalypse and Millennium in English Romantic Poetry*. Oxford: Clarendon, 1999.

———. *The Continuing City: William Blake's* Jerusalem. Oxford: Clarendon P, 1983.

———. "William Blake, the Prince of the Hebrews, and the Woman Clothed with the Sun." *William Blake; Essays in Honour of Sir Geoffrey Keynes*. Ed. Morton D. Paley and Michael Phillips. Oxford: Clarendon, 1973. 274–75.

Palgrave, Francis Turner, ed. *A Golden Treasury of English Songs and Lyrics*. Cambridge: Macmillan, 1861–91.

Parrini, Elena. "La Storia per la storia" "Dalla narrazione alla storia" *La narrazione della storia nei* Promessi Sposi. Florence: Le Lettere, 1996. 61–115; 179–219.

Pascoe, Judith. *The Hummingbird Cabinet: A Rare and Curious History of Romantic Collectors*. Ithaca: Cornell UP, 2006.

Pautasso, Sergio. *I promessi sposi. Appunti e ipotesi di lettura*. Milan: Arcipelago, 1988.

Pedrocco, Filippo. "Iconografia delle Cortigiane di Venezia." *Il Gioco dell'Amore*.

Peer, Larry H. *(Roman)ticism*. New York : UP of America. 2008.

Pemble, John. *Venice Rediscovered.* Oxford: Clarendon, 1995.
Peterfreund, Stuart. *William Blake in a Newtonian World.* Norman: U of Oklahoma P, 1998.
Phillips, Mark Saber. *Society and Sentiment: Genres of Historical Writing in Britain, 1740–1820.* Princeton: Princeton UP, 2000.
Plant, Margaret. *Venice: Fragile City.* New Haven: Yale UP, 2002.
Porter, Roy. *Doctor of Society: Thomas Beddoes and the Sick Trade in Late-Enlightenment England.* London: Routledge, 1992.
———. *Flesh in the Age of Reason: The Modern Foundations of Body and Soul.* New York: Norton, 2003.
———. *Health for Sale: Quackery in England, 1660–1850.* Manchester: Manchester UP, 1989.
Porter, Roy, and Dorothy Porter. "The Rise of the English Drugs Industry: The Role of Thomas Corbyn." *Medical History* 33.3 (1989): 277–95.
Porter, Roy, and Mikuláš Teich, ed. *Drugs and Narcotics in History.* Cambridge: Cambridge UP, 1995.
Potter, Franz. *The History of Gothic Publishing, 1800–1835: Exhuming the Trade.* New York: Palgrave, 2005.
Poulet, Georges. "Criticism and the Experience of Interiority." *Reader-Response Criticism.* Ed. Jane P. Tompkins. Baltimore: Johns Hopkins UP, 1980.
Prickett, Stephen. *Words and* The Word*: Language, Poetics and Biblical Interpretation.* Cambridge: Cambridge UP, 1986.
Punter, David, and Glennis Byron, eds. *Spectral Readings: Towards a Gothic Geography.* New York: St. Martin's P. 1999.
Radcliffe, Mary Anne. *The Female Advocate; or An Attempt to Recover the Rights of Women from Male Usurpation.* 1799. *The Longman Anthology of British Literature.* Ed. Susan Wolfson and Peter Manning. Vol. 2A. New York: Pearson, 2006. 332–38.
Raimondi, Ezio. "L'osteria della retorica." *La dissimulazione romanzesca. Antropologia manzoniana.* Bologna: Il Mulino, 2004. 81–110.
Raine, Kathleen. *Golgonooza, City of Imagination.* Ipswich: Golgonooza P, 1991.
Rajan, Tilottama. "Imagining History." *PMLA* 118 (2003): 427–35.
Redford, Bruce. *Venice and the Grand Tour.* New Haven: Yale UP, 1996.
Reed, Mark L. "Wordsworth's Surprisingly Pictured Page: *Select Pieces*," *Book Collector* 46 (1997): 69–92.
Richardson, Ruth. "Landseer's Apothecary." *The Lancet.* Feb. 24, 2001: 646.
Richmond, Leslie, Julie Stevenson, and Alison Turton, ed. *The Pharmaceutical Industry: A Guide to Historical Records.* Aldershot: Ashgate, 2003.
Richter, David. *The Progress of Romance: Literary Historiography and the Gothic Novel.* Columbus: Ohio State UP, 1996.
———. "The Reception of the Gothic Novel in the 1790s." *The Idea of the Novel in the Eighteenth Century.* Ed. Robert Uphaus. East Lansing: Colleagues, 1988. 117–37.
Robinson, Henry Crabb. *Diary, Reminiscences, and Correspondence.* Ed. Thomas Sadler. 2 vols. London: Macmillan, 1872.

Roedel, Reto. "La folla nei *Promessi Sposi*." *Note manzoniane*. Turin: Chiantore, 1934. 5–104.
Ronell, Avital. *Crack Wars: Literature, Addiction, Mania*. Lincoln: U of Nebraska P, 1992.
Rousseau, G. S. "Nerves, Spirits, and Fibres: Towards Defining the Origins of Sensibility." *Studies in the Eighteenth Century III: Papers Presented at the Third David Nichol Smith Memorial Seminar*. Ed. R. F. Brissenden. Toronto: U of Toronto P, 1976. 137–57.
Rousseau, Jean-Jacques. *The Confessions*. Trans. J. M. Cohen. New York: Penguin, 1953.
———. *Discourse on the Origins of Inequality among Men. The Discourses and Other Early Political Writings*. Trans.Victor Gourevitch. Cambridge: Cambridge UP, 1997.
———. *Italian Journey*. Trans. W. H. Auden and Elizabeth Mayer. New York: Penguin, 1970.
———. *Oeuvres complètes*. Ed. Bernard Gagnebin and Marcel Raymond. Paris: Gallimard, 1959.
Rowden, Maurice. *The Silver Age of Venice*. New York: Praeger, 1970.
Roy, G. Ross. "Some Notes on Scottish Chapbooks." *Scottish Literary Journal* 1 (1974): 50–60.
"Royal Pharmaceutical Society of Great Britain." Royal Pharmaceutical Society of Great Britain, 2009. Web. Dec. 23, 2009. <http://rpsgb.org/>.
Rzepka, Charles J. *Sacramental Commodities: Gift, Text, and the Sublime in De Quincey*. Amherst: U of Massachusetts P, 1995.
Said, Edward. *Orientalism*. New York: Vintage, 1978.
Saprykina, E. IU. "Gogol' i Traditsii italiianso I Satiry." *Gogol' I Mirovaia Literatura*. Moscow: Nauka. 1998. 62–83.
Scarabello, Giovanni. "Le 'Signore' della Repubblica." *Il Gioco dell'Amore: Le Cortigiane di Venezia dal Trecento al Settecento*. Milan: Berenice, 1990.
Schama, Simon. *Landscape and Memory*. New York: Knopf, 1995.
Schenk, H. G. *The Mind of the European Romantics*. New York: Doubleday, 1969.
Schnapp, Friedrich, ed. *E. T. A. Hoffmanns Briefwechsel*. Vol 2. München: Winkler, 1968.
Schorer, Mark. *William Blake: The Politics of Vision*. New York: Vintage, 1946.
Serres, Michel. *Le contrat naturel*. Paris: Bourin, 1990.
Shackford, Martha Hale. *Wordsworth's Interest in Painters and Pictures*. Wellesley: Wellesley P, 1945.
Shambinago, S. K. *Trilogiia Romantizma: N. V. Gogol'*. Moscow: n.p. 1911.
Shelley, Percy Bysshe. *Letters*. Ed. Frederick L. Jones. Vol. 2. Oxford: Clarendon, 1964.
Shenrok, V. I. *Materialy dlya Biografii Gogolia, IV*. Dusseldorf: Brucken. 1970.
Sheringham, Michael. *French Autobiography: Devices and Desires*. Oxford: Oxford UP, 1993.

Shirilan, Stephanie. "Francis Bacon, Robert Burton, and the Thick Skin of the World." *English Studies in Canada* 34:1 (2008): 59–83.

Simonini, Augusto. *L'ideologia di Alessandro Manzoni.* Ravenna: Longo, 1978.

Simonsen, Peter. *Wordsworth and Word-Preserving Arts.* Basingstoke: Palgrave, 2007.

Simonson, George. *Francesco Guardi.* London: Metheun, 1904.

Sinnema, Peter W. *Dynamics of the Pictured Page: Representing the Nation in the Illustrated London News.* Aldershot: Ashgate, 1998.

Slinn, Judy. "Research and Development in the UK Pharmaceutical Industry from the Nineteenth Century to the 1960s." Porter. 168–86.

Smith, Laurie. "Seeing the City." Seeing the City," *Magma Poetry* 21. <http://www.magmapoetry.com/archive/magma-21/articles.html>.

Smith, Suzanne. "The New Atlantis: Francis Bacon's Theological-Political Utopia." *Harvard Theological Review* 101 (2008). 97–125.

Southcott, Joanna. *A Continuation of the Prophecies.* Exeter, 1802.

———. *Song of Moses and the Lamb.* London, 1804.

Southey, Robert. *Letters from England.* Ed. Jack Simmons. London: Cresset, 1951.

St. Clair, William. *The Reading Nation in the Romantic Period.* Cambridge: Cambridge UP, 2004.

Stadler, Ulrich. "Die Aussicht als Einblick. Zu E. T. A. Hoffmanns später Erzählung *Des Vetters Eckfenster.*" *Zeitschrift für deutsche Philologie* 105.4 (1986): 498–515.

Starobinski, Jean. *Transparency and Obstruction.* Trans. Arthur Goldhammer. Chicago: Chicago UP, 1971.

Steigerwald, Jörn. *Die fantastische Bildlichkeit der Stadt. Zur Begründung der literarischen Fantastik im Werk E. T. A. Hoffmanns.* Würzburg: Königshausen, 2001.

Stelzig, Eugene. *All Shades of Consciousness: Wordsworth's Poetry and the Self in Time.* Hague: Mouton, 1975.

Stendhal. *De L'Amour.* Ed. Henri Martineau. Paris: Le Divan, 1957.

Stone, Lawrence. "Literacy and Education in England, 1640–1900." *Past & Present* 42 (1969): 109–25.

Succi, Dario. *Francesco Guardi: itenarario dell'avventura artistica.* Milan: Silvana, 1993.

Sullivan, Walter. *Black Holes: The Edge of Space, the End of Time.* New York: Anchor, 1979.

Summers, Montague. *The Gothic Quest: A History of the Gothic Novel.* London: Fortune, 1938.

Tanner, Tony. *Venice Desired.* Cambridge, MA: Harvard UP, 1992.

Taylor, Anya. *Magic and English Romanticism.* Athens: U of Georgia P, 1979.

Taylor, Charles. *A Secular Age.* Cambridge, MA: Harvard UP, 2007.

Thompson, E. P. *The Making of the English Working Class.* London: Gollancz, 1963.

Thomson, James. "City of Dreadful Night." *The Poetical Works.* Ed. Bertram Dobell. Vol. 1. 2 vols. London: Reeves, 1895.
Timothy, H. B. *The Galts: A Canadian Odyssey: John Galt, 1779–1839.* Toronto: McClelland and Stuart, 1977.
Transactions of the Royal Sciety of Edinburgh. N.p. 1788.
Trott, Nicola. "Wordsworth: The Shape of the Poetic Career." *The Cambridge Companion to Wordsworth.* Ed. Stephen Gill. Cambridge: Cambridge UP, 2003. 5–21.
Trotter, Thomas. *A View of the Nervous Temperament* [...]. Troy: Wright, 1808.
Trudnyi Put': Zarubeznaia Rossiia I Gogol': Sostavitel' M. D. Filin. Moscow: Russkii Mir. 2002.
Tucker, Jennifer. "Voyages of Discovery on Oceans of Air: Scientific Observation and the Image of Science in an Age of 'Baloonacy.'" *Osiris* (Second Series) XI (1996): 144–76.
The Use of Circulating Libraries Considered. The Evergreen Tree of Diabolical Knowledge. Ed. Devendra Varma. Washington: Consortium, 1972. 195–203.
Vaiskopf, Mikhail. *Siuzhet Gogolia: Morfologiia, Ideologiia, Kontekst.* Moscow: TOO Radiks, 1993.
Velkley, Richard. *Freedom and the End of Reason.* Chicago: Chicago UP, 1989.
Vickers, Neil. *Coleridge and the Doctors.* Oxford: Clarendon, 2004.
———. "Coleridge, Thomas Beddoes and Brunonian Medicine." *European Romantic Review* 8:1 (1997): 47–94.
Vinogradov, I. A. "Ot 'Nevskogo Prospekta' do 'Rima' Petergurgska i a Tema v Tvorchestve Gogolia." In *Gogol'—Khudozhnik I Mylsitel': Khristianskie Osnovy Mirosozertsaniia.* Moscow: ILMI RAN, 2000. 204–74.
Virolainen, Maria. "Mify goroda v mire Goglia." In Bocharov, S. G. *Gogol' v Russkoi Kritike: Antologi I a Sostavitel.* Moscow: Fortuna EL, 2008. 652–62.
Wallen, Martin. *City of Health, Fields of Disease: Revolutions in the Poetry, Medicine, and Philosophy of Romanticism.* Aldershot: Ashgate, 2004.
Waterston, Elizabeth. Ed. *John Galt: Reappraisals* Guelph: U of Guelph P, 1987.
Watt, William. *Shilling Shockers of the Gothic School: A Study of Chapbook Gothic Romances.* New York: Russell, 1932.
Weber, Max. "Science as a Vocation." 1919. *Max Weber: Essays in Sociology.* Trans. and ed. H. H. Gerth and C. Wright Mills. New York: Oxford UP, 1958. 129–56.
Weedy, John, ed. *The Illustrated London News.* Web. Jan. 25, 2007. <http://www.iln.org.uk/iln_years/earlyhistiln.htm>.
Weiskel, Thomas. *The Romantic Sublime.* Baltimore: Johns Hopkins UP, 1986.
———. *The Romantic Sublime: Studies in the Psychology of Transcendence.* Baltimore: Johns Hopkins UP, 1976.
Weller, Toni. "Preserving Knowledge through Popular Victorian Periodicals: An Examination of *The Penny Magazine* and the *Illustrated London News*," *Library History* 24 (2008): 200–207.
Wicks, Robert. "Kant on Beautifying the Human Body." *British Journal of Aesthetics* 39.2 (1999): 163–78.

Wiley, Michael. *Romantic Migrations: Local, National, and Transnational Dispositions*. New York: Palgrave Macmillan. 2008.
Wilkinson, Sarah. *The Spectre of Lanmere Abbey; or, The Mystery of the Blue and Silver Bag: A Romance*. 2 vols. London: Mason, 1820.
———. "The White Pilgrim." *Varieties of Female Gothic*. Ed. Gary Kelly. Vol. 2. London: Pickering, 2002. 307–36.
Williams, Nicholas M. *Ideology in the Poetry of William Blake*. Cambridge: Cambridge UP, 1998.
Wilner, Joshua. "The Stewed Muse of Prose: Wordsworth, De Quincey, Baudelaire," *Feeding on Infinity: Readings in the Romantic Rhetoric of Internalisation*. Baltimore: Johns Hopkins UP, 2000. 68–77.
Wollstonecraft, Mary. *Mary, A Fiction and The Wrongs of Woman, or Maria*. 1788 and 1798. Ed. Gary Kelly. Oxford: Oxford UP, 1976.
———. *The Vindications: The Rights of Men and the Rights of Woman*. 1790 and 1792. Ed. D. L. Macdonald and Kathleen Scherf. Peterborough: Broadview, 1997.
Wood, Gillen D'Arcy. *The Shock of the Real: Romanticism and Visual Culture 1760–1860*. Basingstoke: Palgrave, 2001.
Wordsworth, William. *The Excursion*. Ed. Sally Bushell, James A. Butler, and Michael C. Jaye. Ithaca: Cornell UP.
———. *Last Poems, 1821–1850*. Ed. Jared Curtis. Ithaca: Cornell UP, 1999.
———. *The Major Works*. Ed. Stephen Gill. Oxford: Oxford UP, 1984.
———. Preface to *Lyrical Ballads* (1800). *Prose Works*. Ed. W. J. B. Owen and Jane Worthington Smyser. 3 vols. Oxford: Oxford UP, 1974.
———. *The Prelude*. Ed. Ernest De Selincourt. Rev. Helen Darbishire. 2nd ed. Oxford: Oxford UP, 1959.
———. *The Prelude 1799, 1805, 1850*. Ed. Jonathan Wordsworth, M. H. Abrams, and Stephen Gill. New York: Norton, 1979.
———. *The Prelude: A Parallel Text*. Ed. J. C. Maxwell. Harmondsworth: Penguin, 1971.
———. *The Prose Works of William Wordsworth*. Ed. W. J. B. Owen and Jane W. Smyser. 3 vols. Oxford: Clarendon, 1974.
———. *William Wordsworth: The Oxford Authors*. Ed. Stephen Gill. Oxford: Oxford UP, 1984.
Wordsworth, William, and Dorothy Wordsworth. *The Letters of William and Dorothy Wordsworth, The Later Years, Part 1, 1821–1828*. Ed. Ernest De Selincourt. Rev. Alan G. Hill. 2nd ed. Oxford: Clarendon, 1978.
———. *The Letters of William and Dorothy Wordsworth, The Later Years, Part 4, 1840–1853*. Ed. Ernest De Selincourt. Rev. Alan G. Hill. 2nd ed. Oxford: Clarendon, 1988.
———. *The Letters of William and Dorothy Wordsworth, The Middle Years, Part 1, 1806–1811*. Ed. Ernest De Selincourt. Rev. Mary Moorman. 2nd ed. Oxford: Clarendon, 1969.
———. *The Letters of William and Dorothy Wordsworth, The Middle Years, Part 2, 1812–1820*. Ed. Ernest de Selincourt. Rev. Mary Moorman and Alan G. Hill. Oxford: Clarendon, 1970.

Wordsworth, William, and Samuel Taylor Coleridge. *Lyrical Ballads*. Ed. R. L. Brett and A. R. Jones. London: Methuen, 1968.

Worrall, David. *Radical Culture: Discourse, Resistance and Surveillance, 1790–1820*. London: Harvester, 1992.

Youngquist, Paul. *Monstrosities: Bodies and British Romanticism*. Minneapolis: U of Minneapolis P, 2003.

Zen'kovskii, V. V. "N. V. Gogol'." *Trudnyi Put': Zarubezhnaia Rissiia I Gogol': Sostavitel' M. D. Filin*. Moscow: Russkii Mir. 2002. 288–305.

Zimmerman, Michael E. *Contesting Earth's Future: Radical Ecology and Postmodernity*. Berkeley: U of California P, 1994.

Zuckert, Rachel. "Boring Beauty and Universal Morality: Kant on the Ideal of Beauty." *Inquiry* 48.2 (2005): 107–30.

Index

Aikin, John
   "Sir Bertrand: A Fragment," 63
Apel, Johann August
   Das Gespensterbuch, 56
Austen, Jane
   Mansfield Park, 29

Bacon, Francis
   The New Atlantis, 43, 44–5
Barbauld, Anna Letitia
   "On the Pleasure Derived from Objects of Terror," 63
Baudelaire, Charles, 114, 122
Beddoes, Thomas, 13, 19, 20, 21
   Hygeia: or, Essays Moral and Medical on the Causes Affecting the Personal State of our Middling and Affluent Classes, 9, 14
Beethoven, Ludwig, 2
Bell, John, 217
   The Pharmaceutical Journal, 218
Berkeley, George, 29
Bevan, Silvanus, 219
Blake, William, 4, 197, 247–8
   America, A Prophecy, 197
   The Book of Ahania, 198
   The Book of Urizen, 198
   "Elohim Creating Adam," 198
   Europe, A Prophecy, 198
   Jerusalem, 198
   Milton, 198
   "Nebuchadnezzar," 198
   "Newton," 198
Bronte, Emily, 1, 2
Brullov, Karl, 161
Bürger, Gottfried August
   "Lenore," 60

Burney, Francis
   Evelina, 10, 14–15, 16, 19–21
Byron, George Gordon, 55, 83, 199
   Beppo, 176–7

Callot, Jacques, 110, 111
Canel, Giovanni Antonio ("Canaletto"), 94
Carelevaris, Luce, 94
Chateaubriand, François-René, 1, 157
Chodowiecki, Daniel, 110, 111
Cities
   Bath, 73
   Berlin, 73, 105–30
   Birmingham, 73
   Bristol, 73
   Edinburgh, 73
   Genoa, 174
   Glasgow, 73
   London, 4, 5, 16, 73, 108, 181–94, 199–206, 241–56
   Manchester, 73
   Milan, 135–50
   New York City, 73, 201
   Paris, 73, 108, 123
   Philadelphia, 73
   Rome, 4, 73, 157–77
   St. Petersburg, 175
   Venice, 3, 87–99
Clairmont, Claire, 55
Coleridge, Samuel Taylor, 13, 25–6, 29, 33, 74, 78
   "The Devil's Thoughts," 213–14
Constable, John, 1, 83
Corbyn, Thomas, 219

Corri, William
Harlequin and Sinbad the Sailor; Or, The Genii of the Diamond Valley, 46
Cowper, William, 236, 243–4
The Task, 75, 225–6
Crabbe, George
"The Newspaper," 225
Crookenden, Issac, 65
Cuvier, George, 81

D'Alembert, Jean le Rond, 5
Dante Alighieri, 160
Darwin, Charles
Origin of Species, 79
De Quincey, Thomas, 4, 185, 217–19, 221, 228, 231–2, 242, 251
Confessions of an English Opium Eater, 4, 209–13, 248–50, 252–6
Dibdin, Charles
Harlequin and Humpo: Or, Columbine by Candlelight, 46
Dickens, Charles
David Copperfield, 189
Pictures From Italy, 176
Döblin, Alfred
Berlin Alexanderplatz, 106
Dostoevsky, Fyodor, 176
The Idiot, 158

Eyriès, J. B. B.
Fantasmagoriana; ou Recueil d'Histoires d'Apparitions, 56

Fichte, Johann Gottlieb, 1
Franklin, Benjamin, 76, 78

Galt, John, 3
The Apostate; Or, Atlantis Destroyed, 3, 45–6, 49–53
The Canadas: As They At Present Commend Themselves to The Enterprise Of Emigrants, Colonists, And Capitalists, 52
Letters from the Levant, 52–3
Love, Honor and Interest, 46, 48
The New British Theatre 46, 47, 48
The Prophetess, 48
A Search After Perfection, 47–8
Selim and Zuleika, 48
Sixteen and Sixty, 48
Giordano, Lucca
Diana and Endymion, 233
Girtin, Thomas, 5
Goethe, Johann Wolfgang, 1, 83
Gogol, Nikolai, 4, 157–77
The Carriage, 163
The Dead Souls, 157, 158, 168
The Inspector General, 158
The Last Day of Pompeii, 161
Nevsky Prospect, 161, 163–4
The Nose, 157
An Ode to Italy, 160
The Overcoat, 157
Rome, 163, 164–8, 172–4
Graham, James, 79
Grimm, Jacob Ludwig, 5
Guardi, Francesco, 94, 95, 96

Hegel, Georg Wilhelm Friedrich, 3
Lectures on Aesthetics, 171
Heidegger, Martin, 57
Herschel, William, 76
Hoffmann, Ernst Theodor Wilhelm, 4, 57, 105–30
and *Biedermeier*, 110–13, 122, 126–7
"Letter to the Publisher," 115–17
Master Flea, 124
My Cousin's Corner Window, 106–30
The Serapion Brothers, 117–20
Hogarth, William, 110, 111
Hölderlin, Friedrich, 1
Howard, Luke
The Climate of London, 83
Essay on the Modification of Clouds, 83
Hume, David, 238

Illustrated London News, 237–8
Inchbald, Elizabeth
 A Simple Story, 10, 14–15, 16, 18–19, 21–2
Ivanov, Alexander
 The Appearance of Christ before the People, 160

Jefferson, Thomas
 Declaration of Independence, 77

Kant, Immanuel, 87
 Kritik der Urteilskraft, 93
Keats, John, 210, 214
 "Ode on Melancholy," 210

Lamb, Charles, 181, 248
Lane's Circulating Library, 64–5
Laun, Friedrich, 56
Lemoine, Ann
 Tell-Tale Magazine, 65
Leopardi, Giacomo, 1
Lessing, Doris
 The Four-Gated City, 204
Lewis, Isabella
 Terrific Tales, 60
Lichtenberg, Georg Christoph, 242–3
Longhi, Pietro, 96

The Man in the Moon, 77
Manzoni, Alessandro, 1, 4
 I promessi sposi, 4, 135–50
 La Rivoluzione Francese del 1789 e la rivoluzione italiana del 1859. Saggio comparative, 141
 Storia della Colonna Infame, 136–7
Marieschi, Michiel, 94
Martin, John
 Belshazzar's Feast, 248
 The Fall of Babylon, 248
Maupassant, Guy, 57
Milton, John, 230, 231
 Paradise Lost, 185
More, Hannah
 Cheap Repository Tracts, 62

Mudford, William
 "The Iron Shroud, or Italian Revenge," 57

Nazareners, 160

Pergolesi, Giovanni Battista, 5
Perugino, Pietro
 Annunciation, 161
Petöfi, Sandor, 1
photosynthesis, 78
Pixerécourt, René-Charles Guilbert
 Le Pélerin Blanc, 65
Poe, Edgar Allan
 "The Man of the Crowd," 107, 113
 "The Pit and the Pendulum," 57
 "The Tell-Tale Heart," 57
Polidori, John, 55
 The Vampyre, 56
Pre-Raphaelites, 160
Priestley, Joseph, 76, 78
Pushkin, Alexander, 159

Radcliffe, Mary Anne
 The Female Advocate; or An Attempt to Recover the Rights of Women from Male Usurpation, 17
Raphael, Santi da Urbino
 Annunciation, 161
Reign of Terror, 77
Richardson, Jonathan, 230
Robinson, Henry Crabb, 181, 231, 236
Romanticism
 and the chapbook, 54–70
 and discourse, 2, 4
 and dreams, 157–60
 and drugs, 4
 and gender, 9–11, 12, 14
 and the gothic, 3, 55–70
 and history, 30–41
 and the natural world, 1–2
 and nervous disorders, 11–12, 21–2

Romanticism—*Continued*
  and science, 3, 73–84
    balloon flight, 78
    electricity, 78–9
    meteorology, 82–3
    and sensibility, 13–16
    and social order, 2
    and the theater, 47–53
    and the transcendental, 2
    and the urban reader, 3, 55–70
    and urban space, 2, 3, 5
    and visual art, 5
Rousseau, Jean-Jacques, 3, 5, 87–99
  Du contrat social, 89
  Julie ou la Nouvelle Héloïse, 89
  Les Confessions, 3, 87–99
  L'origine et les fondements de l'inegalité parmi les homes, 2
  Réveries du promeneur Solitaire, 76
  Si le rétablissement des sciences et des arts, 88

Scarlatti, (Giuseppe) Domenico, 5
Schelling, Friedrich Wilhelm Joseph, 1
Schiller, Friedrich
  aesthetic education, 2
  Über naïve und sentimentalische Dichtung, 2
Scott, Walter, 65
Shelley, Mary, 55, 79
  Frankenstein, 56
Shelley, Percy, 55, 65, 83
  Alastor, 76
  Prometheus Unbound, 81
Southey, Robert, 65, 213–14
  Letters from England, 241
Stendhal (Henri Beyle)
  Chartreuse de Parme, 165
Sturm und Drang, 1

Tales of Superstition: or Relations of Apparitions, 60–2
Tarkovsky, Andrei
  Nostalgia, 161

Tokyo, 73
Trotter, Thomas, 19, 20, 21
  A View of the Nervous Temperament, 9, 12–13
Turgenev, Ivan, 158
Turner, Joseph Mallord William, 1, 2
The Use of Circulating Libraries Considered, 64

Utterson, Sarah
  Tales of the Dead, 56

Vico, Giambattista
  La scienza nuova prima, 2

Wakefield, Pricilla Bell
  Reflections on the Present Condition of the Female Sex, 17
Walker, Adam, 77
Waren, Louise, 88
Whewell, William, 74
Wilkinson, Sarah Scudgell, 65
  The Spectre of Lanmere Abbey; or, The Mystery of the Blue and Silver Bag: A Romance, 66
  "The White Pilgrim," 65–70
Wittgenstein, Ludwig, 57
Wollstonecraft, Mary
  A Vindication of the Rights of Women, 15
Wordsworth, William, 2, 3, 5, 25, 26–41, 181, 229
  "Composed Upon Westminster Bridge, September 3, 1802," 182–3
  The Excursion, 75, 250–1, 253
  "Expostulation and Reply," 37–8
  "Frost at Midnight," 75
  "Illustrated Books and Newspapers," 5, 223–38
  Last Poems, 76
  "To Lucca Giordano," 232
  Lyrical Ballads, 33, 35–6, 63, 75, 84, 226–7

"Ode on the Intimations of Immortality," 30–3, 34
"Old Man Travelling," 37, 39
The Prelude, 3, 4, 28, 34, 37, 38–41, 81, 181–94, 236, 243, 251
The Recluse, 27

"Tintern Abbey," 75
"The Two April Mornings," 37

Yeats, William Butler
A Vision, 205

Zoological Society of London, 80